Taxation of Individuals

BY STEVEN A. BANK

University of California, Los Angeles

Twenty-First Edition

THOMSON
BAR/BRI

EDITORIAL OFFICES: 111 W. Jackson Blvd., 7th Floor, Chicago, IL 60604
REGIONAL OFFICES: Chicago, Dallas, Los Angeles, New York, Washington, D.C.

PROJECT EDITOR
Carol D. Olbinsky, B.A., J.D.
Attorney At Law

SERIES EDITOR
Elizabeth L. Snyder, B.A., J.D.
Attorney At Law

QUALITY CONTROL EDITOR
Sanetta M. Hister

Summary of Contents

Text Correlation Chart

Gilbert Law Summary **TAXATION OF INDIVIDUALS**	Freeland, Lathrope, Lind, Stephens *Fundamentals of Federal Income Taxation* 2006 (14th ed.)	Graetz, Schenk *Federal Income Taxation* 2005 (5th ed.)	Gunn, Ward *Federal Income Taxation* 2006 (6th ed.)	Klein, Bankman, Shaviro *Federal Income Taxation* 2006 (14th ed.)
I. IS IT INCOME?				
A. Constitutional Background	Page 11-17	Page 56-61	Page 1-5	Page 1-6, 194-206, 210
B. Definition of "Gross Income"	46-66	22-23, 89-91, 124-127, 138-139	33-34, 151-153	8-9, 22-24, 37-38, 54-55, 63-73, 159-160
C. Exclusions from Gross Income	63-64, 67-113, 152-161, 179-191, 224-225, 228-229, 340-341, 535, 541-542	91-138, 164-171, 183, 208-218, 497	33-34, 73-87, 100-102, 136-151, 163-164, 174-199	37-63, 73-105, 109-121, 141-146, 185-191, 206-211
D. Inclusions in Gross Income	46-66, 99-103, 162-178, 192-217, 233-237	91-96, 112-121, 171-190, 469-478	33-34, 40-62, 87-93, 119-136, 140-141, 235-248	37-48, 63-73, 105-109, 120-126, 145-185, 191-192, 311-318
E. Tax-Exempt Organizations	781-803	133, 443-447	205-225	366-367, 376-384, 719-720
II. TO WHOM IS THE INCOME TAXABLE?				
A. Income Splitting by Gifts	240-273, 285-294, 307, 379-381, 491, 850-851	454, 478-514, 520-525	453-469, 473-494, 497-507	66-68, 599-608, 610-630, 639-656
B. Statutory Divisions of Income	241-242, 912-922	455-478	455-461, 469-473, 494-495	14-15, 600, 604-606, 608-610, 618
C. Below-Market Interest on Loans	483-504	112, 357, 733-736	433-436	
D. Taxation of Trusts	277-294	514-519	473-475, 495-497	29, 630-639, 656-664
III. IS IT DEDUCTIBLE OR IS IT A CREDIT?				
A. Introduction	312-314, 540-542, 925-926	23-24, 219-220	34-36	339-342, 401-403, 491
B. Business and Investment Deductions	312-539, 767-781, 804-814, 864-873	23, 220-341, 363-375, 379-414	102-103, 257-298, 301-407, 525-530, 547-555, 558-563, 617-619, 627-635, 679-690	120-121, 302-307, 401-588
C. Personal Deductions	195-197, 230-232, 473-504, 540-577, 600, 664-668, 767-814	23, 342-363, 375-379, 413-453, 474	34-35, 38-40, 63-71, 199-248, 409-443, 580-586, 620-626, 664-665, 685-689, 820-822	13, 22-24, 94, 285-286, 311-318, 339-397, 401-403, 487-488
D. Tax Rates	912-924	24-27	14-21, 232-233, 469-473	13-16
E. Credits	226-228, 925-932	24, 257-258, 418-423, 425-426	35-36, 228, 248-255	24, 397-399, 456-459, 487
IV. GAIN OR LOSS ON SALE OR EXCHANGE OF PROPERTY				
A. Computation of Basis, Gain, or Loss	114-131	139-147, 190-208	50-51, 525-547, 563-599, 703-704	95-96, 170, 193-211
B. The Requirement of Realization	131-151, 834-842	147-164, 190-208, 351, 379-385	43-46, 106-119, 510-522	27-28, 159-163, 170, 173-179, 211-224, 245-250, 302-307
C. Nonrecognition of Gain or Loss	126-128, 205-209, 218-224, 874-910	478, 625-636	45, 565-580, 601-618	190-191, 224-237, 302-307, 585-587
V. WHAT KIND OF INCOME IS IT? CAPITAL GAINS AND LOSSES AND TAX PREFERENCES				
A. Introductory Material	674-699	24, 526-540	637-648	25, 665-671

Gilbert Law Summary TAXATION OF INDIVIDUALS	Freeland, Lathrope, Lind, Stephens *Fundamentals of Federal Income Taxation* 2006 (14th ed.)	Graetz, Schenk *Federal Income Taxation* 2005 (5th ed.)	Gunn, Ward *Federal Income Taxation* 2006 (6th ed.)	Klein, Bankman, Shaviro *Federal Income Taxation* 2006 (14th ed.)
B. Is It a Capital Asset?	691-699, 733-750	540-608	654-673, 691-718	667-668, 671-749
C. Was There a "Sale or Exchange"?	699-708	592, 608-624	648-654, 679-690	666-668, 749-750
D. Was There a Sufficient "Holding Period"?	708-715	624-625	638	665
E. Gains on Small Business Stock	685, 908, 937	573, 636	616-617, 641	667
F. Special Computations	751-766, 864-873	335, 557-558, 728-736	410, 639-645, 674-678, 721-722	241-245, 249-251, 547, 550, 572
G. Alternative Minimum Tax	932-944	26, 453, 767-779	445-452, 482-488, 643	24, 588-597
VI. TAX ACCOUNTING PROBLEMS				
A. Accounting Method—When Is an Item Taxable or Deductible?	580-642, 656-668, 816-851	26-27, 637-640, 661-766	50-51, 64-71, 298-301, 719-730, 762-829	25-27, 250-302, 322-335, 497
B. The Annual Accounting Period	580, 643-655, 668-671	26, 637-661	737-762	27, 126-141

Capsule Summary

loan, return of invested capital), from borrowing money, or from receiving money as a trustee. The receipt must increase net worth to be considered income.

b. "Income" that is not cash §19
Income need not be received in cash to be taxable. The receipt of property or services is frequently treated as taxable income.

c. Windfalls §20
Windfalls (*e.g.*, winning the lottery or finding money) are taxable.

d. Unsolicited property §21
Unsolicited property is not taxable until the taxpayer indicates an intent to retain it (*e.g.*, by donating and claiming a charitable deduction).

e. All-inclusive definition §22
Any increment in net worth is presumed income unless: (i) it is specifically excluded by the Code, or (ii) it falls within a nonrecognition provision. Note that taxation depends on *realization*.

4. Imputed Income §23
Imputed income arises when a taxpayer ***works for himself or uses his own property*** (*e.g.*, housekeeping services done for one's own family). This type of income has never been taxed.

a. Working for oneself §24
If one renders services to himself and an ***employment relationship is also involved***, that benefit is held to be gross income. And ***interest income*** often must be imputed.

b. Exchange of services §26
If two taxpayers exchange goods or services, ***both*** have gross income, unless an exclusion applies.

C. EXCLUSIONS FROM GROSS INCOME

1. Gifts and Inheritances §28
Gross income does not include the value of property received by gift, devise, bequest, or inheritance.

a. What is a "gift"? §29
The donor's ***motive*** must have been one of ***"detached and disinterested generosity."*** If there are mixed motives, the "primary" motive controls. The concept of a "gift" is narrowly construed for income tax purposes.

b. Gift vs. compensation §31
A problem arises when a payment is made without a legal obligation to one who has rendered services to the payor. The donor's primary motivation will determine the taxability. Payments by employer to employee are not gifts.

(1) Deduction by donor §35
An attempted deduction does not rule out a gift.

(2) Death made benefits §36
Payments made by an employer "on behalf of" an employee are not considered gifts. Whether or not death benefits qualify as these types of payments has not been determined.

(3) Gratuities §38
Tips and gratuities are *not gifts,* nor in most cases are *strike benefits* paid by a union.

(4) Gifts to spouses §40
Transfers to spouses are not taxable as income, even if they were not intended as gifts.

(5) Bargain purchases §41
When property is sold for less than fair value, the excess value may be a gift depending on the seller's motive. However, bargain purchases by an employee from an employer generally produce income to the employee.

c. What is "inheritance"? §43
Any payment "referable" to an inheritance is excluded (*e.g.*, money received in settlement of a will contest). However, bequests to employees are taxable as income, as are bequests to executors that are intended as a substitute for their fees.

d. Income derived from gifts §47
Although the property transferred is a gift, all income derived from the gift is taxable to the donee. All money received from a gift of future income is taxable to the donee.

2. Awards and Scholarships

a. Prizes and awards §50
Prizes and awards are *included in gross income*.

b. Scholarships and fellowships §53
A scholarship or fellowship is taxable unless it must be applied to tuition or books ("qualified scholarship").

3. Contributions to Capital §56
Amounts received by partnerships and corporations as capital contributions are not taxable. Government inducements and amounts contributed by customers, however, are taxable.

4. Life Insurance §58
Amounts paid by reason of the *insured's death* are excluded.

a. "Life insurance" defined §59
A "life insurance" contract *shifts the risk* of premature death to the insurance company.

(1) Employer-paid benefits §60
Death benefits paid by an employer are taxable.

(2) Debtor's insurance §61

When a creditor takes out insurance on the life of a debtor, the amount received by the creditor is **not excludible** life insurance. This money is treated as payment of a debt.

(3) Accelerated death benefits §62

Life insurance amounts payable before death to a terminally or chronically ill individual are treated as if paid by reason of death.

b. Premium payments §63

An exclusion is generally available to a recipient of insurance proceeds, **regardless of who paid** the premiums.

c. Purchasers of existing policies §65

Purchasers of existing policies do **not** qualify for the life insurance exclusion, unless the purchaser is the insured, his partner or partnership, or a corporation in which the insured is a shareholder or officer.

d. Installment payments §67

Benefits payable in installments are taxed to the extent that they represent **interest** on the unpaid balance.

5. Annuities §68

The portion of an annuity payment that represents the **taxpayer's investment** in the policy is exempt as a return of capital. The excluded portion is computed by dividing the consideration paid for the policy by the total expected return.

a. Employees' annuity plans §72

Annuity rules apply to amounts received from employee pension plans. If the employee has a nonforfeitable right to the policy, she is taxed on the purchase price when the employer purchases it. However, tax on **qualified pension or profit-sharing plans** is **deferred** until payments are made.

6. Interest on State and Local Bonds §75

Interest on state and local bonds is **excluded** from the income tax; however, interest received on **federal** obligations (*e.g.*, treasury bonds or notes) is **included**.

7. Government Benefits

a. Social Security benefits §79

A portion of Social Security benefits (old age and disability) is included in income if the taxpayer's **modified** adjusted gross income plus 50% of his Social Security benefits exceed $25,000 ($32,000 on a joint return). A greater portion is included in income if this sum exceeds $34,000 ($44,000 on a joint return). However, Supplemental Security Income ("SSI") payments are nontaxable.

b. Welfare benefits §82

Government benefits based on need (*e.g.*, welfare) are **excluded** from income—even payments for government work required of welfare recipients.

c.   Unemployment compensation   §83
These payments are taxable.

8. Medical Insurance and Private Disability Payments

a.   Medical insurance—employee-paid premiums   §84
When the employee paid for medical or disability insurance, any benefit payments received under the policy are excluded from income. However, if the employee **deducted** the medical expenses and then was **reimbursed** for them, these reimbursements must be included in income.

b.   Employer-paid premiums   §86
If the employer pays for health and accident insurance for its employees, the employees are **not** taxed on the premiums. Nor are they taxed on direct payments of medical expenses by the employer if the payments are made pursuant to a nondiscriminatory plan. All other **disability** payments are included in income.

9. Damage Payments

a.   Payments for personal injuries   §89
Under the Code, damages received, in lump sum or periodic payments, as a result of a judgment or settlement on account of personal physical injuries or physical sickness are **excluded**. Punitive damages are not excluded.

  (1) Scope of exclusion   §90
  Damages for **emotional distress alone** are income unless a physical injury was also involved. Damages for **illegal discrimination** are also taxable.

  (2) Attorneys' fees, costs, and taxable tort recoveries   §97
  Since the taxpayer owns the tort claim, attorneys' costs and fees must be included in income and then claimed as a deduction.

b.   Damages for business injuries   §100

  (1) The recovery for damage to goodwill was originally held excludible, but it was later held taxable to the extent that it exceeds the basis of the goodwill.

  (2) Damages for lost profits are income.

  (3) The Code partially excludes damages for patent infringement, breach of contract, breach of fiduciary duty, and antitrust violations. The amount excludible is the compensatory amount or the unrecovered losses, whichever is less. (The effect is an exclusion if there was no benefit from the prior losses.)

10. Meals and Lodging Furnished for Convenience of Employer   §107
The value of meals and lodging received by an employee and his family is **excluded** from gross income if the meals and lodging are furnished on the employer's business premises and, in the case of lodging, is accepted as a condition of employment.

a. **Convenience of employer** §110

Under the Regulations, the "convenience of the employer" requires a *"substantial noncompensatory business reason."* However, a recent Supreme Court case indicates a narrower *"business necessity" test*.

b. **Campus lodging** §112

The value of "qualified campus lodging" received by an employee of an educational institution is *excluded* from gross income if it is located on or near the campus and the employee pays "adequate rent."

c. **Fixed charges for meals** §113

An employee can *exclude* fixed charges for meals furnished for the convenience of the employer; however, she *cannot exclude cash reimbursements* for meals and lodging paid for by the employer.

11. **Fringe Benefits** §115

Fringe benefits are generally taxable, but employees may exclude "no additional cost" services, qualified employee discounts, working condition fringes (*e.g.*, car provided for business use), qualified transportation fringes (*e.g.*, vanpool), de minimis fringes (*e.g.*, on-premises gym), qualified moving expense reimbursement (*e.g.*, expenses employee would have been allowed to deduct if paid herself), qualified retirement advice (if the employer has a qualified retirement plan), and group term life insurance premiums (up to $50,000). "Employee" includes an employee's spouse and dependent children, and also a retired or disabled former employee.

12. **Miscellaneous Other Exclusions**

a. **Foreign earned income** §125

Taxpayers working abroad may exclude up to $80,000 of their service income from a foreign source.

b. **Frequent flier miles** §126

The value of frequent flier miles earned by an employee for a business trip is *excluded*, even if the employee subsequently applies the miles toward a personal trip. However, if the miles are turned into cash, it is taxable.

c. **Lessee's improvements** §127

Lessee's improvements on leased property are *not* income to the landlord unless they are intended as *substitutes for rent*.

d. **Insurance reimbursements for above-normal living expenses** §128

Expenses resulting from fire, storm, or other casualty losses to a *taxpayer's home* are excludible.

e. **Investment interest—higher education** §129

Income from redemption of savings bonds, purchased after 1989 by a taxpayer at least 24 years old, that is used for higher education purposes is excluded. The exclusion is phased out as AGI exceeds $60,000 ($40,000 for singles).

f.   Compensation for Holocaust victims   §130
Excluded compensation includes direct payments, returned assets, and
certain interest payments from funds arising from Holocaust litigation.

g.   Other items   §131
A minister's rental allowance, payments to foster parents, and combat and mustering-out pay to those in the service are excluded.

D.   INCLUSIONS IN GROSS INCOME

1.   Compensation for Services Rendered   §135
Irrespective of the form of the payments, compensation for services rendered is includible in gross income.

a.   Payment of employee's income taxes   §136
The payment of an employee's income taxes or debts by an employer
increases the employee's taxable income.

b.   Reimbursements or expense payments by employer   §138
Reimbursement for *travel, meals, and entertainment* costs is not income if the employee is primarily engaged in the employer's business
and the reimbursement is made pursuant to an accountable plan.

2.   Income from Cancellation of Indebtedness   §142
Unless within an exception (below), or unless the taxpayer had no net economic benefit, cancellation of debts is treated as income.

a.   Exception as to insolvent taxpayers   §143
No income exists to the extent that a debtor is insolvent before the
debt cancellation (including discharge in bankruptcy). Note that other
tax benefits are correspondingly reduced.

b.   Exception for qualified real property business indebtedness   §146
A taxpayer can elect to exclude debt cancellation from income where
the debt is secured by real property used in a trade or business.

c.   Exception for deductible payments   §147
Income is not recognized on cancellation of a debt to the extent that
payment of the debt would have given rise to a deduction.

d.   Cancellation as a "gift"   §148
If the cancellation is a gift to the debtor, there is no income. There is
rarely a gift motive unless there is a personal or family relationship.

e.   Student loans   §149
A student loan made by the government, a charitable hospital, or an
educational institution that has been forgiven because the borrower
has met certain conditions (*e.g.,* worked in certain areas or for certain
employers), does not give rise to income.

f.   Shareholder debt forgiveness   §151
If a shareholder cancels a debt owed her by the corporation (either in
exchange for stock or as a contribution to capital), the cancellation is

treated as giving cash to the shareholder, and the corporation will also have debt cancellation income.

    g.   **Reduction in purchase money debt**   **§155**

            A reduction in purchase money debt by the *seller* is treated as a reduction in the basis, not as debt cancellation income.

    h.   **Settlement of disputed claim**   **§156**

            A compromise of a disputed claim does *not* produce income.

3.   **Illegal Increases in Net Worth**   **§158**

    Money or property received through illegal activities is *included* in gross income irrespective of a promise to repay (*e.g.*, extortion money or embezzled money is included).

4.   **Gambling Winnings**   **§160**

    Gambling winnings are included in gross income. Gambling losses are deductible to the extent of the winnings.

5.   **Spousal and Child Support Payments**   **§161**

    Generally, payments by a separated or divorced spouse to the other spouse are *taxable to the recipient* and *deductible by the payor*. *But note:* Child support payments are *not deductible* to payor *nor are they taxable* to recipient.

E.   **TAX-EXEMPT ORGANIZATIONS**

1.   **Charitable Organizations**   **§171**

    To qualify, an organization must be organized and operated for religious, charitable, scientific, educational, etc., purposes; it must be nonprofit; no substantial part of its activities can include attempts to influence legislation. Contributions to such organizations are deductible.

    a.   **Other tax-exempt organizations**   **§174**

            Organizations such as unions, fraternities, civic leagues, etc., are exempt but contributions to them are *not* deductible.

    b.   **Discrimination disqualifies organization**   **§175**

            Organizations engaging in racial discrimination are not tax-exempt.

2.   **Unrelated Business Income**   **§176**

    Income from an activity substantially different from the nonprofit, charitable purpose is *not exempt*.

    a.   **Rental income**   **§177**

            Rental income from *real property* is exempt; however, rental income from personal property is not.

    b.   **Debt-financed property**   **§178**

            Investment income is taxed if the property involved was acquired with borrowed funds (unless the property is used solely for the purposes substantially related to the organization's charitable purposes).

3.   **Private Foundations**   **§179**

    Foundations are subject to special restrictions; in any event, a blanket 2% tax is imposed on net investment income.

4. Political Organizations §180

These organizations are taxed like corporations on *investment* income, but they are not taxed on *"exempt function income."*

II. TO WHOM IS THE INCOME TAXABLE?

A. INCOME SPLITTING BY GIFTS

1. Gifts of Income vs. Gifts of Income-Producing Property §183

Income remains taxable to the *donor* if she retains ownership of the property to which she has transferred income.

a. Transfers of property §184

When the donor transfers income-producing property, income from the property is taxed to the donee. However, income accrued prior to the transfer is taxed to the donor. (Transfers of income-producing property are subject to gift tax.)

b. Sham transfers §190

A transfer lacking donative intent, delivery, and acceptance does *not* shift the income to the donee; nor will a transfer be effective if the donor retains *excessive controls*.

c. Transferring income while retaining property §191

Generally, if a donor transfers income from property while retaining the property itself, the income is taxed to the *donor* at the time the donee collects it.

(1) Rental income §193

Rental income is taxable to the *owner* of the reversion even though he has gratuitously assigned his right to another.

(2) Assignments of trust income §194

A trust beneficiary can shift trust income by assigning the *entire beneficial interest* (or an *undivided portion* thereof) to the donee. But no shift occurs if the interest transferred is considered insignificant (*e.g.*, shift for only one year).

(3) Distinguish—assignments for consideration §195

The tax burden on income *always shifts* when the transfer of the income right is supported by bona fide consideration.

d. No realization of income to donor making gift §196

Even if the donor receives an immediate tax benefit (*e.g.*, a charitable deduction), he realizes no gain or loss.

(1) Exception—gifts to political organizations §199

A taxpayer will recognize gain, but not loss, from a transfer of property to a *political organization*.

(2) Exception—certain gifts §200

Realization can also occur from gifts of *mortgaged property* or gifts upon which the donee *pays gift tax*.

2. Personal Service Income §201

Generally, personal service income is taxed to the person who earned it, even if an agreement exists splitting it.

a. Obligatory assignments §203
Results are unclear when the employer is willing to make payments only to someone **other than the employee.** The decision may turn on whether the employment relation was a regular one, or whether the payment is pursuant to a "one-shot situation" wherein services do not resemble normal employment services (*e.g.,* father enters contest, but prize is paid to child). *Note:* I.R.C. section 83(a) requires that the service provider be taxed on compensation, regardless of who receives the payment, making even the exception for one-shot situations unclear.

b. Working for charity §204
A taxpayer can work for free without being taxed on the value of her services. But she cannot avoid taxation on income from employment by diverting it to a charity.

c. Working for oneself §205
If the taxpayer creates something and then gives it away, this is treated as a **transfer of property** and the income shifts to the donee.

d. Commonly controlled businesses §206
To clearly reflect the income of two or more businesses where there is common control, the IRS can allocate income, deductions, or credits.

3. Excessive Controls §209
Generally, the retention of excessive controls over transferred property causes income to be taxed to the transferor. (For example, in *Helvering v. Clifford*, the grantor remained subject to the tax on the income from the trust property because he retained a reversion and broad managerial powers, including the right to control when the wife-beneficiary would receive the income.) The law is now codified in "grantor trust rules" (*infra*).

a. Transfers of patents §211
A taxpayer who licenses his patent to a manufacturer **that he controls** is taxed on the royalty income; but the income shifts if the taxpayer does not control the donee-manufacturer.

b. Gift and leaseback §213
A taxpayer can give away a business asset and **lease it back,** and then deduct the rental as a business expense only if there is a transfer considered effective for tax purposes.

c. Family partnerships §214
When a parent seeks to make her children her partners, the income will shift as long as the capital is a **"material income-producing factor"** in the partnership; if not, the income shifts only if the donee contributes capital or services.

B. STATUTORY DIVISIONS OF INCOME

1. Income Earned by Children §220
Income earned by a child is taxable to the child even though it is paid to the parent. It is the parent's responsibility to file a tax return for the child.

Unearned income of a child under age 18 over $850 is taxed in the parents' bracket.

2. **Income of Husbands and Wives**

    a. **Right to file joint return**   §227

    Husbands and wives can *elect* to file a joint return, the effect of which is to tax the income one-half to each spouse, irrespective of which spouse earned it. *Note:* The option to file jointly is available only to married persons. Domestic partners cannot elect to file jointly.

    b. **Marriage penalty and single penalty**   §232

    The tax rate is structured so that single people are taxed more than a joint return for the same income. However, where married people have substantial income, they could pay less combined tax if they were single.

        (1) **"Quickie" divorce**   §233

        Obtaining a "quickie" divorce each year to avoid the marriage penalty will be ignored as a sham for tax purposes.

        (2) **Reduction of marriage penalty**   §234

        The standard deduction and the maximum income in the 15% tax bracket for married taxpayers filing joint returns was increased so that the resulting amounts are the same for each joint taxpayer as they would be for a single taxpayer.

    c. **Liability for tax due on joint return**   §235

    Each spouse is *jointly and severally* liable for the payment of the income tax reported on a joint return.

        (1) **Exception—"innocent spouse" rule**   §236

        A spouse *without knowledge* of an omission can escape liability for the tax, as long as he did not benefit from the item.

3. **Income Earned by Head of Household**   §238

Unmarried persons who maintain a household for qualified relatives can file a special return where, in effect, 25% of the income is split with the dependents.

C. BELOW-MARKET INTEREST ON LOANS

1. **In General**   §239

Interest is imputed (income to lender, deduction to borrower) if there is a failure to charge the applicable federal rate ("AFR").

    a. **De minimus exception**   §241

    The rule is inapplicable to gift loans any time the balance is *$10,000* or less *unless* the loan is used to purchase income-producing assets. For loans under $100,000, the imputed amount is limited to the borrower's net investment income, absent tax avoidance purposes. Several loans between the same parties must be aggregated to determine the dollar amount ceilings.

(1) *Distributable to the grantor or spouse* (even if the income is not in fact distributed);

(2) *Accumulated for future distribution to the grantor or spouse;*

(3) *Used to pay premiums on life insurance policies* of the grantor or spouse unless a charity is the beneficiary of the policy; or

(4) *Used to support dependents* whom the grantor is legally obligated to support, but only to the extent that the income is so applied. (*Note:* Alimony trusts do shift the tax burden to the beneficiary.)

e. Administrative powers that may benefit grantor §269
Where administrative control is or may be exercised for the grantor's benefit, the income is taxed to the grantor (*e.g.,* where the grantor or a nonadverse party, or both, have the power to deal with trust property or income for less than adequate consideration, without the approval of an adverse party in interest).

f. Trust income taxable to person other than grantor §277
If a person other than the grantor has a general power of appointment, the trust income is taxed to her, whether or not she takes it, subject to the following limitations:

(1) *If the power is for the support of dependents* of the third party, the income is taxed to her only to the extent it is so applied;

(2) *If the income is taxed to the grantor* under the grantor trust rules, it is not taxed to the third party. Nor is a taxpayer taxed when she disclaims a power within a reasonable time after becoming aware of its existence.

2. Trusts Recognized for Tax Purposes §278
A trust is the recognized taxable entity where the grantor has **not** retained any substantial "strings."

a. Taxability of income §279
The income is taxed to the beneficiaries when it is distributed to them, and to the trust when it is retained by it. The beneficiaries are not taxed on distributions of the **corpus**.

b. Distributable net income ("DNI") §280
To prevent trust income from being taxed twice, a special deduction is allowed for distributions. (Distributions out of income or principal may be included in the deductible amount to the extent the deductible amount does not exceed DNI.) DNI is the maximum amount includible in a beneficiary's income and deductible by the trust. DNI for the trust is the trust's **taxable income** before the deductions for the distributions to the beneficiaries, the trust's personal exemption, or the undistributed capital gains or losses allocated to the corpus.

c. "Simple trusts" §281
Simple trusts are trusts that **must distribute all the current income** to the beneficiaries, but cannot distribute the corpus or deduct charitable

contributions. The beneficiaries are taxed on the amounts distributed, or required to be distributed, and a corresponding deduction is given to the trust. Note that the deduction cannot exceed DNI. The trust is taxed on capital gains allocated to the corpus.

d. **"Complex trusts" and estates**

 (1) **First tier**   **§284**
  All the income *required* to be distributed is taxed to the beneficiaries who are entitled to receive it, to the extent of DNI.

 (2) **Second tier**   **§285**
  If DNI exceeds the amount required to be distributed, then *additional payments* (*e.g.,* discretionary income payments) to the beneficiaries become taxable. Note that the includible amount *cannot exceed DNI less the amount taxed to first tier beneficiaries*.

 (3) **Tax to trust**   **§287**
  The trust may deduct the amounts includible in the income of the first and second tier beneficiaries; however, if taxable income remains, the trust is taxed thereon.

  (a) **Exemptions**   **§288**
   Simple trusts have a $300 personal exemption, complex trusts have a $100 personal exemption, and estates have a $600 personal exemption.

e. **Throwback rule**   **§289**
A distribution in excess of the current DNI is "thrown back" into the accumulated income of the preceding years. It is treated as if it had been distributed in those years to the extent of the undistributed income of those years.

 (1) **Taxing beneficiaries**   **§291**
  The beneficiary is taxed on the accumulated distribution in the year made, but the tax is determined by the amount the beneficiary would have paid had a distribution been made in prior years. A credit is given for taxes previously paid by the trust.

III. IS IT DEDUCTIBLE OR IS IT A CREDIT?

A. INTRODUCTION

1. **Deductions and Credits Defined**   **§292**
A *"deduction"* is subtracted *from gross income* or adjusted gross income to arrive at *taxable income*. *"Credits"* are subtracted *from taxes* due.

2. **Business vs. Personal Deductions**   **§293**
Generally, business costs are deductible, while personal costs are not.

3. **No Shifting of Deductions**   **§294**
Payment of *another's liabilities* is not deductible, unless it serves an independent business purpose (*e.g.,* protecting taxpayer's job).

B. BUSINESS AND INVESTMENT DEDUCTIONS

1. Business Expenses §296

All *"ordinary and necessary expenses* paid or incurred during the taxable year in carrying on any trade or business" are deductible.

a. "Trade or business" defined §298

The Code does not define a "trade or business," but it generally requires an expectation of profit, regular and continuous operation, and the active pursuit thereof.

(1) Legality of business §299

The legality of the business is not per se relevant, but certain illegal expenses are not deductible.

(2) Nature of taxpayer §300

Expenses incurred in connection with a trade or business are deductible by any kind of taxpayer—corporation, trust, or individual. However, a stockholder is not in business merely because his corporation is in business.

(3) Tax shelters §301

Activities involving flagrant tax shelters do not meet the "trade or business" requirement; therefore expenses arising from these activities are not deductible.

b. Business vs. personal expenses §302

Individual taxpayers must prove that the particular expense was incurred *in connection with* the taxpayer's trade or business. Corporate taxpayers have the benefit of a *presumption*.

(1) Requirement of proximate relationship to trade or business §303

If several purposes are involved, the *predominant* one controls.

(2) Travel expenses §304

Travel expenses incurred while *away from home in pursuit of a trade or business* are deductible.

(a) Pursuit of trade or business

1) Commuting to and from work §306

Costs for commuting to and from work are *not* deductible.

2) Combined business and pleasure trips §311

The entire cost of the transportation is deductible if the *primary* purpose of the trip was business, but lodging and meal expenses must be allocated.

3) Foreign meetings §312

Certain limitations are placed on expense deductions for attendance at foreign conventions.

4) **Presence of spouse** §313
A spouse's expenses are deductible only if there is a sufficient business connection.

(b) **"Away from home"** §314
There has been considerable controversy over whether this phrase means away from *business headquarters* or away from the *residence*.

1) **"Homeless" taxpayers** §315
If no business headquarters exist, the taxpayer's permanent residence can be "home." However, if the taxpayer has neither, there are no deductions for travel expenses.

2) **Taxpayers with several offices** §316
If the taxpayer has several business headquarters, he can deduct expenses of traveling between them.

3) **Deductibility of meals** §317
Only **50%** of meal costs are deductible, and that deduction is available only if the taxpayer is away from home for a time requiring *"sleep or rest."*

4) **"Temporary" vs. "indefinite" rule** §318
Deductions are not allowed when the taxpayer is away on an assignment of an *indefinite* duration, but are allowed for temporary assignments.

(3) **Expenses of "businesses" operated for pleasure—hobby farm problem** §319
Expenses are generally not deductible unless a *significant purpose* of the business is to earn a profit. However, interest and property taxes are deductible since they do not require profit-seeking, and if income exceeds this amount, expenses up to this balance can be deducted.

(4) **Moving expenses** §325
Employees or self-employed persons can deduct the costs of moving family and furniture to a new home, subject to certain limitations: The new job site must be more than **50 miles** farther from the old home than the old home was from the old job site; the taxpayer must work full-time; and the new place of work must be permanent.

(5) **Entertainment expenses** §331
Entertainment expenses are deductible only if they are *directly related* to the active conduct of the taxpayer's business. Only 50% of entertainment is deductible.

(6) **Business gifts** §337
Business gifts are generally deductible up to $25.

(7) Litigation expenses §338

Whether legal fees or other costs incurred in a lawsuit are deductible depends on the nature of the dispute. If the **origin of the dispute is related to a trade or business** and the expenses are **"ordinary and necessary,"** they are deductible. Litigation expenses incurred for the **production of income** are deductible, but only as miscellaneous itemized deductions. Special provisions allow a deduction for costs in connection with tax matters.

(8) Educational expenses §342

Educational expenses that qualify the taxpayer for a **new** trade or business, or constitute the **minimum education requirement** for qualification in her job, are **not** deductible. However, costs to **maintain or improve** skills required in a taxpayer's job, or for education that is required as a condition to retention of the job, are deductible.

(9) Insurance premiums §344

The cost of insurance on business **property** is an ordinary and necessary business expense. **Life** insurance premiums for a "key person" (*i.e.*, officer or employee) are deductible only if the taxpayer is not the beneficiary.

(10) Offices at home §347

Generally, **no** deductions are given for a taxpayer's residence. There is a special exception for **certain business uses** if a portion of the home is used **exclusively** for business (*e.g.*, principal place of business, certain storage use, or if the residence is used as a day care facility). The deductible amount is limited to the gross income from such use, less the nonbusiness deductions.

(11) Vacation homes §356

Generally, no deduction is allowed in excess of the income if the dwelling unit is used **as a "residence"** (*i.e.*, if used for personal purposes for more than 14 days or 10% of the days rented, whichever is greater). Also, expenses must be prorated between rental and personal use.

(a) Limited rental use §363

If the dwelling unit is rented fewer than 15 days, no deduction is allowed, and the rental income is excluded from gross income.

(12) Clothing §364

Clothing is **not** deductible unless it cannot appropriately be worn for nonbusiness purposes (*e.g.*, firefighter's uniform).

c. Current expense vs. capital outlay §365

To be deductible as a business expense, an item must be an **expense**, rather than a **capital outlay**.

(1) Test §366

An expense is considered a "capital outlay" if it brings about the *acquisition of an asset or some advantage* to the taxpayer having a *useful life in excess of one year*.

(a) "Capitalization" distinguished §367

A *capital asset*, when sold, qualifies for capital gain or loss treatment (*infra*). However, expenditures must be *capitalized* if they create an asset or advantage lasting beyond the taxable year, whether or not a capital asset is produced (*i.e.*, match up income with costs of earning that income).

(b) Future benefit §369

An outlay must be capitalized if it produces significant long-term benefits (*INDOPCO* case). Thus, the costs of arranging a friendly corporate takeover must be capitalized because the benefits will inure into the future, but the costs of resisting a hostile takeover can be deducted currently because there is no long-term benefit created by the expenses.

(c) Ramifications §374

The *INDOPCO* case has cast doubt on many decisions that allowed expensing, rather than capitalization, of business expansion costs because no distinct asset resulted, although a long-term benefit was produced.

(2) Repairs of property vs. capital improvement §376

Maintenance and repairs are current expenses and are deductible in the year paid *unless they improve* the value of the original property, make it suitable for a different purpose, or extend its original useful life. Certain *environmental cleanup costs* also may be deducted instead of capitalized.

(3) Property produced or sold §380

Taxpayers must capitalize the direct and indirect costs of producing property, including materials, labor, rent or depreciation on equipment, etc. *Interest* allocable to produced property must be capitalized only if the property has a long useful life or production period.

(a) Resale property §384

Costs associated with property acquired for resale (*e.g.*, inventory storage costs) are capitalized if the taxpayer has average gross receipts of more than $10 million.

(b) Exception for authors §385

Mandatory capitalization rules are inapplicable to the "qualified creative expense" of authors, artists, or photographers (*i.e.*, costs are deductible).

(4) Rent payments §386

Rental payments for the use of another's property are deductible. But **prepayments** of rent are **not** currently deductible, nor are **leases** that are actually payments towards the **purchase price** of the property.

(5) Acquisition costs §391

Amounts paid to **purchase** a business or an asset are capital outlays, as are "start-up" costs. However, costs of expanding an existing business are deductible. To equalize this situation between new and existing businesses, **section 195** was enacted to allow **amortization over a 15-year period** of the costs of investigating and starting up a new business. However, the purchase price must still be capitalized.

(a) Finding employment §398

Employment agency fees are deductible (except the costs of seeking a **first** job).

1) Distinguish—running for office §399

Costs of running for office are **nondeductible**.

(b) Corporate organization and reorganization §400

Legal fees connected with the organizing or reorganizing of a business are capital outlays but can usually be amortized over a 15-year period.

(c) Patents, copyrights, and trademarks §401

The purchase of patents, copyrights, and trademarks are **capital outlays**; but costs in creating them are currently deductible.

(d) Bar exam §402

Bar exam costs must be capitalized.

(e) Selling costs §403

Commissions paid on the sale of property are **not** deductible as expenses, but they do decrease the amount realized on the sale.

(f) Acquiring goodwill §404

The costs of acquiring goodwill in a new business are nondeductible. But amounts paid for the **protection or improvement** of the goodwill may be deductible. Purchased goodwill can be amortized over a 15-year period.

(g) Short-term prepayments §407

Routine and recurring payments lasting into the following year may be entirely deducted in the year in which they are made.

d. "Ordinary and necessary" expense §408

An expense must be: (i) of a type encountered by other businesses in the community, and (ii) appropriate or helpful to the business.

(1) Determinative factors §410
The following are the chief factors in determining if an expense is in fact "ordinary and necessary": the **voluntariness** of the payment, the **customariness** of the payment, and whether it is **"reprehensible"** (e.g., legal kickback).

(2) Compensation §415
"Reasonable" compensation costs for services rendered are deductible. A court considers the value of the service to the business and what similar businesses would pay for like services.

(a) Tests for reasonableness §418
Salary based on a **percentage of income** may be suspicious. Some courts consider what an **independent investor** would pay for the services. A salary **unrelated to the value** of the services may be disallowed on the basis that it is a "constructive dividend." A few cases have disallowed a reasonable salary to the extent the employee-shareholder has not received a reasonable return on her investment.

(b) Salaries in excess of $1 million §423
A publicly held corporation cannot deduct remuneration in excess of $1 million per year to certain top executives unless payments are commissions actually earned or are based on achievement of performance goals.

e. Public policy limitation §424
Bribes to government employees, payments **illegal under the criminal law, fines** paid for a violation of the law, and payments in connection with **political campaigns or lobbying are not** deductible.

(1) Damages §435
Civil penalties or damages paid to a victim are usually **deductible**, but two-thirds of the payments made in connection with antitrust violations are not.

2. "Nonbusiness" Expenses—Expenses for Production of Income

a. General rule §437
An **individual** taxpayer can deduct expenses paid or incurred for **production or collection** of income; for management, conservation, or maintenance of **property held for the production of income;** or in connection with the **determination, collection, or refund of any tax.**

(1) Scope of deductible expenses §440
Expense must be **current, ordinary and necessary, not violative of public policy,** and **not incurred for personal reasons**.

(2) Illustrations §441
Proxy fight expenses are deductible; stockholders' expenses for travel to stockholder meetings are generally deductible; litigation expenses are **not** deductible if the **primary purpose** is to establish or defend title or ownership; divorce and property settlement expenses are generally nondeductible personal expenses.

3. **Depreciation and Amortization** §450
Reasonable deductions are allowed for exhaustion and wear and tear of property used in a trade or business, or held for the production of income (depreciation). If an asset is intangible, the deduction is known as ***amortization***.

   a. **Limitations** §451

      (1) ***Passive loss deductions*** cannot exceed income from those activities;

      (2) ***The "at risk limitation"*** (*infra*); and

      (3) ***Depreciation is not deductible*** if the property is worth less than the amount of a nonpersonal liability mortgage.

   b. **Depreciable property** §455
   All physical property, except land, that is used in a trade or business, or held for the production of income, and that has a ***limited useful life***, may be depreciated. Many intangibles (*e.g.*, goodwill) can be amortized over a 15-year period.

      (1) **Books, films, sound recordings, software** §457
      Production costs are amortized over the period that these items are expected to produce income.

      (2) **Unlimited useful life** §458
      Assets other than intangibles (*e.g.*, works of art, land) cannot be depreciated.

   c. **Who is entitled to depreciation deduction** §459
   Generally, the person suffering the economic loss due to the decreased value of the property from depreciation can claim the deduction.

      (1) **Landlord-tenant** §460
      The landlord gets the deduction if he improves the land and leases it to the tenant except when the ***tenant is required to maintain*** the land so that when it is returned it will be of equivalent value. If the tenant erects a building on unimproved land or constructs improvements in a leased building, the tenant gets the deduction.

      (2) **Sale-leaseback** §461
      The investor in a sale-leaseback transaction is entitled to the deduction if he is treated as the ***owner***.

      (3) **Purchaser** §462
      The purchaser under an executory sale contract gets the deduction on the property after the ownership burdens and benefits pass to him.

      (4) **Future interest holder** §463
      A life tenant is entitled to the deduction.

      (5) **Trustee-beneficiary** §464
      In trusts, the deduction is apportioned among income beneficiaries and the trustee.

d. **Computation of depreciation**

(1) **Recovery periods** §465
The accelerated cost recovery system ("ACRS") provides "recovery periods" of certain assets. These recovery periods are: for residential buildings—27.5 years; for nonresidential buildings—39 years; for tangible personal property—3, 5, 7, 10, 15, or 20 years.

(2) **Salvage value** §466
ACRS ignores salvage value and makes no distinction between new and used property.

(3) **Methods of depreciation** §467
ACRS provides two types of depreciation: straight-line and accelerated. *Straight-line depreciation* is computed by dividing the cost (or other basis) by the useful life. This method results in the same deduction for every year during the recovery period. *Accelerated depreciation* provides for a greater deduction in the early years and a lower deduction in later years.

(4) **Personal property—accelerated depreciation** §468
Double-declining balance is permitted for most personal property.

　　(a) **Half-year convention** §470
　　Regardless of when personal property is purchased, it is treated as if it were purchased halfway through the year. If more than 40% of assets are bought during the last quarter of the year, *all* assets acquired during the year are considered purchased in the middle of the *quarter* in which they are purchased.

　　(b) **Straight-line election** §471
　　A taxpayer may elect to use *straight-line depreciation*.

(5) **Stimulus bill** §472
To stimulate the local economy after Hurricane Katrina, Congress passed legislation to provide financial incentives for taxpayers who invest in new property in the devastated region.

(6) **Amortization of intangibles** §473
Under section 197, many intangibles (*e.g.*, purchased goodwill, licenses, covenants not to compete, and franchises) are amortized over a 15-year period. Intangibles not covered by section 197 (*e.g.*, interests in companies, land, software, sports franchises, films) can be amortized only according to their proved useful lives.

(7) **Real property** §476
Depreciation is calculated on a monthly basis in the year in which the buildings are purchased or constructed (purchase is deemed

to occur at mid-month in year of purchase). Only straight-line depreciation is permitted.

e. Election to expense purchase price §477

A small business taxpayer may elect to "expense" (*i.e.*, to deduct immediately) a certain amount of the purchase price of tangible personal property. The maximum amount that can be expensed is $108,000.

f. Limitations on consumer items §478

Limitations on depreciation and rental expense deductions apply to "listed property" (*e.g.*, cars, cellular telephones, home computers used for business). Only straight-line depreciation can be used for listed property used less than 50% for business.

g. Caution—ultimate effect of deduction §482

A depreciation deduction *reduces basis;* hence, the more depreciation taken, the greater the taxable gain (or less loss) is when the property is sold.

4. Depletion §483

The owner of the *economic interest* in a wasting asset (*e.g.*, oil, gas, or minerals) is entitled to a reasonable annual allowance to compensate for the diminution of the asset.

a. Methods of computing depletion

(1) Cost method §486

The cost or other basis of the wasting asset is allocated to each unit of the mineral deposit. Then, the depletion allowable for each year is computed by multiplying this amount by the number of units actually sold or withdrawn during the year.

(2) Percentage method §487

Under this more popular method, the deduction is a fixed percentage of the property's gross income during the taxable year. *Note:* With respect to *oil and gas*, the percentage depletion cannot exceed 50% of the taxpayer's net income from the property. *And note:* Percentage depletion is especially attractive because greater income results in a greater deduction and the deduction goes on *indefinitely*.

b. Drilling costs §490

The costs of production are deductible as *expenses.* Intangible drilling and development expenses (*i.e.*, wages, supplies, etc., in locating sites and preparing for production) in connection with oil and gas wells may be deducted as current expenses or capitalized and recovered through subsequent depletion and depreciation deductions.

5. Losses §493

A loss occurs when a transaction ends and the taxpayer has not recovered her basis for the assets involved. Corporate losses are generally deductible as business losses. Individuals can deduct only limited losses.

a. **Types of losses allowed to individuals**

 (1) **Losses incurred in a trade or business**   §497
  Any loss incurred in a trade or business is deductible.

 (2) **Losses incurred in transactions entered into for profit**   §498
  These are generally deductible. For example, losses from the sale of securities or other investments are deductible (as capital losses—the deductibility of which is limited); however, losses suffered on the sale of a **personal residence** are **not** deductible.

 (3) **Wagering**   §501
  Wagering losses are deductible to the extent of any winnings.

 (4) **Demolition losses**   §502
  Losses from the demolition of a structure are not deductible **unless the loss was incurred before the demolition** (e.g., the building was damaged by a tornado and then demolished—the casualty loss is deductible).

b. **When loss allowable—"realization"**   §504
 Generally, a loss must be realized (evidenced by a closed and completed transaction in the current tax year) to be deductible. A mere decline in value is **not** enough.

 (1) **Time of realization**   §506
  The realization on a tangible asset usually occurs in the year of the intention to abandon **and** the affirmative act of abandonment. The remote possibility of recoupment is irrelevant.

 (2) **Exchanges**   §509
  For loss to be realized on an exchange of property, the property received must differ materially either in kind or in extent from the property transferred.

 (3) **Exceptions**   §510
  Theft losses are deductible the year in which the taxpayer discovers the loss. Casualty losses from natural disasters are deducted either in the year of occurrence or on the return for the prior year. Declines in value in inventory may be deducted in the year they occur. The year they become worthless is the year of loss for stocks and securities.

c. **Disallowed losses**

 (1) **Losses between related taxpayers**   §511
  Losses arising from a sale or exchange **directly or indirectly** of property between related taxpayers are not allowed. However, **gain** upon such transactions is taxable.

 (2) **Losses from "wash sales" of securities**   §517
  When a taxpayer sells stocks or securities and **buys** substantially identical assets within 30 days before or after the sale, the transaction is ignored, and losses are not deductible.

(3) Sham transactions §518

If, in reality, there was no real interruption of the taxpayer's beneficial ownership, despite the appearance of a sale, losses from this "sham transaction" are disallowed.

(4) Public policy §519

Loss deductions violative of public policy are disallowed.

6. Bad Debts

a. "Bad debt" defined §520

A "bad debt" arises when an obligation owed to the taxpayer becomes uncollectible.

b. Requirements for deductibility §521

There must be a *valid debt* owing that arose from a *debtor-creditor relationship,* and the debt must have become unenforceable or uncollectible *during the tax year* for which the deduction is claimed.

c. Business and nonbusiness bad debts §528

Business bad debts are fully deductible, and a deduction is allowed for "partial worthlessness." Nonbusiness bad debts are deductible as *short-term capital losses* (*e.g.*, a loan to a friend or family, or most shareholder loans to corporations (*Whipple* rule)).

d. Amount deductible §533

The amount deductible is *limited to the basis* of the debt. Uncollectible *accounts receivable* are deductible only if the taxpayer is on the accrual basis.

e. Recovery of bad debts §536

If a bad debt is deducted and then recovered, it must be included in the *gross income* in the year it is received. But to the extent that the previous bad debt deduction failed to effect a *tax benefit,* the income can be excluded.

7. "At Risk" Limitation on Tax Shelter Deductions §538

Deductions from operating losses for all investments *except real estate* are limited to the amount "at risk," *i.e.*, the amount of investment in the property excluding nonpersonal liability money loans. Operating losses are the excess of deductions from the activity over income from the activity during the year.

8. Passive Losses §543

Taxpayers who do not *materially participate* in a business cannot deduct losses from such "passive" activities except against income from such activities. Deductions are deferred until future years when there is passive income or the activity is disposed of.

a. Exceptions for real estate rentals §549

A taxpayer may deduct up to $25,000 in losses from real estate *rental activity* if he *actively participates*. The deduction is phased out when adjusted gross income ("AGI") exceeds $100,000. A taxpayer who is a *real estate professional* can deduct all losses if the taxpayer spends more than 750 hours a year materially participating in the business.

(1) Identifying interest §583

Payments for the *use* of borrowed money are interest and deductible (*e.g.*, "points"), while payments for a lender's *services* are *not* interest. Interest may be *imputed* in some situations when interest charged is less than the applicable federal rate.

b. Nondeductible interest

(1) Personal interest §591

Personal interest (*e.g.*, on credit cards) is not deductible. *Exception:* Interest on certain educational loans or on acquisition debt (cannot exceed $1 million), and home equity debt (cannot exceed $100,000) is deductible if *secured* by a principal residence (or a second residence).

(a) Interest on education loans §596

A taxpayer can deduct *from gross income* interest on educational loans (up to $2,500) incurred to pay higher education expenses for the taxpayer, her spouse, or a dependent. The deduction begins phasing out when AGI exceeds $50,000 on a single return or $105,000 on a joint return.

(2) Expense allocable to exempt income §601

Interest expenses attributable to the production of tax-exempt income are disallowed.

(3) Tax-exempt interest §602

Interest on debts incurred to purchase or carry tax-exempt state and municipal bonds is not deductible.

(4) Loans to purchase insurance §603

No interest deduction is allowed on a debt incurred to buy "single premium" life insurance, endowment, or annuity contracts, or on loans made as part of a systematic plan of financing insurance premiums. *Exception:* The disallowance rule is inapplicable if: (i) no part of four of the first seven premiums is borrowed; (ii) the amount disallowed would be less than $100, if borrowing occurred because of unforeseen financial problems; or (iii) the borrowing was incurred in connection with a trade or business.

(5) Unpaid interest §604

Unpaid interest owed by a debtor on an accrual basis to a related creditor on the cash basis is not deductible *until paid*.

(6) Prepaid interest §605

Prepaid interest must be capitalized and deducted in the years the underlying loan is outstanding (except that *points* paid on a loan secured by a principal residence are immediately deductible).

(7) Excess investment interest §607

If the interest deductions on investments exceed the net investment income, the excess is *disallowed*, but may be *carried forward* and deducted against investment income in future years.

donated property would (if sold) produce **long-term capital gain** and is donated to a **public charity.** However, the amount of the deduction is limited to 30% of the donor's AGI.

(a) **Amount limitations** §631
The amount deductible is reduced by the capital gain if the gift is to a **private foundation** (unless an **"operating"** foundation), the gift is of **tangible personal property unrelated** to the charity's charitable purpose, or the gift is of a patent, copyright, or other intellectual property.

(b) **Gift that would not produce long-term capital gain** §635
If the property would produce short-term capital gain or **ordinary income,** then only the donor's basis, in effect, is deductible. However, if the gift is of inventory to a public charity to be used solely for the care of the ill, needy, or infants (and the charity does not resell the property), an amount in excess of basis is deductible.

(3) **Property description and appraisals** §638
Taxpayers must submit property descriptions if the contribution is worth more than $500, and an appraisal if the contribution is worth more than $5,000.

(4) **Contributions of used cars, boats, and airplanes** §639
The taxpayer must receive a written acknowledgment of the vehicle's identification number if it is worth more than $500.

b. **Bargain sales** §640
When property is **sold** to a charity **below** the fair market value, the difference between the fair market value and purchase price is deductible, but the basis must be **apportioned** between the gift and sale elements.

c. **Contribution of services or use of property** §642
The value of **personal services** donated to a charity is nondeductible; **out-of-pocket expenses** (e.g., automobile expenses) can be deducted. If the taxpayer donates the use of his property, he cannot deduct the value of the use.

d. **No deduction if taxpayer benefits** §648
Contributions made with the anticipation of future economic benefit are not deductible.

6. **Medical Expenses** §653
Amounts paid for the "**diagnosis, cure, mitigation, treatment or prevention of disease,** or for the purpose of affecting any structure or function of the body" are specifically deductible, as is the cost of prescription drugs. **Transportation** costs for essential medical care and the amounts paid for **medical insurance** (not disability insurance) are also deductible.

a. **Borderline expenses** §655
The deductibility of borderline expenses (e.g., long-term care costs) turns on the relationship of the expense to health needs.

b. Health savings accounts   §663
Contributions made to health savings accounts are deductible by the employee. The contributions are used to reimburse the employee for her medical expenses, and any excess at the end of the year carries over to the next year.

c. Effect of insurance   §664
If an expense is compensated by insurance, it is *not* deductible.

d. Limitation on deductible amount   §665
Only medical costs in *excess of 7.5% of AGI* are deductible.

e. Self-employed persons   §666
Self-employed persons are entitled to deduct their medical insurance premiums.

7. Personal and Dependency Exemptions and Child Tax Credits

a. Personal exemptions   §667
Taxpayer is entitled to an exemption of $3,300 (indexed for inflation) for herself.

b. Exemption for dependents   §668
An exemption is provided for each "dependent." A person is a dependent if:

(1) *"Dependent's" gross income is less than the exemption amount* (unless taxpayer's child is either under age 19 or a full-time student under age 24);

(2) *Taxpayer supplies over half of the dependent's support;* and

(3) *"Dependent" is a close relative* or has his principal abode with the taxpayer.

c. Special rules concerning dependents

(1) **Support in kind**   §669
Support in kind (*e.g.*, housing, food) is included in determining the amount of support taxpayer provided, but scholarships are ignored. If a *state* provides more than 50% of the total support costs, an exemption cannot be claimed by a parent.

(2) **Multiple support agreement**   §670
If several people contribute to the dependent's support, any one of them can claim the exemption pursuant to a multiple support agreement.

(3) **Divorced parents**   §672
In cases of divorce, generally the parent with custody is given the exemption unless she waives the right to claim it.

d. Phaseout   §674
Personal exemptions are phased out at the rate of two percentage points for each $2,500 by which the taxpayer's AGI exceeds the threshold amount. However, these are scheduled to be phased out between 2006 and 2009.

8. Casualty and Theft Losses §676

Individuals can deduct each casualty and theft loss to the extent it *exceeds $100* but *only if the damage is to taxpayer's own property.* And the *total* of casualty and theft losses is deductible only if it is *in excess of 10% of AGI.* Any insurance recoveries reduce casualty losses.

a. Amount deductible §683

Taxpayer can deduct the *lesser* of:

(1) *The adjusted basis* of property; or

(2) *The difference between the value* of the property before and after the casualty.

b. Personal casualty gains and losses in the same year §686

If the gains exceed the losses, the gains are treated as capital gains and the losses (in excess of $100 per loss) are deductible. If the losses exceed the gains, both the gains and losses are ordinary, not capital. The losses (in excess of $100 per loss) are deductible to the extent of the gains.

9. Other Personal Deductions §688

Nonbusiness bad debts, alimony payments, and certain contributions to retirement plans are allowed.

a. Contributions to retirement plans §690

A taxpayer may establish an individual retirement account ("IRA") and contribute and deduct up to $4,000 per year ($5,000 for taxpayers age 50 and older). Investment gains are not currently taxed, but are taxed when withdrawn. The deduction begins phasing out for single taxpayers when AGI reaches $50,000 ($75,000 for married taxpayers) *if* the taxpayer is covered by an employer-maintained retirement plan, but there is no phaseout for taxpayer not covered by such a plan.

(1) Roth IRAs §692

Contributions to Roth IRAs are not currently deductible, but like regular IRAs, investment gains are not taxed. Moreover, *none of the distributions* are taxed if made after the taxpayer reaches age 59½ and more than five years after the first contribution.

(2) Education IRAs §693

A taxpayer can contribute up to $2,000 per year to an education IRA for a beneficiary under age 18. The contributions are not deductible but investment income and distributions are not taxable.

D. TAX RATES §694

The tax rates depend on marital status. Married taxpayers may file joint or separate returns. Singles may qualify for the head of household rate. There are six tax brackets: 10%, 15%, 25%, 28%, 33%, and 35% for the year 2006.

E. CREDITS §696

Credits reduce the tax payable dollar for dollar.

1. **Credit for Taxes Withheld and Prepaid** §697

   The taxpayer is entitled to a credit against taxes payable for all sums withheld from wages and for all amounts prepaid in connection with declarations of estimated tax.

2. **Foreign Tax Credit** §698

   The taxpayer may elect to take as a credit in lieu of a deduction from income the amount of income and similar taxes paid or accrued during the year to foreign countries or possessions of the United States.

3. **Credit for the Elderly** §699

   Taxpayers who are age **65 *or over*** (or retired on total or permanent disability) receive a credit of 15% of their "section 22 amount" ($5,000 for singles, $7,500 on a joint return if both spouses are eligible, or $3,750 for a married person filing separately). However, the "section 22 amount" must be reduced by excludible Social Security or other amounts excluded from gross income. And if gross income exceeds $7,500 ($10,000 on joint return, $5,000 for a married person filing separately), there is a further reduction of one-half of the excess.

4. **Work Incentive Credit** §703

   The Code allows a credit of 50% of the salaries paid to disadvantaged employees (*e.g.,* welfare recipient).

5. **Child or Dependent Care Credit** §704

   A credit is given for at least 20% (35% for lower income taxpayers) of expenses for household services and care of a "qualifying individual" (dependent under age 13 or unable to care for himself or herself). But the expenses must be incurred to enable the taxpayer to be gainfully employed.

   a. **Dollar limit** §709

      Expenses for which the credit is allowed cannot exceed earned income (if married, income of lower earning spouse used) or $3,000 for one qualifying individual or $6,000 for two or more.

   b. **Divorced parents included** §711

      Even though the parent is not entitled to claim the exemption, she can take the child care credit.

6. **Child Tax Credit** §712

   A taxpayer who claims a ***child under age 17 as a dependent*** is entitled to a child tax credit of $1,000 per child. The credit is gradually phased out when AGI exceeds $110,000 on a joint return, $75,000 on a single return, and $55,000 for a married person filing separately. The child tax credit is refundable even if it exceeds an individual's tax liability for the year.

   a. **Divorced parents** §717

      A noncustodial parent can receive the credit if the custodial parent signs a written waiver.

7. **Earned Income Credit** §718

   A lower-income taxpayer with one child under age 19 can claim a credit of 34% of earned income (the percentage is 40% if he has two or more children) up to a threshold amount (adjusted for inflation). The credit is less for tax-payers without children and is phased out above certain income levels.

8. **Adoption Tax Credit** §721

A taxpayer can claim a credit for adoption expenses up to $10,960 per child in 2006, although the credit phases out when AGI exceeds $164,410.

9. **Education Credits** §722

The HOPE credit is available for the first $1,650 of expenses for the first two years of post-secondary education (100% of the first $1,100 and 50% of the next $1,100 in tuition expenses). The lifetime learning credit, which applies in years when the HOPE credit is not claimed, is equal to 20% of the first $10,000 of tuition and related expenses. These credits begin to phase out when AGI reaches $45,000 on a single return and $90,000 on a joint return.

IV. GAIN OR LOSS ON SALE OR EXCHANGE OF PROPERTY

A. COMPUTATION OF BASIS, GAIN, OR LOSS

1. **Computation Formula** §726

   a. *Adjusted basis = unadjusted basis + additions - reductions*

   b. *Gain = amount realized - adjusted basis*

   c. *Loss = adjusted basis - amount realized*

2. **Basis**

   a. **Unadjusted basis** §728

   This is usually cost. However, there are special rules for *gifts, inheritances,* and *tax-free exchanges*.

   (1) **Cost basis** §729

   Generally, the basis of property is the cost thereof. It includes cash, mortgages, or other property paid to obtain the asset. Income charged to the taxpayer in acquiring the property also is added to the basis.

   (2) **Inter vivos gifts** §737

   For the purpose of computing *gain,* the donee takes the *donor's basis;* but for *loss* purposes, the donee's basis is the *fair market value* at the time of the gift or the donor's basis, whichever is less.

   (a) **Increase by gift tax paid** §738

   The basis is increased by the gift tax the donor paid, which is attributable to an appreciation in property, but not in excess of the fair market value at the time of the gift.

   (3) **Tax-free exchanges** §739

   The basis of property in a tax-free exchange is that of the property transferred—adjusted upward for gain recognized and downward for money received on the exchange.

(4) Inherited property §740

The basis of inherited property in the hands of decedent's estate or the person inheriting it is the property's value at the date of death of decedent (or six months later if the alternate valuation date is elected).

(a) Form in which property is held

1) Community property §743

If decedent and her surviving spouse owned the property as community property, both halves receive a new basis.

2) Tenants in common §744

On the death of one tenant in common, the person inheriting the decedent's interest receives a new basis, but the surviving tenants in common do not.

3) Joint tenancy §745

Property owned as joint tenants receives a new basis if includible in the estate for estate tax purposes, and maintains its former basis if excluded from the estate.

(b) Term interests §746

"Term interests" include life estates, term for years, or an income interest in a trust. Special rules apply to determining the recipient's basis in the term interest.

(c) Income in respect of a decedent §751

This refers to situations wherein income is not taxed to the decedent even though events leading to its realization occurred prior to his death. In these cases income is taxed to the recipient, but a deduction is available if the item was subject to estate tax.

b. Adjusted basis §755

Adjusted basis is determined by *adding* to the unadjusted basis all subsequent expenditures chargeable to the asset that were not deductible as current expenses. From the sum is subtracted (i) receipts, losses, or other items properly chargeable to a capital account; and (ii) depreciation, depletion, amortization, or obsolescence allowed.

c. Allocation of basis §759

Where the taxpayer sells or exchanges only a *part* of her asset, she must allocate the basis between the part sold and the part retained. Allocation also applies when *several assets* are purchased for a lump sum.

B. THE REQUIREMENT OF REALIZATION

1. In General §761

A *realization* must occur prior to the taxation of the increase in the net worth.

2. **Realization in Property Transactions** §762
The owner of property realizes gain or loss only on the *sale or other disposition* of the property.

   a. **Mortgages** §763
   Mortgaging alone and *gifts alone* are *not* realizing transactions, but if *both* are combined, there may be a realization.

     (1) **Mortgage foreclosure** §767
     Foreclosure is a realization; it is treated as a sale by the debtor to the creditor, and a transfer in satisfaction of a claim.

     (2) **Exchanges** §768
     An exchange is a realization if the properties *differ materially*.

3. **Amount Realized** §769
The amount realized is the sum of money, plus the fair market value of any other property, received by the taxpayer in the realizing transaction.

   a. **Mortgaged property** §770
   The amount realized on mortgaged property is cash received *plus* the amount of any debt secured by the property for which the taxpayer is no longer liable.

   b. **Sale for future payments** §778
   Where the sale price for the property sold consists of payments to be made in the future, the amount realized is the full sale price unless the *fair market value* of the future payments is less than the sale price.

C. NONRECOGNITION OF GAIN OR LOSS

1. **In General** §784
Generally, all gain or loss is *recognized* (taxed), subject to certain exceptions.

2. **Nonrecognition Provisions** §785
In certain transactions, gain or loss is *not* recognized, and the basis of new property is the same as the transferred property. Gain or loss is merely *deferred* until the acquired property is sold.

   a. **Like kind exchanges** §786
   No gain or loss is recognized where the property held for investment or a business use is exchanged *solely for like kind property*. Note that "like kind" is strictly interpreted for *personal property*.

     (1) **Coverage limited to tangible property other than inventory** §789
     Stocks and bonds, partnership interests, stock in trade, or other property held for sale to customers in the ordinary course of a trade or business is *not* included.

     (2) **Sale and leaseback** §793
     If the lease is for *more than 30 years,* the IRS considers it a fee interest and the "like kind" requirement is met. However, the judicial approach is contra.

(3) Effect of "boot" §796

If a taxpayer receives like kind and non-like kind property in an exchange, the non-like kind property is considered "boot," and the *realized gain is recognized* to the extent of the boot. The basis is adjusted: new basis = old basis + gain recognized - money received.

(4) Effect of mortgages §799

For tax purposes, an exchange subject to an outstanding mortgage is treated the same as if the acquiring party paid cash.

(5) Exchanges between related persons §801

If a relation with whom taxpayer exchanged property disposes of the property *within two years* (or vice versa), the taxpayer must recognize gain or loss on the original exchange.

(a) Exceptions §802

Dispositions after the death of either the taxpayer or related person, involuntary conversion of the property, or a transaction that satisfies the IRS that tax avoidance is not a principal purpose do not trigger recognition of gain or loss.

b. Involuntary conversions §803

If the converted property is replaced with "similar or related in service or use" property *within two years* after the close of the tax year in which the insurance proceeds were received, gain is recognized only to the extent the amount realized exceeds the replacement cost. Nonrecognition under this section is *elective*.

(1) Special rules for condemnation of business real property §809

Condemnations (or threat of) causing sale of *business real property* results in no gain if the proceeds are reinvested in like kind property, whether or not it is similar or related in service or use. The replacement period is three years.

c. Nonrecognition of gain on sale of principal residence §810

No loss can be recognized on the sale of a personal residence. Gain from the sale of a principal residence generally is not recognized unless in excess of $250,000 (or $500,000 on a joint return), which excess is taxable as capital gain. To qualify for the exclusion, the taxpayer must have *owned and used* the dwelling as a *principal residence* for periods aggregating *two years or more in the five-year period* ending on the date of the sale or exchange.

(1) Married couples §813

To qualify for the $500,000 exclusion, a married couple must file a joint return for the year in which the sale or exchange occurs and must still be married on the last day of the taxable year. Either spouse can be the record owner of the house, but *both* spouses must meet the two-year use and two-year prior sale requirement.

therefrom is given ***ordinary income treatment*** (*e.g.*, compensation paid for the sale of one's right of privacy).

d. Classification through correlation with related transaction §869

A transaction may be classified as ordinary or capital because it is part of a related transaction.

(1) Tax benefit rule §870

If taxpayer deducts certain notes as bad debts and later recovers on the notes, the recovery produces ordinary income. Thus, if taxpayer sells these notes, it would result in ordinary income, not capital gain.

4. Sale of Business Interests

a. Sole proprietorships §873

In determining capital gain vs. ordinary income on the sale of a proprietorship (or the sale of assets by a partnership or corporation), each asset is examined separately to determine if it qualifies as a capital asset (***fragmentation theory***). The parties can make a ***reasonable allocation*** of price to each asset.

(1) Goodwill §875

Goodwill is a capital asset and is depreciable by the buyer over a 15-year period.

(2) Covenant not to compete §876

Payment for a covenant not to compete is ordinary income to the seller. The amount paid is an asset to the buyer, which can be amortized over a 15-year period.

b. Partnerships and corporations §878

A partnership ***interest*** or corporate stock is generally a capital asset. ***Sale of assets*** is treated the same as in a proprietorship.

5. Assets Used in Trade or Business—Quasi-Capital Assets §881

Real property and depreciable personal property ***used in a trade or business*** and ***held for more than one year*** are "quasi-capital assets."

a. Other assets §884

Quasi-capital assets also include ***unharvested crops*** sold with the land, ***livestock herds*** held at least 24 months, and in certain cases, ***coal, timber, and minerals***.

b. Computation §886

If the gains exceed the losses, all the transactions are ***long-term capital transactions.*** If the losses exceed the gains, all the transactions are ***ordinary***. Losses within the preceding five years will result in treating current gain as ordinary income to the extent of previously unrecaptured losses (***recapture of losses***).

c. Special rules for casualties §888

If the taxpayer has recognized gains and losses from business or investment casualties and gains exceed losses, all such casualties are included in the section 1231 calculation.

d. Limitation—recapture of depreciation §891

Recapture of depreciation provisions **supersede** section 1231, turning capital gain into ordinary income. However, capital gains treatment for *any depreciable property* (not just section 1231 assets) is **not** allowed in sales or exchanges **between "related" taxpayers**, and **losses** are **not** deductible (*supra*).

C. WAS THERE A "SALE OR EXCHANGE"?

1. In General §896

Usually, there must be a "sale or exchange" of a capital asset for the transaction to be taxed as a capital gain or loss.

a. Aborted sales §897

If a "sale" occurred and the seller repossessed the property because of failure to pay the entire price, the amount that the seller keeps is capital gain.

b. Transfer of mineral interest §898

A mineral interest is a capital asset, but if the seller retains an *economic interest,* she is treated as not having sold the minerals (she can deduct depletion).

c. Transfers of franchises, trademarks, and trade names §899

Capital gains treatment is available on the transfer of a franchise, trademark, or trade name **only if** the transferor retains **no significant interest or power** therein. *Note: Sport franchises* are always entitled to capital gains treatment.

d. Contract rights §901

Generally, the transfer of contract rights between contracting parties is considered a "sale" and is given capital gains treatment. However, a minority of jurisdictions hold that this transfer does not constitute a "sale or exchange."

e. Foreclosure §903

Foreclosure is treated as a sale or exchange by the debtor; consequently it is given capital gain or loss treatment. But the *abandonment* of worthless property is **not** a sale or exchange and thus is an ordinary loss.

2. Special Situations in Which "Sale or Exchange" Deemed to Occur

a. Worthless debts and securities §906

Nonbusiness bad debts and worthless securities are deductible as capital losses.

b. Payments to creditors §907

Ordinarily, amounts paid by a debtor to a creditor are a return of capital and *not* a "sale or exchange." This general rule has been partially superseded by statute in that collection of a debt instrument (*e.g.,* bond, promissory note) is treated as a sale or exchange by the creditor.

c. Involuntary conversion §910
This is deemed equivalent to a "sale or exchange."

3. Validity of "Sale or Exchange" Not Affected by Seller's Retention of Control §911
If there is a complete transfer of title for a fair consideration, there is a sale. If the purchase price exceeds the value of the assets sold, the excess is ordinary income. Note that the grantor trust rules do not apply.

D. WAS THERE A SUFFICIENT "HOLDING PERIOD"?

1. In General §915
A capital asset must be held **more than 12 months** prior to a "sale or exchange" to qualify for a **long-term** capital gain; if held 12 months or less, it is a short-term gain.

2. "Tacking" of Holding Period Where Substituted Basis §917
A holding period commences only on a **change in basis** on the property. If there is no change, the taxpayer acquires the holding period of the transferor and can "tack" it to the time he holds the property.

E. GAINS ON SMALL BUSINESS STOCK

1. General Rule §918
A taxpayer (other than a corporation) can exclude from income 50% of the gain on the sale of qualified small business stock that has been held for at least five years.

2. Limit §919
The amount of gain subject to the 50% exclusion cannot exceed the greater of $10 million or 10 times the adjusted basis of the stock.

3. Qualified Small Business Stock §920
The stock must have been **issued after August 1993**, taxpayer must be the **original purchaser**, and the corporation must conduct an **active business** (excluding most service and real estate businesses) with **assets** after stock issuance **not exceeding $50 million**.

F. SPECIAL COMPUTATIONS

1. In General §922
Special rules may turn capital gain into ordinary income or require the deferral of certain losses.

2. "Imputed Interest" §923
Interest is imputed on sales wherein the payments are **deferred** and interest is charged at less than the prescribed rate. Interest produces ordinary income.

a. Exceptions §929
Total and partial exceptions to imputed interest rules include a selling price of $3,000 or less (**de minimus rule**) and **intrafamily real estate deals** (imputed interest cannot exceed 7%). The rules also are inapplicable to **buyers of personal use property**.

3. Recapture of Depreciation §933

Long-term or short-term gain attributable to prior depreciation may have to be reported as ***ordinary income*** if subject to special provisions.

a. Personal property §934

The realized gain on most depreciable tangible personal property is treated as ordinary income to the extent of all depreciation previously deducted by a taxpayer.

b. Real property (buildings) §937

Depreciation deductions in excess of straight-line rate (available only under prior law) taken with respect to buildings are recaptured.

c. Certain transfers not subject to depreciation recapture §938

Depreciation is recaptured on any sale or disposition of property ***except***:

(1) ***Transfers by reason of death or gift;*** and

(2) ***Most nonrecognition transfers.***

4. Disallowed Losses

a. Losses between related taxpayers §940

Losses between "related" taxpayers are not deductible, even if it was a bona fide transaction.

b. Personal losses §941

Personal expenses or losses not in connection with a trade or business or investments are not deductible.

c. Losses on "wash-sales" §942

These are not recognized and cannot be deducted.

d. Passive losses §943

Loss on passive activity is deductible only to the extent of income from that activity.

e. "At risk" rules §944

For certain investments, annual operating losses are limited to the amounts "at risk."

G. ALTERNATIVE MINIMUM TAX

1. Computation §946

Start with AGI, less certain deductions, plus "tax preferences" to arrive at alternative minimum taxable income ("AMTI"). Then subtract an exemption ($62,550 on joint returns, $42,500 on single). The exemptions are phased out for higher income taxpayers. The balance is taxed at a rate of 26% or 28%. If the alternative minimum tax ("AMT") exceeds the taxpayer's regular income tax, she must pay the AMT instead of the regular tax.

a. Capital gains §948

AMT on net capital gain is computed separately from the AMT on ordinary income. The AMT on net capital gain is at the same rate as for regular tax purposes.

c. **Property transferred in connection with performance of services—"timing rule"** §983

I.R.C. section 83 gives rules for the "timing" of an employee's income when the employer uses property (including stock) as compensation. Generally, the employee is taxed when he receives the property. However, if the property is subject to **both** a substantial risk of forfeiture **and** is nontransferable, the employee is not taxed (and the employer does not claim a deduction) until the first year in which the property is either nonforfeitible or transferable. The amount includible is the value of the property at the later date.

(1) **Nonlapse restrictions** §986

If the property is subject to a restriction that will never lapse, the includible amount is the formula price.

(2) **Other restrictions** §987

Restrictions on property not amounting to a substantial risk of forfeiture or a nonlapse restriction are ignored in valuing the property.

(3) **Employee election** §990

In any event, the taxpayer can elect to include value in income when the property is received.

d. **Employee's stock options** §992

Generally, stock or an option to buy stock issued by an employer is taxed as **ordinary income** to the employee. The **exercise** of the option is usually the taxable event unless it has an ascertainable value, in which case it can be included in income when received.

(1) **Employer's deduction** §997

The employer gets a deduction when the employee has income.

(2) **Incentive stock options** §998

If a stock option qualifies as an "incentive stock option" based on certain requirements, there is no tax on either the grant or exercise of the option. The employee is taxed when he sells the stock. The employer receives no deduction at any time.

e. **Claim of right doctrine** §999

If a taxpayer receives money or property and claims she is entitled to it and can freely dispose of it, it is immediately taxable, despite the fact that she might have to give it back.

(1) **Repayment** §1001

If repayment is made, the taxpayer receives a deduction in the year of repayment.

f. **Prepaid income** §1002

Prepayments are income when received.

(1) **Deposits** §1003

An advance payment for goods or services is currently taxable to the seller even if the goods or services are to be furnished in a later year. A security deposit, however, is not currently taxable.

g. **Prepaid expenses**   §1004
Amounts prepaid for goods or services to be received in later tax years must be *capitalized* and deducted ratably in future tax years.

h. **Credit card payments**   §1013
Payment for any deductible item by a credit card gives rise to a deduction when the item is charged, not when the bill is paid.

3. **Accrual Method**   §1014
The taxpayer reports income in whatever year it is *earned* (not necessarily paid) and deducts expenses in the year *incurred.* This method is required in all cases where *inventories* are a material factor affecting income, and for corporations, partnerships with a corporate partner, and tax shelters.

a. **Exceptions**   §1017
Important exceptions to the accrual method requirement include *S corporations*, corporations or partnerships with *average annual gross receipts of less than $5 million*, *qualified personal service corporations*, and *farming businesses*.

b. **Special problems with income under accrual method**

   (1) **Deferred income**   §1018
The test applied is whether *all events have occurred* that establish a right to income and the amount is reasonably determinable.

   (2) **Prepaid income**   §1023
Supreme Court cases hold that prepaid income is taxable *when received;* the IRS permits deferral of advance payments from sale of goods and limited deferral for advance payments for services.

   (3) **Dividends**   §1029
Taxpayer is treated as having no income until dividends are actually received.

   (4) **Increasing rents**   §1030
When a lease calls for increasing payments with total rent payments in excess of $250,000, both lessor and lessee must account for the rent on an accrual basis.

c. **Deductions under accrual method**   §1033
The criteria for deductibility are whether: (i) all events have occurred that establish an *unconditional duty to pay*; (ii) *economic performance* has occurred; and (iii) the amount is *reasonably ascertainable*.

   (1) **Fixed duty to pay**   §1034
It must be established that there is an unconditional duty to pay a reasonably determinable amount. Contingent liabilities and reserves are therefore not deductible.

(2) Economic performance rule   §1038
The all events test is not met until economic performance occurs. Economic performance occurs when services or property are actually provided to, or used by, the party obligated to pay for them.

(3) Disallowance of deduction for amount owed to related taxpayer   §1044
The Code *disallows* the accrual of such a deduction *until paid*. *Note:* No deduction is allowed until "economic performance" has occurred.

d. Inventories   §1047
When inventories are an income-producing factor, the taxpayer *must* account for purchases by using an *inventory.* The effect is that the taxpayer cannot deduct the cost of goods or materials in the year of the purchase *unless he sells them that year.* There are two methods by which the taxpayer may take his inventory:

(1) First-in, first-out ("FIFO")   §1049
The theory is that the goods first acquired were those that were first sold. The "cost" of the goods on hand at the close of the tax year is the cost of the goods last purchased.

(2) Last-in, first-out ("LIFO")   §1052
The last items placed in inventory are assumed to be the first sold. LIFO can be used for tax purposes only if also used for financial purposes.

4. Installment Method   §1055
This method is intended to allow sellers of *property* (other than "dealers") who are receiving payments on a deferred basis to include their gain only as they receive cash from the sale. The mechanics involve a fraction of the "gross profit" over "total contract price" being applied to each installment payment to determine how much of the payment is income (but interest payments are entirely includible). The installment method can be used only for sales of non-dealer property, not services, and only if the transaction produces a gain.

a. Restrictions   §1061
The installment method cannot be used for *debts payable on demand* (or readily transferable), *sales to related persons*, *dealer property*, or *sale of assets of an accrual method business*.

b. Interest on deferred income   §1064
When the installment sale price *exceeds $150,000*, the taxpayer must pay interest to the government on the deferred tax liability if the face amount of *all* such obligations held by the taxpayer and that arose during, and are still outstanding at the close of, the taxable year, exceeds *$5 million*.

c. Mortgaged property   §1068
When a buyer takes subject to a mortgage, the mortgage is not considered in determining the seller's total contract price or payments received in the year of the sale, unless the seller's basis is less than the mortgage.

Approach to Exams

In spite of the great complexity in the income tax field, you will find that tax issues can be broken down into a relatively small number of areas. In resolving tax problems on your exam, it may be helpful to focus on each issue within the following analytical framework:

I. IS IT INCOME?

A. Does the particular item fall within the *definition* of income used under I.R.C. section 61?

B. Does it fall within any of the statutory *exclusions* from income?

II. TO WHOM IS THE INCOME TAXABLE?

If a gift has been made, is income shifted to the donee? Consider the following:

A. Was the gift of *property* or of the *income from property*?

B. Was the gift of income from *services*?

C. Did the donor retain *excessive controls*?

D. If the gift was in *trust*, is income taxed to the grantor, the beneficiary, or the trust?

III. IS IT DEDUCTIBLE?

A. Does it qualify as a *business or investment* deduction?

  1. Is the item *business or personal*?

  2. Is it a *current expense or a capital outlay*?

  3. Is it *ordinary and necessary*?

  4. Is it *barred by public policy*?

  5. If it is not an expense, can it be deducted as *depreciation, depletion, a loss, or a bad debt*?

  6. Is the deduction *above the line or below the line*, and is it limited by the restriction on "*miscellaneous itemized deductions*"?

B. Does it qualify as a *personal deduction*? If so, it must fit within the statutory provisions for interest, charitable contributions, etc.

IV. DOES A SALE OF PROPERTY PRODUCE GAIN OR LOSS?

A. How much was the *gain or loss*?

    1. What was the *basis*? Are there any adjustments to basis?

    2. Was there a *realization*? If so, what was the amount realized?

    3. Does the transaction qualify for *nonrecognition*?

B. Is the asset a *capital asset*? If so, was there a *"sale or exchange"*?

V. DOES THE ALTERNATIVE MINIMUM TAX ("AMT") APPLY?

A. What is the taxpayer's "alternative minimum taxable income"?

B. What is the taxpayer's exemption under the AMT?

C. What is the taxpayer's AMT?

D. Is the AMT greater than the taxpayer's "regular" tax?

VI. WHEN IS THE ITEM INCOME OR DEDUCTIBLE?

A. Does the taxpayer use the *cash* method, the *accrual* method, or the *installment* method?

B. If the transaction spans *several years*, should *each* year be taken separately, or can the *entire* period be considered?

STEPS FOR DETERMINING TAX LIABILITY

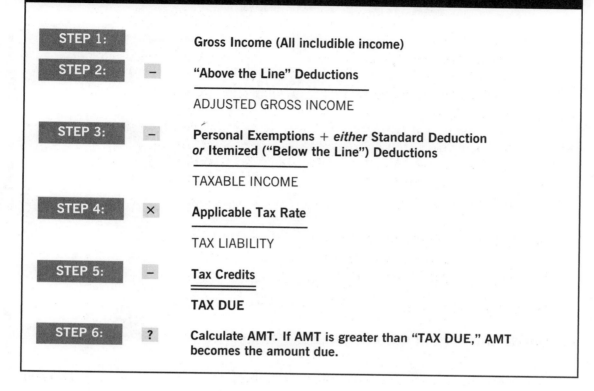

STEP 1:   **Gross Income (All includible income)**

STEP 2:   −   **"Above the Line" Deductions**

ADJUSTED GROSS INCOME

STEP 3:   −   **Personal Exemptions + *either* Standard Deduction *or* Itemized ("Below the Line") Deductions**

TAXABLE INCOME

STEP 4:   ×   **Applicable Tax Rate**

TAX LIABILITY

STEP 5:   −   **Tax Credits**

TAX DUE

STEP 6:   ?   **Calculate AMT. If AMT is greater than "TAX DUE," AMT becomes the amount due.**

Chapter One:
Is It Income?

CONTENTS

Chapter Approach

One of the most basic questions in a tax situation is whether an item is income. Therefore, you will almost certainly see a question that requires you to make such a determination. In considering whether an item is income, use the following checklist:

1. Is an item *income under I.R.C. section 61*? To decide, ask:

   a. Did the item increase the taxpayer's *net worth*?

   b. Or did it merely involve a *change of form*, like borrowing money or recovering basis?

2. Does the item fall under a *statutory exclusion* from gross income? Is it:

   a. *Gift or inheritance* (as opposed to compensation for services)?

   b. *Award or scholarship*?

   c. *Contribution to capital*?

   d. *Life insurance recovery*?

   e. *Recovery of the cost of an annuity contract*?

   f. *Interest on state or local bonds*?

   g. *Government benefits*? (*But note:* Some benefits, *e.g.*, unemployment compensation and a part of Social Security, are taxed.)

   h. *Medical insurance recovery*?

   i. *Damages for personal physical injuries or damages for business injuries*?

   j. *Meals and lodging for the convenience of the employer*?

3. Is it a taxable *form of compensation* for services? Most compensation (whether paid in cash or property) is taxable, including employer payment of employee expenses, but some forms of compensation are specially treated. Thus, is the item:

   a. A tax-free *fringe benefit*?

   b. *Employer-paid health insurance* or medical reimbursement?

   c. *Group term life insurance*?

4. Is the item *debt cancellation income* and, if so, does it qualify for exclusion? Remember:

a. *Insolvent and bankrupt taxpayers* can avoid debt cancellation income but must reduce tax attributes.

b. *Shareholder debt forgiveness* has special rules.

5. Is the item *spousal or child support*? Keep in mind that:

a. *Spousal support* is taxable to the recipient, deductible by the payor.

b. *Recapture* is possible if the amount declines during the first three years.

c. *Child support* is neither taxable nor deductible.

A. Constitutional Background

1. Constitutional Provisions [§1]

The Constitution provides that Congress "shall have power to lay and collect taxes . . . ." [Art. I, §8, cl. 1] However, "[n]o capitation, *or other direct*, tax shall be laid unless in proportion to the census . . . ." [Art. I, §9, cl. 4; Art. I, §2, cl. 3] The meaning of the second provision is that a "direct" tax has to be apportioned among the states so that a state with 1% of the population will bear 1% of the tax.

a. Income tax held unconstitutional [§2]

An income tax statute was struck down in 1895 as an unapportioned direct tax. [**Pollock v. Farmers Loan & Trust Co.,** 157 U.S. 429 (1895)] The idea was that a tax on rents, interest, or dividends was equivalent to a tax on the underlying real or personal property and thus was a "direct" tax. In the same case, the Court also held unconstitutional a federal tax on the interest from state or municipal bonds. For this and other reasons, such interest is still not subject to federal taxation.

2. Sixteenth Amendment [§3]

The requirement of apportionment among the states made a federal income tax completely impractical. However, this problem was solved by the adoption in 1913 of the Sixteenth Amendment, which states: "The Congress shall have power to lay and collect taxes *on incomes, from whatever source derived,* without apportionment among the several states, and without regard to any census of enumeration."

3. *Eisner v. Macomber* [§4]

In only one case since 1913 has the Supreme Court held an income tax provision unconstitutional. Congress had attempted to tax a dividend of common stock distributed to existing holders of common stock. The Court held that the Sixteenth

Amendment requires a *realization*, an element lacking in a stock dividend. [**Eisner v. Macomber**, 252 U.S. 189 (1920); *see infra*, §§762 *et seq.*] Many but not all stock dividends are excluded from tax by the present statute. (*See* Taxation of Business Entities Summary.)

4. **Remaining Constitutional Issues [§5]**

Since the adoption of the Sixteenth Amendment, constitutional issues have been of much less importance. However, certain constitutional issues can still be raised:

a. **Due process violation [§6]**

A tax imposing unreasonable or arbitrary distinctions could be a violation of the Due Process Clause of the Fifth Amendment. Thus, a now repealed provision on child care deductions was held unconstitutional because of arbitrary distinctions between men and women. [**Moritz v. Commissioner**, 469 F.2d 466 (10th Cir. 1972), *cert. denied*, 412 U.S. 906 (1973)]

b. **Tax not on income [§7]**

If a particular tax is not "on income," it is not legitimated by the Sixteenth Amendment. While courts have traditionally allowed Congress to define "income" virtually without constitutional review, one court has recently called this practice into question. [*See* **Murphy v. United States**, 2006 WL 2411372 (D.C. Cir.); *and see infra*, §96] However, such a tax could be valid as an *indirect* tax under Article I, Section 8, Clause 1, as to which there was never an apportionment requirement. [**Penn Mutual Indemnity Co. v. Commissioner**, 277 F.2d 16 (3d Cir. 1960)]

c. **Tax procedures invalid [§8]**

Constitutional issues frequently arise in connection with tax procedures. These can include unlawful search and seizure, right to counsel, and the like.

B. Definition of "Gross Income"

1. **I.R.C. Definition [§9]**

The definition of "gross income" set forth in Internal Revenue Code ("I.R.C.") section 61 echoes the language of the Sixteenth Amendment. Some cases have said that this section is intended to reach every transaction that it constitutionally could. It provides: "Gross income means *all income from whatever source derived* . . . ."

a. **Specific items included**

Section 61 lists many specific items that are gross income: interest, rents, dividends, business profits, salaries, gain on sale of property, alimony, etc.

b. **Not exclusive list**

However, as section 61 makes clear, this list is *not exclusive*. Many other transactions produce gross income although not mentioned in I.R.C. section 61.

2. **Early Attempts to Define Income [§10]**

In **Eisner v. Macomber,** *supra,* the Court held that gross income (in both the constitutional and statutory senses) meant a gain "derived from capital, from labor, or from both combined . . . ." However, this definition proved far too narrow; it was difficult to stretch it to cover debt cancellation income or windfalls (both discussed *infra*). Consequently, it has now been abandoned.

3. **Net Worth Concept [§11]**

The prevailing definition of income is that any item that increases a taxpayer's **net worth** is gross income. [*See* **Commissioner v. Glenshaw Glass Co.**, 348 U.S. 426 (1955)—punitive damages taxable as income] One's net worth (or **wealth**) is the difference between **assets and liabilities**. Anything that increases that difference is potentially income. Anything that decreases it is potentially deductible. (However, deductions must be specifically provided for by statute.)

a. **Change in form [§12]**

There is no income from a receipt that does not increase net worth.

(1) **Loan repayment [§13]**

The *repayment of a loan* does not produce income to the lender, because it does not increase her net worth. There is simply a change in the form of her property—from a loan receivable to cash.

(a) **Interest is income [§14]**

Interest paid to the lender for the use of her money is income.

> **Example:** Donny Debtor repays a note for $500 plus $50 interest to Larry Lender. Larry Lender must report $50 as taxable income (the interest), but he does not have to report the $500 repayment.

(b) **Repayment when note purchased for less than face value [§15]**

If the creditor bought the debt for *less than its face value,* its repayment by the debtor would produce a profit, which would be income.

> **Example:** Before repayment, Larry Lender sells the $500 note to Tom Transferee for $300. Tom collects full repayment ($500) from Donny Debtor, plus $50 in interest. Tom must report $200 (the difference between the face value of the note and the amount he paid for the note) and the $50 interest as taxable income.

(2) **Return of capital [§16]**

Similarly, a *return of invested capital* is not income; the taxpayer has merely recovered his cost, not increased his net worth. [**Doyle v. Mitchell Bros.**, 247 U.S. 179 (1918)]

Example: If Warren buys a share of stock for $30 and sells it for $32, his income is only $2; he is entitled to get back the $30 without tax.

b. Borrowing [§17]

There is no income from borrowing money. Borrowing increases assets and liabilities by the same amount and thus does not create net worth. However, monies obtained by *embezzlement or extortion* are treated as income. (*See infra,* §§158-159.)

c. Trust income [§18]

Amounts received by a taxpayer as a trustee do not increase the trustee's wealth because the trustee must use the amounts for a particular purpose that does not primarily benefit the trustee. Thus, these amounts are not income to the trustee. But note that a trust itself may be a taxable entity. (*See infra,* §278.)

Example: A political candidate is not taxed on political contributions because they must be expended for campaign purposes. However, if the candidate diverts the contribution to his personal use, it becomes taxable. [Rev. Rul. 74-22, 1974-1 C.B. 16; Rev. Rul. 74-23, 1974-1 C.B. 17]

d. "Income" need not be received in cash [§19]

The receipt of property or services is frequently treated as income. Thus, for example, noncash benefits and services received by an *employee* (*e.g.,* company car or free housing) may be taxable (*see infra,* §§135-141). Debt cancellation income is another example of noncash income (*see infra,* §142).

e. Windfalls [§20]

Under authority of *Glenshaw Glass, supra,* "found money" or windfalls (*e.g.,* winning the lottery or finding money in a piano bought at a garage sale) are taxable. [**Cesarini v. United States,** 296 F. Supp. 3 (N.D. Ohio 1969), *aff'd,* 428 F.2d 812 (6th Cir. 1970)]

EXAM TIP   **gilbert**

For exam purposes, remember that *all* income from *whatever source* must be declared as income, even if, as a practical matter, the Internal Revenue Service would probably not be aware of the income, as in the piano windfall case above.

---

f. Unsolicited property [§21]

An item received involuntarily is not taxable until the taxpayer indicates that he intends to retain it.

Example: A school principal received unsolicited books from publishers and then donated them to charity. He claimed that the books were not includible in income but took a charitable deduction for their value. The court disagreed; the books must be included in income. Possession of them increased the taxpayer's wealth, and his donation of the books, when coupled with the act of claiming a charitable deduction, indicated that he intended to accept them. [**Haverly v. United States,** 513 F.2d 224 (7th Cir.), *cert. denied,* 423 U.S. 912 (1975)]

---

(1) Note

The court in *Haverly, supra,* commented that the result might be different if the taxpayer did not accept the books but merely held them for the publishers. Indeed, the court did not decide whether the books would be income had the taxpayer *not claimed a charitable deduction.* Failure to claim the deduction could suggest that he failed to exercise "complete dominion" over the books—something that might be required by the realization requirement.

(2) And note

In *Haverly, supra,* the Internal Revenue Service ("IRS") conceded that it made no effort to tax unsolicited samples unless the taxpayer sought a double deduction (*e.g.,* by giving them to charity and claiming a deduction after excluding them from income). The court said that the IRS's decisions concerning allocation of enforcement resources were none of its concern.

g. All-inclusive definition [§22]

Any increment in net worth is presumed to be income unless specifically excluded (*see infra,* §§27 *et seq.*) or unless a nonrecognition section applies (*see infra,* §§784 *et seq.*). In other words, Congress is presumed to have fully used its constitutional power to tax income. However, a *realization* (*see infra,* §§762 *et seq.*) must occur before an increase in net worth becomes taxable. This means that some event must occur so that it is appropriate to tax the increase in wealth *now.*

Example: In Year 1, Paul buys an "Elvis on Black Velvet" painting for $1 at a garage sale. In Year 2, he has it appraised and discovers its value is $1,000. In Year 3, he sells the painting for $1,000. Paul has $999 of income *in Year 3* because that is when he realized his gain.

---

(1) Note

Eisner v. Macomber (*supra,* §10) held that a realization was a *constitutional* requirement. The courts today would probably permit Congress to dispense with the requirement of realization [*see* **Commissioner v. Glenshaw Glass Co.,** *supra,* §11], but Congress has not done so.

4. Imputed Income [§23]

According to many economists, imputed income should be treated as gross income.

Imputed income is created when the taxpayer *works for himself or uses his own property*—for example, lives in his own house. Conceptually, this could be said to create rental income (and other countries have treated it as such). The point can be illustrated this way: If two taxpayers each own a house and rent it to the other, each one will have rental income. Why should it be any different if each lives in his own house? However, with the exception noted below, Congress has never sought to tax imputed income. Thus, for example, the value of housekeeping services to one's own family is not taxed.

a. Working for oneself [§24]
However, if one renders services to himself *and an employment relationship is also involved*, the courts have held that the benefit produced is income. [**Commissioner v. Minzer**, 279 F.2d 338 (5th Cir. 1960)]

> **Example:** If a real estate *broker* buys a house for himself and splits the commission with the broker for the seller, the reduction in purchase price is not income. But if a real estate *salesperson* employed by a broker does the same thing, he does have income. The bargain purchase is seen as part of the employment relationship and thus produces taxable income.

b. Exception—interest income may be imputed [§25]
I.R.C. sections 483, 1274, and 7872 *require that interest income be imputed* in certain situations (*see infra, §923*).

c. Exchange of services [§26]
If two taxpayers exchange goods or services, both will have income unless some exclusion applies. Such a transaction is treated as though each taxpayer had charged an appropriate fee (thus receiving income) and then used the money to pay the other one. [Treas. Reg. §1.61-2(d)(1)]

> **Example:** If a lawyer and a plumber each work for the other for five hours without any cash changing hands, each will have income equal to the value of services provided to him. [Rev. Rul. 79-24, 1979-1 C.B. 60]

C. Exclusions from Gross Income

1. In General [§27]
The scope of the Sixteenth Amendment and I.R.C. section 61 has been sharply limited by a long list of *exclusions*—items that would be income except that Congress has chosen to exclude them.

2. Gifts and Inheritances [§28]
Gross income does not include the value of property received by a gift, devise, bequest, or inheritance. [I.R.C. §102(a)]

a. **What is a "gift"? [§29]**
The *motive of the donor* determines whether the transaction results in a tax-free "gift" to the donee. If the donor had mixed motives, his primary motive controls. There must be a showing of *"detached and disinterested generosity."* The transfer must be made "out of affection, respect, admiration, charity or like impulses." [**Commissioner v. Duberstein,** 363 U.S. 278 (1960)]

(1) **Rule of construction [§30]**
The concept of "gift" is *narrowly* applied by the courts, so as to limit the scope of the exclusion.

(a) **Distinguish—gift tax construction**
For *federal gift tax* purposes, the opposite is true: A broad construction of "gift" is adopted in order to reach as many transactions as possible.

(b) **Note—different results**
Hence, a particular transaction could be a taxable gift for gift tax purposes, but not a gift for income tax purposes. In such event, the donor would have to pay a gift tax and the recipient would have to pay income tax! [*See* **Farid-Es-Sultaneh v. Commissioner,** 160 F.2d 812 (2d Cir. 1947)]

(2) **Gift vs. compensation [§31]**
Amounts transferred by an employer to, or for the benefit of, an *employee* cannot be excluded as gifts. [I.R.C. §102(c)] Such transfers are taxable regardless of whether the employer intended to compensate the employee or whether the employer made the transfer solely out of affection or other disinterested generosity. However, a transfer to an employee who is also a relative can be treated as a gift if "the purpose of the transfer can be substantially attributed to the familial relation of the parties and not to the circumstances of their employment." [Prop. Reg. §1.102-1(f)(2)] *But note:* Many transfers to persons who are *not* employees involve mixed motivations by the transferor. It is often difficult to decide whether such transfers should be classified as gifts.

(a) **Background—leading cases**

1) *Commissioner v. Duberstein* **[§32]**
The *Duberstein* case, *supra,* presented this problem. Duberstein had frequently told Berman of potential customers for Berman's products. Berman sent Duberstein a Cadillac. Obviously, this represented both recognition of Duberstein's past services to Berman and also was designed to encourage future referrals. The Supreme Court held that it was not a gift. As to the past

referrals, Berman owed Duberstein a moral obligation (although not a legal obligation) for the valuable favors. As to the future referrals, Berman was actuated by self-interest. In both cases, Berman's primary motivation was not "detached and disinterested generosity" or "affection, respect, admiration, charity or like impulses."

2) *Stanton v. United States* [§33]

Yet in **Stanton v. United States,** 287 F.2d 876 (2d Cir. 1961) (which was decided with *Duberstein*), the Court declined to rule as a matter of law that a gift can never arise from an employment relationship. Stanton was a church treasurer who was given a bonus by the church when he retired. The Court held that it was for the trier of fact to decide the church's primary motivation; it was possible that the church could meet the "detached and disinterested generosity" test. In fact, it was subsequently held that the payments were gifts.

a) Note

Under section 102(c) (above), which was enacted in 1986, the transfer to Stanton would be treated as income regardless of the church's motivation, because a transfer to an employee cannot be excluded as a gift.

3) Effect [§34]

When a transfer falls outside the terms of section 102(c), because it does not arise out of employment, the law is very unclear. The result of *Duberstein* and *Stanton* is to leave great discretion with the trier of fact. Inconsistent and unpredictable results are inevitable.

---

e.g. Example: A man made large transfers of cash and property to his mistress, who did not include them in income. The mistress was convicted of criminal tax evasion. The conviction was reversed; the court held that she could not have had the requisite willfulness to be guilty of tax evasion because she could not know whether the man made the transfers out of affection or to compensate her. Yet this distinction, based on the transferor's intention, is critical in deciding whether the transfers were taxable under section 102. In dictum, the court suggested that such payments should generally be treated as gifts under section 102. [**United States v. Harris,** 942 F.2d 1125 (7th Cir. 1991)]

(b) Deduction by donor [§35]

Ordinarily, if a transfer is a "gift," it could not also be deductible as a business expense to the transferor because it would lack sufficiently close connections to business. (*See infra,* §303.) However, the income issue and deduction issue are not inseparably connected and it is possible that an item could be *both* a gift and deductible, especially if the issues are considered by different courts. If the transferor deducts the payment to the transferee, this fact is relevant, but not conclusive, in ascertaining the transferor's motive. The transferor's action in taking the deduction suggests that there was a business reason for making the transfer, which would negate its being treated as a gift to the transferee. [**Commissioner v. Duberstein,** *supra,* §32]

1) Note
If the recipient is entitled to exclude the payment as a gift, the payor's deduction is limited to $25. [I.R.C. §274; *see infra,* §337]

(c) Death benefits [§36]
Many cases have considered whether a payment by an employer to an employee's surviving spouse (or other beneficiary) can be treated as a gift. It might be argued that the payment is motivated by sympathy rather than by a desire to provide additional compensation for the decedent's services. [*See* **Estate of Carter v. Commissioner,** 453 F.2d 61 (2d Cir. 1971); **Poyner v. Commissioner,** 301 F.2d 287 (4th Cir. 1962)] Section 102(c) might render all such payments *taxable* to the recipient, regardless of the employer's motivation. Section 102(c) provides that a payment cannot be treated as a gift if paid by an employer "on behalf of" an employee; it could be argued that a payment to a surviving spouse is such a payment. The point has not yet been settled.

1) Deductibility by employer [§37]
If found to be taxable to the surviving spouse, the payment is probably deductible as a business expense. However, if the payment is found to have been a gift to the recipient, the payment is probably nondeductible to the employer. If the payment were found to be a gift to the recipient but also deductible to the employer, the deduction is limited to $25. [*See* I.R.C. §274(b)(1); *infra,* §337]

(d) Gratuities [§38]
Tips and gratuities, such as those received by waiters or taxi drivers, are compensation for services rather than gifts, and hence taxable to the recipient. [**Roberts v. Commissioner,** 176 F.2d 221 (9th Cir. 1949)]

Example: "Tokes" received by gambling dealers are not gifts. Because gamblers pay them out of a superstitious belief that they produce good luck, they are not paid from detached or disinterested generosity. They are taxable even though they are not payment for any special service and there is no social compulsion to pay them. [**Olk v. United States,** 536 F.2d 876 (9th Cir. 1976)]

(e) Strike benefits [§39]
Benefits paid to striking union members by their union are ordinarily taxable income. Such benefits are paid to further the union's objectives and to induce persons to join the union; they are not "gifts" from the union. [**Hagar v. Commissioner,** 43 T.C. 468 (1965)]

1) Distinguish—benefits paid to nonmembers
In one case, the Supreme Court upheld a jury's finding that strike benefits paid by a union to *nonmembers* were "gifts" from the union, ". . . proceeding primarily from generosity rather than from the incentive of anticipated economic benefit." [**United States v. Kaiser,** 363 U.S. 299 (1960)]

(3) Gifts to spouses [§40]
While gifts to family members generally fall within the "detached and disinterested generosity" standard in *Duberstein* (*see supra*, §35), transfers to spouses are specifically excluded from income by statute, and this exclusion applies even if the transfer was not made from detached and disinterested generosity. [I.R.C. §1041(a)(1)]

(4) Bargain purchases [§41]
When a person "sells" property to another for less than the property's value, an issue arises whether the difference between the value and the amount paid should be treated as a gift to the "buyer," as income to the "buyer," or as an ordinary purchase transaction that is neither a gift nor income to the "buyer." This issue depends on the "seller's" motives and the circumstances of the parties.

(a) Application

1) *If the "seller" is misinformed as to the value,* or knows the value but must make a *distress sale,* there is no income or gift. The "buyer" has merely made an advantageous purchase.

Example: To pay off a note that is about to come due, Sam sells an antique that he had appraised at $5,000 to Bart for $3,500. Sam had earlier purchased the antique for $300. Sam and Bart are not related and do not know each other, and the sale to Bart occurs on an Internet auction site. The difference between market value and sale price ($1,500) is neither income nor a gift to Bart. Also, Sam has a gain of $3,200 on the sale to Bart.

2) *If the "seller's" motives proceed from disinterested generosity,* the "bargain" element is an excludible gift. Also, if the "buyer" is a recognized charity, the "bargain" element may be *deductible* by the seller as a *charitable contribution* (*see infra,* §640).

> **e.g.** **Example:** Mary sells her car (actually worth $2,000) to her granddaughter, April, for $800. April has probably received a gift of $1,200.

(b) Distinguish—compensation cases [§42]
Bargain purchases that are compensation for services produce income to the person who rendered the services. [I.R.C. §83(a), discussed *infra,* §§983-991] However, certain bargain purchases are excluded fringe benefits. [I.R.C. §132(c), discussed *infra,* §117]

> **e.g.** **Example:** As part of his employment, Eastco grants Paul a nontransferable *option* to purchase shares of Eastco's stock at $5 per share. Because the option is difficult to value, the receipt of the option is not a taxable event. [I.R.C. §83(e)(3)] Paul exercises the option, purchasing 100 shares for $500. The stock is then worth $2,000. Paul has received income of $1,500. [**Commissioner v. LoBue,** 351 U.S. 243 (1956)] In *LoBue,* the Court held it immaterial that the employer's purpose was to give its employee a proprietary interest in the business. *Note:* Certain stock options that meet precisely defined criteria do not produce income when exercised (*see infra,* §§992-998).

b. What is "inheritance"? [§43]
The inheritance exclusion applies not only to property received under a will or through intestate succession, but also to any other payment that is "referable" to such an inheritance.

(1) Will contest settlement [§44]
Money received by an heir in settlement of a will contest has been held tantamount to receiving an inheritance and, therefore, excluded from income. [**Lyeth v. Hoey,** 305 U.S. 188 (1938)]

(2) Compensation for past services [§45]
But a bequest from an employer to an employee is taxable. [I.R.C. §102(c)]

EXAM TIP	gilbert

On your exam, be sure to remember that *all* "gifts" or "bequests" *from employers to employees are taxable* under section 102(c), no matter how much the facts of the problem try to point you in the other direction. Thus, if Faithful Butler has worked for Testator for 20 years, tending to Testator's every need, while Testator's children could not be bothered even to visit Testator during the past 10 years, and, as a result, Testator leaves all of his estate to Faithful Butler, the "bequest" is taxable income to Butler.

(3) Payment for services to estate [§46]

Similarly, a *"bequest" made to an executor* is not exempt if intended as a *substitute* for the fees payable for his services to the estate. The test is whether the beneficiary was required to perform the services as an executor to obtain the bequest. [*See* **United States v. Merriam,** 263 U.S. 179 (1923)]

(a) Note

An executor who *waives* the commissions due him for his services to the estate will not be taxed on the value of his services, even though he is also a legatee, provided the waiver is "within a reasonable time after entering upon his duties." [Rev. Rul. 66-167, 1966-1 C.B. 20]

c. Income derived from gifts [§47]

Even when property is transferred as a tax-free gift, any *income subsequently derived* by the donee from the property is taxable. [I.R.C. §102(b)(1)]

Example: Father conveys to son (by inter vivos or testamentary gift) an apartment building worth $500,000. Son is not required to include the value in his gross income. However, the rentals thereafter received from the apartment building are income to son.

(1) Distinguish—gift of future income [§48]

If the gift involved is *solely of future income,* then *all* money received is taxable to the donee. [I.R.C. §102(b)(2)—codifying **Irwin v. Gavit,** 268 U.S. 161 (1925)] However, if a donor gives the donee income from the property but retains the property for herself, the donor is taxed on the income (*see infra,* §191). (*See also* the discussion of the taxation of trusts, *infra,* §§249 *et seq.*, as to dividing the income from the gift between the trust and beneficiaries.)

Example: If Andy bequeaths to Betty the income for life from certain stocks, remainder to Clyde, the dividend income thereafter received by Betty is taxable to her, even though she received it as a gift.

3. Awards and Scholarships [§49]

Under present law, most awards and scholarships do *not* qualify for exclusion and thus are taxable.

a. Awards and prizes [§50]

Awards and prizes are taxable to the recipient. [I.R.C. §74(a)] Thus, for example, the Nobel Prize is taxable. (It was excludible prior to 1987.)

(1) Exception—charitable transfer [§51]

A prize is not taxable to the recipient if: (i) it was received for scientific, educational, or similar achievements, and (ii) the recipient orders that it be transferred to a charity. [I.R.C. §74(b)]

Example: If the winner of the Nobel Prize orders the Nobel committee to transfer her award to the American Cancer Society, the recipient would not include the award in income (but also would not be entitled to a charitable deduction for the transfer).

---

(2) Exception—employee achievement awards [§52]

An award to an employee for length of service or safety achievement is not taxable unless it cost the employer more than $400. [I.R.C. §§74(c), 274(j)]

b. Scholarships and fellowships [§53]

With certain exceptions, scholarships and fellowships are taxable to the recipient. [I.R.C. §117]

(1) Exception—qualified scholarship [§54]

An amount received as a "qualified scholarship" is excluded from income. A qualified scholarship is an amount that can be used only to pay *tuition and fees* or for *required books or supplies*. Only degree candidates at tax-exempt educational organizations are entitled to this exclusion. [I.R.C. §117(b)] An amount received in payment for teaching, research, or other services, required as a condition for receiving the grant, does not qualify for the exclusion. [I.R.C. §117(c)]

Example: Sandra receives a scholarship of $8,000 per year to attend law school. The school requires that $6,500 of this grant be applied to tuition and books. Of the $8,000, $6,500 is excludible, but the remaining $1,500 of the grant (which defrays Sandra's living expenses) is taxable.

---

(2) Exception—tuition reduction [§55]

With some qualifications, a tuition reduction plan does not result in taxable income. Generally, such plans must not discriminate in favor of highly compensated employees. Also, the tax benefit applies only with respect to undergraduate, not graduate, education. [I.R.C. §117(d)]

 Example: The child of Tina, a Princeton professor, is an undergraduate at Stanford. There is a plan by which the children of full-time employees of either school can attend the other school free of tuition. The tuition reduction at Stanford is not taxable to Tina.

---

4. Contributions to Capital [§56]

If an investor contributes capital to a corporation or partnership, the amount received is *not* taxable to the recipient (whether or not the investor receives stock or a partnership interest in exchange). [I.R.C. §§118(a), 1032]

a. Distinguish—contributions by government or customers [§57]

Amounts received from a government to induce business construction in a particular area are taxable. Similarly, any amount contributed to a business by a customer or potential customer is taxable. [I.R.C. §118(b)]

Example: Wisconsin gives $2.5 million to Cheesy, Inc. to locate one of its plants in the state. The amount is taxable.

---

5. Life Insurance—Amounts Paid by Reason of Insured's Death [§58]

Benefits paid under an insurance contract, by reason of the death of the insured, are *excluded* from gross income. [I.R.C. §101(a)]

a. "Life insurance" defined [§59]

Neither the Code nor the Regulations defines what constitutes "life insurance" as used in section 101(a). However, the Supreme Court has indicated that "life insurance historically and commonly *involves risk-shifting and risk-distributing.*" [**Helvering v. Le Gierse,** 312 U.S. 531 (1941)] Therefore, if the particular contract does not shift any risk of premature death to the insurance company, it is not life insurance. [Rev. Rul. 65-57, 1965-1 C.B. 56]

(1) Distinguish—employer-paid benefits [§60]

Death benefits paid by an employer, whether voluntarily or under a plan, are taxable (*see supra*, §36).

(2) Debtor's insurance [§61]

Creditors often take out life insurance on the life of the debtor. If the debtor dies, the insurance is applied to pay off the debt. The amount thus received by the creditor is treated as payment of the debt (which might be taxable if it exceeds the basis of the debt), *not* as excludible life insurance. [Rev. Rul. 70-54, 1970-1 C.B. 218]

(3) Accelerated death benefits [§62]

Life insurance amounts payable before death to a terminally or chronically ill individual are treated as if paid by reason of death. For this purpose, a terminally ill individual is one certified by a physician as having less than 24 months to live. A chronically ill individual is one unable to perform at least two of the activities of daily living without assistance. Similarly, amounts received by reason of the sale of a life insurance policy to a "viatical settlement provider" is treated as if paid by reason of death. A "viatical settlement provider" is in the business of purchasing life insurance policies from terminally or chronically ill insured persons. [I.R.C. §§101(g), 7702B(c)]

EXAM TIP   **gilbert**

Remember that although life insurance death benefits, inheritance, and gifts are **excluded** from income **for income tax purposes**, they may be subject to **estate or gift taxes**.

---

b. Premium payments [§63]

Life insurance proceeds are excluded regardless of **who** paid the premiums on the policy. And it does not matter that the proceeds are paid to the insured's estate, her family, or creditors (except as discussed *supra,* §61), or to the partnership or corporation of which she was a member. [Treas. Reg. §1.101(a)]

(1) Policy owned by corporation [§64]

If a corporation owns and pays the premiums on an insurance policy on the life of its controlling shareholder, the proceeds are subject to **estate tax** in the shareholder's estate. [Treas. Reg. §20.2042-l(c)(6); *and see* Estate and Gift Tax Summary] But payment of the proceeds will **not** be taxed as a **dividend** to the beneficiary, even if he is himself a shareholder. [**Ducros v. Commissioner,** 272 F.2d 49 (6th Cir. 1959); **Estate of Horne v. Commissioner,** 64 T.C. 1020 (1975)]

c. Purchasers of existing policies [§65]

The exclusion for life insurance does **not** apply to a taxpayer who has **purchased** an existing policy for consideration.

---

e.g. **Example:** The owner of an existing policy sells it to Tammy for consideration. Tammy pays additional premiums. The insured dies. The proceeds are taxed to Tammy, except, of course, she can recover her basis—purchase price plus subsequent premiums. [I.R.C. §101(a)(2)]

---

(1) Exception [§66]

The "purchaser" rule does not apply if the purchaser is the insured himself, his partner or partnership, or a corporation in which he is a shareholder or officer. It also does not apply if the person acquiring the policy has a carryover basis from the transferor (as could occur, for example, if the policy was purchased by one spouse from the other; *see infra,* §§816 *et seq.*, discussing I.R.C. section 1041). In these situations, the entire proceeds are excludible, not just the transferee's basis.

d. Installment payments [§67]

If the death benefits are payable by the insurer in installments, and the unpaid balance bears *interest*, that portion of the installment payments that represents interest is taxable, although the balance is exempt. If the insurer simply holds the proceeds and pays interest on the amount held, the interest is taxable. [I.R.C. §101(c), (d)] If the installment payments are computed without a separate allocation of interest in each payment, the amount treated as interest is determined in the same manner as for annuities (*see* below).

6. Annuities [§68]

An annuity contract is one in which the taxpayer invests a fixed sum, which is later paid back, with interest, in installments for a set period or for life. That part of each annuity payment that represents the taxpayer's *investment* in the policy is exempt as a return of capital. The interest portion, however, is income. [I.R.C. §72]

a. Computation of excluded portion [§69]

The excludible portion of an annuity contract payment can be calculated by multiplying the payment by a fraction, the numerator of which is the amount that the taxpayer invested in the annuity contract and the denominator of which is the taxpayer's total expected return from the annuity contract. Mathematically:

$$\text{excludible amount} = \text{annuity payment} \times \frac{\text{investment}}{\text{total expected return}}$$

Example: Thurston purchases an annuity contract for $9,000 (investment). The contract provides that Thurston will receive $1,200 annually for 10 years (a total expected return of $12,000). The excludible amount of each annual payment is $900 ($1,200 × ($9,000 ÷ $12,000)). Thus, only $300 of each annual payment is includible in Thurston's income each year.

(1) Payments "for life" [§70]

Often, annuity contracts provide that payments will be made to the taxpayer "for life." In such cases, the taxable portion of each payment is calculated exactly as explained above, but the total expected return must be calculated by referring to a life expectancy table.

Example: Thurston purchases an annuity contract for $9,000. The contract provides that Thurston will receive $600 annually for life, beginning on his 50th birthday. If tables provide that Thurston can be expected to live 25 more years, his total expected return is $15,000 ($600 × 25). The annual exclusion would be: $600 × ($9,000 ÷ $15,000) = $360.

(2) Limits on proration [§71]

If the recipient outlives his life expectancy, all amounts received thereafter are income. If the recipient fails to reach his life expectancy, however, the unrecovered amount would be *deductible* in the year the recipient dies. [I.R.C. §72(b)(3)]

---

e.g. **Example:** In the scenario set forth in the example above, assume that Thurston lives more than another 25 years; in that case, Thurston would have recovered his entire $9,000 investment, and the entire annual payment of $600 would be taxable (beginning in year 26).

---

e.g. **Example:** Assume now that Thurston lives only to age 56. In that case, he would only have recovered $3,600 of his investment ($600 × 6 years); thus, $5,400 could be deducted from his income in the year of his death.

---

b. Employees' annuity plans [§72]

The annuity rules apply to the taxation of amounts received under pension plans provided by employers for employees.

(1) Nonforfeitable rights [§73]

If the employer purchases an annuity policy for the employee, and the employee has a nonforfeitable right to the policy, the employee is taxed on its purchase price when the employer purchases it, even though payments will not begin until years later. [**United States v. Drescher,** 179 F.2d 863 (2d Cir. 1950); *and see infra,* §§969 *et seq.*] In such a case, the employee's basis, which he can recover tax-free when the payments finally begin, will include the amount previously taxed to him when the employer bought the policy.

(2) Qualified plan [§74]

However, if the annuity is part of a *qualified pension or profit-sharing plan,* no tax is payable in the year in which the employer makes the contribution to the plan. The tax on the employer's contribution is *deferred* until the year in which the annuity becomes payable to the employee, at which time the employee will presumably be in a lower tax bracket. [I.R.C. §402(a)(1); *see infra,* §§977-982]

7. Interest on State and Local Bonds [§75]

Interest earned on bonds and other obligations of state and local governments is *excluded* from federal income taxation. [I.R.C. §103] However, if the proceeds of the bond issue are used for private purposes (*e.g.,* construction of factories), the interest is taxable in most cases. [I.R.C. §§103(b)(1), 141]

a. Background [§76]

This exemption was originally of constitutional origin, required under the doctrine of intergovernment tax immunity (*see supra*, §1, *and see* Constitutional Law Summary). Although no longer constitutionally required [**South Carolina v. Baker,** 485 U.S. 505 (1988)], the exemption now serves the function of encouraging investment by high-bracket taxpayers in state and municipal bonds, thereby allowing these governments to borrow at a reduced rate of interest.

b. Distinguish—federal obligations [§77]

Interest on *federal* bonds, notes, postal savings, etc., is wholly taxable. [I.R.C. §103(b)]

8. Government Benefits [§78]

Certain amounts received from the government as benefits under social programs are *wholly or partially tax-free.*

a. Social Security benefits [§79]

Social Security benefits (both old age and disability benefits) are partially taxable. [I.R.C. §86] Supplemental Security Income ("SSI") payments, which are based on need, are nontaxable. [I.R.C. §86(d)(1)(A)]

(1) Taxable amount at lower levels of modified AGI [§80]

Social Security benefits may be taxable in an amount equal to *the lesser* of (i) one-half of the benefits received during the year *or* (ii) one-half of the amount by which the sum of 50% of Social Security benefits plus taxpayer's *modified* adjusted gross income ("AGI") exceeds a statutory floor. (Modified AGI means AGI increased by tax-exempt interest received during the year.) The floor is $32,000 on a joint return or $25,000 on a single person return. The formula for calculating the excess is:

Excess = (50% of Social Security benefits + Modified AGI) - Floor Amount

The lesser of 50% of excess or 50% of Social Security benefits is taxable.

---

e.g. **Example:** Tammy Taxpayer files a single person return, and she received Social Security benefits of $7,200. Assume that her modified AGI is $22,000. The sum of modified AGI and 50% of Social Security benefits is $25,600. This exceeds the statutory floor by $600. The amount taxable is the lesser of 50% of benefits ($3,600) or 50% of the excess ($300). Thus, Tammy must include $300 in income.

---

(2) Taxable amount at higher levels of modified AGI [§81]

At higher income levels, up to 85% of Social Security benefits received during the year are taxable. The income levels (the "adjusted base amount") are $44,000 on a joint return and $34,000 on the return of a single taxpayer. The calculation of the amount taxable at higher levels involves a complex phase-in as modified AGI rises above the base amount or the adjusted base amount.

b. Welfare benefits [§82]

Governmental payments based on *need*, such as welfare benefits, are excluded from income—even if a welfare recipient must work for the government to get the payments. [Rev. Rul. 71-425, 1971-2 C.B. 26]

c. Unemployment compensation [§83]

Unemployment compensation payments are taxable. [I.R.C. §85]

9. Medical Insurance and Private Disability Payments

a. Employee-paid premiums [§84]

Benefit payments received under a medical or disability insurance policy purchased *by the taxpayer* are *excluded*, whether or not the taxpayer deducted the premiums paid to purchase the insurance. [I.R.C. §104(a)(3)]

(1) Exception—no double exclusion [§85]

If medical expenses were deducted (*see infra,* §§653-666), the insurance reimbursements for these expenses must be included in income.

b. Employer-paid premiums [§86]

If the employer pays for health and accident insurance for its employees, the employees are not taxed on the premiums or on benefits received. [I.R.C. §106] Similarly, if the employer directly pays for medical expenses of employees or their dependents, the employees are not taxed on these payments (except to the extent they also deducted the same costs). [I.R.C. §105(d)] However, a medical reimbursement plan may not discriminate in favor of "highly compensated individuals"; it must cover a broad range of employees or the amounts received will not be excludible. [*See* I.R.C. §105(g)]

(1) Permanent injuries [§87]

An employee may exclude amounts received from the employer (or from insurance paid for by the employer) that are payment for the permanent loss of a member or function of the body or a permanent disfigurement. To be excludible, payments must be based on the nature of the injury without regard to the period the employee is absent from work (*e.g.,* loss of big toe pays $2,000 whether the employee returns to work after a week or after a month). [I.R.C. §105(c)]

(2) Other disability payments [§88]

With the above exceptions, payments received under disability insurance policies paid for by the employer must be *included* in income. [I.R.C. §105(a)]

10. Damage Payments

a. **Payments for personal injuries [§89]**

Damages received, whether in a lump sum or as periodic payments and whether by judgment or settlement, on account of *personal physical injuries* or *physical sickness*, are excluded. However, punitive damages are not excluded [I.R.C. §104(a)(2)]; similarly, amounts received by a plaintiff in a physical injury case for prejudgment interest on damages are not excluded. [**Rozpad v. Commissioner,** 154 F.3d 1 (1st Cir. 1998)]

(1) **Scope of exclusion [§90]**

As long as an action has its origin in physical injury or sickness, all damages received (except punitive damages) are excluded.

(a) **Damages for emotional distress [§91]**

Damages for emotional distress *alone* (*e.g.,* in a suit for intentional infliction of emotional distress) are not the result of a "physical injury" or "sickness," even if the emotional distress is accompanied by a physical manifestation (such as headaches). However, if the tort giving rise to the emotional distress *also involved* a physical injury, damages for emotional distress may be excluded (*e.g.,* in a car accident). [I.R.C. §104(a)]

(b) **Damages for illegal discrimination [§92]**

Damages arising out of illegal discrimination (*e.g.,* race, sex, age, or disability) are taxable because they do not result from a physical injury.

(2) **Prior law [§93]**

Under the prior version of section 104(a)(2), taxpayers could also exclude damages received by reason of intangible injuries, such as injury to reputation or privacy or certain violations of civil rights, if compensated for by tort-type remedies. [*See* **Commissioner v. Burke,** 504 U.S. 229 (1992)] However, punitive damages were taxable even in personal injury cases. [**O'Gilvie v. Commissioner,** 519 U.S. 79 (1996)]

(3) **Common law background [§94]**

Before and after enactment of section 104(a)(2), personal injury recoveries were held not to be income under section 61 by rulings and judicial decisions on the rationale that they did not represent any accretion in net worth; *i.e.,* they "roughly correspond to a return of invested capital." [**Commissioner v. Glenshaw Glass Co.,** *supra,* §22]

(a) **Scope of common law exclusion [§95]**

The early rulings and case law exempted damages recovered for any interference with personal or family rights—*e.g.,* recoveries for alienation of affections or breach of contract to marry, as well as libel and slander. [*See* Sol. Op. 132, I-1 C.B. 92 (1922); Rev. Rul. 74-77, 1974-1 C.B. 33; **McDonald v. Commissioner,** 9 B.T.A. 1340 (1928)]

(b) Probably not excludible now [§96]

Since the sort of damage claims involved in the older cases are not damages for personal physical injuries or sickness, they would not qualify for exclusion under the present version of section 104(a)(2). However, one court has recently held that damages for nonphysical injuries nevertheless should not be taxed because such damages were not considered income when the Sixteenth Amendment was ratified. [*See* **Murphy v. United States**, *supra,* §7—court excluded compensatory damages for nonphysical injuries]

(4) Attorneys' fees, costs, and taxable tort recoveries [§97]

A taxpayer cannot exclude attorneys' fees related to taxable tort recoveries. Under normal assignment of income rules, the taxpayer owns the tort claim and must include the entire amount recovered in income. [**Commissioner v. Banks**, 543 U.S. 426 (2005)] Then she deducts the costs of obtaining the income, subject to the limits on deductibility of personal expenses discussed in Chapter 3. In certain discrimination suits, however, the taxpayer may avoid these limits in deducting attorneys' fees and related costs. [*See* I.R.C. §62(a)(19)]

Example: Assume Travis wins an award of $900,000 in a civil rights case, and that he has a one-third contingent fee arrangement with his attorney. Assume further that $100,000 of court costs were incurred. The entire award of $900,000 is taxable to Travis under section 104(a)(2). The fee of $300,000 and the costs of $100,000 may be deducted, *but not excluded*, under section 212(1). (*See infra,* §§437 *et seq.*)

---

(5) Reimbursed medical expenses [§98]

If the damages compensate the taxpayer for medical expenses that were previously deducted (*see infra,* §§653-666), the damage payment must be included in income.

(6) Periodic payments [§99]

The exclusion under section 104(a)(2) for personal physical injury damages applies to both lump sum and periodic payments. [Rev. Rul. 79-220, 1979-2 C.B. 74—monthly payments to compensate for personal injury, to be paid over a period of 20 years or taxpayer's life, whichever is longer, are fully excluded, including the portion representing interest] Note, however, that the payor of periodic damage payments cannot deduct them until they are actually paid, even when the payor uses the accrual method. [I.R.C. §461(h)(2)(C); *see infra,* §§1038-1042]

b. Damages for business injuries

(1) Damage to goodwill [§100]

Case law also excluded damages for injuries to business goodwill under the "return of capital" theory. [**Farmers & Merchants Bank v. Commissioner,** 59 F.2d 912 (6th Cir. 1932)] But in a later case, this theory was questioned;

if the destroyed goodwill had a tax basis of zero (*i.e.,* no money was paid to acquire it), the amount received as damages for its destruction should be treated as income. [**Raytheon Production Corp. v. Commissioner,** 144 F.2d 110 (1st Cir.), *cert. denied,* 323 U.S. 779 (1944)] Also, damages attributable to *lost profits* (as well as punitive damages) are treated as income.

(a) Note
Sometimes it is necessary to apportion a damage award to ascertain the tax treatment accorded to different elements.

(2) Statutory provision [§101]
A special statute confers a partial exclusion on certain recoveries of damages for business injuries. [I.R.C. §186]

(a) Injuries covered [§102]
The statute covers damages for patent infringement, breach of contract, breach of fiduciary duty, and antitrust violations.

(b) Amount excludible [§103]
The amount that can be excluded is the compensatory amount or the unrecovered losses, whichever is less.

1) "Compensatory amount" [§104]
The "compensatory amount" is the damages recovered minus the amounts paid in securing the judgment or settlement.

2) "Unrecovered losses" [§105]
The "unrecovered losses" are the amount of net operating loss carryovers attributable to the injury that have not been carried to other taxable years. (For explanation of net operating loss carryovers, *see infra,* §1087.)

3) Effect [§106]
The effect of this provision is to allow exclusion of damage recoveries only if the taxpayer had no tax benefit from the prior losses for which he now obtains a recovery. (*See infra,* §§1079-1084, for discussion of the "tax benefit rule.")

Example: As a consequence of violations of the antitrust law by drug companies, Tammy Taxpayer lost $1 million because she had to pay excessive prices for drugs sold at her drugstore. The excessive amounts paid were part of the basis for the drugs that had been sold. However, in each year during which the injury occurred, Tammy Taxpayer had taxable income and therefore received a tax benefit by deducting the cost of the drugs. Upon a successful suit against the drug companies, she cannot exclude any part of the damage recovery.

> **cf.** **Compare:** Suppose in the previous example that Tammy Taxpayer did not have taxable income in the years of the injury but instead had deductions in excess of income. Furthermore, this went on a long time so she could never carry those losses to other years and use them as deductions, and the carryovers have now expired. She can exclude the damage recovery because she received no tax benefit from the losses that she is now recovering.

11. Meals and Lodging Furnished for Convenience of Employer [§107]

The value of meals and lodging furnished by or on behalf of an employer to an employee, his spouse, or dependents *for the convenience of the employer* is excluded from gross income. [I.R.C. §119(a)] This section codifies prior case law that allowed employees to exclude meals and lodging furnished for the convenience of the employer. [**Benaglia v. Commissioner,** 36 B.T.A. 838 (1937)]

a. Business premises requirement [§108]

The meals or lodging must be furnished *on the business premises of the employer.* In the case of lodging, it must be accepted as a condition of employment, *e.g.,* meals and quarters furnished to firefighters at the station house.

> **e.g.** **Example:** A house provided for a hotel manager located across the street from the hotel and next to an overflow parking lot was held to be on the business premises. [**Lindeman v. Commissioner,** 60 T.C. 609 (1973)]

b. "Meals" and "lodging" [§109]

The terms "meals" and "lodging" are broadly construed. Thus, groceries supplied to an employee, including nonfood items such as soap and toilet paper supplied to an employee residing on the employer's premises, can be treated as "meals" or "lodging." [**Jacob v. United States,** 493 F.2d 1294 (3d Cir. 1974)]

c. Convenience of employer [§110]

The "convenience of the employer" provision requires a *"substantial noncompensatory business reason"* for providing meals and lodging. [Treas. Reg. §1.119-l(a)(2)]

(1) "Substantial noncompensatory business reasons" [§111]

Substantial noncompensatory business reasons for providing meals include situations in which employees must be present to deal with emergencies or in which employees must take short lunch breaks because that time of day is the busiest for the employer. [**Boyd Gaming Corp. v. Commissioner,** 177 F.3d 1096 (9th Cir. 1999)—casino's requirement that all employees stay on premises during their entire shift provided substantial noncompensatory business reason for free meals in employee cafeteria even though there was sufficient time for most of them to leave the casino and eat elsewhere] Substantial noncompensatory business reasons for supplying lodging include situations in which no accommodations are available in the vicinity or in which an employee must be on call 24 hours a day. [Treas. Reg. §1.119-1(a)(2), (b)]

(a) Note

In the case of meals, if more than half of the employees receiving meals qualify for exclusion, meals provided to the rest of the employees will qualify as well (even if those employees could not meet the convenience of the employer test on their own). [I.R.C. §119(b)(4)]

(b) But note—"business necessity" test

The Supreme Court has suggested that convenience of the employer means "business necessity"—*i.e.,* that the job could not be performed unless meals or lodging were supplied. [**Commissioner v. Kowalski,** 434 U.S. 77 (1977)] This is seemingly a much narrower test than the "substantial noncompensatory business reason" test of the regulations.

d. Campus lodging [§112]

An employee of an educational institution (and her family) can exclude the value of "qualified campus lodging" provided on or near the campus. Because of the conditions placed on this exclusion, it is best to think of it as a type of tax-free employee discount. The exclusion applies if the lodging is on or near the employer's campus and the employee pays "adequate rent." Rent is deemed adequate if it is equal to the lesser of: (i) 5% of the appraised value of the lodging, or (ii) the average rent paid by individuals other than employees or students for similar housing owned by the educational institution. If rent is inadequate (*i.e.,* the employee pays less than the lesser of (i) or (ii) above), the taxpayer must treat the difference between what he pays and adequate rent as income. Note that the exclusion does not require the lodging to be furnished for the convenience of the employer and that the lodging does not have to be on the employer's premises; it need only be nearby.

Example: Faber College owns an apartment building near its campus. The college rents apartments in the building to its faculty members and students for $500 per month ($6,000 per year), while it charges the general public $1,000 per month ($12,000 per year) for similar apartments. The appraised value of each apartment is $120,000 (5% of which would be $6,000). Bluto Blutarsky, a distinguished history professor at Faber College, rents one of the apartments for $500 per month. Bluto does not owe any tax on account of the $6,000 annual discount in rent because the rent that he pays is (at least) equal to 5% of the appraised value of the housing.

cf. **Compare:** Same facts as above, but in order to convince Bluto to teach at Faber, the college agreed to rent him an apartment for $1 per year. Bluto will be taxed on $5,999, the difference between the rent that he pays and 5% of the appraised value of the apartment.

e. **Fixed charges for meals [§113]**

Fixed charges for meals furnished for the convenience of the employer are excluded from the employee's gross income, provided the employee is required to make the payment whether or not he accepts the meals. This rule applies whether the employee pays the charge out of his compensation or out of his own funds. [I.R.C. §119(b)(3)]

f. **Distinguish—cash payments for meals and lodging [§114]**

Amounts paid *in cash* to compensate an employee for meals or lodging must be included in income. They cannot be excluded under section 119, because that section covers only meals and lodging furnished *in kind*. Nor can the payments be excluded by applying a nonstatutory convenience of the employer test. [**Commissioner v. Kowalski,** *supra*]

e.g. **Example:** In *Kowalski*, state police troopers were reimbursed for meals taken during midshift breaks. The Court held that section 119 does not cover cash payments of any kind. Even assuming the payments were made for the convenience of the employer (so as to be excludible under the law in effect prior to adoption of section 119), that section was intended to *narrow the circumstances* in which meals could be excluded, and hence to *replace* prior law. Therefore, the payments were includible as gross income and not excludible under section 119 or otherwise.

(1) **Note**

The troopers in *Kowalski* could not *deduct* the payments they made for meals because they could not meet the "overnight" rule of section 162(a)(2). (*See infra*, §317.)

EXAM TIP   gilbert

On your exam, be sure to remember the difference between employer-provided meals and lodging *furnished for the convenience of the employer* for (at least) a *substantial noncompensatory business reason* and employer reimbursement for expenses incurred on *business trips* (see *infra*, §§314 et seq.). The former implies a more permanent arrangement (*e.g.*, hotel manager lives at the hotel) and *must* be furnished *in kind* to be *excluded* from gross income. The latter implies a more temporary arrangement (*e.g.*, the traveling salesperson), and generally may be *excluded* from gross income.

12. Fringe Benefits [§115]

Some "fringe benefits" furnished by employers are specifically excludible, *e.g.*, group term life insurance coverage up to $50,000 per year and employer-paid accident and health insurance. (*See supra,* §86, *and infra,* §123.) Congress has set forth the following rules for determining whether other fringe benefits should be excludible. [I.R.C. §132]

a. "No additional cost" service [§116]

A "no additional cost" service is excludible from income. This term refers to a service provided to the employee if the same service is routinely offered for sale to customers and the employer incurs no substantial additional cost (and forgoes no revenue) in providing the service to the employee (*e.g.*, allowing a flight attendant to fly free if she goes on standby). [I.R.C. §132(b)]

b. Qualified employee discount [§117]

A qualified employee discount is excludible from income. This term refers to allowing an employee to purchase a good or service routinely sold by the employer at a price at least equal to cost (in the case of products) or at not more than a 20% discount (in the case of services). In the case of this and the preceding paragraph, the fringe benefit must be offered on a nondiscriminatory basis to the employees—not just to highly compensated ones. [I.R.C. §132(c), (h)(1)]

> **e.g.** **Example:** Big-Mart allows employees to buy goods at a 10% discount (so that the price received exceeds Big-Mart's cost). The employee is not taxed on the discount.

c. Working condition fringe [§118]

A working condition fringe is excludible from income. This term refers to any property or services provided to an employee which, if the employee had paid for the item herself, would have been deductible to the employee (or depreciable by the employee). [I.R.C. §132(d)]

> **e.g.** **Example:** If an employer furnishes an employee salesperson with a car that she uses *exclusively* for business, the value of the car is not taxable to the employee.

d. Qualified transportation expense [§119]

The cost of commuting to work is not deductible (*see infra,* §306), but a qualified transportation fringe benefit is not taxable. A qualified transportation fringe benefit includes an employer-provided vanpool (in a vehicle holding at least six persons), a transit pass, and free parking. The amount that can be excluded, however, cannot exceed $100 per month (in the case of vanpool and transit pass) and $185 per month (in the case of free parking). [I.R.C. §132(f)] These figures are adjusted for inflation. In 2006, the amount that can be excluded cannot exceed $105 per month (in the case of vanpool and transit passes) and $200 per month (in the case of free parking). In the case of parking, an employer may offer the employee a choice of free parking or additional compensation in lieu of free parking. An employee who chooses the free parking is not taxed on the forgone extra compensation. [I.R.C. §132(f)(4)]

e. De minimis fringe [§120]

A de minimis fringe is excludible from income. This term refers to a fringe that is so small as to make accounting for it unreasonable or administratively impracticable. [I.R.C. §132(e), (h)(5)]

---

e.g. **Example:** A company cafeteria open to all employees sells lunch for a price that is less than those of comparable eating facilities, but still high enough for the cafeteria to break even. The value of the reduced lunch price is not taxable. Similarly, an employee is not taxed on the value of an on-premises gym.

---

cf. **Compare:** Airline distributed American Express vouchers to its employees entitling them to $50 worth of restaurant meals. Employees used 97% of the vouchers. This was not a de minimis fringe because it was administratively practical for Airline to account for and value each voucher. [**American Airlines, Inc. v. United States**, 204 F.3d 1103 (Fed. Cir. 2000)]

---

f. Qualified moving expense reimbursement [§121]

To the extent that the employee would have been entitled to a moving expense deduction had she paid for the moving expenses herself (*see infra*, §325), she will have no tax if the employer pays or reimburses her moving expenses. [I.R.C. §132(g)]

g. Qualified retirement advice [§122]

A taxpayer can exclude the value of qualified retirement planning services provided by the employer, provided that the employer also maintains a qualified retirement plan for its employees. [I.R.C. §132(m); *see infra*, §977, for treatment of qualified retirement plans] For purposes of I.R.C. section 132, the term "employee" includes an employee's spouse or dependent child. It also includes a former employee who has retired or is disabled. [I.R.C. §132(h)(2)]

h. Group term life insurance premiums [§123]

The cost of group term life insurance (up to a maximum coverage of $50,000 per employee) purchased by an employer for employees is not includible in the employee's income as compensation, even though the employer receives a deduction for the premiums. However, benefits must be provided to all employees on a nondiscriminatory basis. [I.R.C. §79]

NONTAXABLE FRINGE BENEFITS **gilbert**

THE FOLLOWING ARE EXCLUDED FROM INCOME:

☑ *"No additional cost" service—if* the employer (i) routinely offers the services for sale to customers, and (ii) does not incur any substantial additional cost

☑ *Qualified employee discount—if* discount does not (i) reduce sale price to below cost of products, or (ii) exceed 20% of the normal price for services

☑ *Working condition fringe—if* item or service would have been deductible to or depreciable by the employee had the employee paid

☑ *Qualified transportation expense—if* the amount does not exceed the statutory amount (for 2006, (i) $105 per month for vanpools or transit passes, or (ii) $200 for parking expenses)

☑ *De minimis fringe—if* fringe is too small to track

☑ *Qualified moving expense reimbursement—if* the amount does not exceed the employee's actual expenses and employee would have been able to deduct the expense if employee paid

☑ *Qualified retirement advice—if* employer maintains a qualified retirement plan for its employees

☑ *Group term life insurance premiums* up to $50,000

☑ Employer-paid *accident and health insurance premiums and benefits received*

---

13. Miscellaneous Other Exclusions [§124]

A variety of other exclusions are available.

a. Foreign earned income [§125]

Taxpayers working abroad can exclude up to $80,000 per year of their service income from foreign sources. To qualify, the taxpayer must be either a bona fide foreign resident for an uninterrupted period that includes an entire taxable year or present for 330 days in a foreign country during a period of 12 consecutive months. [I.R.C. §911] In addition, such taxpayers can exclude substantial amounts of housing reimbursements (or deduct a substantial part of their housing costs). [I.R.C. §911(c)]

b. Frequent flier miles [§126]

Because of the practical difficulties of doing so, the IRS does not tax the value of frequent flier miles credited by an airline to an employee for a trip paid for by the employer and personally used by the employee. [*See* Announcement 2002-18, 2002-10 I.R.B. 621]

(1) Exception

If frequent flier miles are turned into cash, the cash is taxed to the employee. [**Charley v. Commissioner,** 91 F.3d 72 (9th Cir. 1996)]

Example: In *Charley*, taxpayer frequently flew on business. His employer would bill its clients for the cost of taxpayer's first class tickets, but taxpayer had instructed his travel agent to purchase coach tickets, upgrade taxpayer with the frequent flier mileage taxpayer earned on previous business trips, and forward the difference in ticket prices to him. In effect, taxpayer had exchanged his miles for cash. These amounts were taxable to the employee/taxpayer on either of two theories: (i) he had sold zero basis miles for cash, or (ii) he received additional compensation from his employer because the employer allowed him to cash in his miles—miles that were both earned and used in traveling on business.

---

c. Lessee's improvements [§127]

The value of a lessee's improvements on leased property is *not* income to the landlord, either at the time of the improvement or on termination of the lease, even though the improvement increases the value of the property. [I.R.C. §109] And the lessor makes no adjustments to the tax basis of the property. [I.R.C. §1019]

(1) Exception—disguised rent

A contrary result is reached, however, if the landlord and tenant intend the improvements as a substitute for rent. [Treas. Reg. §1.109-1(a)]

d. Insurance reimbursements for above-normal living expenses [§128]

Insurance reimbursements for above-normal living expenses, resulting from fire, storm, or other casualty loss to the *taxpayer's home,* are excludible. [I.R.C. §123]

e. Investment interest—higher education [§129]

The Code excludes the income resulting from the redemption of United States savings bonds if a taxpayer spends an amount equal to the redemption proceeds for "qualified higher education expenses." The bonds must be purchased after 1989 and the taxpayer must be at least 24 years old when the bonds are purchased. The exclusion is phased out as AGI exceeds $60,000 ($40,000 for singles). This exclusion is designed to give a tax break to middle-class parents for higher education expenses of their children; it will seldom apply to bonds purchased by the students themselves (since to take advantage of the exclusion a taxpayer must be at least 24 years old when the bonds are issued, as opposed to when they are redeemed). [I.R.C. §135] (*Note:* When the proceeds are not used for higher education expenses, the rising redemption value of the savings bonds is deferred until the bonds are cashed in, unless the taxpayer elects to include the interest in income during the year. [I.R.C. §454])

f. Compensation for Holocaust victims [§130]

Certain forms of reparation received by persons persecuted by Nazi Germany (or other Nazi-allied countries) on the basis of race, religion, physical or mental disability, or sexual orientation, are excluded from income. The exclusion covers direct payments as well as the assets (or their value) stolen from victims of Nazi persecution and returned to the victim. In addition, certain interest payments on funds arising out of Holocaust litigation are excluded. [Economic Growth and Tax Relief Reconciliation Act of 2001, Pub. L. No. 107-136, §803, 115 Stat. 38 (2001)]

g. Parsonage exclusion [§131]

In the case of a "minister of the gospel," a rental allowance or the rental value of a home paid to him as compensation is excludible from gross income. However, such amount is excluded only if it is actually directed for housing in the minister's employment documents or the board minutes and if it is indeed used to pay rent or to provide for a house. [I.R.C. §107; Treas. Reg. §1.107-1(a); **Toavis v. Commissioner**, 67 T.C. 897 (1977)]

h. Combat pay [§132]

Active duty military personnel are entitled to exclude from gross income up to the maximum enlisted pay received while serving in a combat zone or while hospitalized during the two-year period following service in a combat zone. [I.R.C. §112] Note also that currently, income excluded for this reason may be considered included for purposes of calculating earned income in order to receive the earned income tax credit. [I.R.C. §32; Gulf Opportunity Zone Act of 2005, §302(a); *see infra*, §718]

i. Payments to foster parents [§133]

Government payments to foster parents for the care of foster children are excluded from gross income. [I.R.C. §131]

D. Inclusions in Gross Income

1. In General [§134]

As discussed in the initial definition of "gross income" (*supra*, §11), it is generally held that any increase in net worth is income. Certain includible items, however, merit special consideration.

2. Compensation for Services Rendered [§135]

As previously noted, cash or property received as compensation for services rendered is includible in the gross income of the recipient, irrespective of the form such payments take.

a. Payment of employee's income taxes [§136]

If an employer (whether or not pursuant to contract) pays an employee's income taxes (or any other debts of the employee), the amount of the tax payment is considered additional compensation to the employee and is taxable as income. [**Old Colony Trust Co. v. Commissioner,** 279 U.S. 716 (1929)]

b. Reimbursements or expense payments by employer [§137]

Employers often pay travel or entertainment expenses of employees (or prospective employees), or reimburse them for such expenses. Whether such reimbursements and expense payments are income depends on the employer's motive. If the motive was to award additional compensation to the employee, the reimbursement or expense payment is taxable to the employee. But if the payment was designed to serve the employer's business (or was for the convenience of the employer), it is not taxable to the employee.

Example: A free trip to a company convention in New York was taxable because the purpose was to reward an insurance salesman for a job well done. [**Rudolph v. United States,** 291 F.2d 841 (5th Cir. 1961), *aff'd,* 370 U.S. 269 (1962)]

Compare: A free trip to Germany provided by Volkswagen to a potential dealer was not taxable because it was provided for Volkswagen's business purposes. [**United States v. Gotcher,** 401 F.2d 118 (5th Cir. 1968)— note that the value of spouse's trip was taxable because there was no business reason for her to go]

(1) Travel, meal, and entertainment expenses [§138]

Reimbursements of employees for travel, meal, and entertainment expenses incurred in pursuit of the employer's business are not taxable. [Treas. Reg. §162-2(c)(4)] However, they are included in gross income if they are not made pursuant to an accountable plan. (See *infra,* §§139-140.)

(a) Accountable plans [§139]

The most common practice is for the employer to reimburse the employee for expenses and not include the reimbursement amount on the employee's W-2 form. This practice is authorized if: (i) the expense is related to business; (ii) the employee substantiates, or is deemed to have substantiated, the claim; and (iii) the employee returns payments in excess of the amount substantiated. This type of arrangement is called an "accountable plan." Additionally, the 50% limit on these deductions (see *infra,* §331) applies to the employer.

(b) Nonaccountable plans and unreimbursed expenses [§140]

The employer must include the amount of reimbursement as income on the employee's W-2 form if the reimbursement is not made pursuant to an accountable plan (*see supra*, §139). The employee may take a deduction for the business-related expenses, provided she can substantiate them. Unreimbursed expenses are treated in the same manner—the employee may take a deduction for them if she can substantiate them. *Note:* A 50% limit and a 2% floor applies to these types of deductions. (*See infra*, §§331 *et seq.*).

---

e.g. **Example:** Tom Taxpayer travels from his office in Chicago to New York to attend company meetings. He stays one night at a hotel (cost, $200) and orders three meals (cost, $100). After returning to Chicago, Tom submits receipts to his employer for reimbursement, and his employer reimburses him with a check for $300 from an accountable plan. The reimbursement is not taxable.

EXAM TIP **gilbert**

On your exam, be sure to remember that an employee may have reimbursed expenses under an accountable plan, reimbursed expenses under a nonaccountable plan, and unreimbursed expenses from the same trip. *Each type of expense is treated separately* and is subject to the rules and limits stated above.

(2) Distinguish—reimbursement for routine meal and lodging [§141]

Recall that cash reimbursements for everyday meal and lodging expenses generally are not deductible or excludible from income (*see supra*, §114); the above rules apply only to amounts reimbursed as expenses incurred in pursuit of the employer's business.

3. Income from Cancellation of Indebtedness [§142]

The reduction or cancellation of a person's debts increases his net worth. Therefore, it is treated as income, unless it falls within one of several possible exceptions.

---

e.g. **Example:** A corporate taxpayer issues bonds (evidence of indebtedness) having a face value of $12 million. Later, it is able to purchase a number of bonds on the open market at a discount from face value, totaling $137,000. Thus, its assets went down but its liabilities went down more—creating an increase in net worth and hence income. [**United States v. Kirby Lumber Co.,** 284 U.S. 1 (1931)]

EXAM TIP **gilbert**

On your exam, be alert to *cancellation of debt* that results in an *increase of the taxpayer's net worth*. The cancellation may be a taxable event, subject to exceptions (see chart, *infra*, after §157).

a. Cancellation of indebtedness income exceptions

(1) Insolvent taxpayers [§143]

To avoid hardship, a cancellation of debt is not taxable if the taxpayer is insolvent immediately before the cancellation (*i.e.,* liabilities exceed the value of the taxpayer's assets). However, the exclusion cannot exceed the amount by which the taxpayer is insolvent. [I.R.C. §108(a), (d)(3)] In addition, a taxpayer whose debts are discharged in a statutory bankruptcy proceeding is not subject to debt cancellation income.

(a) Definition of assets [§144]

For purposes of the insolvency exception, the term "assets" includes assets that are exempt from execution under state law. [**Carlson v. Commissioner,** 116 T.C. 87 (2001)—taxpayers had to include their valuable fishing license in calculating their assets for purposes of determining whether they were insolvent, even though such licenses are exempt from execution by creditors under state law]

(b) Price tag [§145]

In both insolvency and bankruptcy cases, the Code exacts a price: The taxpayer must *reduce certain tax benefits* by the amount of the debt cancellation income not recognized. These benefits include: net operating loss carryovers (*see infra,* §1087), disallowed passive loss carryovers (*see infra,* §547), and capital loss carryforwards (*see infra,* §826). In the event these are insufficient to absorb the entire amount of untaxed income, the basis of assets must be reduced in accordance with section 1017. [I.R.C. §108(b)]

> **Example:** Before a debt cancellation, Teri Taxpayer's assets are worth $1,000 and her liabilities total $1,600. One of her debts, in the amount of $900, is canceled upon payment of $100. Ordinarily this would result in debt cancellation income of $800. However, Teri is insolvent to the extent of $600, and so $600 of the income is not taxed. Consequently, her income on the transaction is only $200. Teri must reduce tax benefits (such as loss carryforwards) by the remaining $600.

(2) Qualified real property business indebtedness [§146]

A taxpayer can elect to exclude debt cancellation from income when the debt is secured by real property used in a trade or business. If the debt arose after 1993, to qualify for this election it must have been incurred in connection with the acquisition or improvement of the real property. The basis of all real property owned by the taxpayer is reduced by the amount of debt cancellation income that was excluded by the election. A taxpayer cannot exclude more than the difference between the debt (before reduction) and the value of the property (reduced by the amount of any other debt to which it is subject). [I.R.C. §108(a)(1)(D), (c)]

---

e.g. **Example:** Teri Taxpayer is solvent and owns an apartment building worth $12 million that is subject to a debt owed to Bank of $17 million. The debt was incurred in connection with acquisition of the apartment building. Rather than foreclose, Bank reduces the debt to $11 million. Teri can exclude $5 million from income, but she must reduce the basis of all of her realty by $5 million. The remaining $1 million is taxable as debt cancellation income.

---

(3) Deductible payments [§147]

Income is not recognized on cancellation of a debt to the extent that payment of the debt would have given rise to a deduction. [I.R.C. §108(e)(2)]

(4) Cancellation as a "gift" [§148]

A creditor's reduction or cancellation of indebtedness may be a gift to the debtor, in which case the resulting increase in net worth would be excluded from income. However, unless the creditor and debtor have a personal or family relationship, the creditor's intent would seldom be the "detached generosity" required to establish a gift (*see supra,* §29). Rather, the creditor usually intends either to keep the debtor in business so that he may remain as a customer in the future or to get as much as possible out of a debtor in precarious financial circumstances. [**Commissioner v. Jacobson,** 336 U.S. 28 (1949)]

(5) Student loans [§149]

Some student loans are discharged if the borrower works for a certain time for certain employers. For example, a government loan might provide that if the student graduates and teaches in the inner city, the loan will be forgiven. Such loan discharges do *not* give rise to income. [I.R.C. §108(f)(1)] The lender must be the government, a charitable hospital, or an educational institution. In the case of an educational institution, the forgiveness must be pursuant to a program designed to encourage its students to serve in occupations or geographic areas with unmet needs. [I.R.C. §108(f)(2)]

(6) Net benefit [§150]

If a taxpayer does *not* benefit economically from the debt cancellation, he has no income.

---

e.g. **Example:** Taxpayer Corp. issued preferred stock in exchange for $100. When the stock was worth $165, it exchanged the stock for a bond that was also worth $165. Later it bought back the bond for $118. The issue was whether the $118 should be compared to the $100 that the company originally received or the $165 that the stock was worth when the bond was exchanged for it. The court held that the company had no debt cancellation income because the $118 should be compared to the $100 originally received. When the entire transaction is viewed together, the taxpayer had no net economic benefit. [**United States Steel Corp. v. United States,** 848 F.2d 1232 (Fed. Cir. 1988)]

(7) Shareholder debt forgiveness [§151]

Special rules govern a discharge of corporate debt by a shareholder. Such transactions may produce income to the corporation and gain or loss to the shareholder.

(a) Income of corporation [§152]

If a corporation transfers stock in discharge of its debt, it is treated as having satisfied the debt with money equal to the value of the stock.

Example: Car Corp. owes Kirk $1,000. Kirk cancels the debt in exchange for stock worth $600. The company has debt cancellation income of $400. The usual exceptions to debt cancellation income (*see supra,* §143, relating to insolvency or bankruptcy) can apply in this situation where stock is substituted for debt.

(b) Treatment of shareholder [§153]

If a shareholder receives stock in exchange for a corporate debt, the shareholder will recognize gain or loss, unless a nonrecognition section is applicable.

Example: Assume in the previous example that Kirk's basis for the Car Corp. debt was $860. Kirk would have a bad debt of $260. (*See infra,* §531, for discussion of bad debt deductions.) [I.R.C. §351(d)] However, such loss might be nondeductible if the exchange was part of a corporate recapitalization. (*See* Taxation of Business Entities Summary for discussion of corporate recapitalization and other reorganizations.)

(c) Contribution to capital [§154]

Suppose a shareholder forgives a corporate debt as a "contribution to capital" (*i.e.,* gets nothing in exchange). In this situation, the corporation is treated as having satisfied the debt with an amount of money equal to the shareholder's basis in the debt.

Example: In the previous example, in which Kirk has an $860 basis for a $1,000 debt of Car Corp., assume Kirk simply cancels the debt. Kirk already owns most of the stock of Car Corp. The company is treated as having satisfied the $1,000 debt for $860. Car Corp. has debt cancellation income of $140. [I.R.C. §108(e)(6)] Kirk adds $860 to the basis of his Car Corp. stock.

(8) Reduction in purchase money debt [§155]

A reduction in a purchase money debt is treated as a reduction of basis, not as debt cancellation income. The theory is that the purchase price has been retroactively adjusted downward. [I.R.C. §108(e)(5)] The debt reduction must, however, come from the *seller*, not from a third-party lender. [**Preslar v. Commissioner**, 167 F.3d 1323 (10th Cir. 1996); Rev. Rul. 92-99, 92-2 C.B. 35]

e.g. **Example:** Bill buys a house from Sally, giving Sally a $20,000 mortgage. Bill claims that the purchase was fraudulently induced. As a compromise, Sally reduces the purchase money debt by $5,000. Consequently, the basis in the house is reduced by $5,000, but the $5,000 is *not* treated as income.

(9) Settlement of disputed claim [§156]

There is *no* income where the cancellation or reduction was in reality a settlement of a disputed claim, rather than a fixed indebtedness.

e.g. **Example:** Plaintiff sues Taxpayer for $10,000 for personal injuries. Taxpayer settles Plaintiff's claim for $1,000 without admitting liability. Because Taxpayer never acknowledged a fixed indebtedness of $10,000 to Plaintiff, the compromise of Plaintiff's claim for $1,000 does *not* result in $9,000 income to her.

e.g. **Example:** Taxpayer incurred debts to a gambling casino of $3.4 million. The debt was unenforceable under state law. Nevertheless, Taxpayer and the casino settled for $500,000. *Held:* Taxpayer does not have debt cancellation income because the debt was disputed. [**Zarin v. Commissioner**, 916 F.2d 110 (3d Cir. 1990)] This holding is remarkable because taxpayer actually received $3.4 million in chips, which he gambled away; when he was not required to pay for the chips, he should have income. (Alternatively, he should have had income when he received the chips in exchange for a nonenforceable promise to pay for them.) In most cases involving disputed debts, like the personal injury claim in the first example, the taxpayer never actually received cash or a cash equivalent.

(a) *Zarin* disapproved [§157]

Another court has disapproved of *Zarin*. It held that the disputed debt doctrine should apply only when the *amount* of the original debt is *unliquidated,* meaning uncertain or disputed in amount, as in the personal injury case in the first example. If the amount is liquidated, but the liability to pay it is disputed, as in *Zarin,* the normal debt cancellation rules should apply. [**Preslar v. Commissioner,** *supra*—taxpayer has debt cancellation income when he pays less than the amount of a $1 million debt that was subject to a liability dispute]

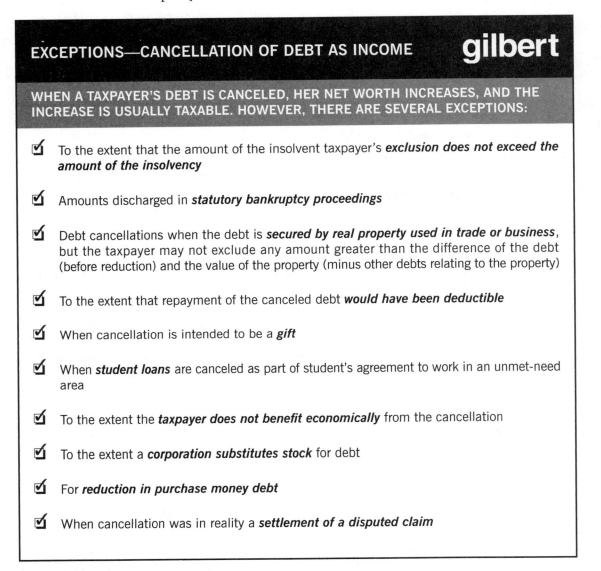

EXCEPTIONS—CANCELLATION OF DEBT AS INCOME gilbert

WHEN A TAXPAYER'S DEBT IS CANCELED, HER NET WORTH INCREASES, AND THE INCREASE IS USUALLY TAXABLE. HOWEVER, THERE ARE SEVERAL EXCEPTIONS:

☑ To the extent that the amount of the insolvent taxpayer's *exclusion does not exceed the amount of the insolvency*

☑ Amounts discharged in *statutory bankruptcy proceedings*

☑ Debt cancellations when the debt is *secured by real property used in trade or business,* but the taxpayer may not exclude any amount greater than the difference of the debt (before reduction) and the value of the property (minus other debts relating to the property)

☑ To the extent that repayment of the canceled debt *would have been deductible*

☑ When cancellation is intended to be a *gift*

☑ When *student loans* are canceled as part of student's agreement to work in an unmet-need area

☑ To the extent the *taxpayer does not benefit economically* from the cancellation

☑ To the extent a *corporation substitutes stock* for debt

☑ For *reduction in purchase money debt*

☑ When cancellation was in reality a *settlement of a disputed claim*

4. Illegal Increases in Net Worth [§158]

Money or property that the taxpayer obtains through illegal activities is includible in gross income. *Rationale:* Such property is taxable because, as a practical matter, the criminal derives readily realizable *economic value* from it. The fact that the money really belongs to another is immaterial.

 Example: *An embezzler* is taxable on the amount of money embezzled. [**James v. United States,** 366 U.S. 213 (1961)]

---

e.g. **Example:** *A swindler who "borrows" money* from his victims, *never intending to repay*, has immediate income. [**United States v. Rochelle,** 384 F.2d 748 (5th Cir. 1967), *cert. denied,* 390 U.S. 946 (1968)] *But note:* A loan that was illegal under corporate law, but which the taxpayer intends to repay and expects he can repay, is not treated as income. [**Gilbert v. Commissioner,** 552 F.2d 478 (2d Cir. 1977)]

---

a. Promise to pay irrelevant [§159]

It is immaterial that the criminal is under an obligation to restore the money on which he is taxed. Even the taxpayer's promise to repay the money, made in the same year as his embezzlement, is unavailing to avoid tax. [**Buff v. Commissioner,** 469 F.2d 847 (2d Cir. 1974)] However, if in fact he does make restitution, he can deduct the amount in the year in which restitution is made. [*See* **James v. United States,** *supra*]

5. Gambling Winnings [§160]

Gambling winnings are includible in the gross income of the gambler. This is true whether or not the gambling is illegal. Gambling losses are deductible to the extent of the winnings. [I.R.C. §165(d)]

6. Spousal Support Payments [§161]

Payments of spousal support (sometimes called "alimony" or "maintenance") are treated consistently with respect to the spouses: If the payor can deduct the payment, it is taxable to the payee, but if the payor cannot deduct the payment, it is not taxable to the payee.

a. Spousal support—general rule [§162]

A cash payment by a separated or divorced spouse to the other spouse is *generally taxable to the recipient* and *deductible by the payor*. [I.R.C. §§71(a), 215] The payor deducts the payment in computing adjusted gross income. [I.R.C. §62(a)(10)] However, child support is generally not taxable/deductible. (*See infra,* §169.)

(1) Instrument requirement [§163]

To be deductible by the payor (and thus taxable to the payee), the spousal support payment must be required by a "divorce or separation instrument." An "instrument" is a judicial decree of divorce or separate maintenance or a decree for temporary support. An instrument also includes a written agreement incident to a divorce or written separation agreement. [I.R.C. §71(b)(2)]

(2) Designated payment [§164]

The instrument can designate that otherwise taxable and deductible payments will not be taxable and deductible. [I.R.C. §71(b)(1)(B)] This provision gives the spouses flexibility in negotiating the treatment of support payments.

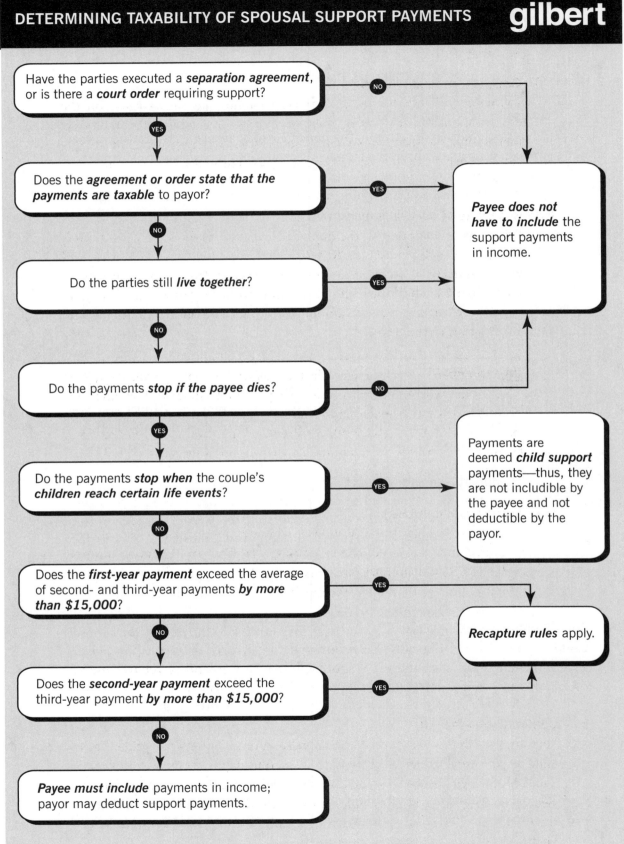

Have the parties executed a *separation agreement*, or is there a *court order* requiring support?

Does the *agreement or order state that the payments are taxable* to payor?

Do the parties still *live together*?

Do the payments *stop if the payee dies*?

Do the payments *stop when* the couple's *children reach certain life events*?

Does the *first-year payment* exceed the average of second- and third-year payments *by more than $15,000*?

Does the *second-year payment* exceed the third-year payment *by more than $15,000*?

Payee must include payments in income; payor may deduct support payments.

Payee does not have to include the support payments in income.

Payments are deemed *child support* payments—thus, they are not includible by the payee and not deductible by the payor.

Recapture rules apply.

NO   YES   YES   NO   NO   YES   YES   NO   NO   YES   YES   NO

(3) Cohabitation [§165]

A payment is not deductible to the payor or taxable to the payee if the parties are living in the same household after being legally divorced. [I.R.C. §71(b)(1)(C)]

(4) Cessation at death [§166]

Payments will not be deductible/taxable unless payments cease on the recipient's death. Moreover, there cannot be any liability to make payments after the recipient's death as a substitute for payments cut off because of her death. [I.R.C. §71(b)(1)(D); *see* Treas. Reg. §§1.71-1T, A-13, A-14]

(5) Recapture of spousal support [§167]

When the amount paid in the first year exceeds average second- and third-year payments by more than $15,000, the excess is recaptured in the third year. Similarly, if second-year payments exceed third-year payments by more than $15,000, the excess is recaptured in the third year. The term "recapture" means that the amount is ordinary income to the payor and a deduction to the payee.

---

e.g. **Example:** An instrument calls for Husband to make payments to Wife of $24,000 in Year 1 and $1 per year in Years 2 and 3. Payments in Year 1 exceed average payments in Years 2 and 3 by $23,999. The excess over $15,000 ($8,999) is recaptured as income in Year 3. Thus, Husband has $8,999 of income in Year 3, and Wife has an $8,999 deduction.

---

(6) Alimony trusts [§168]

When a trust is used to pay spousal support, the recipient's only income is limited to the taxable income of the trust. The payor gets no alimony deduction. Child support payments from the trust are not taxable to the recipient but are taxable to the grantor of the trust. [I.R.C. §682]

7. Child Support [§169]

Child support, which basically is any amount that the divorce or separation instrument **designates** as for the support of a child, is **not taxable to the recipient** or the child, and is **not deductible by the payor**. [I.R.C. §71(c)(1)]

a. Contingencies [§170]

Any amount that is reduced on the happening of a contingency related to the child or at a time associated with such a contingency is deemed child support. Thus, if payments decline around the time a child reaches majority or gets married, they are treated as child support no matter how the instrument describes them. [I.R.C. §71(c)(2)] This provision changes prior law. [**Commissioner v. Lester,** 366 U.S. 299 (1961)—overruled]

INCLUDIBLE VS. EXCLUDIBLE INCOME ITEMS **gilbert**

THE FOLLOWING SHOWS WHETHER CERTAIN ITEMS ARE INCLUDIBLE OR EXCLUDIBLE AS INCOME TO THE RECIPIENT:

INCLUDIBLE	EXCLUDIBLE
• Compensation for services	• Meals and lodging for employer's convenience
• Gratuities and tips	• Gifts and inheritance
• Most interest payments	• Interest on state and local bonds
• Punitive damages	• Damages for personal physical injury
• Spousal support	• Child support
• Cancellation of indebtedness	• Repayment of indebtedness
• Prizes	• Contribution to capital
• Gambling winnings	• Life and medical insurance recovery
• "Earnings" from illegal activities	• Recovery of cost of annuity contract

E. Tax-Exempt Organizations

1. Charitable Organizations [§171]

Certain types of organizations are *exempt* from income tax. To be exempt under I.R.C. section 501(c)(3), an organization must be organized and operated for religious, charitable, scientific, educational, etc., purposes. The organization's status must also be determined by the IRS. [I.R.C. §501] No part of the net earnings can inure to a private shareholder, and no substantial part of the organization's activities can include carrying on propaganda or otherwise attempting to influence legislation.

a. Charitable purposes [§172]

Tax exemption is not available if the organization is primarily dedicated to providing social or recreational opportunities for its members. [**Wayne Baseball, Inc. v. Commissioner**, T. C. Memo. 1999-304—organization devoted to sponsoring particular amateur baseball team is not exempt; *but see* **Hutchinson Baseball Enterprises, Inc. v. Commissioner**, 73 T.C. 144 (1979), *aff'd*, 696 F.2d 757 (10th Cir. 1982)—exemption granted to an organization that sponsors a team but that also showed dedication to promoting amateur baseball in the area in other ways, such as by operating a field for and coaching the local little league team]

b. Other effects of status [§173]

Exemption from tax is not the only benefit of a section 501(c)(3) organization. Contributions to such organizations are also deductible for income, estate, and gift tax purposes. (*See infra,* §618; *and see* Estate and Gift Tax Summary.)

c. Other tax-exempt organizations [§174]

Many other kinds of organizations are also exempt from tax, such as unions, fraternities, civic leagues, chambers of commerce, etc. [*See* I.R.C. §501(c)(4) - (6)] However, contributions to them are *not* deductible.

d. Discrimination disqualifies organization [§175]

Organizations that practice racial discrimination cannot qualify as tax-exempt organizations. [**Bob Jones University v. United States**, 461 U.S. 574 (1983)—college that banned interracial dating not exempt]

2. Unrelated Business Income [§176]

The exemption from tax is limited to the income derived by eligible organizations from their nonprofit, charitable activities or their investments (interests, rents, dividends, etc.). It does *not* extend to "unrelated business income"—*i.e.,* income from an activity substantially different in purpose from the organization's nonprofit, charitable purpose. [I.R.C. §511]

Example: The American Bar Association ("ABA") sells life insurance to its members. Because it keeps the "dividends" refunded by the life insurance companies, the ABA makes a large profit on its insurance programs. Because this profitable business is unrelated to its charitable activity, it gives rise to unrelated business income. [**United States v. American Bar Endowment**, 477 U.S. 105 (1986)]

a. Rental income [§177]

Rental income from a tax-exempt organization's *real property* is generally treated as investment income and therefore exempt from tax. But rental income from a tax-exempt organization's *personal property* is treated as unrelated business income.

b. Debt-financed property [§178]

Investment income is also taxable as unrelated business income if the property involved was acquired with *borrowed funds*, unless it is used solely for purposes "substantially related" to the organization's charitable purposes. [I.R.C. §514] Only that portion of the income that results from investment of borrowed funds is taxed. *Gain* on the sale of any such property is also taxed. (This section was designed to prevent the tax avoidance scheme involved in the *Brown* case; *see infra*, §§911-913.)

3. Private Foundations [§179]

Nonpublic charitable organizations (other than churches) are subject to special restrictions. Generally speaking, if the organization receives more than one-third of its support from the general public, it is not a private foundation. [I.R.C. §509] The charter of a private foundation must require the prompt distribution of all income for charitable purposes. It must also prohibit "self-dealing" between the foundation and any substantial contributor, and further prohibit "excess" business holdings and certain types of expenditures (*e.g.*, lobbying). [*See* I.R.C. §508(e)]

a. Note

Even if the organization otherwise qualifies, a blanket 2% tax is imposed on its net investment income. [I.R.C. §4940]

b. And note

Violation of any of the above charter restrictions results in stiff penalty taxes against the foundation and (in certain cases) its management. [*See* I.R.C. §§4941 - 4945]

4. Political Organizations [§180]

To clear up much confusion, Congress passed I.R.C. section 527, detailing the taxation of political organizations. They are taxed like corporations on investment income, but they are not taxed on *"exempt function income."*

a. "Exempt function income" [§181]

"Exempt function income" is contributions of money or property, membership dues, or proceeds from political fundraising or entertainment events, or from sale of political campaign materials (as long as such sales are not in the ordinary course of trade or business). To be excludible, this income must be segregated for an *"exempt function."*

b. "Exempt function" [§182]

An "exempt function" is one that attempts to influence the nomination, election, or appointment of individuals to public office.

Chapter Two:
To Whom Is the
Income Taxable?

CONTENTS

Chapter Approach

Chapter Approach

Assuming that a particular item is income, the question then becomes to whom is it taxable? In general, income is taxed to the person who earned it, to the owner of the property that produced it, or to the person who controls it. Problems arise when taxpayers spread income by making gifts among several persons or entities, so as to minimize the tax rates. Exam questions on income splitting are common. Some key things to remember for exam purposes are discussed below.

1. **Income from Property**

   Income is shifted in the case of a gift of the income-producing *property*, but does not shift with a gift of the *income* from the property. If a question involves income from property, ask:

   (i) Does the donor actually *give up control* over the property, or is the transfer a sham? Remember that even if the transfer is effective under state law, the income may be taxed to the donor if he retains *excessive controls* over the management of the property and over who receives the income.

   (ii) Has the income already *accrued or matured*? If so, it may be too late to shift the income.

   Keep in mind that the donor does *not* realize income on a gift of appreciated property.

2. **Income from Services**

   If the question concerns income from personal services, remember that generally this income *cannot be shifted by gift* either before or after services are rendered. Note that it is possible to work for free, without imputed income, but if payment is made to anyone, it is taxable to the *earner*.

   a. **Commonly controlled businesses**

      Code section 482 allows the IRS to reallocate income among businesses controlled by the same people.

3. **Statutory Divisions of Income**

   Watch for the following income-splitting situations that are specifically addressed by the Internal Revenue Code:

   a. **Children's income**

      All of a child's income is taxed to the child [I.R.C. §73], and under what is known as the *"kiddie tax,"* the child's *unearned* income is taxed to her at her parents' top marginal rate [I.R.C. §1(i)].

   b. **Income of husbands and wives**

      The *joint return* privilege allows income splitting between spouses.

c. Income Earned by Head of Household

Taxpayers who qualify to file a "head of household" return are subject to special tax rates that effectively split 25% of their income with qualified relatives.

4. Trust Income

Although the regular trust taxation rules are not often tested in a personal income tax course, you should remember the basic rule that a trust is taxed on its income except to the extent the income is distributable to a beneficiary, in which case the beneficiary is taxed. Also, *grantor trust rules* are more frequently tested. When faced with a question involving a trust, remember that the grantor is taxed on trust income if:

(i)   The grantor or a nonadverse party has *excessive control over distributions* of income or corpus;

(ii) The trust *can be revoked* by the grantor or a nonadverse party;

(iii) The income can be paid for the *benefit of the grantor* or the grantor's spouse;

(iv) The income is actually paid to *discharge the grantor's child support obligation*; or

(v)   The general powers of administration are exercisable by a person in a *nonfiduciary capacity*.

Be aware that the same principles can be applied to third parties with control of a trust. Thus, if a third party has a *general power of appointment* over a trust, the third party is taxed on the trust income.

A. Income Splitting by Gifts

1. Gifts of Income vs. Gifts of Income-Producing Property [§183]

If a taxpayer makes a gift of the *income* from property, but retains ownership of the property, the income remains taxable to the taxpayer/donor. But an effective transfer of the *property itself* shifts the tax burden on the income to the donee, except for income that has already accrued. (Note the special rule for unearned income of a child under age 18, *infra*, §§224-226.)

a. Transfers of property [§184]

As stated, a transfer of income-producing property shifts the subsequent income to the donee. Similarly, a transfer of an *undivided interest* in the property shifts the appropriate *fraction of income* to the donee.

> **e.g. Example:** Dad gives Son an undivided one-quarter interest in an apartment house. One-quarter of the rental income is taxed to Son from that time onward. If the building is sold, Son is taxed on one-quarter of the gain (or deducts one-quarter of the loss).

(1) Right to receive income [§185]

Even if the donor owns only a right to receive income, the donor can shift part or all of that income to the donee by giving away that right. [**Blair v. Commissioner,** 300 U.S. 5 (1937)]

---

e.g. Example: Dad owned the right to receive income from a trust for his life. He gave Daughter the right to $9,000 per year of this income. *Held:* The $9,000 is taxable to Daughter because Dad parted with ownership of an undivided interest in his property. [**Blair v. Commissioner,** *supra*]

EXAM TIP   gilbert

On your exam, be sure to remember that if the income is *derived from property that the taxpayer owns*, the taxpayer *must give away the property* itself to avoid the tax consequences of the income—transfer of the income alone would be ineffective in this situation. However, if the taxpayer "merely" has the *right to receive income*, a gift of that income would be effective to avoid the income tax consequences of that income to the extent that the income has not yet accrued (*see infra*, §§187 *et seq.*).

(2) Other consequences of transfer [§186]

Transfers of income-producing property are subject to gift tax. (*See* Estate and Gift Tax Summary.) The property will usually have the same basis in the donee's hands as the donor had (*see infra*, §737). The donee does not treat the receipt of the property as income, because it will generally be excludible as a gift under I.R.C. section 102 (*see supra*, §28). However, section 102 does not protect the donee from taxation on the income subsequently produced by the gifted property (*see supra*, §47).

CONSEQUENCES OF GIFT OF PROPERTY   gilbert

TO DONOR	TO DONEE
• Will not be taxed on income generated by the property after the transfer.	• Will be taxed on income generated by the property after the transfer.
• Will not be liable for any capital gain, or benefit from any capital loss, as a result of the transfer.	• Usually will take the same basis in the property as the donor had.
• May be liable for gift tax on the transfer.	• Will not be taxed on receipt of property because it will be treated as a gift.

(3) Accrued income [§187]

A gift of property does not shift income that has already accrued as of the date of the gift. When the donee ultimately collects the accrued income, it will be taxed to the *donor* and treated as an additional gift to the donee.

Example: Alice gives a corporate bond to Bob on June 1. Interest accrues on the bond on a daily basis and is actually paid on January 1 and July 1. When Bob collects interest on July 1, Alice is taxed on the interest that accrued from January 1 to June 1; Bob is taxed on the interest that accrued from June 2 to June 30. Note that this result occurs whether Alice uses the cash or the accrual methods of taxation (which are discussed *infra,* §§958 *et seq.*).

(a) Shift of dividend income [§188]

There are conflicting decisions about whether a transferor can shift dividend income on stock after the dividend is declared but before the "record date." (The "record date" is the date on which a person must be a registered holder of the security in order to, among other things, collect the dividend.)

Example: Wiley owns preferred stock in Acme Corp. worth $100. On January 5, Acme Corp. declared a $50 dividend on the stock, payable to holders of record on January 15. On January 10, Wiley gave the stock to a qualified charity. The charity then collected the dividend. The law is unsettled as to whether Wiley can avoid paying tax on the dividend.

1) Better view—dividend cannot be shifted

The better view is that the dividend income cannot be shifted. The declaration creates a fixed obligation to pay the dividend and, at that point, it becomes too late to transfer the income to a donee to avoid income taxation. [**Estate of Smith v. Commissioner**, 292 F.2d 478 (3d Cir. 1961), *cert. denied*, 368 U.S. 967 (1962)]

2) Contrary view

The contrary view is that the dividend income can be shifted because the transfer occurred before the record date. Under state corporate law, the holder on the record date is entitled to a dividend. Moreover, for tax purposes, even an accrual method taxpayer is not required to accrue a dividend on the declaration date, only on the due date (*see infra,* §1029). [**Caruth v. United States,** 865 F.2d 644 (5th Cir. 1989)]

(b) Gift of contingent contracts [§189]

A similar problem arises when a taxpayer transfers a contingent contract that has not yet been paid off. Whether income is shifted to the donee depends on just how certain it was that the contingency would occur and the income would be realized. These cases are difficult to predict.

Example: A gift of an endowment insurance contract that would certainly mature later that year does not shift income to the donee. [**Friedman v. Commissioner,** 41 T.C. 428 (1964)]

Example: Johnson & Son, Inc. had a contract to sell British pounds at $2.80 each. After devaluation of the pound, this contract had great value, and Johnson donated the contract to a charity. *Held:* Johnson had accrued no income on the contract when it gave the contract away—so it could not be taxed on any gain from the sale of the contract by the charity—because it did not yet have a "fixed legal right" to the profit when it gave away the contract. For example, the pound could have been revalued upward or the dollar devalued before the contract was sold, which would have wiped out the profit. Thus the case is no different from a gift of appreciated stock, which successfully shifts income to the donee. [**Johnson & Son, Inc. v. Commissioner,** 63 T.C. 778 (1975)]

b. Sham transfers [§190]

Frequently, the courts hold that a purported gift to the donee does not shift income because there has been no real transfer. The transfer must be actually effective from a *state law* point of view. This means that there must be donative intent, delivery, and acceptance by the donee—the usual property law requirements.

(1) But note

Even if the transfer is actually effective from the point of view of state law, it will not be effective for income tax purposes if the donor retained *excessive controls*. (*See infra,* §209.)

c.   **Transferring income while retaining the property**

(1) **General rule [§191]**
     If the donor transfers the income from property to the donee *while retaining the income-producing property*, the income is taxed to the donor at the time the donee collects it. For tax purposes, income is to be taxed to the person who bears the risks of *gain or loss* from the investment that produces the income.

---

e.g.   **Example:** In the leading case, Father owned a coupon bond. He removed the coupons (*i.e.*, the rights to collect interest) from the bond and gave them to Son. Father was taxed on the income when Son collected the interest. [**Helvering v. Horst,** 311 U.S. 112 (1940)] If Father had given Son both the bond and coupons, the income would have been shifted to Son at least as to the income that *accrued* after the date of the gift (*see supra*, §187).

(a) **Note—coupon bonds [§192]**
     The Code has changed the outcome of *Horst*. It now requires the donor of coupons stripped from a bond to take into income on a daily basis the increase in value of the bond and the donee to take into income on a daily basis the increase in value of the coupons. [I.R.C. §1286]

(2) **Rental income [§193]**
     Rental income remains taxable to the *owner* of the reversion who has given away the right to the income. [**Galt v. Commissioner,** 216 F.2d 41 (7th Cir. 1954)]

(3) **Assignments of trust income [§194]**
     The beneficiary of a trust can shift the income from the trust to a donee if he assigns his *entire* beneficial interest to the donee. Similarly, he can shift a portion of the income if he assigns an *undivided portion* of the *entire interest*.

---

e.g.   **Example:** The owner of a life estate in trust transferred $9,000 per year of income to his daughter. The gift was effective for the life tenant's *entire life*. The court held that $9,000 per year of income was shifted to the daughter for income tax purposes. [**Blair v. Commissioner,** *supra*, §185]

---

cf.   **Compare:** Where the owner of a life estate in trust transferred the income from the trust for only *one year*, the income was held not to have shifted—because the interest transferred was too insubstantial. [**Harrison v. Schaffner,** 312 U.S. 579 (1941)]

---

(4) Note—assignments for consideration [§195]

The rules above apply only to *gifts* of income. If a transfer of an income right is supported by bona fide consideration received from the transferee (*e.g.*, it is a sale), the tax burden on income thereafter received is shifted to the transferee. [**Commissioner v. P.G. Lake,** 356 U.S. 260 (1958)]

(a) But note

The seller's profit will be ordinary income, not capital gain. (*See infra*, §855.)

d. No realization of income to donor making gift [§196]

The donor does not realize *gain or loss* when she makes a gift of property.

Example: Mother owns stock for which she has paid $5,000, but which is now worth $2,000. Mother makes a gift of the stock to Daughter. Mother cannot deduct the capital loss; she should have sold the stock and given the proceeds to Daughter. Daughter's basis for the stock is $5,000 for purposes of computing gain but only $2,000 for computing loss. (*See infra*, §737.)

---

(1) Charitable contributions [§197]

Gain or loss is not realized when a taxpayer gives an asset to a charity, even though the making of the gift results in immediate tax benefits to the donor-taxpayer.

Example: Trent purchased a residence for $100,000. Years later, when the house was worth $1 million, Trent gave it to Charity (a recognized charitable organization). On the same day Charity received the residence, Charity sold the residence to a third party for $1 million. Trent is entitled to a $1 million charitable contribution deduction. Trent does not realize the $900,000 gain on the house, and Charity does not pay tax on the gain because it is a tax-exempt organization (*see supra*, §171).

(a) "Ripened" gifts [§198]

In a transaction such as the one described in the above example, the IRS may contend that the taxpayer made the sale before making the charitable gift and merely transferred the proceeds of the sale to the charity. This is a distinct possibility if the donor prearranged the sale or if the charity was required by the terms of the gift to sell the property. It is also a possibility if the donor's business premises are used for the purposes of making the sale. [*See* **Kinsey v. Commissioner,** 477 F.2d 1058 (2d Cir. 1973)]

Example: Wally owns stock of Beaver Corp., a publicly traded corporation. On August 3, Eddie makes an offer to purchase in cash (a "tender offer") all shares of Beaver. The tender offer was contingent on Eddie being able to purchase at least 50% of Beaver's shares. On August 31, more than 50% of the shares are tendered, although numerous corporate formalities have not yet been performed. On September 8, Wally transfers his shares of Beaver to a charity. The charitable gift is too late, and Wally will be taxed on his capital gain. The stock "ripened" into a right to receive cash on August 31. [*See* **Ferguson v. Commissioner,** 174 F.3d 997 (9th Cir. 1999)]

(2) Exception—gifts to political organizations [§199]

A gain *is* recognized when a taxpayer transfers property to a political organization—although a loss is not recognized. The political organization receives a basis equal to the transferor's basis, plus gain recognized to the transferor. [I.R.C. §84]

(3) Exception—certain gifts [§200]

Realization can occur by reason of gifts of *mortgaged* property or gifts for which the donee *pays gift tax.* (*See infra,* §§765-766.)

2. Personal Service Income

a. General rule [§201]

The income from personal services is taxed to the person who earns it.

Example: In the leading case, an attorney and his wife agreed that income from their future services would be owned by them as joint tenants. (This case arose before the joint return privilege made it pointless to split income with a spouse.) The Court held that Congress had intended to tax personal service income to the person who had performed the work. Consequently, it was taxed to the husband; the transfer of half of the money to the wife was treated as a gift to her. [**Lucas v. Earl,** 281 U.S. 111 (1930)]

(1) Time agreement made immaterial [§202]

The same rule applies if the income-splitting agreement is made *after the work is done*: It is still taxed to the person who did the work. [**Helvering v. Eubank,** 311 U.S. 122 (1940)]

EXAM TIP	gilbert

On your exam, be sure to remember that *income from services* generally *cannot* be shifted by gift.

b. Obligatory assignments [§203]

If an employer is willing to make payments only to someone *other than the employee*, the result is not clear under present law.

Example: An employer made payments to an educational benefit trust. Payments from the trust could be made only for the college expenses of an employee's child. *Held:* These payments were simply substitutes for salary and were taxable to the employee at the time payments were made to the employee's child. [**Armantrout v. Commissioner,** 67 T.C. 996 (1977), *aff'd,* 570 F.2d 210 (7th Cir. 1978)]

Compare: In an earlier case, a father entered a contest, the terms of which were that the prize could be paid only to a child. The court held the prize taxable to the child and not the father. [**Teschner v. Commissioner,** 38 T.C. 1003 (1962)]

---

(1) Distinction between *Armantrout* and *Teschner*

Armantrout dealt with a regular employment relation, and it seems reasonable that all of an employee's earnings be taxed to him, whether or not he receives them. The employee probably perceived the educational benefit payments as a substitute for salary and conceivably could have bargained to receive the payments himself. *Teschner,* on the other hand, dealt with a one-shot situation in which payment to the child was not perceived as a substitute for anything. Moreover, the services rendered in *Teschner* (submitting a jingle) did not resemble normal employment services and no bargaining was possible. Note also that the explicit language of I.R.C. section 83(a) (adopted after *Teschner*) requires that the service provider be taxed on compensation, regardless of who receives the payment. As a result, it is unclear whether *Teschner* would be followed under existing law.

c. Working for charity [§204]

A taxpayer can work for free without being taxed on the dollar value of services rendered. However, income from employment cannot be diverted to charity to avoid income taxation. [Treas. Reg. §1.61-2(c)]

Example: Tonya, a rock star, volunteers to entertain at a benefit for a political candidate. The candidate is the promoter of the concert. Tonya is not taxed on the value of her services.

Compare: Theresa, a nun who is under a vow of poverty, is a nurse at a public hospital. Her entire salary is paid to her order. Theresa is taxed on the salary because she is an agent of the hospital, not of the order. The salary is treated as if paid to her, then contributed to the order. She can deduct the payment to the order, but is subject to the percentage limitations on charitable contributions (*see infra*, §§619-621). [**Schuster v. Commissioner**, 800 F.2d 672 (7th Cir. 1986); **Fogarty v. United States**, 780 F.2d 1005 (Fed. Cir. 1986)]

d. Working for oneself [§205]

Suppose a taxpayer invents something or constructs a building for himself and then gives the invention or building to his child. The child derives income from the property. This is treated as a transfer of *property*, thus shifting income to the child for income tax purposes. It is not treated as an assignment of rights to personal service income since the *services* involved were *rendered to the taxpayer himself*, not to another. [**Heim v. Fitzpatrick**, 262 F.2d 887 (2d Cir. 1959)] However, in an earlier case, a taxpayer rendered *personal services* to a group of inventors. Later he became entitled to a share of the royalties, which he sought to shift to other family members. It was held that this income stream derived from personal services rendered *to others*; consequently, the resulting income could not be shifted. [**Strauss v. Commissioner**, 168 F.2d 441 (2d Cir.), *cert. denied*, 335 U.S. 858 (1948)]

e. Commonly controlled businesses [§206]

I.R.C. section 482 applies to situations in which there is common control of two businesses (whether or not incorporated). To clearly reflect the income of the businesses, the IRS can allocate income, deductions, or credits between them. This section provides the IRS with a potent weapon to challenge income-splitting schemes.

(1) Intercorporate transactions [§207]

When two companies are controlled by the same people and deal with each other, section 482 is frequently employed. For example, if one company is profitable but the other is not, the profitable company might sell goods to the unprofitable company at an unrealistically low price. Alternatively, the profitable company might loan money interest-free to the unprofitable company. Both have the effect of shifting income. Using section 482, the IRS is permitted to allocate income to the profitable company from the unprofitable one by requiring that the bargain between the companies be at arm's length. [**Latham Park Manor, Inc. v. Commissioner**, 69 T.C. 199 (1977)—interest-free loan between related corporations; IRS can require interest to be charged]

(2) Services [§208]

I.R.C. section 482 has frequently been employed in situations in which an individual seeks to shift income to her corporation.

(a) Illustration

Tina is a management consultant. She forms a corporation, Consult Corp. Consult Corp. arranges to supply Tina to Acme Co., a business that needs her help. Acme Co. pays Consult Corp. for Tina's services, but Consult Corp. does not pay Tina any salary.

(b) **IRS position**

The IRS contends in this situation that Consult Corp. should be ignored entirely and the money paid by Acme Co. should be directly taxed to Tina. However, the courts say that section 482 offers a more discriminating approach to the problem. When the arrangement between Tina and Consult Corp. is analyzed under this approach, Tina is charged with the income that an unrelated management consultant would have required as a salary, and this same amount is then allowed to Consult Corp. as a deduction. [**Rubin v. Commissioner,** 429 F.2d 650 (2d Cir. 1970)] However, there is a split in authority as to whether section 482 applies. [*See* **Fogelsong v. Commissioner,** 691 F.2d 848 (7th Cir. 1982)—section 482 not applicable to employee who works exclusively for controlled corporation; **Haag v. Commissioner,** 88 T.C. 604 (1987), *aff'd,* 855 F.2d 855 (8th Cir. 1988)—section 482 applies in this situation]

(c) **Rationale**

According to the decisions applying section 482 in this situation, Tina's work as a consultant and Consult Corp.'s activity in lending Tina out are considered two separate businesses—both controlled by Tina. Consequently, I.R.C. section 482 applies. Since the arrangement between Tina and Consult Corp. does not clearly reflect income, the IRS can require an allocation that does clearly reflect income, which, in this situation, means requiring payment of compensation for Tina's services.

3. **Excessive Controls [§209]**

In general, if a taxpayer makes a legally valid transfer of property, but retains "excessive" controls over how the property is managed and who gets the income from it, the taxpayer will be taxed on the income.

Example: In **Helvering v. Clifford,** 309 U.S. 331 (1940), the grantor made a transfer *in trust*, giving income to his wife but retaining a *reversion* after five years. The wife was entitled to the income, but the grantor retained control over *when* she would get it. In addition, he retained broad managerial powers over the trust. Tax avoidance was concededly involved. The Court held that the grantor remained subject to tax on the income. *Rationale:* On the facts, this transfer did not appreciably change the way in which grantor had always held this property. Consequently, in substance he was still the owner and should be taxed as such.

---

a. Statutory codification [§210]

Clifford has now been codified by an elaborate body of statutes that leave it intact in some respects and change it in others. These statutes—the grantor trust rules, discussed *infra*, §§253 *et seq.*—are the exclusive source of law concerning whether a transfer to trust shifts income. However, the *Clifford* rationale is still applicable to transfers not in trust in which controls have been retained.

b. Transfers of patents [§211]

When a taxpayer licenses his patent to a manufacturer, and then gives away all his retained rights, he can shift the royalty income to the donee. However, if the taxpayer controls the manufacturer, he has power to decide how to use the patent and thus can control the stream of royalties to the donee. This retained control causes the royalties to be taxed to the donor. [**Commissioner v. Sunnen,** 333 U.S. 591 (1948)]

(1) Distinguish—effect if no controlling interest [§212]

If the donor owns stock in the manufacturing corporation but does *not control it*, he is not treated as having retained excessive control. Thus, the transfer of the patent *does* shift the income to the donee. [**Heim v. Fitzpatrick,** *supra*, §205]

c. Gift and leaseback [§213]

In many cases, taxpayers (particularly doctors and dentists) have given business assets to their children (or to trusts for their children) and *leased them back*. They have sought to deduct the rentals as business expenses. This plan will work if the gift and leaseback are upheld as valid business transactions—if, in other words, it is not a sham. One of the factors that courts have looked to is whether an independent trustee for the children is used; hypothetically, at least, such an independent trustee will force the grantor-lessee to pay the rent if he defaults. [**Van Zandt v. Commissioner,** 341 F.2d 440 (5th Cir. 1965), *cert. denied*, 382 U.S. 814 (1966)]

d. Family partnerships [§214]

Many of the ingredients of the cases above are involved when a parent seeks to make her children into her *partners*, hopefully causing partnership distributive shares to be taxed to the children instead of the parent.

(1) Judicial response [§215]

The Supreme Court held that this device would work if the taxpayers had an "intention" to be partners together. In general, this would require some significant contribution by the children of either services or capital to the partnership. [**Commissioner v. Culbertson,** 337 U.S. 733 (1949)]

(2) Statutory change [§216]

Congress has substantially relaxed the requirements of *Culbertson*. When capital is a *"material income-producing factor"* in the partnership, the gift of a partnership interest will effectively shift income, even though the children contribute neither capital nor services. [I.R.C. §704(e)]

(a) Reasonable compensation [§217]

The Commissioner can require that the donor receive reasonable compensation for her services before anything is left to be divided with the children. [I.R.C. §704(e)(2)] This is to ensure that personal service income is taxed to the one doing the work; only the return from capital supposedly can be divided with the children.

(b) Sham transfers [§218]

However, the Commissioner frequently attempts to circumvent section 704(e) by arguing that there has been *no real transfer* of partnership interests to the children—thus the transfer is a sham and the parent still owns the business. The regulations supply the standards for determining whether the transfer is a sham. [Treas. Reg. §1.704-1(e)(2)]

(3) Materiality of capital [§219]

If capital is not a "material income-producing factor," section 704(e) is not applicable and the *Culbertson* standards apply.

EXAM TIP   **gilbert**

Watch for fact patterns in which a parent makes his child a partner. This is an effective way to shift income if **capital** is used **to produce income**. However, if partnership income is generated by fees, commissions, or personal services, the income is taxable **only to the service provider/parent**, even if large amounts of capital are otherwise employed. (Thus, for example, the doctor or dentist in §213, *supra*, could not form a family partnership with her children.)

B. Statutory Divisions of Income

1. Income Earned by Children [§220]

Income earned by a child is taxable to the child. [I.R.C. §73] This is true even though the income is paid to the parent rather than the child, and even though under state law such income may be the property of the parent rather than the child. However, if a parent agrees to do a job, and puts his child to work on the job but does not pay the child a salary, the income is taxed to the parent, not to the child. The rationale is that the third party contracted with the parent, not the child, to do the work. [**Fritschle v. Commissioner**, 79 T.C. 152 (1982)]

a. Filing of return [§221]

The *parent* has the responsibility to see that an income tax return is filed on behalf of the child. [I.R.C. §6201(c)]

b. Expenditures [§222]

Expenditures made by the parent in connection with the business or activity from which the child's income is derived are treated as if made by the child and are deductible on the child's tax return. [I.R.C. §73(b)]

c. Dependency [§223]

As to the effect of a child's earnings on the parent's right to a dependency exemption, *see infra*, §668.

2. Kiddie Tax [§224]

All *unearned* income of a child under age 18 in excess of $850 (in 2006) is taxed to the child at the top marginal rate *of her parents*. The figure is *indexed for inflation.* This provision is often referred to as the "kiddie tax." [I.R.C. §1(g)]

a. Unearned income [§225]

Unearned income refers to rent, dividends, interest, and similar items that are *not produced by rendering personal services*. [I.R.C. §911]

b. Allocable parental tax [§226]

If a child's parents are not married, the tax bracket of the *custodial* parent is used. If the parents are married but file separately, the bracket of the parent with the greater income is used.

Example: Claudia is 16 years old. Last year, Claudia's grandfather gave her bonds that produce interest income of $5,000. Claudia's parents are divorced; she lives with her mother. Her mother's top tax bracket is 28%. Claudia must pay an income tax of 28% of $4,150 ($5,000 minus $850).

---

3. Income of Husbands and Wives

a. Right to file joint return [§227]

A husband and wife may elect to file a joint income tax return. [I.R.C. §§2, 6013] The effect of such a return is to tax income one-half to each spouse, irrespective of which spouse actually earned it. This generally reduces the overall tax liability of the spouses, since it has the effect of using the lower brackets twice.

(1) Background [§228]

The joint return privilege was enacted in 1948 to eliminate the special tax advantage that had theretofore existed for spouses in community property states. Because husbands and wives in a community property state had a vested, equal interest in each other's earnings, the Supreme Court held that one-half of the earnings of one spouse were taxable to the other spouse. [**Poe v. Seaborn,** 282 U.S. 101 (1930)] However, spouses in non-community property states were *not* permitted to split personal service income. [**Lucas v. Earl,** *supra,* §201—husband taxable on his earnings although he had assigned one-half to wife]

(2) Elective community property [§229]

Later, other states enacted statutes under which spouses could "elect" to make their earnings community property, but the Court held that such local statutes were not binding for tax purposes, so that the income would remain taxable to the one who earned it. [**Commissioner v. Harmon,** 323 U.S. 44 (1944)]

(3) Effect of joint return [§230]

A joint return treats the spouses as if their incomes were equal. Thus, it achieves the same result as if all of their income were community property.

(4) Domestic partnership laws [§231]

The creation of domestic partnership laws in states such as California has led some to conclude that the participants in a domestic partnership may file a joint return under the authority of **Poe v. Seaborn** (*see supra*). The IRS has ruled, however, that *Poe* only applies to married persons and therefore joint filing of federal tax returns is unavailable to domestic partners. [Chief Counsel Advisory 200608038 (Feb. 24, 2006)]

b. Marriage penalty and single penalty [§232]

The rate structure can penalize both married and single people. Single people are penalized because the tax on a given income is lower on a joint return than on a separate return. But married people can also be penalized when each of them has substantial income. In that situation, they would pay less combined tax if they were single rather than married.

(1) "Quickie" divorce [§233]

To avoid the marriage penalty, some taxpayers get divorced at the end of the year (thus allowing them to file as singles), then remarry. This technique is in considerable doubt—either because the "quickie" divorce may be invalid under state law or because the divorce and remarriage will be ignored as a sham for tax purposes. [*See* **Boyter v. Commissioner,** 668 F.2d 1382 (4th Cir. 1982)]

(2) Reduction of the marriage penalty [§234]

Two measures have been enacted recently to reduce the marriage penalty problem: First, beginning in 2005, the standard deduction for married taxpayers was increased to twice the standard deduction for single filers. [I.R.C. §63(c)(2)(A)] Second, beginning in 2004, the maximum income in the 15% bracket for married persons filing joint returns was raised to double the maximum income in the 15% bracket for single persons. [I.R.C. §1(f)(8)]

c. Liability for tax due on joint return [§235]

If spouses file jointly, each is jointly and severally liable for the payment of income tax on *all* income reported. Thus, the husband becomes liable for payment of tax on his wife's earnings, and vice versa. [I.R.C. §6013(d)] Both spouses are liable for penalties if the return is fraudulent.

(1) Exception—innocent spouse rule [§236]

Under the "innocent spouse" rule, a spouse who signs a joint return is relieved of liability for tax, interest, and penalties if she establishes that in signing the return she did not know, or have reason to know, of the understatement. The "innocent spouse" is entitled to this relief only if it would be inequitable to hold her liable. [I.R.C. §6015(b)] In addition, a spouse who is divorced or has been living apart from the other spouse for 12 months can file an election to be taxed only on that portion of a deficiency attributable to items on the joint return that are attributable to the electing spouse. [I.R.C. §6015(c), (d)]

d. Joint return not mandatory [§237]

Spouses do not have to file joint returns. However, it is almost always advantageous for them to do so because a special table of higher rates applies to married persons filing separately. [I.R.C. §1(d)]

4. Income Earned by Head of Household [§238]

A "head of household" is an unmarried individual who maintains for more than one-half of the year a household for qualified relatives (such as children). "Maintaining a household" means supplying over one-half of the cost of running the household. By filing a "head of household" return, special tax rates are provided that in effect split 25% of taxpayer's income with the relatives (as contrasted with the 50% split allowed between spouses filing joint returns, above). [I.R.C. §2(b)] Even if a taxpayer is married at the close of the year, she can be treated as a head of household if she files separately and her spouse was not a member of the household during the last six months of the taxable year. [I.R.C. §§2(c), 7703(b)]

C. Below-Market Interest on Loans

1. In General [§239]

Loans that carry no interest (or interest below prevailing rates) were once a useful income-splitting device (as well as a valuable way to compensate employees or reward corporate shareholders). However, the Code now requires that interest be *imputed* to the lender, thus wiping out the income tax advantage of the plan. It also subjects below-market interest loans to the gift tax. [I.R.C. §7872]

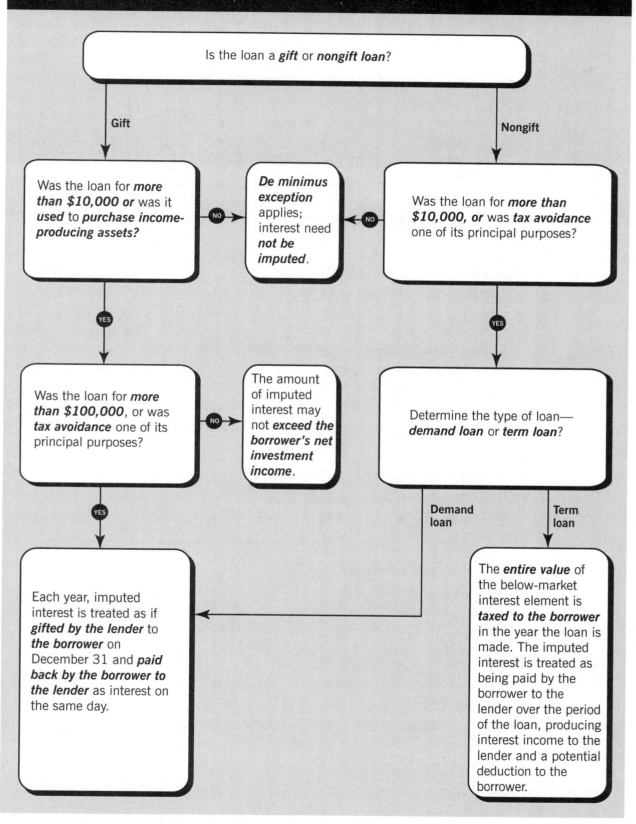

Is the loan a *gift* or *nongift loan*?

Gift

Nongift

Was the loan for *more than $10,000 or* was it *used* to *purchase income-producing assets?*

NO → De minimus exception applies; interest need *not be imputed*. ← **NO**

Was the loan for *more than $10,000, or* was *tax avoidance* one of its principal purposes?

YES

YES

Was the loan for *more than $100,000*, or was *tax avoidance* one of its principal purposes?

NO → The amount of imputed interest may not *exceed the borrower's net investment income*.

Determine the type of loan— *demand loan* or *term loan*?

Demand loan

Term loan

YES

Each year, imputed interest is treated as if *gifted by the lender* to *the borrower* on December 31 and *paid back by the borrower to the lender* as interest on the same day.

The *entire value* of the below-market interest element is *taxed to the borrower* in the year the loan is made. The imputed interest is treated as being paid by the borrower to the lender over the period of the loan, producing interest income to the lender and a potential deduction to the borrower.

> **Example:** Suppose that on January 1, Mother loans Daughter $150,000 interest free. Daughter puts the money in the bank and earns interest of $12,000 on it. She uses the $12,000 to pay her college expenses. Formerly, the interest would be taxed to Daughter in her low tax bracket, rather than to Mother. When Daughter finishes college, she repays the loan. Now, however, Daughter is treated as if she had paid interest to Mother at the applicable federal rate (*infra,* §242) minus the interest Daughter actually pays (if any). Additionally, Mother is subject to gift tax for the value of the interest-free loan.

2. Coverage [§240]

The imputed interest rule of section 7872 applies to gift loans (as in the example in §239). It also applies to compensation loans, to corporation-shareholder loans, to any loan that has tax avoidance as one of its principal purposes, or to any other loan that has a significant effect on the tax liability of the lender or borrower. [I.R.C. §7872(c)]

a. De minimis exception [§241]

Section 7872 will not apply to gift loans on any day when the loan balance does **not exceed $10,000**—**unless** the loan is used to purchase or carry income-producing assets. Of course, that is exactly what the loan is used for in the Mother-Daughter example (*supra,* §239). Also, if a gift loan is $100,000 or less, the amount of imputed income may not exceed the borrower's net investment income ($12,000 in the example)—**unless** tax avoidance was one of the principal purposes. Finally, the section will not apply to compensation or corporate loans that do not exceed $10,000—**unless** one of the principal purposes for the arrangement is tax avoidance.

(1) Note

In all these cases, if there are several outstanding loans between the parties, they must be added together to see whether the loans in total exceed the ceilings. [I.R.C. §7872(c)(2) - (3), (d)]

3. Measurement of Market Interest [§242]

Section 7872 is triggered if an interest rate is below the "applicable federal rate." These rates, which differ depending on the maturity of the loan, are set periodically by the IRS. The rates require semi-annual compounding.

4. Mechanism for Imputing Interest [§243]

If section 7872 applies, interest must be imputed. This will require the lender to include imputed interest income. However, because of the prohibition on deducting personal interest (except some mortgage interest), the borrower will probably be denied a deduction.

a. Gift loans [§244]

When interest is set below market as a gift (as in the Mother-Daughter example above), each year's forgone interest is treated as if it were transferred on December 31 by the lender to the borrower (as a gift), *then retransferred as an interest payment* by the borrower to the lender. [I.R.C. §7872(a)]

---

e.g. Example: Assume the example *supra*, §239, and that the applicable interest rate is 6% compounded semi-annually. Mother is treated as having made a $9,135 transfer to Daughter on December 31 (this is $150,000 at 6% interest compounded semi-annually). Then Daughter is treated as having paid back $9,135 to Mother as interest. Mother has $9,135 in interest income. Daughter is denied an interest deduction because the interest is personal. [I.R.C. §163(h); *see infra*, §591]

---

(1) Term of loan [§245]

The same rules apply to all *gift loans* whether they are "demand loans" (*i.e.*, repayable on the lender's demand) or "term loans" (*i.e.*, repayable at a fixed date). However, in the case of the other kinds of loans covered by section 7872 (such as compensation, corporate, or tax-avoidance loans), there are different rules depending on whether the loan is a demand loan or a term loan.

b. Nongift demand loans [§246]

Nongift *demand* loans are treated much like gift loans. The forgone interest each year is treated as if it were paid by the lender to the borrower, then re-transferred from the borrower to the lender. [I.R.C. §7872(a)]

---

e.g. Example: John works for Kap Co. On January 1, Kap Co. loans John $80,000 at 2% interest, repayable when Kap Co. demands it. Assume the applicable federal rate is 6%. On December 31, Kap Co. is treated as having transferred $3,264 to John (*i.e.*, the difference between 6% and 2% of $80,000 compounded semi-annually). This is treated as compensation income to John and a compensation deduction to Kap Co. John is then treated as having paid the $3,264 back to Kap Co. This payment is interest income to Kap Co. Whether John is entitled to an interest deduction depends on his use of the borrowed funds. If the interest is personal, it is not deductible.

---

e.g. Example: Suppose in the previous example that John was a stockholder of Kap Co. In that case, the $3,264 would be considered a dividend to John (nondeductible to Kap Co. but taxable to John). John would then be treated as having retransferred the $3,264 to Kap Co. as interest.

---

c. Nongift term loans [§247]

Different rules apply to nongift loans for a *fixed term*. In that case, the *entire value* of the below-market interest element is treated as transferred from the lender to the borrower as soon as the loan is made. The value of the below-market feature is equal to the difference between the amount of the loan and the present value of the interest and principal payments the borrower is to make. [I.R.C. §7872(b)]

> **e.g.** **Example:** John is an employee of Kap Co. On January 1, Kap Co. loans John $80,000 at an interest rate of 3% for five years. Assume that the applicable federal rate is 6%, and that the present value of the principal and interest payments John will make over the term of the loan (using present value tables) is $69,000. Kap Co. is treated as having transferred $11,000 to John on January 1 ($80,000 minus $69,000). John has compensation income of $11,000 (bunched in the first year of the loan), and Kap Co. has a compensation deduction of $11,000 (assuming that the deduction is not disallowed as unreasonable compensation). John is then treated as paying interest on the loan over the five-year period the loan is outstanding. The amount of interest is computed according to a formula that produces an ascending amount each year. For example, in the first year, the interest would be 3% (*i.e.*, 6% less 3%) of $69,000 compounded semi-annually, or about $2,085. In the second year, the interest would be 3% of $71,085 compounded semi-annually, or about $2,148. These amounts would be interest income to Kap Co. and an interest deduction (if otherwise allowable) to John.

---

5. **Imputed Interest Under Other Code Sections [§248]**

I.R.C. sections 483 and 1274 likewise provide for imputed interest, also called "original issue discount" or "OID" (*see infra*, §§923 *et seq.*). These sections come into play in cases of *sales* of property in exchange for deferred payments if an obligation fails to call for interest at the applicable federal rate. When the rules of section 483 or 1274 are applicable, section 7872 is not applicable.

D. Taxation of Trusts

1. **Introduction [§249]**

A brief summary of the taxation of trusts is provided here. There are two different schemes for trust taxation: the *grantor trust rules* (which provide for taxing the trust's income to the grantor) and the rules for *dividing trust income between the trust and the beneficiaries*.

2. **Grantor Trust Rules—In General [§250]**

The *Clifford* case (*see supra*, §209) established a rather vague principle under which the grantor of property to a trust would be taxed on the trust's income if he retained excessive controls. The IRS adopted regulations spelling out the *Clifford* principle, and these later became the statutory grantor trust rules. They are now the *exclusive* criteria for deciding whether the income of a trust should be taxed to the grantor. [I.R.C. §671] However, the vague *Clifford* rule is still applicable to gifts that are not in trust.

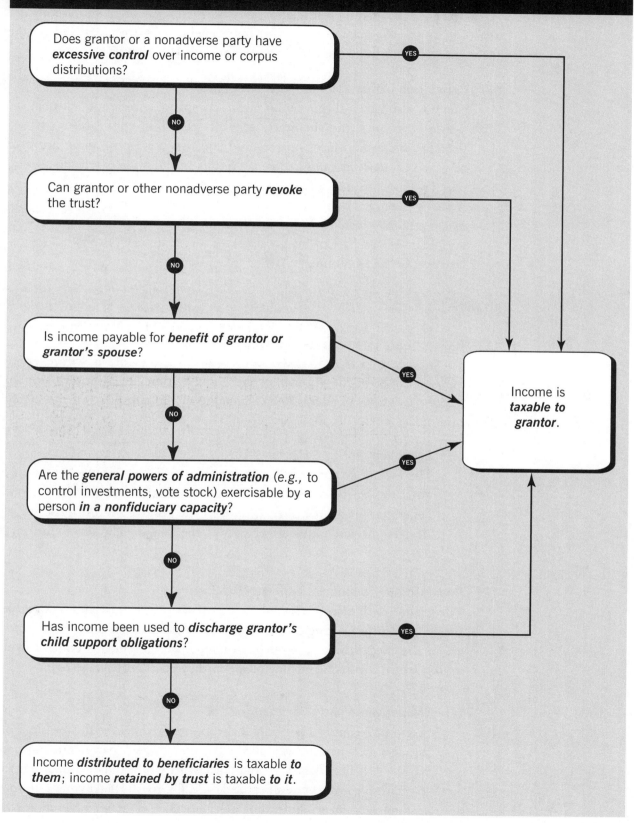

Does grantor or a nonadverse party have **excessive control** over income or corpus distributions?

NO

Can grantor or other nonadverse party **revoke** the trust?

NO

Is income payable for **benefit of grantor or grantor's spouse**?

NO

Are the **general powers of administration** (e.g., to control investments, vote stock) exercisable by a person **in a nonfiduciary capacity**?

NO

Has income been used to **discharge grantor's child support obligations**?

NO

Income **distributed to beneficiaries** is taxable **to them**; income **retained by trust** is taxable **to it**.

YES → YES → YES → YES

Income is **taxable to grantor**.

a. Tax effect [§251]

When the grantor is treated as the "owner" of a trust, he is taxed in the same way as if the trust did not exist: The grantor must include all the "trust" income in his gross income but is allowed whatever deductions and credits are attributable to that income. The trust and beneficiaries are not taxed on the income and cannot take the deductions or credits. [I.R.C. §671]

(1) Correlation with estate and gift taxes [§252]

There is a substantial (but by no means complete) correlation between the income tax rules and the estate and gift tax rules applicable to trusts. Broadly, the retention of powers and controls that cause the grantor to be taxed on trust income frequently results in the transfer's being considered an "incomplete" gift so that it is *not* subject to the federal gift tax. And the retention by the trustor of such powers and interests in the trust assets generally results, on the death of the grantor, in the trust assets being includible as part of his gross estate for estate tax purposes. (*See* Estate and Gift Tax Summary.)

b. Grantor trust rules

(1) Reversionary interest retained [§253]

The income of a trust is taxed to the grantor if the corpus will revert to the grantor or to the grantor's spouse at any time, and the reversionary interest is worth at least 5% of the value of the corpus as of the inception of the trust. [I.R.C. §§672(e), 673]

(a) Exception

The income is not taxed to the grantor if: (i) the corpus reverts only after the death of the trust's income beneficiary; (ii) the income beneficiary is a *lineal descendant* of the grantor; and (iii) the reversionary interest takes effect only if the beneficiary dies *before age 21*.

(2) Power to alter beneficial enjoyment [§254]

The grantor will also be treated as the owner of the trust and be taxable on the trust income if he or his spouse or a "nonadverse party" has *powers of disposition* over the corpus or income. This means control over *who* gets the corpus or income or *when* they get it. [I.R.C. §674]

(a) "Nonadverse party" defined [§255]

Section 674 applies not only if the grantor retains the power himself, but also if the control is lodged in a "nonadverse" party. An "adverse party" is a beneficiary of the trust who would have something to lose if the power were exercised. [I.R.C. §672(a)] Anyone else (including a trustee who is not a beneficiary) is a nonadverse party.

[I.R.C. §672(b)] Section 674 is *not applicable* if the power involved can be exercised *only* with the consent of *an adverse party*.

(b) Exception—retention of certain powers not subject to rule [§256]

In the following situations, the grantor will not be taxed on the trust income even though he or a nonadverse party has retained powers of disposition:

1) Certain powers of independent trustees [§257]

Where *independent trustees* have the power to *apportion income or pay out principal* among the beneficiaries, the income will not be taxed to the grantor. However, the grantor cannot be a trustee, and not more than half the trustees can be his relatives or subordinates *subservient* to his wishes. [I.R.C. §674(c)]

2) Power limited by standard [§258]

If a reasonably definite external *standard* for apportionment of trust income (or accumulation of trust income) is spelled out in the trust instrument, the grantor will not be treated as owner of the trust even if the trustees are relatives or subordinates subservient to him. However, none of the trustees can be the grantor or the grantor's spouse living with him. [I.R.C. §674(d)]

 Example: A trust that allows a trustee to distribute the corpus for the medical bills of the beneficiaries is one subject to *reasonably definite external standards*.

---

3) Reasonable alterations of beneficial enjoyment [§259]

The following powers are deemed reasonable controls and will not cause the trust income to be taxed to the grantor—even if retained by the grantor himself [I.R.C. §674(b)]:

a) *Power to invade corpus* for the benefit of a designated beneficiary, if limited by a *reasonably definite standard* [I.R.C. §674(b)(5)];

b) *Power to postpone payments* of income to a beneficiary who is under 21 years old or under a legal disability [I.R.C. §674(b)(7)];

c) *Power to change the distribution* of income by will [I.R.C. §674(b)(3)];

d) *Power to either distribute or accumulate income*, provided that the accumulated income is certain eventually to be paid to the person who would have received it currently (or to his estate or appointees) [I.R.C. §674(b)(6)].

(3) Power to revoke [§260]

The income of a trust is taxable to the grantor if either the grantor, his spouse, or a nonadverse party (*see* definition, above) has the power to *revoke* the trust and revest all or part of the *corpus* in the grantor. [I.R.C. §676; **Corliss v. Bowers,** 281 U.S. 376 (1930)]

(4) Income for benefit of grantor or spouse [§261]

The trust income is also taxable to the grantor if it is, or *may be* in the *discretion* of the grantor or any nonadverse party, applied to any of the following purposes [I.R.C. §677]:

(a) Distributable to grantor or spouse [§262]

If any part of the income *may* be distributed to the grantor or his spouse (without the consent of the beneficiary), such income is taxable to him, even though none of it is in fact so distributed.

1) Note

Income is considered distributable to the grantor if it can be used to pay his debts. [**Morrill v. United States,** 228 F. Supp. 734 (D. Me. 1964)]

(b) Accumulated for future distribution to grantor or spouse [§263]

If income is accumulated for future distribution to the grantor or his spouse, it is taxable to the grantor.

(c) To pay premiums or insurance policies on life of grantor or spouse [§264]

If trust income is used to pay for insurance policies on the life of the grantor or his spouse, it is taxable to the grantor even if the policy was taken out by the trustee and belongs to the trust.

1) Distinguish—charity as beneficiary [§265]

If a recognized *charity* is the beneficiary of the policy, then the trust income is not taxed to the grantor. [I.R.C. §677(a)(3)]

(d) To support other dependents [§266]

Trust income is also taxable to the grantor if it may be used for the support of any beneficiary whom the grantor is legally obligated to support—*but only to the extent that the income is actually so applied.*

1) Distinguish—support of spouse [§267]

The mere fact that income *may* be used to support the grantor's *spouse* renders trust income taxable to the grantor (*see* above). But as to other dependents, the income is taxed to the grantor only to the extent that it is **actually so used**.

2) Distinguish—alimony trusts [§268]

The grantor trust rules are superseded in divorce cases. For example, assume Husband creates a trust whose income is payable to Wife. After Husband and Wife are divorced, the income is taxable to Wife, not to Husband. [I.R.C. §682—overrides I.R.C. §677(a)(1)] Similarly, if Husband sets up a trust for Wife as part of their divorce agreement, the income is taxed to Wife under the usual trust rules, not to Husband. However, child support paid through such a trust is taxable to Husband, not to Wife. [I.R.C. §682—overrides the rules of I.R.C. §71]

EXAM TIP   **gilbert**

For your exam, remember that a trust that was initially set up to support the grantor's spouse may "morph" into an alimony trust after divorce. Thus, trust income that was initially taxable to the grantor because it was used to support the grantor's spouse **may become taxable to the spouse** after the parties divorce.

---

(5) Administrative powers that may benefit grantor [§269]

The grantor is taxable on the income of a trust where the administrative control of the trust is, or may be, exercisable primarily for the benefit of the grantor or his spouse instead of the beneficiaries. [I.R.C. §675] The following are the kinds of administrative powers that will cause the trust income to be taxed to the grantor:

(a) Dealing not at arm's length [§270]

The trust income will be taxed to the grantor if the grantor or a nonadverse party, or both, have the power to **deal** with the trust property or income for **less than an adequate consideration** without the approval of an adverse party. [I.R.C. §675(1)]

(b) Borrowing not at arm's length [§271]

The grantor will also be taxed on trust income if the grantor or a nonadverse party, or both, have the power to **borrow** the corpus or income, directly or indirectly, **without adequate interest or security**. [I.R.C. §675(2)]

(c) Borrowing part of corpus or income [§272]

If the grantor directly or indirectly borrows any part of the income or corpus and does not repay the loan **before the beginning of the year**, he will be taxed on the appropriate portion of the trust income (*e.g.*, if he borrows half the corpus, he is taxed on half the income). This rule applies even though the grantor has given *adequate security* and is paying *adequate interest*. [I.R.C. §675(3)]

1) Exception [§273]

This rule does not apply if the loan was made by a trustee other than the grantor or a related or subordinate trustee subservient to him, and the loan provides for adequate interest and security.

2) Tax to grantor [§274]

If the grantor borrows a portion of trust *income*, he is taxed on the appropriate percentage of the income until the year following the year in which the loan is repaid. In each year, the appropriate percentage is determined by dividing the amount of the loan by the sum of the trust's total income for all the years that the loan was outstanding. [*See* **Bennett v. Commissioner,** 79 T.C. 470 (1982)]

Example: Gina Grantor established a trust. She borrowed $10,000 from the trust for three years—Year 1, Year 2, and Year 3. In each year that the loan was outstanding, the trust made $20,000 in income. Gina would be taxed on 50% of the Year 1 income ($10,000/$20,000), 25% of the Year 2 income ($10,000/$40,000), and 16.67% of the Year 3 income ($10,000/$60,000).

3) "Borrowing" from trust [§275]

A grantor is treated as borrowing from a trust if a loan is made to the grantor's partnership, but *not* if the loan is made to a corporation of which the grantor is the majority stockholder. [**Bennett v. Commissioner,** *supra*]

(d) Powers exercised by nonfiduciary [§276]

Trust income will be taxed to the grantor if general powers of administration are exercisable by anyone in a *nonfiduciary capacity*. These include powers to control investments, vote stock in the trust, or reacquire assets in the trust. However, if these powers can be exercised by someone only in a *fiduciary capacity*, they will not cause the income to be taxed. [I.R.C. §675(4)]

c. Trust income taxable to person other than grantor [§277]

The *Clifford* principle (*see supra*, §209) is also applied when a person *other than the grantor* has a *general power of appointment*. In other words, if a grantor sets up a trust for a beneficiary, but gives a third party the power to *vest in herself the trust income or corpus*, the third party is taxed on the income whether or not she takes it. [I.R.C. §678]

(1) Rationale

This statute is derived from the *Mallinckrodt* doctrine—the third party's power to control the flow of income is tantamount to ownership of the income for tax purposes. [**Mallinckrodt v. Nunan,** 146 F.2d 1 (8th Cir.), *cert. denied*, 324 U.S. 871 (1945)]

(2) Note

If the third party has the power only to apply the trust income for the *support of her dependents*, the income is not taxable to her except to the extent that she actually applies the income to their support. [I.R.C. §678(c)]

(3) And note

Section 678 is not applicable to powers over income if the *other grantor trust rules* would *cause the income to be taxed to the grantor*. It is also inapplicable if the third party *renounces or disclaims* the power within a reasonable time after becoming aware of its existence. [I.R.C. §678(b), (d)]

3. Trusts Recognized for Tax Purposes [§278]

If the grantor has not retained substantial "strings" on the trust, the trust itself will be recognized as a separate taxable entity. Trust income will be taxable to the trust itself or to the beneficiaries, rather than to the grantor. A decedent's estate computes its taxable income in the same manner as a trust. The following is an abbreviated treatment of the taxation of trusts and estates (often called "fiduciaries"). A more complete discussion appears in the Taxation of Business Entities Summary.

a. Taxability of income [§279]

In general, either the trust or the beneficiaries will pay tax on the income earned by the trust. If the income is distributed to the beneficiaries, it is includible in their income and deductible by the trust. If the trust retains the income, it pays tax thereon.

(1) Note

Distributions of *corpus* by the trust are not taxed to the beneficiaries. However, the precise rules for distinguishing income from corpus are quite complex.

b. Distributable net income [§280]

The concept of distributable net income ("DNI") is an essential element of the taxation of trusts and estates. DNI is the "measuring rod" to determine the maximum amount that can be included in the beneficiary's income and be deducted as a distribution by the trust. It is defined as the trust's *taxable income*, with the following special adjustments (among others) [I.R.C. §643(a)]:

(1) *No deduction for distributions to beneficiaries*;

(2) *No deduction for the trust's personal exemption* (*see* below); and

(3) *No deduction for undistributed capital gains or losses allocated to corpus.*

c. "Simple trusts" [§281]

A simple trust is basically a conduit for moving current trust income to the beneficiaries. A trust will be treated as a simple trust if it is *required to distribute* all of its current income to the beneficiaries, makes no distribution of corpus, and claims no deduction for charitable contributions. [I.R.C. §651(a)]

(1) Taxation of simple trusts [§282]

The beneficiaries of a simple trust are taxed on the income of the trust that is distributed or (if not actually distributed) *required to be distributed*. The amount taxed to the beneficiaries is deducted by the trust. However, the amount included in income cannot exceed the trust's DNI. The trust will be taxed on capital gains allocated to corpus. [I.R.C. §652(a)]

d. "Complex trusts" and estates [§283]

A complex trust is any trust that does not fall within the definition of a simple trust (above). Decedent's estates are treated as complex trusts, as are all trusts that accumulate income, trusts that distribute corpus, or trusts in which the trustee has discretion in distributing income. Taxation of complex trusts is as follows:

(1) First tier [§284]

All of the income *required* to be distributed is included in the income of the beneficiaries entitled to it, whether or not distributed. However, the amount taxed can never exceed DNI. [I.R.C. §662(a)(1)]

(2) Second tier [§285]

If DNI exceeds the amount *required* to be distributed, then *additional payments to beneficiaries become taxable*. These would include discretionary income payments or distributions from corpus or accumulated income. Again, however, the amount includible *cannot exceed DNI less the amount that was taxed to first tier beneficiaries*. DNI is allocated among the second tier beneficiaries in proportion to the amounts they receive. [I.R.C. §662(a)(2)]

(3) Nonperiodic payments [§286]

Even if there is available DNI, certain nonperiodic distributions are not taxed to second tier beneficiaries: If the governing instrument requires payment of a lump sum (or payments of a set amount in not more than three installments), this payment is treated as a tax-exempt gift, even if there is DNI available. [I.R.C. §663(a)]

(4) Tax to trust [§287]

To the extent that amounts are includible in income of first and second tier beneficiaries, the trust deducts these amounts from its own income. If these deductions leave taxable income above zero, the trust pays tax on these amounts.

(a) Exemptions [§288]

A simple trust has a $300 personal exemption, a complex trust has a $100 personal exemption, and an estate has a $600 personal exemption. Trust and estate exemptions are not indexed for inflation (in contrast to individuals, who have an indexed $1,000 personal exemption). [I.R.C. §642(b)]

e. Throwback rule

(1) The problem—tax avoidance through delay [§289]

If the trust is in a low bracket and the beneficiaries are in a high bracket, considerable tax savings could be obtained by delaying distributions. For example, assume that in 2004 and 2005, DNI of the trust is $20,000. The trust makes no distribution in 2004 (and therefore has taxable income of $20,000 less a $100 personal exemption). But in 2005, it distributes $40,000. Since DNI is only $20,000 in 2005, the beneficiary would have to include only $20,000 in income.

(2) Taxing the trust—throwback rule [§290]

The throwback rule is designed to prevent such avoidance. It provides that a distribution in excess of current DNI is "thrown back" to the accumulated income of any preceding years. It is treated as though it had been distributed in those years, to the extent of the undistributed income in those years. The tax that the trust previously paid on the income is also treated as though it had been distributed in the prior years. [I.R.C. §§665 - 669]

(3) Taxing beneficiaries [§291]

The beneficiary is taxed on the accumulation distribution in the year in which it is made. The procedure involves a shortcut method so that the tax of each prior year in which there was undistributed net income does not have to be recomputed. Instead, the accumulation distribution (plus the taxes previously paid by the trust), divided by the number of years to which it is being thrown back, is added to taxable income of three of the preceding five taxable years. (Of the five preceding taxable years, the highest and lowest are disregarded and the remaining three are used.) The average increase in tax for each of those three years is then multiplied by the total number of years to which the distribution is thrown back.

[*See* I.R.C. §667—described in much greater detail in the Taxation of Business Entities Summary]

(a) Note

The amount distributed includes the tax paid by the trust during the years in which there was undistributed net income. However, the beneficiary is given a *credit* for the amount of those taxes.

Chapter Three:
Is It Deductible or Is It a Credit?

CONTENTS

Chapter Approach

The income tax is a tax on *net* income, not on gross income. Therefore, after gross income is determined (Chapter I, *supra*) and after it is assigned to the proper taxpayer (Chapter II, *supra*), the next set of questions relates to deductions from income and credits against the tax. Deductions are a favorite exam topic.

1. Business and Investment Deductions

When a potentially deductible item appears on your exam, you should first determine whether it qualifies as a business or investment deduction—*i.e.*, as expense, depreciation, depletion, loss, or bad debt.

a. Expense

If the item might be a business or investment expense, ask whether it was paid or incurred: (i) in connection with a *trade or business* [I.R.C. §162], (ii) for the *production of income* [I.R.C. §212(1)], or (iii) for the management, conservation, or maintenance of *income-producing property* [I.R.C. §212(2)].

(1) The next issue to address is whether the item is *business or personal*. Ask yourself:

    (a) Was it a deductible *traveling expense* or personal commuting? If a meal, does it satisfy the "overnight" test or meet the test for entertainment? (Note that only 50% of meal and entertainment costs are deductible.) If a meals and lodging expense, is the taxpayer "away from home"?

    (b) If expenses arise from a business that might be a hobby, does it meet the test of *intention to make a profit* under section 183?

    (c) If it is an *educational expense*, does it qualify the taxpayer for a new trade or business?

    (d) If it involves a *home office* or a rented *vacation home*, does it meet all the requirements of section 280A?

    (e) If it involves *attorneys' fees*, what was the origin of the dispute? If the origin was personal (*e.g.*, divorce), the fees are not deductible.

(2) To determine whether an item is an *expense* or must be *capitalized*, ask:

    (a) Is it a *repair* or a *permanent improvement*?

(b)   Is it a *cost* of purchasing or producing property? Watch here for the strict requirements of section 263A for capitalization of *interest and overhead*.

(c)   If the item involves *rent with an option* to purchase, analyze whether it is a concealed purchase.

(d)   Is it a *start-up cost* or a cost of searching for a new business? Apply section 195.

(e)   Is it a *selling cost*? If so, it reduces the amount realized on the sale.

(f)   Is it a cost of *acquiring goodwill*? Distinguish from the cost of maintaining existing goodwill, which is deductible.

(g)   If it is an *attorneys' fee* incurred in litigation relating to property, distinguish disputes over title (not deductible) from disputes concerning income (deductible).

(3)   The item must be *ordinary and necessary* to qualify as a deductible expense. Ask yourself whether the expense helps the business and whether other businesses in the community would, under similar circumstances, incur this expense. If the item involves compensation, it must be reasonable.

(4)   Certain expense items are disallowed if a deduction would be contrary to *public policy*, so watch for: bribes to government officials and any other type of illegal payment; fines or similar penalties paid to the government; certain punitive antitrust damages; and ballot initiatives or political campaigns (but distinguish lobbying expenses, which are deductible at the local level).

b.   Depreciation and amortization

If the item might be deductible as depreciation or amortization, consider:

(1)   The item's *useful life*. An arbitrary 15-year useful life is provided for many intangibles.

(2)   Who is seeking the deduction; *i.e.*, is the taxpayer the *owner* of the property? Generally only one who has a capital investment in the property is entitled to claim a deduction.

(3)   Whether the item is *"listed property"* (*e.g.*, cars, home computers). If so, the deduction is limited.

(4)   Which depreciation *method* (accelerated or straight-line) should be used, and whether the election to deduct up to $108,000 (for 2006) in the year of purchase can be used.

c.   Depletion

If the taxpayer owns an asset subject to depletion, important issues will be whether he can use *percentage* depletion, and whether he can deduct *intangible drilling costs*.

d.   Loss

If the item might be deductible under I.R.C. section 165 as a loss, you will want to ask:

(1)   If the taxpayer is an individual, is it a *business or investment loss*? Personal losses are not deductible except for casualty losses.

(2)   Was the loss *realized*?

(3)   Was the loss *ordinary or capital*? The deduction of capital losses is restricted.

(4)   What is the *amount* of the loss? It is limited to a taxpayer's basis in the asset.

(5)   Will the deduction be *disallowed* because of sale to a *related party*? Because the transaction was motivated by *tax avoidance*? Because of *public policy*?

e.   Bad debt

If you suspect the item might qualify for a bad debt deduction, ask:

(1)   Was there a *bona fide debt*? Intrafamily debts are suspect.

(2)   Did it become *worthless in the taxable year*? Remember, however, that a deduction for partial worthlessness is permitted for business debts.

(3)   What was the *basis* of the debt? No bad debt deduction is allowed if the debt had no basis, as in the case of the account receivable of a cash-basis taxpayer.

(4)   Is the deduction *ordinary or capital*? Nonbusiness bad debts produce capital loss.

f.   Limitations on deductibility

Finally, you will want to determine whether there are any rules that limit the deductibility of the item in question. You must consider:

(1)   *The at-risk rules:* Operating losses cannot be deducted beyond the amount at risk in the activity.

(2)   *The passive loss rules:* Loss from passive activity can be deducted only against passive income. There are, however, exceptions to this rule for

certain real property rentals by moderate income taxpayers and for real estate professionals.

(3) The limitations on *excess investment interest*.

(4) The rule that the cost of earning *tax-exempt interest* is not deductible.

2. Personal Deductions

Certain items are deductible even though they have no connection to business or investment. These items fall into two categories: "above-the-line" deductions, which are deducted from gross income; and "below-the-line" deductions, which are deducted from adjusted gross income ("AGI"). *Below-the-line deductions must exceed the standard deduction.* Be aware that certain below-the-line deductions (such as employee business expenses and most expenses deductible under section 212) are subject to a 2% floor; *i.e.*, they are deductible only to the extent they exceed 2% of AGI. Note also that itemized deductions are further reduced by 3% of the excess of AGI over the applicable amount. The following are personal deductions that are popular exam subjects:

a. Qualified residence interest

Most personal interest is not deductible. When you encounter the issue of whether the interest on a debt secured by a residence is deductible, the important issues will be:

(1) Whether the debt is secured by a *personal* residence or a designated second residence.

(2) Whether it is *acquisition* debt or *home equity* debt.

(3) Whether it is *within the monetary limits* ($1 million on acquisition debt, $100,000 on home equity debt).

b. Taxes

When the item in question is taxes, remember that *state and local taxes* on income, real property, and personal property are deductible.

c. Charitable contributions

When the item in issue is a gift to charity, ask:

(1) Is it within the applicable *percentage limits*? Taxpayers may deduct up to 50% of their AGI for gifts to most charities.

(2) If a gift of *appreciated property*, does it encounter any of the limits on deducting fair market value? To deduct the fair market value, the property must have been a long-term capital asset and donated to a public charity. Also, the deduction for gifts of property is limited to 30% of AGI.

    (3)   Does the taxpayer receive any *benefit* from the transfer that *exceeds* that which would inure to the general public? If so, it is not deductible.

d. Medical expenses

Most medical expenses are deductible to the extent that they exceed 7.5% of AGI. However, expenses compensated by insurance are not deductible.

e. Casualty loss

If an exam question concerns an item that might be a casualty loss, remember that the loss must be over $100 and exceed 10% of AGI. In addition, consider whether the requisite element of suddenness is present. Finally, note that the amount deductible is the lesser of the adjusted basis or the difference in the value of the property before and after the casualty.

f. Personal and dependency exemptions

A taxpayer is entitled to a personal exemption for himself (and another for a spouse on a joint return). The question most likely to arise on an exam in this area is whether the taxpayer can claim an exemption for a dependent. If you encounter this situation, ask:

(i)   Is the person in question a *close relative* of the taxpayer or does he have his principal place of abode with the taxpayer?

(ii)   Is the "dependent" person's *gross income less than the exemption* amount? (Note that there are important exceptions to this requirement.)

(iii)   Does the taxpayer supply *over one-half of the person's support*?

(iv)   If the exemption is for a *child of divorced parents*, which parent is entitled to the exemption? Absent a waiver of the exemption, the custodial parent is entitled to the exemption.

Watch out for the phaseout of exemptions when AGI exceeds various thresholds.

3. Personal Credits

Taxpayers are entitled to a number of *credits*—meaning that the item reduces the tax due *dollar for dollar*. Important personal credits include (i) credits for low-income elderly persons, (ii) the child care credit, (iii) the child tax credit, (iv) the earned income credit, and (v) education credits.

A. Introduction

1. Deductions and Credits Defined [§292]

A *deduction* is subtracted either from gross income or from adjusted gross income (*see infra*, §§553 *et seq.*). In either case, the deduction reduces **taxable income**. A **credit**, on the other hand, reduces the **tax** that is payable dollar for dollar.

 Example: What is the difference between a $1,000 deduction and a $1,000 credit? Assume that Tom's taxable income is $25,000 and the tax is $5,000 (in both cases, before taking the $1,000 into account). Assume further that Tom is in the 28% tax bracket. If the $1,000 is a **deduction**, it will reduce his taxable income to $24,000 and reduce his tax by $280 (*i.e.*, 28% of $1,000) to $4,720. However, if the $1,000 is a **credit**, it will reduce his tax from $5,000 to $4,000.

---

2. Business vs. Personal Deductions [§293]

As a broad general principle, the costs of doing business (or of otherwise making money through investments) are deductible. The costs of a taxpayer's personal life are not deductible, with a few exceptions (*e.g.*, medical expenses or charitable contributions).

3. No Shifting of Deductions [§294]

In general, payment of **another's liabilities** (*e.g.*, paying interest on someone else's loans) will not create a valid deduction for the taxpayer. [*See* **United States v. Davis**, 370 U.S. 65 (1962)]

a. Exception—separate business purpose [§295]

Payment of another's debt may be deductible if it serves **independent business purposes** of the taxpayer.

 Example: Taxpayer Gould owned all of the stock of insolvent Gould Plumbing & Heating, Inc. and was an employee of Industrial Mechanical Contractors, Inc. Unless the debts of Gould Plumbing & Heating, Inc. were cleared up, he was in danger of losing his job with Industrial Mechanical Contractors, Inc. He paid Gould Plumbing & Heating's debts. Ordinarily, a stockholder cannot deduct the payment of any corporate debts or expenses, but here the deduction was allowed because the payment was related closely enough to protecting the taxpayer's job with Industrial Mechanical Contractors. [**Gould v. Commissioner**, 64 T.C. 132 (1975)]

B. Business and Investment Deductions

---

1. Business Expenses [§296]

The most important provision for deducting the costs of doing business is set forth in I.R.C. section 162, which provides that all "ordinary and necessary **expenses**

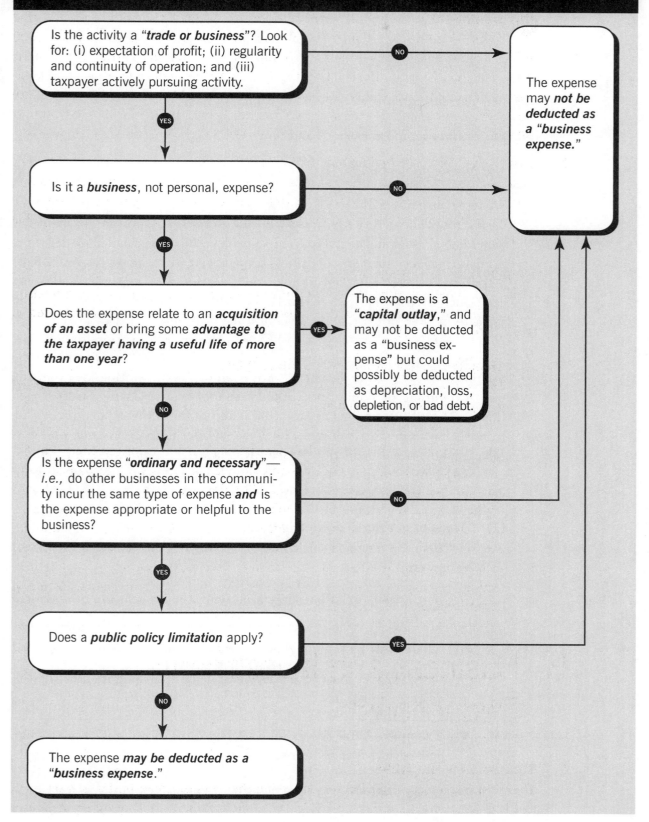

OVERVIEW OF BUSINESS DEDUCTIONS

gilbert

Is the activity a *"trade or business"*? Look for: (i) expectation of profit; (ii) regularity and continuity of operation; and (iii) taxpayer actively pursuing activity.

NO →

The expense may *not be deducted as a "business expense."*

YES ↓

Is it a *business*, not personal, expense?

NO →

YES ↓

Does the expense relate to an *acquisition of an asset* or bring some *advantage to the taxpayer having a useful life of more than one year*?

YES →

The expense is a *"capital outlay,"* and may not be deducted as a "business expense" but could possibly be deducted as depreciation, loss, depletion, or bad debt.

NO ↓

Is the expense *"ordinary and necessary"*—*i.e.,* do other businesses in the community incur the same type of expense *and* is the expense appropriate or helpful to the business?

NO →

YES ↓

Does a *public policy limitation* apply?

YES →

NO ↓

The expense *may be deducted as a "business expense."*

paid or incurred during the taxable year in carrying on any trade or business" are deductible. Thus, to be deductible under this section, an expense must meet several criteria. It must:

(i) Be paid or incurred during the year in connection with a *trade or business*;

(ii) Be a *trade or business*, rather than a *personal,* expense;

(iii) Be a *current expense*, as opposed to capital outlay;

(iv) Be *"ordinary and necessary"*; and

(v) *Not violate public policy.*

a. Trade or business [§297]

Characterization of an activity as a *trade or business* is important for many tax provisions. For example, a taxpayer in a trade or business can deduct depreciation on business property, business expenses, and business losses. [I.R.C. §§167(a)(1), 162, 165(c)(1)] Alternatively, depreciation, expenses, and losses can be deducted with respect to transactions entered into for profit, even though the activity does not rise to the level of trade or business. [I.R.C. §§167(a)(2), 212(1) - (2), 165(c)(2); *see infra*, §§437-440] However, for various reasons, the treatment of a "transaction entered into for profit" is not as favorable as the treatment of a "trade or business." For example, net operating losses arising out of nontrade or nonbusiness activity cannot be carried forward or back [I.R.C. §172(d)(4); *and see infra*, §1087], and some of the deductions arising from such activity are "below the line" and subject to the restriction on "miscellaneous itemized deductions" [*see* I.R.C. §§62, 67; *and see infra*, §§555, 562-564]. Similarly, the costs of a home office devoted to nontrade or nonbusiness activity cannot be deducted. (*See infra*, §§347-348.)

(1) "Trade or business" defined [§298]

The I.R.C. never defines "trade or business," but the most important factors are:

(i) The activity must be entered into with the *expectation of making a profit*;

(ii) There must be some *regularity and continuity* in its operation; and

(iii) The taxpayer must be *actively* engaged in pursuing it (either herself or through agents).

Example: A full-time gambler is in a trade or business, even though he provides no goods or services to others. Note, however, that gambling losses in excess of gains are not deductible. [**Commissioner v. Groetzinger**, 480 U.S. 23 (1987); I.R.C. §165(d)—*see infra*, §501]

---

(2) Legality of business [§299]

An illegal business (*e.g.*, bookmaking) is entitled to deduct its operating expenses, like any legitimate business enterprise. [**Commissioner v. Sullivan**, 356 U.S. 27 (1958)] However, certain *illegal expenses* (violative of public policy) are *not* deductible (*see infra*, §§424-435).

EXAM TIP   gilbert

For your exam, remember it is the *legality of the expense*, *not* the legality of the *business*, that governs whether the expense is deductible. Thus, the legitimate operating expenses of an illegal business are deductible.

---

(3) Nature of taxpayer [§300]

Expenses incurred in connection with a trade or business are deductible by any kind of a taxpayer—individual, trust, or corporation. *Employees* are in a "trade or business" and can deduct the costs incurred in connection with their jobs. Thus, union dues or the costs of uniforms are deductible as business expenses—usually from adjusted gross income (*see infra*, §554) and only to the extent they exceed 2% of adjusted gross income (*see infra*, §§562-564). However, a *stockholder* is not treated as being in business merely because his corporation is in business. [**Whipple v. Commissioner**, 373 U.S. 193 (1963)] The costs of *investment*, such as holding stock, are deductible under I.R.C. section 212 (*see infra*, §§437-440).

(4) Tax shelters [§301]

The courts have frequently characterized activities involving flagrant tax shelters as not meeting the "trade or business" requirement. Thus, deductions arising out of such activities are denied. [**Rose v. Commissioner**, 88 T.C. 386 (1987), *aff'd*, 868 F.2d 851 (6th Cir. 1989); *see infra*, §§322-323]

b. Business vs. personal expenses [§302]

Expenses incurred by a *corporate* taxpayer are *presumed* to have been incurred "in connection with" its trade or business—since a corporation normally exists only for business purposes. However, corporate outlays for the personal benefit of the shareholders are treated as nondeductible dividends (*e.g.*, paying for shareholder's house). *Individual* taxpayers must prove that the particular expenditure was incurred *in connection with* the taxpayer's trade or business—rather than as a personal, family, or living expense, which is expressly *not* deductible. [I.R.C. §262]

EXAM TIP   gilbert

For your exam, remember that an *individual must be able to prove* that an expense was incurred "in connection with" his trade or business in order to deduct the expense, but that *a corporation's expenses are presumed* to be incurred in connection with its trade or business.

---

(1) Requirement of proximate relationship to trade or business [§303]

A remote connection to business is not enough. There must be a direct, *proximate* relationship between the business and the purpose of the expenditure. If the expenditure is for several purposes, and is not susceptible to proration, the *predominant* purpose determines deductibility.

---

e.g. Example: Taxpayer is sued for *personal injuries* resulting from an auto accident that occurred while he was driving between two jobs. Although the driving cost is deductible in this situation (*see infra*, §316), the costs of settling the lawsuit were held not proximately connected to either of the jobs and thus nondeductible. [**Freedman v. Commissioner**, 301 F.2d 359 (5th Cir. 1962)]

---

cf. Compare: On the other hand, expenses incurred in defending an action brought by a former business partner *have* been held to be "trade and business" expenses. Although the partnership was dissolved, and the taxpayer was no longer in business at the time of the suit, the Court declared that the expenses bore a "proximate relationship" to a *former* business and were deductible. [**Kornhauser v. United States**, 276 U.S. 145 (1928)]

---

(2) Travel expenses [§304]

I.R.C. section 162(a)(2) allows deduction of "traveling expenses (including amounts expended for meals and lodging if not lavish and extravagant under the circumstances) while *away from home* in the *pursuit of a trade or business*." In the case of food or beverages, however, only 50% of their cost is deductible. [I.R.C. §274(n)]

(a) "Pursuit of trade or business" [§305]

The expenses must have been incurred primarily in furtherance of business rather than personal objectives.

1) Commuting to and from work [§306]

Expenses incurred in traveling to or from the taxpayer's place of business or employment are *not* deductible. Commuting represents a *personal* choice to live far from work. [**Commissioner v. Flowers**, 326 U.S. 425 (1946)—lawyer lived 250 miles from employer's office; expenses in traveling to and from office held not deductible]

a) Involuntary commuting [§307]

The same rule applies even if there is not a place closer to work for the taxpayer to live. Commuting, even from the closest possible dwelling place, is still nondeductible. [**Sanders v. Commissioner**, 439 F.2d 296 (9th Cir. 1971)]

b) Transportation between businesses [§308]

If a taxpayer has several business locations, the costs of traveling between them are deductible, regardless of distance. For example, an attorney can deduct the cost of traveling from her office to a courthouse or a doctor can deduct the cost of traveling from his office to a hospital.

1/ Home-to-business commutes [§309]

The rules are not clear when a taxpayer travels from home to business and the trip does not meet the normal pattern of commuting. According to the IRS, the cost of a home-to-business commute is generally nondeductible, except in the following situations [Rev. Rul. 99-7, 1999-1 C.B. 361]:

a/ A taxpayer *may deduct* the cost of travel from home to a temporary work location *if the commute is outside of the metropolitan area* in which the taxpayer normally lives and works. A temporary work location means a location where the work is realistically expected to last for less than one year (*see infra*, §318). However, unless the taxpayer falls under b/ or c/, below, he *may not deduct* the cost of travel from home to a temporary work location *if the commute is within the same metropolitan area* in which the taxpayer normally lives and works.

b/ If a taxpayer has at least *one regular workplace away from home*, he *may deduct* the cost of a commute *from home to a temporary work location that is in the same trade or business.*

---

e.g. **Example:** An attorney who travels from home to the courthouse without stopping first at the office may deduct the cost of the trip.

---

c/ If a taxpayer's home is also his *principal place of business* as defined by I.R.C. section 280A(c)(1) (*see infra*, §351), his home becomes a "business location." Thus, he may deduct the cost of travel from home to a secondary place of business—a regular or temporary workplace without regard to distance—as a *cost of traveling between several business locations* (*see supra*, §308).

WHEN THE TAXPAYER'S HOME IS ALSO A PLACE OF BUSINESS, CONSIDER THE FOLLOWING:

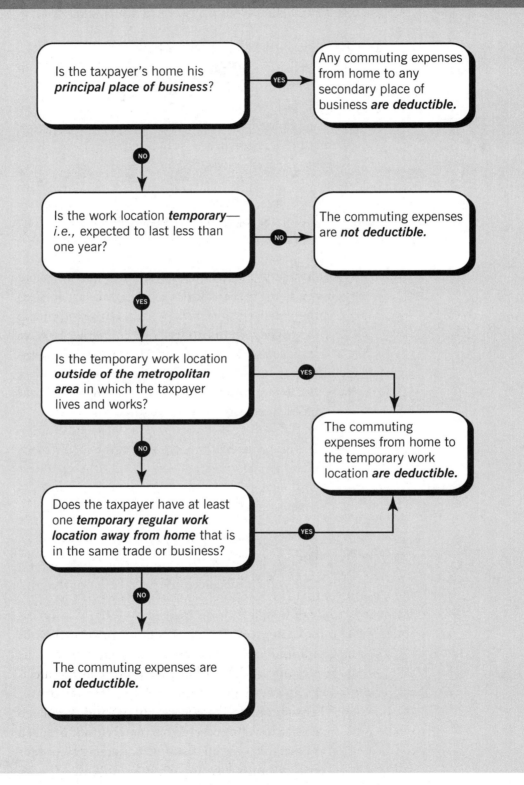

Is the taxpayer's home his *principal place of business*?

YES → Any commuting expenses from home to any secondary place of business *are deductible.*

NO ↓

Is the work location *temporary*—*i.e.,* expected to last less than one year?

NO → The commuting expenses are *not deductible.*

YES ↓

Is the temporary work location *outside of the metropolitan area* in which the taxpayer lives and works?

YES → The commuting expenses from home to the temporary work location *are deductible.*

NO ↓

Does the taxpayer have at least one *temporary regular work location away from home* that is in the same trade or business?

YES → The commuting expenses from home to the temporary work location *are deductible.*

NO ↓

The commuting expenses are *not deductible.*

> **EXAM TIP** | **gilbert**
>
> On your exam, remember that a "principal place of business" means something other than just any old place of business. If the specific conditions for *a principal place of business* cannot be met (*see infra*, §§347-355), the home-to-work commuting expenses *within the same metropolitan area* in which the taxpayer normally lives and works are *not deductible*.

c) Transporting equipment [§310]

Even if a taxpayer has to transport heavy tools to work, he still cannot deduct the cost of commuting by car. However, if he can show that he incurred additional costs (like trailer rental) for the purpose of transporting the tools, the additional costs are deductible. [**Fausner v. Commissioner,** 413 U.S. 838 (1973); Rev. Rul. 75-380, 1975-2 C.B. 59]

2) Combined business and pleasure trips [§311]

Transportation expenses incurred on a combined business-pleasure trip are entirely deductible if the *primary purpose* of a trip was business, *but lodging and meals* must be fairly allocated between business and pleasure. If the primary purpose was pleasure, then no part of the transportation expense is deductible (although any meals or lodging attributable to business would be). [Treas. Reg. §1.162-2] Note that travel costs are nondeductible if the travel is engaged in as a form of professional education (*e.g.*, high school French teacher visits France in the summer). [I.R.C. §274(m)(2)]

3) Foreign meetings [§312]

Section 274(h) imposes special limitations on the deduction of expenses of attending foreign conventions, seminars, or other meetings. If the meeting is outside North America, the taxpayer must establish that the meeting is *directly related* to the active conduct of trade or business or investment and that it is as reasonable for the meeting to be held outside North America as inside it. In deciding the reasonableness question, consider the purpose of the meeting and activities taking place at the meeting, the purposes and activities of the sponsors, the residences of active members of sponsoring organizations, and the places where other meetings have been held. No deduction is allowed for meetings on cruise ships, except for American registered ships sailing between American ports.

4) Presence of spouse [§313]

No deduction is allowed for the travel expenses of a person (such as a spouse) accompanying the taxpayer (or an officer or employee of the taxpayer), unless that person is an employee of the taxpayer, the person's travel had a bona fide business purpose, and the expenses would otherwise be deductible by that person. [I.R.C. §274(m)(3)] Prior law allowed deduction of a spouse's expenses if there was a valid reason for the spouse to come along, such as assisting with entertainment of clients. [**United States v. Disney,** 413 F.2d 783 (9th Cir. 1969)]

EXAM TIP   **gilbert**

On your exam, if you encounter a question that has a married couple traveling together, be sure to check if *each has an independent basis* for claiming a deduction for a business trip. Only if each spouse has an independent basis will both be able to claim a deduction.

(b) "Away from home" [§314]

The meaning of the phrase "away from home" is the subject of considerable controversy. The Commissioner and the Tax Court hold that it means away from the taxpayer's *business headquarters*. [Rev. Rul. 75-432, 1975-2 C.B. 60] However, some courts of appeal have held that it means away from the taxpayer's *residence*. [**Rosenspan v. United States,** 438 F.2d 905 (2d Cir. 1971)—taxpayer without permanent residence cannot be "away from home"] The Supreme Court has not squarely ruled on this point, except in the case of military personnel, as to whom "home" means the duty station to which the taxpayer is assigned. [**Commissioner v. Stidger,** 386 U.S. 287 (1967)]

1) "Homeless" taxpayers [§315]

If the taxpayer has no business headquarters, the Commissioner will permit the taxpayer's residence to be treated as his "home," provided it is a "regular abode in a real and substantial sense." [Rev. Rul. 73-529, 1973-2 C.B. 37]

a) Note

A taxpayer who does not have a "business headquarters" or a permanent "residence" (such as a transient worker) is not entitled to deduct travel expenses because he does not have duplicated living expenses. [**Henderson v. Commissioner,** 143 F.3d 497 (9th Cir. 1998)]

2) Taxpayers with several offices [§316]

Conversely, if the taxpayer has *several* "business headquarters" (*e.g.*, several offices or several different businesses), the expenses of traveling *between them* are deductible. Moreover, it is necessary to decide which of them is his principal business, since meals and lodging would be deductible only when he is away from the principal business. This should be done by an "objective" test—the business that produces the most money and consumes the most time is usually considered the principal business. [**Markey v. Commissioner,** 490 F.2d 1249 (6th Cir. 1974)]

3) Deductibility of meals—the "sleep or rest" rule [§317]

To limit claims for deduction of every meal taken by the taxpayer while away from home (business headquarters *or* residence), the Commissioner ruled that the cost of meals may be deducted only when the taxpayer is away from home on an *overnight trip*—or if not actually overnight, at least for such a period of time as requires "*sleep or rest.*" The validity of this rule was upheld by the Supreme Court. [**United States v. Correll,** 389 U.S. 299 (1967)] Recall that only 50% of the cost of meals or beverages is deductible. [I.R.C. §274(n)]

4) "Temporary" vs. "indefinite" rule [§318]

Suppose the taxpayer is sent to work at a distant job site. Instead of commuting to and from his residence, he chooses to live at the job site. Are his *food and lodging* there deductible? In other words, is he "away from home" or does his "home" shift to the job site where he is living?

a) Rule

A taxpayer is entitled to deduct his transportation, food, and lodging if the job assignment is *temporary*, but not if the assignment is of *indefinite* duration. [**Peurifoy v. Commissioner,** 358 U.S. 59 (1958)] The theory is that when the work is temporary in nature, it is unrealistic to expect the taxpayer to uproot his family and home and take them with him, as he might do when the work is indefinite. In no event is an assignment temporary if it exceeds one year. [I.R.C. §162(a)]

b) Application of one-year rule

If the taxpayer realistically expects that the job assignment will last more than one year, the living expenses at the job site are not deductible, even if, in fact, the job lasts one year or less. On the other hand, if the taxpayer realistically expects the job to last one year or less, but, in fact, it lasts more than one year, the living expenses are deductible up until the date that the taxpayer's realistic expectation changes. [Rev. Rul. 93-86, 1993-2 C.B. 71]

c) Business reason for maintaining home

To deduct expenses at the temporary job location, there must be a *business* reason for maintaining a home at the permanent location. [**Henderson v. Commissioner**, *supra*, §315—lighting technician, who is usually on the road but sometimes stays rent-free in his parents' home in Boise, had no duplicated living expenses and no business reason to maintain Boise home and was thus not "away from home"; **Hantzis v. Commissioner**, 638 F.2d 248 (1st Cir.), *cert. denied*, 452 U.S. 962 (1981)—law student who takes summer job in New York cannot deduct costs there because she had no *business* reason for maintaining permanent home in Boston, where her husband remained and where she attended law school]

TRAVEL-RELATED EXPENSES · gilbert

DEDUCTIBLE EXPENSES	NONDEDUCTIBLE EXPENSES

• Home-to-business commute *if*:
   (i) "Home" is principal place of business and "work" is second place of business;
   (ii) "Work" is temporary location *outside* the metropolitan area in which the taxpayer lives; or
   (iii) The taxpayer has a regular workplace away from home and travels to a temporary work location.
 • Commute *between* business locations.
 • Meals falling under *sleep or rest* rule.
 • Lodging for a *temporary* (one year or less) job assignment.
 • Travel to out-of-town locations for business purposes where an overnight stay is necessary.
 • Transportation to a foreign meeting if *directly related* to the active conduct of trade or business.
	• "Normal" home-to-work commute.
	 • Meals and lodging that are allocated to "pleasure" in a mixed-purpose trip.
	 • Travel expenses of person accompanying taxpayer (*e.g.,* spouse) *unless* that person has an independent basis for a deduction.

(3) **Expenses of "businesses" operated for pleasure—hobby farm problem [§319]**
A frequent problem is the deductibility of the expenses of a hobby farm or other business that produces some income but consistently operates at a loss because expenses exceed income. [I.R.C. §183] To deduct the annual loss, the taxpayer must demonstrate that at least a *significant* purpose of the venture was to earn a profit. Some cases hold that profit must be the *primary* purpose. [**Nickerson v. Commissioner,** 700 F.2d 402 (7th Cir. 1983)] The intended profit need not be reasonable or immediate; long-run profitability is sufficient. [**Nickerson v. Commissioner,** *supra*] Note that the deduction of expenses incurred on hobby farms or similar businesses may well be disallowed under the provisions restricting deduction of passive losses. (*See infra*, §§543-551.)

EXAM TIP   gilbert

On your exam, don't be fooled by facts indicating that the business run by the taxpayer is also a hobby. A hobby *could* be a business, so long as profit was a *significant* (some courts say *primary*) *purpose* of the venture.

(a) **Determinative factors [§320]**
The taxpayer's purpose is determined by the particular facts. If the taxpayer hired professional help to operate his farm, made marketing surveys, purchased the best available machinery, and personally involved himself in the details of the farm's operation, these factors would indicate a purpose to make a profit. But if he built a lavish home on the property in which he lived on weekends and took little interest in financial details, this would show a purpose of operating the farm for pleasure rather than profit. Horse breeding and racing are particularly apt to be treated as a personal rather than business venture. [*See* Treas. Reg. §1.183-2]

1) **Actual profit-and-loss history**
The actual profit-and-loss history of the enterprise is an important factor in determining its purpose. If the activity occasionally produces a profit, this tends to show that the taxpayer did have a reasonable expectation of profit. By statute, if the activity produced a profit (*i.e.*, income exceeded expenses) in three or more of the five years ending with the taxable year, there is a rebuttable presumption that the activity was engaged in for profit. [I.R.C. §183(d)]

 Example: A middle-income taxpayer lost money for several years running a pet store. His recordkeeping was very sloppy and the store was run incompetently. In overturning a Tax Court decision treating the business as a hobby, the appellate court stressed (i) the store had once been profitable; (ii) the taxpayer had previously changed locations to cut costs; (iii) the poor recordkeeping and failure to improve business methods could be explained by time constraints—the taxpayer had several other jobs; (iv) the taxpayer had real out-of-pocket loss—not just depreciation; (v) the taxpayer was not wealthy; (vi) the taxpayer had no other obvious purpose in mind such as pleasure; (vii) a retail business run by the taxpayer and his family is hard work and very different from a pleasurable activity like weekend farming or horse breeding. In short, a businessperson's incompetence does not turn his business into a hobby. [**Ranciato v. Commissioner,** 52 F.2d 23 (2d Cir. 1995)]

(b) Amounts deductible [§321]

If it is found that the activity was *not* for profit, the taxpayer can still deduct items, such as property taxes, that are deductible regardless of whether the activity was profit-seeking. However, as to expenses without an independent basis for deduction, the expenses of an activity not engaged in for profit can be used to offset the income it produces, but no more. [I.R.C. §183(b)] The deduction for hobby expenses up to hobby income is a miscellaneous itemized deduction, and miscellaneous itemized deductions in total must exceed 2% of adjusted gross income to be deductible (*see infra,* §§562 *et seq.*) [I.R.C. §67]

Example: Steve raises race horses as a hobby. Last year, he had no income from horse racing. However, he incurred property taxes of $5,000, groomer fees of $7,000, and feed expenses of $10,000. The property taxes are deductible (*see infra,* §§612-613). However, none of the other costs are deductible.

Compare: Same facts as above, except that one of Steve's horses earns $6,800 in prize money. Steve can deduct the property tax ($5,000) and $1,800 of his other costs (to offset his winnings). The $1,800 is a miscellaneous itemized deduction.

(c) Tax shelters [§322]

The courts have decided numerous cases in which taxpayers claimed deductions for flagrant "tax shelters," *i.e.,* gimmicky transactions that give rise to deductions far in excess of cash investment and which are heavily motivated by tax avoidance. The Tax Court has characterized such deals as "generic tax shelters" and disallowed all deductions in excess of income. [**Rose v. Commissioner,** *supra,* §301]

1) *Rose* decision [§323]

In *Rose, supra,* taxpayers claimed large deductions and credits arising out of the purchase of rights to make reproductions (prints, posters, etc.) from works of art. Finding that the tax savings were the focus of the deal, that the investors accepted the deal without investigation or price negotiation, that the assets were substantially overvalued, and that the bulk of the consideration was paid through nonrecourse notes, the Tax Court simply disallowed all deductions. This approach seems not only to be based partly on section 183, but also on a holding that the activity is not a "trade or business" (*see supra,* §§298-301) and a holding that the activity is so lacking in economic substance that it should be ignored for tax purposes. *Rose* was affirmed by the court of appeals on the latter ground, finding that the deal had no practicable economic effect (and no purpose) other than the creation of tax deductions. [**Rose v. Commissioner**, 868 F.2d 851 (6th Cir. 1989)] Note that deductions based on such deals would now be disallowed under the passive loss rules. (*See infra,* §§543-551.)

2) Economic substance rule [§324]

Be wary of any transaction that generates tax benefits but is motivated only by tax avoidance and lacks nontax economic consequences. The transaction will probably be ignored and the tax benefits denied. [*See, e.g.,* **Yosha v. Commissioner**, 861 F.2d 494 (7th Cir. 1988)—commodity transactions arranged so that taxpayer could not make or lose money but could get tax benefits]

(4) Moving expenses [§325]

Ordinarily, moving costs are personal expenditures. However, a limited exception exists for employees (existing or newly hired) *or* self-employed individuals. They are permitted to deduct expenses of moving their family and furniture to their new home. [I.R.C. §217]

(a) Distance limitation [§326]

However, the new job site must be at least *50 miles* farther from the old home than the old home was from the old job site. [I.R.C. §217(c)]

Example: Courtney commutes 55 miles per day to her job at a downtown Chicago law firm. If she finds another position with a law firm in Los Angeles, her moving expenses from Chicago to Los Angeles are deductible. However, if she finds a job with a law firm across the street and moves downtown in order to devote more time to her new job, her moving expenses would not be deductible.

(b) Full-time employee [§327]

In addition, the taxpayer must be a full-time employee during at least *39 weeks* of the 12-month period following the move. If self-employed, the taxpayer must perform services during at least 78 weeks of the succeeding 24-month period. [I.R.C. §217(c)(2), (d); *and see* **Muse v. Commissioner,** 76 T.C. 574 (1981)]

(c) Allowable deductions [§328]

A taxpayer may deduct any amount for moving her household goods and for traveling (including lodging) from the former residence to the new residence. However, meals consumed during travel cannot be deducted. The moving expenses of individuals other than the taxpayer can be deducted only if the individuals had both the former residence and the new residence as their principal place of abode. Other costs relating to the move, such as costs of searching for a new residence, living in temporary quarters before finding a new residence, or selling the old house and buying or renting a new one, are not deductible. [I.R.C. §217(b)]

JOB-RELATED MOVING EXPENSES	gilbert
MOVING EXPENSES ARE DEDUCTIBLE FOR EMPLOYEES OR SELF-EMPLOYED PERSONS IF 50-MILE DISTANCE LIMITATION MET (*see supra*, §326). *EXAMPLES:*	
DEDUCTIBLE EXPENSES	**NONDEDUCTIBLE EXPENSES**
• Cost of moving household goods from old residence to new residence • Traveling expenses (including lodging but *not* meals) incurred during move from old residence to new residence	• Meals taken during travel from old residence to new residence • Costs of searching for a new residence • Temporary lodging while searching for a new residence • Costs of selling, buying, or renting a new or old residence

(d) Reimbursement by employer [§329]

Employer reimbursement of deductible moving expenses is not taxed to the employee, but employer reimbursement of *nondeductible* moving expenses is taxable to the employee. [I.R.C. §§82, 132(g)]

(e) Permanent place of work [§330]

A taxpayer cannot deduct moving expenses when she is away from home "temporarily" on business; such expenses are deductible only if the taxpayer moves to a new *permanent* place of work. [Treas. Reg. §1.217-1(c)(3)(iii); **Goldman v. Commissioner**, 497 F.2d 832 (6th Cir.), *cert. denied*, 419 U.S. 1021 (1974)]

(5) Entertainment expenses [§331]

Expenses incurred with respect to entertainment, amusement, or recreation are deductible only if the taxpayer can establish that the expenses were *directly related* to the active conduct of her business. The costs of socializing (*e.g.*, by attending sports events or nightclubs) are deductible only if it immediately precedes or follows a *substantial and bona fide business discussion*. [I.R.C. §274(a)] Only 50% of the cost of entertainment expense (or of any food or beverage) is deductible. [I.R.C. §274(n)]

(a) Entertainment expenses defined [§332]

"Entertainment" expenses include those associated with entertaining at nightclubs, cocktail lounges, theaters, country clubs, golf and athletic clubs, sporting events, and on hunting, fishing, vacation, and similar trips. They also may include providing food and beverages, a hotel suite, or an automobile to a business customer or her family or to an employee while on vacation. An objective test is used to determine whether an activity is of a type generally thought to constitute entertainment, which is in part designed to preclude the argument that an expense should be characterized as advertising or public relations rather than entertainment. [*See* **Churchill Downs, Inc. v. Commissioner**, 307 F.3d 423 (6th Cir. 2003)—parties for the press and others at the Kentucky Derby and Breeders' Cup races constituted entertainment rather than attempts to "showcase" the host's product because there was no information imparted at the parties about the races and there were no parties conducted at the track during the races]

(b) Entertainment facilities [§333]

No deduction is allowed for costs relating to entertainment "facilities," such as yachts or hunting lodges, or for amounts paid for membership in any club organized for business, pleasure, recreation, or other social purpose. [I.R.C. §274(a)(1)(B), (2)(A), (3)]

(c) Burden of proof [§334]

The Code imposes a special requirement that travel and entertainment expenses be substantiated either by adequate records or by sufficient evidence corroborating a taxpayer's own statement. The evidence must substantiate the amount of the expense, the time and place, the business purpose, and the business relationship to the taxpayer of the persons entertained or using the facility. [I.R.C. §274(d)]

(d) Business meals [§335]

To deduct the cost of a meal as an entertainment expense, the taxpayer must meet the general standards set forth for entertainment expenses: The taxpayer must be present, and the meal must be related to the active conduct of a trade or business (or precede or follow a substantial and bona fide business discussion). Note that only 50% of meal and beverage costs are deductible. [I.R.C. §274(k), (n)]

(e) Caution—taxpayer's own meal [§336]

The cost of a taxpayer's own meal is generally not deductible, even if business is discussed, because the taxpayer would have eaten the meal anyway. The cost is deductible only if the business aspects somehow increase the cost of the meal, as when the taxpayer pays for a client's meal at the same time. [**Moss v. Commissioner,** 758 F.2d 211 (7th Cir. 1985)—lawyer cannot deduct cost of daily lunches with his partners even though business is discussed]

(6) Business gifts [§337]

Logically, it is not likely that an item could be both a deductible business expense and also excludible as a gift to the recipient, because the "disinterested generosity" necessary under I.R.C. section 102 is inconsistent with the business motivation necessary to deduct an item under I.R.C. section 162. In the event that this unlikely combination emerges, however, I.R.C. section 274(b) limits the deduction to $25.

(7) Litigation expenses [§338]

Whether legal fees or other costs incurred in a lawsuit (including payments made by way of judgment or settlement) are deductible depends on the nature of the dispute.

(a) Business expense [§339]

If litigation costs are related to the taxpayer's trade or business, they may be deductible if *"ordinary and necessary"* (*see infra,* §408).

(b) Personal litigation [§340]

Costs of *personal litigation* are *not deductible*. Costs of litigation incurred as part of the taxpayer's trade or business are deductible under section 162. Costs of litigation incurred for the *production of taxable income* (but not as part of a trade or business) are deductible under section 212, but only as miscellaneous itemized deductions. The test for distinguishing between personal litigation and business (or income production) litigation is the origin of the dispute. For example, the costs of divorce litigation are *generally* not deductible as a business expense since the origin of the dispute lies in the personal life of the taxpayer. This is true even if the taxpayer's sole reason for contesting the divorce is to protect his business from the community property claims of his wife. [**United States v. Gilmore,** 372 U.S. 39 (1963); *and see infra,* §§446-449]

(c) Distinguish—tax matters [§341]

I.R.C. section 212(3) specifically allows a deduction for expenses "in connection with the determination, collection or refund of any tax" *whether or not* related to a trade or business. This covers costs of tax litigation and having tax returns prepared. It also permits deduction for legal fees and related expenses in connection with *tax planning.* However, costs of estate planning (other than the tax aspects) are personal, nondeductible items. [**Merians v. Commissioner,** 60 T.C. 187 (1973)] Note that this deduction is a "miscellaneous itemized deduction." Such deductions are subject to a floor; *i.e.,* they can be deducted only to the extent that they exceed 2% of adjusted gross income. [I.R.C. §67, *see infra,* §§564-565; Rev. Rul. 89-68, 1989-1 C.B. 82—cost of obtaining IRS ruling is deductible subject to 2% floor]

EXAM TIP   gilbert

For your exam, be sure to remember the rules of deductibility for litigation costs. If the litigation relates to the taxpayer's *business*, the costs could possibly be *deducted* as an "ordinary and necessary" business expense under I.R.C. section 162. If the litigation relates to *the production of income* or to a *tax matter*, the costs could possibly be *deducted* under I.R.C. section 212. Otherwise, the litigation is most likely *personal* in nature, and the costs *may not be deducted*.

---

(8) Educational expenses

(a) General rule [§342]

Educational costs that either qualify the taxpayer for a *new* trade or business or that constitute the *minimum educational requirement* for qualification in her job are not deductible. [Treas. Regs. §1.162-5(b)(2), (3)]

Example: The costs of going to law school are not deductible. Similarly, the cost of a bar review course is not deductible, even if the taxpayer is already admitted to practice in another state, since practicing in a new state is considered a new business. [**Sharon v. Commissioner,** 66 T.C. 515 (1976), *aff'd,* 591 F.2d 1293 (9th Cir. 1978)]

Compare: The cost of taking the bar exam is not considered an educational expense; it produces an economic benefit that lasts for more than a year, and hence may be capitalized and amortized and deducted over its useful life—the taxpayer's life expectancy. (*See infra*, §§402, 450.) [**Sharon v. Commissioner,** *supra*]

(b) Deductible educational costs [§343]
Certain kinds of educational costs are deductible, *as long as they do not qualify the taxpayer for a new trade or business* or constitute the *minimum educational requirement* for her job. These include:

(i) *Education that maintains or improves* skills required by the individual in her job or other trade or business; or

(ii) *Education that meets the express requirements* of the individual's employer, or the requirements of law, as a condition to *retention* of a job or an increase in the rate of compensation.

 Example: Continuing education courses for lawyers and summer courses for teachers are deductible under this provision.

Compare: An IRS agent who goes to law school cannot deduct the costs on the argument that law school improves her skill as an accountant. Since it is also the minimum educational requirement for a *new* profession, the costs are automatically nondeductible.

(9) Insurance premiums

(a) Property insurance [§344]
The cost of insurance on business *property* is an ordinary and necessary business expense.

(b) Life insurance [§345]
Premiums for insurance on the *life* of an officer or employee are deductible *provided* the taxpayer-employer is *not* the direct or indirect beneficiary of the policy. [I.R.C. §264(a)(1)] If the taxpayer-employer is the beneficiary, the proceeds of the policy are tax-exempt income to the taxpayer-employer, and the expenses allocable to the production of tax-exempt income are not deductible.

1) Note
If the taxpayer-employer is not the beneficiary, so that the premiums may be deductible, the amount of the premium payments will then probably constitute taxable income to the insured (*e.g.*, as additional compensation to the employee-insured; as

DEDUCTIONS FOR "HOME OFFICE" COSTS—AN APPROACH

gilbert

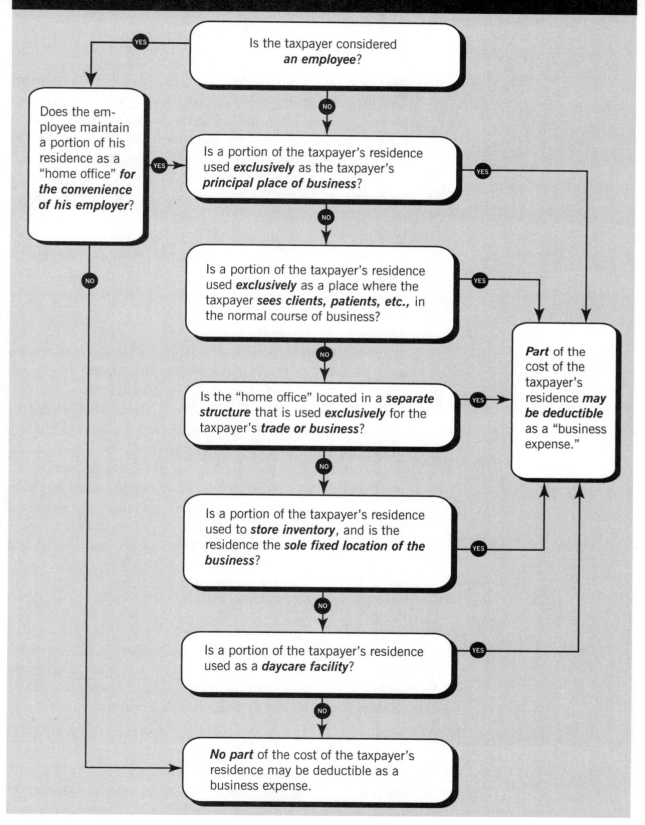

Is the taxpayer considered **an employee**?

Does the employee maintain a portion of his residence as a "home office" **for the convenience of his employer**?

Is a portion of the taxpayer's residence used **exclusively** as the taxpayer's **principal place of business**?

Is a portion of the taxpayer's residence used **exclusively** as a place where the taxpayer **sees clients, patients, etc.,** in the normal course of business?

Is the "home office" located in a **separate structure** that is used **exclusively** for the taxpayer's **trade or business**?

Is a portion of the taxpayer's residence used to **store inventory**, and is the residence the **sole fixed location of the business**?

Is a portion of the taxpayer's residence used as a **daycare facility**?

Part of the cost of the taxpayer's residence **may be deductible** as a "business expense."

No part of the cost of the taxpayer's residence may be deductible as a business expense.

a dividend to the shareholder-insured, etc.; *see supra*, §115). However, if the insurance is group term life insurance, the employer can deduct premiums and the employees can exclude them to the extent of $50,000 worth of insurance. (*See supra*, §123.)

Example: Corporation hires Perry Taxpayer as its president and agrees to pay him $1 million per year and to pay for a $10 million life insurance policy that names Perry's wife as the beneficiary. The life insurance premiums are deductible by the corporation and probably constitute income to Perry (except to the extent they constitute $50,000 of group term life insurance). If the corporation purchased a similar policy naming itself as the beneficiary (to cover potential losses that will arise from changes in leadership after Perry's death), the premiums will not be deductible by the corporation and will not constitute income to Perry.

---

2) Split dollar life insurance [§346]

In split dollar life insurance, the employer pays part of the annual premium of a whole life policy covering the life of the employee, and the employee pays the balance. When the employee dies, the employer receives the cash surrender value of the policy and the employee's beneficiary receives the balance of the payout. Under this arrangement, the employer cannot deduct its premium payments as compensation because it is a partial beneficiary of the policy. Assuming the employee pays the correct proportion of the annual premium, the employee has no income from the arrangement. If the employee pays less than the cost of the insurance protection received during the year, the employee has income in an amount equal to the difference. [Rev. Rul. 64-328, 1964-2 C.B. 11]

(10) Offices at home [§347]

Generally, no business deductions are allowable for part or all of the costs relating to a taxpayer's personal residence. [I.R.C. §280A] (Of course, this does not preclude deduction of qualified residence interest, real estate taxes, or casualty losses, which need not be connected to business or investment.)

(a) Exception for certain business use [§348]

However, costs of a portion of a taxpayer's residence can be deducted if that portion is used *exclusively* [I.R.C. §280A(c)(1)]:

1) *As the taxpayer's principal place of business* (if the taxpayer has several businesses, the residence qualifies for the deduction if it is the principal location of any of the businesses); or

2) *As a place of business used by patients, clients, or customers,* when visiting the taxpayer in the normal course of business; or

3) *In the case of a separate structure not attached to the dwelling,* in connection with the trade or business.

(b) Principal place of business [§349]

The test set forth in section 280A requires a taxpayer with several business locations to establish that her home is the "principal" location.

1) Factors considered [§350]

Two factors are significant when determining whether the taxpayer's at-home office qualifies as her principal place of business: (i) the relative importance of the activities performed at home and elsewhere, and (ii) the amount of time spent working at home and elsewhere. [**Commissioner v. Soliman**, 506 U.S. 168 (1993)]

Example: A musician spends five hours per day practicing in her home studio (used exclusively for business) and much less time actually performing at different concert halls or movie studios. The court thought that the relative importance of practice and performance were about equal. Thus, the time factor was determinative, and the studio was treated as the principal place of business. [**Popov v. Commissioner**, 246 F.3d 1190 (9th Cir. 2001)]

2) Management at home [§351]

A home office qualifies as a principal place of business if it is used to conduct administrative or management activities of the taxpayer's trade or business and there is no other fixed location where such administrative or management activities can be performed. [I.R.C. §280A(c)(1)]

Example: An anesthesiologist renders services to patients at a hospital, but performs all of the managerial tasks (such as billing insurance companies) in his home office because the hospital provides no office space. The home office is used exclusively for this purpose. The home office is treated as the taxpayer's principal place of business. [I.R.C. §280A(c)(1)—*superseding* **Commissioner v. Soliman**, *supra*]

(c) Exception for certain other uses [§352]

A taxpayer can deduct the costs of a portion of his residence if that portion is used for storage of an inventory held for sale in his business—but only if the dwelling is the sole fixed location of the business. Also, a portion of the costs can be deducted if the residence is used as a daycare facility. [I.R.C. §280A(c)(2), (4)]

(d) Employees [§353]

If a taxpayer is an employee, there is an *additional* requirement: The exclusive use of the residence must be for the *convenience of the employer.* [I.R.C. §280A(c)(1); *and see supra,* §§107-111] For example, if no space is provided at work for necessary tasks, the home office would serve the convenience of the employer. [**Drucker v. Commissioner,** 715 F.2d 69 (2d Cir. 1983)—concert violinist's home practice studio deductible because no practice space available at concert hall]

(e) Investors [§354]

The management of investments is not a trade or business. Therefore, a taxpayer cannot deduct any portion of a home office used exclusively to manage an investment portfolio—even though he does it 40 hours per week. [**Moller v. United States,** 721 F.2d 810 (Fed. Cir. 1983), *cert. denied,* 467 U.S. 1251 (1984)] Most of the costs of investing, such as subscriptions to business periodicals, are deductible under I.R.C. section 212 (*infra,* §§437-445) but not the costs of a home office. *Moller* distinguished the case of a *trader* in securities, who might be in a trade or business. The difference between an "investor" and a "trader" is that a trader looks to quick turnover and short-term profits rather than to long-term profits or to earning dividends and interest. [*See* **Estate of Yaeger v. Commissioner,** 889 F.2d 29 (2d Cir. 1989)]

(f) Limitation on the amount deductible [§355]

Even if the taxpayer falls within one of the exceptions, he cannot deduct any more than the gross income from such use, less the deductions (*e.g.,* qualified residence interest or property tax) allowed without regard to business. [I.R.C. §280A(c)(5)]

(11) Vacation homes [§356]

Section 280A imposes limitations on deductions with regard to dwellings that are rented out. There are two rules: (i) deductions must be *prorated between personal and rental use,* and (ii) if the dwelling is "*used as a residence,*" business and investment deductions are *limited to income generated by the property.*

(a) Caution—some items may be otherwise deductible [§357]

Deductions that need not be connected to profit-making activities— *e.g.*, qualified residence interest, property tax, or casualty losses—are deductible in full.

(b) "Used as a residence" defined [§358]

A dwelling is used *as a residence* if it is used for *personal purposes* by any of its owners, or their relatives, for more than 14 days *or* more than 10% of the days it was rented at a fair rental, whichever figure is *greater*. [I.R.C. §280A(d)]

> **e.g.** **Example:** Bob lived in his ski condominium seven days last year. He rented it (at a fair rental) to nonfamily members for 40 days. Since he did not use it for the greater of 14 days or 10% of the rented days (four days), he did not use it "as a residence."

> **cf.** **Compare:** Alice and Sally own a beach house as tenants in common. Alice used it one day, Sally eight days, and Sally's daughter six days. It was rented to others (at a fair rental) for 85 days. Since personal use for 15 days exceeds the greater of 14 or 8.5 days (10% of 85), the house was "used as a residence."

1) Exception [§359]

If the dwelling is rented for at least one year, the taxpayer's personal use before or after the rental period is ignored. Similarly, if the dwelling is sold at the end of the rental period, personal use before the rental period is disregarded. [I.R.C. §280A(d)(3)]

2) Exception [§360]

A dwelling is not "used as a residence" if rented at a fair rental to a relative of the owner as the occupant's principal residence. [I.R.C. §280A(d)(3)]

(c) Proration [§361]

If the dwelling was used at all for personal purposes (*whether or not* it was "used as a residence," *supra*, §358), the various expenses (other than qualified residence interest on a second home or property taxes) must be *prorated*. Only the portion allocable to rental use is deductible. [I.R.C. §280A(e)]

> **e.g.** **Example:** Thus in Bob's case above, 40/47ths of the expenses (other than qualified residence interest or taxes) is deductible, as that is the amount attributable to rental use.

Example: In the case of Alice and Sally (*supra*), 85/100ths of the expenses (other than qualified residence interest or taxes) would be deductible, but in their case, there is an additional limitation (*see* below).

(d) Limitation on amount [§362]

The expenses prorated to rental use are deductible only in part if the dwelling was "used as a residence." In that case, the owners cannot deduct more than the gross rental income less a prorated share of the qualified residence interest and taxes.

Example: This limitation does not apply to Bob (*supra*), since the ski condominium was not "used as a residence."

Compare: This limitation does apply to Alice (*supra*). Assume that her share of the qualified residence interest and taxes for the year is $1,200 and 85/100ths of her share of the other expenses (such as depreciation and repairs) is $2,000. Her share of gross rentals is $2,800. She can deduct all of the qualified residence interest and taxes. In addition, she can deduct only $1,600 of the remaining expenses (*i.e.*, $2,800 less $1,200). [I.R.C. §280A(c)(5)]

(e) Special rule for limited rental use [§363]

If a dwelling unit is rented fewer than 15 days during the year, no deductions are allowed and the income from rental is not included in gross income. [I.R.C. §280A(g)] While the denial of a deduction should usually balance out the exclusion of rental income, this provision provides a substantial benefit involving short-term high-demand events, such as the Olympics or a political convention, when the owner can demand above-market rent.

EXAM TIP	gilbert

Remember that if the vacation home is rented out for *fewer than 15 days* per year, *neither income nor expenses* are taken into account.

(12) Clothing [§364]

Most clothing costs are not deductible because clothing bought for business use (like a three-piece suit) can be used for nonwork purposes. However, if the clothing *cannot appropriately be worn for nonbusiness purposes* (*e.g.*, a firefighter's uniform), its cost is deductible. [*See* **Pevsner v. Commissioner**, 628 F.2d 467 (5th Cir. 1980)—designer clothes not deductible since they could be worn on the street even though taxpayer's lifestyle precluded such use; **Deihl v. Commissioner**, T.C. Memo 2005-287—refusing to accept the notion that a "one-wear policy" for formal dress at conventions would necessarily render the clothing unsuitable for personal use]

c. Current expense vs. capital outlay [§365]

To be deductible as a business expense, the item must be an *expense*, as distinguished from a *capital outlay*. A capital outlay is expressly not deductible. [I.R.C. §263]

(1) Test [§366]

The distinction between an "expense" and a "capital outlay" is often difficult to draw. Generally, an expenditure should be treated as being of a *capital* nature if it brings about the *acquisition of an asset or some advantage to the taxpayer having a useful life in excess of one year*. [Treas. Reg. §1.263(a)] In that situation, the taxpayer has purchased an *asset*, not incurred an expense. The business cost can be deducted through depreciation, loss, depletion, or bad debt (all discussed *infra*) but not as a business expense.

(a) Caution—distinguish "capitalization" from "capital assets" [§367]

Do not confuse "capitalization" with "capital assets." A capital asset is one which, when sold, qualifies for capital gain or loss treatment. (*See infra*, §§821 *et seq.*) But expenditures must be "capitalized" if they create an asset or advantage lasting beyond the taxable year—whether or not they produce a "capital asset." [**Georator Corp. v. United States**, 485 F.2d 283 (4th Cir. 1973), *cert. denied*, 417 U.S. 945 (1974)]

(2) Purpose of rule [§368]

The idea of capitalization is to match up income with the costs of earning that income. Outlays that produce long-term benefits must be capitalized, not deducted, in order to match the costs with future income that they will produce. [**Encyclopedia Britannica v. Commissioner**, 685 F.2d 212 (7th Cir. 1982)—publisher must capitalize cost of acquiring manuscript] A factor to be considered in a close case is whether the item is recurring as opposed to extraordinary; recurring items are more likely to be expenses. Another factor is whether the administrative burden of allocating costs to particular assets outweighs the benefit of improved matching. [**Encyclopedia Britannica v. Commissioner,** *supra*]

(3) Future benefit [§369]

An outlay must be capitalized if it produces significant long-term benefits. [**INDOPCO, Inc. v. Commissioner**, 503 U.S. 79 (1992)]

(a) "Long-term benefit" does not have to be an asset [§370]

In *INDOPCO*, a corporation incurred substantial costs in arranging to be taken over in a friendly corporate acquisition. This takeover was expected to produce important long-term benefits for the corporation because of the superior financial strength of the acquiring corporation. Additionally, the takeover reduced the number of public shareholders by 3,500, saving the corporation substantial expenses. The Supreme Court rejected the idea that an outlay had to produce some specific, identifiable asset in order to be capitalized rather than deducted. The costs of arranging the takeover did not produce any specific asset, but they did produce long-term benefits for the corporation that were more than "incidental." That was sufficient to require the costs to be capitalized.

(b) Distinguishing *INDOPCO* [§371]

The exact scope of *INDOPCO* is very uncertain. Several cases have distinguished *INDOPCO* and did not require the taxpayer to capitalize certain expenses.

1) *Wells Fargo* case [§372]

In **Wells Fargo & Co. v. Commissioner,** 224 F.3d 874 (8th Cir. 2000), officers of the company spent time evaluating and negotiating a friendly takeover. The IRS required the acquired company to capitalize the salaries that it paid to its officers while they worked on the acquisition, but the court held that the salaries were deductible, and it distinguished *INDOPCO*. The court observed that the officers' salaries were regular and recurring costs that would have been paid notwithstanding the acquisition. The salaries were "merely incidental" to the future benefit to be obtained through the acquisition. Moreover, the salaries would have been difficult to allocate between work on the acquisition and other work. The court also held that legal expenses for the proposed transaction were deductible up to the time that the companies entered into a definitive agreement; and that legal fees incurred after that date must be capitalized.

2) *PNC Bancorp* case [§373]

In **PNC Bancorp, Inc. v. Commissioner,** 212 F.3d 822 (3d Cir. 2000), a bank incurred various costs (*e.g.,* investigating borrowers) in making loans. Some of the costs included payments to outsiders for such items as property reports and appraisals, while other costs included such items as the regular salaries of employees. For financial reporting purposes, the bank must capitalize these costs as part of the acquisition cost of valuable assets (the loans made by the bank). However, the court held these costs were deductible for tax purposes because they were ordinary, recurring expenses in operating the bank.

(c) Ramifications [§374]

The *INDOPCO* case casts doubt on many lower court decisions in which the courts allowed expensing, rather than capitalization, of business expansion costs because the costs did not yield a separate and distinct asset (despite the fact that they produced a long-term benefit). [*See, e.g.,* **Briarcliff Candy Corp. v. Commissioner,** 475 F.2d 775 (2d Cir. 1973)] On the other hand, *Wells Fargo* and *PNC Bancorp* suggest that cases such as *Briarcliff* were correctly decided. The Supreme Court may have to reconsider this area in order to make clear how far *INDOPCO* was intended to reach.

(d) Resisting a hostile takeover [§375]

The costs of unsuccessfully resisting a hostile takeover are deductible because these costs do not produce a long-term benefit and cannot be defined as the costs associated with facilitating a capital transaction. Instead, such costs are incurred in defending the business against attack, which makes them currently deductible. [**A.E. Staley Manufacturing Co. v. Commissioner,** 119 F.3d 482 (7th Cir. 1997)]

(4) Repairs of property vs. capital improvement to property [§376]

Maintenance and repair costs are "current expenses," and hence entirely deductible in the year paid. [Treas. Reg. §1.162-4] This rule was not altered by the *INDOPCO* case, *supra*. [Rev. Rul. 94-12, 1994-1 C.B. 36] However, what is a "repair" and what is an "improvement" could be at issue.

(a) Capital improvements [§377]

If the "repairs" actually make the property more valuable than it was originally, or make it suitable for a different use, or extend its useful life beyond what it was originally, the cost is regarded as a capital improvement, not an expense. [Treas. Reg. §1.162-4]

(b) Environmental remediation costs [§378]

Taxpayers may deduct certain environmental cleanup costs that would otherwise have to be capitalized. [I.R.C. §198] These are expenditures incurred in connection with the abatement or control of hazardous substances at a qualified contaminated site. A qualified site is one that a state environmental official has certified as located in an area where there has been a release (or threatened release) of a hazardous substance on the site. Additionally, the site must be in a targeted area, meaning one with a poverty rate of at least 20%, an empowerment zone, or a site announced as being included in a brownfields pilot project of the Environmental Protection Agency.

(c) **Nonstatutory authority for deduction of environmental remediation costs [§379]**

Section 198 apparently does not erase a series of rulings and cases that allowed deductions for certain environmental cleanup costs. Under this authority, cleanup costs which do not meet the precise definitions of section 198 may still be deductible because the cleanup restores the property to the value it had before the problem arose (but does not otherwise significantly enhance the value of the property). [**Midland Empire Packing Co. v. Commissioner,** 14 T.C. 635 (1950)—cost of installing concrete basement to stop oil seepage is currently deductible repair; Rev. Rul. 94-38, 1994-1 C.B. 35—costs of removing toxic substances from land and groundwater are deductible]

(5) **Property produced or sold by taxpayer [§380]**

A taxpayer must capitalize all of the direct or indirect costs of producing property. [I.R.C. §263A]

(a) **Direct cost [§381]**

The direct cost of producing property is the materials and labor consumed in producing it.

(b) **Interest [§382]**

A taxpayer is required to capitalize any interest incurred during the production period that is allocable to produced property. [I.R.C. §263A(f)—applies only to property with a long useful life or a long production period]

(c) **Overhead [§383]**

Section 263A requires capitalization of various items of "overhead," such as the rent or depreciation on buildings and equipment used to produce property. [*See* **Commissioner v. Idaho Power Co.,** 418 U.S. 1 (1974)—depreciation on construction machinery cannot be deducted but must be added to the basis of produced property]

Example: The costs of designing a package for a new product must be capitalized under section 263A. Since these costs will benefit sales for both the current and future years, the IRS will allow amortization of the costs over an arbitrary five-year period. [Rev. Rul. 89-23, 1989-1 C.B. 85; Rev. Proc. 89-17, 1989-1 C.B. 827]

(d) **Property acquired for resale [§384]**

The rules of section 263A also apply to property acquired for resale, but only if the taxpayer has average annual gross receipts of more than $10 million [I.R.C. §263A(b)(2)], in which case the taxpayer would have to add to the basis of his inventory (rather than deduct) the cost of guards or storage of the inventory.

(e) Exception for authors [§385]

The mandatory capitalization rules of section 263A do not apply to the "qualified creative expense" of individual authors, artists, and photographers. Thus, for example, research costs for an uncompleted book can be deducted rather than capitalized. [I.R.C. §263A(h)]

(6) Capitalization of rental payments [§386]

Rental payments for the use of property belonging to another are a deductible business expense unless they must be capitalized as part of the cost of production. [I.R.C. §§162(a)(3), 263A—*see supra*, §§380 *et seq.*] However, deductions for lease payments for automobiles used in business, or for home computers, are limited in amount. They cannot exceed the amounts that would be deductible as depreciation if the car or computer were purchased rather than rented. [I.R.C. §280F(c); *see infra*, §§478 *et seq.*]

(a) Prepayments [§387]

Prepayments of rent in excess of one year *cannot* be deducted currently. They must be capitalized because they create an asset having a useful life extending into future years. [**University Properties, Inc. v. Commissioner,** 45 T.C. 416 (1966); *and see infra*, §1007]

(b) Lease vs. sale [§388]

"Rental" payments that are in reality payments toward the *purchase price* of the asset are treated similarly; *i.e.,* when the form of the transaction is a lease but its substance is a *purchase*, no "expense" deduction is allowed.

1) Determinative factors [§389]

While not conclusive, the courts are apt to treat the lease *as a sale* if:

(i) The payments are *higher than normal rent* for the property involved;

(ii) The amount of "rental" payments over the term of the lease *equals the value of the property plus financing charges*; or

(iii) The "lessee" has the *option to acquire title* at the end of the "lease" for *only a nominal payment*.

[**Starr's Estate v. Commissioner,** 274 F.2d 294 (9th Cir. 1959)]

gilbert

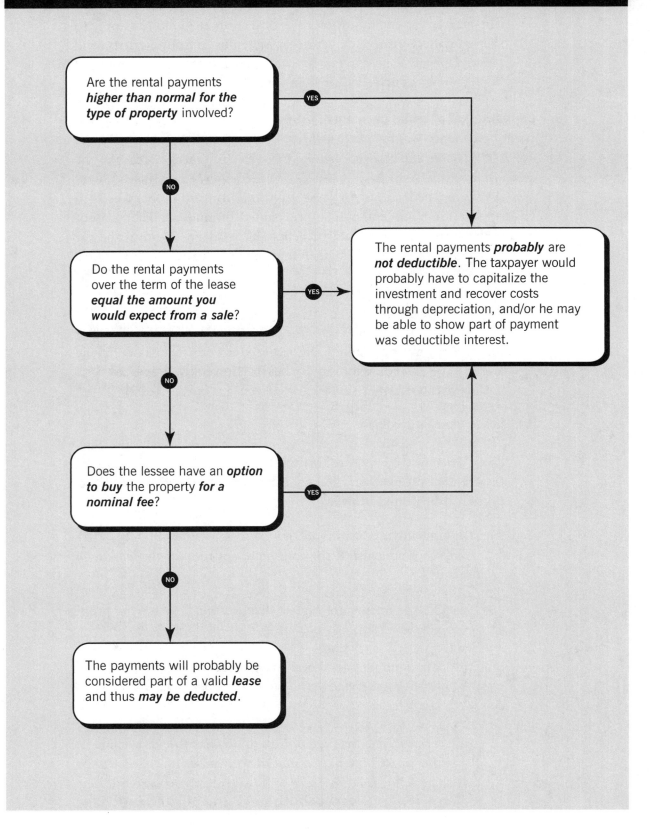

Are the rental payments **higher than normal for the type of property** involved?

NO

Do the rental payments over the term of the lease **equal the amount you would expect from a sale**?

NO

Does the lessee have an **option to buy** the property **for a nominal fee**?

NO

The payments will probably be considered part of a valid **lease** and thus **may be deducted**.

YES

The rental payments **probably** are **not deductible**. The taxpayer would probably have to capitalize the investment and recover costs through depreciation, and/or he may be able to show part of payment was deductible interest.

2) Tax consequences [§390]

In such cases, the "rental" payments are probably not deductible. However, the taxpayer may capitalize his investment and recover the cost through depreciation over the useful life of the property involved (*see infra*, §§455-460). He might also be able to show that part of the payments were deductible interest.

(7) Capitalization of acquisition costs [§391]

Amounts paid to *purchase* a business or asset (tangible or intangible) are clearly capital outlays and not deductible. [**Woodward v. Commissioner**, 397 U.S. 572 (1970)—costs of litigation incurred in acquiring stock from minority stockholders under state law must be capitalized along with the cost of the stock]

(a) Start-up costs [§392]

Start-up costs of a new business are not currently deductible. [**Richmond Television Corp. v. United States,** 345 F.2d 901 (4th Cir. 1965)—costs of starting new television business before license obtained must be capitalized] Under prior law, start-up costs could not be depreciated or amortized because they have no determinable useful life. As a result, these costs would be permanently nondeductible. However, an existing business that is expanding could currently deduct the costs of expansion. To partially equalize the situation of new and existing businesses, Congress enacted section 195.

1) Scope of I.R.C. section 195 [§393]

A taxpayer may currently deduct up to $5,000 of the costs of investigating the creation or acquisition of an active trade or business and the costs of actually creating a new trade or business, reduced by the amount such costs exceed $50,000. Thus, there is no deduction if the total start-up cost exceeds $55,000. Any amounts not deducted currently may be deducted ratably over the 15-year period beginning on the date the active trade or business commences.

2) Distinction between investigation and purchase costs [§394]

Section 195 covers the costs of deciding whether to enter a new business and which new business to enter. However, once the taxpayer decides which business to purchase, the costs of purchasing the business are not covered by section 195. Instead, they must be capitalized as part of the cost of purchasing the assets of that business. [Rev. Rul. 99-23, 1999-1 C.B. 998]

 Example: U Corp. hired an investment banker to evaluate the purchase of a new business. The banker considered various industries and zeroed in on one of them. He then evaluated several businesses within that industry. So far, these investigatory costs are covered by section 195—the costs must be capitalized, but they may be amortized over a five-year period. The banker then decided that V Corp. was the best bet and appraised V Corp.'s assets to determine the purchase price. Ultimately, U purchased V. The costs that were incurred after the investment banker had decided that V Corp. was the best bet are not covered by section 195 and must be capitalized as part of the cost of purchasing V Corp. [Rev. Rul. 99-23, *supra*]

3) Exceptions [§395]

The ban on deducting start-up costs does not apply to business interest, deductible taxes (such as property or state income taxes), or research and experimentation expenditures. [I.R.C. §195(c)(1); for discussion of research and experimentation expenditures, *see infra*, §401]

(b) Unsuccessful searches [§396]

The cost of investigating a business opportunity by one not yet in business is not deductible if the deal falls through. [**Frank v. Commissioner,** 20 T.C. 511 (1953)] Moreover, the IRS takes the position that the costs of unsuccessfully trying to buy a business cannot be added to the basis of a different business that the taxpayer successfully locates later on. [Rev. Rul. 57-418, 1957-2 C.B. 143]

1) Effect of I.R.C. section 195 [§397]

It is not clear what effect section 195 will have on the cost of an unsuccessful business investigation. If the taxpayer never finds a business, no amortization would be permitted. However, arguably, if the taxpayer ultimately finds a business, he could capitalize and amortize all the costs of investigation, including the deals that fell through. Clearly, he can amortize the cost of investigating and acquiring the business he actually buys.

(c) Finding employment [§398]

Fees paid to employment agencies are deductible, whether or not a job was actually found. However, the costs of looking for one's *first* job in his trade or business are not deductible—only the costs connected with subsequent jobs. The IRS has also cautioned that expenses are not deductible "where there is a substantial lack of continuity" between the time of a previous job and the beginning of a new job search. [Rev. Rul. 75-120, 1975-1 C.B. 55; **Cremona v. Commissioner,** 58 T.C. 219 (1972)]

1) **Distinguish—running for office [§399]**

The costs of running for office, even for reelection, are not deductible, on the theory that they are costs of obtaining a new position. Neither can such expenses be amortized over the term of office. This rule seems to be based on the notion that the tax system should not subsidize the expenses of wealthy people in running for office. [**McDonald v. Commissioner,** 323 U.S. 57 (1944)]

2) **Criticism**

This position seems inconsistent with the rule that fees paid to employment agencies are deductible, but the Fifth Circuit felt it must adhere to the *McDonald* rule until the Supreme Court changes it. [**Nichols v. Commissioner,** 511 F.2d 618 (5th Cir. 1975)—en banc decision with five dissenters]

(d) Corporate organization and reorganization [§400]

Legal fees in connection with the *organization* of a business (*e.g.,* incorporation and stock issuance) are deemed capital outlays, which generally cannot be deducted currently. Legal expenses in corporate reorganizations [**Bush Terminal v. Commissioner,** 7 T.C. 793 (1946)] and the costs of facilitating a corporate takeover [**INDOPCO, Inc. v. Commissioner,** *supra,* §376] are also generally capital outlays. However, a taxpayer may currently deduct up to $5,000 of corporate organization or business start-up expenses, including legal expenses, reduced by the amount such expenses exceed $50,000. Thus, there is no deduction if the expenses exceed $55,000. Any amounts not deducted currently may be deducted ratably over the 15-year period beginning on the date the active trade or business commences. [I.R.C. §§248, 195; *and see supra,* §393]

(e) Patents, copyrights, trademarks [§401]

Although the cost of *purchasing* patents, copyrights, and trademarks is clearly a capital outlay [Treas. Reg. §1.263(a)], research and experimental expenditures incurred by the taxpayer in creating his own patents, copyrights, etc., may be deducted currently [I.R.C. §174].

EXAM TIP	**gilbert**

On your exam, note that the election to deduct research and experimentation costs is an *exception* to the "current expense" vs. "capital outlay" rule, since the costs of research and experimentation often result in acquisition of an asset having a useful life longer than one year.

1) Note

The benefit of I.R.C. section 174 is available even to a taxpayer with a new invention that has not yet produced any income and thus is not yet a trade or business. [**Snow v. Commissioner,** 416 U.S. 500 (1974)]

2) And note

In addition to the deduction under I.R.C. section 174, there is a *credit* for increased research and experimentation. To compute the credit, take the current year's research expense and compare it to the average for the three preceding years. The credit is 25% of the excess. [I.R.C. §44F]

(f) Bar exam [§402]

The cost of taking the bar exam must be capitalized rather than deducted. It can be amortized over the lawyer's life expectancy. [**Sharon v. Commissioner,** *supra*, §342]

(g) Selling costs [§403]

Commissions paid on the sale of property are not deductible as expenses. However, they decrease the amount realized on the sale and thus decrease the gain (or increase the loss) on the sale of the asset.

(h) Acquiring goodwill [§404]

The cost of acquiring goodwill in a new business is a nondeductible capital expenditure. [Treas. Reg. §1.263(a)]

---

e.g. **Example:** Taxpayer took over a defunct business and paid off the debts of the prior owners for the purpose of acquiring the goodwill of customers. It was held that these expenditures were capital, not expense, because they were in effect the purchase of goodwill. It was also held that they were not "ordinary" (*see infra*, §409). [**Welch v. Helvering,** 290 U.S. 111 (1933)]

---

1) Tax treatment [§405]

Purchased goodwill can be amortized over a 15-year period. [I.R.C. §197; *see infra*, §456]

2) Distinguish—preserving goodwill [§406]

But amounts paid for the *protection or improvement* of the goodwill of a going business (*e.g.*, advertising expenses or public relations) are deductible. [**Dunn & McCarthy, Inc. v. Commissioner,** 139 F.2d 242 (2d Cir. 1943)]

COST	RULE
REPAIR TO PROPERTY	If property's *useful life or value is increased*, the associated cost must be capitalized. Otherwise, cost is deductible as a current expense.
ENVIRONMENTAL CLEANUP	Such cleanup is *specifically deductible* under section 198 (if conditions met). If conditions not met, could still be deductible *as repair*.
PROPERTY PRODUCED OR SOLD BY TAXPAYER	Direct costs (cost of producing property—*e.g.*, materials and labor) and indirect costs (*e.g.*, overhead) must be *capitalized*.
PROPERTY ACQUIRED FOR RESALE	Property acquired for resale is *capitalized*; if the taxpayer has gross receipts of more than $10 million, the cost of maintaining the property is *added to the property's basis*.
RENTAL PAYMENTS	Rental payments are generally *deductible*.
ACQUISITION OF BUSINESS, START-UP OF BUSINESS; SEARCHING FOR NEW BUSINESS	Costs of investigating the creation or acquisition of an active trade or business, or of creating a new trade or business, are deductible up to $5,000, reduced by the amount such costs exceed $50,000. (Costs not currently deductible may be deducted ratably over the 15-year period beginning when the trade or business begins.)
FINDING EMPLOYMENT	Costs of finding a *first job* are *not deductible*. The costs of finding subsequent jobs *may be deductible*—assuming there isn't a long break in employment.
CORPORATE ORGANIZATION	Costs of a corporate organization, including legal expenses, may be currently deducted up to $5,000, reduced by the amount such costs exceed $50,000. (Costs not currently deductible may be deducted ratably over the 15-year period beginning when the trade or business begins.)
PATENTS, COPYRIGHTS, AND TRADEMARKS	Costs of *buying* these items are *capitalized*. Costs of *developing* them are *deducted*.
GOODWILL	Purchased goodwill is a capital outlay that is *amortized* over a 15-year period. (Costs of protecting or improving goodwill of a going business are deductible.)
SHORT-TERM PREPAYMENT	These prepayments may be deducted entirely in the year they were paid, assuming they are *routine and recurring* and cover no more than one year.

(i) Short-term prepayments [§407]

Frequently, taxpayers pay for items in one year that last until sometime during the following year. If a payment is routine and recurring, it does not have to be capitalized, and it may be entirely deducted in the year in which it is made. [*See*, **U.S. Freightways Corp. v. Commissioner**, 270 F.3d 1137 (7th Cir. 2001)—licenses and insurance payments beginning in one year and lasting into the following year are currently deductible; *see infra*, §§1006-1009, for further discussion of prepayments]

d. "Ordinary and necessary" expense [§408]

Even if the expense is of a business (rather than personal) nature, and is a current (rather than a capital) item, it will be deductible only if it is both "ordinary and necessary" in the taxpayer's business.

(1) "Ordinary and necessary" defined [§409]

The terms "ordinary" and "necessary" are given a broad but vague interpretation. An expense is "ordinary" if other businesses in the community, confronted with the same problem, would incur the same type of expense. "Necessary" means that the expense is appropriate or helpful to the business. [**Welch v. Helvering**, *supra*, §404]

EXAM TIP   **gilbert**

On your exam, be sure to remember that an "ordinary and necessary" expense is one (i) that *other businesses would incur* if confronted with a similar problem, and (ii) that is *appropriate or helpful* to the taxpayer's business.

(a) Note

The standard of what is "ordinary and necessary" is "not a rule of law; it is rather a way of life. Life in all its fullness must supply the answer to the riddle." [**Welch v. Helvering**, *supra*]

(2) Determinative factors [§410]

The following are the chief factors relied on by the courts in determining whether a claimed expense is in fact "ordinary and necessary."

(a) Voluntariness of payment [§411]

People in business ordinarily make only those payments they are required to make. Hence, a payment made without legal obligation may not be "ordinary and necessary."

Example: Taxpayer, an attorney, represented that his client would deposit certain funds in court; when the client failed to come up with the funds, the attorney made the deposit on his client's behalf. Since this was a voluntary payment, it was not "ordinary," and hence could not be deducted as a business expense. [**Friedman v. Delaney,** 171 F.2d 269 (1st Cir. 1948), *cert. denied*, 336 U.S. 936 (1949)]

1) Voluntary payments could be deductible [§412]

However, voluntariness does not always disqualify a payment as a deductible business expense—as when an obvious business advantage was gained thereby (*e.g.*, corporate-taxpayer pays off debts of one of its officers in order to preserve corporate goodwill). [**Pepper v. Commissioner,** 36 T.C. 886 (1961), *and see supra,* §295]

(b) Customariness of payment [§413]

The more common the payment in the trade, the more likely it will be deductible. However, an expense may be unusual and nonrecurring, but still be "ordinary and necessary" (*e.g.*, legal fees in a criminal prosecution involving the business), even though the taxpayer may encounter them only once in a lifetime. [**Commissioner v. Tellier,** 383 U.S. 687 (1966)]

(c) Unsavoriness [§414]

Occasionally, courts seem to hold that an expense is not "ordinary" or "necessary" because they find it reprehensible, even though it does not fall within the public policy rules (*see infra,* §424). [**Car-Ron Asphalt Paving Co. v. Commissioner,** 758 F.2d 1132 (6th Cir. 1985)—legal kickbacks not "necessary"; *but see* **Raymond Bertolini Trucking Co. v. Commissioner,** 736 F.2d 1120 (6th Cir. 1984)—different panel holds legal kickbacks "ordinary"; IRS had conceded they were "necessary"]

(3) Compensation [§415]

Compensation costs for services rendered are deductible, but only if "reasonable." [I.R.C. §162(a)(1)]

(a) Reasonableness of compensation—in general [§416]

The reasonableness of salaries or other compensation to executives is often a matter of litigation. For example, corporate taxpayers (particularly closely held corporations) frequently attempt to deduct as business expenses huge salaries paid to executives who are also shareholders of the corporation. The issue in such cases is whether the salary payments are compensation for services or are really nondeductible *constructive dividends*. [**Nor-Cal Adjusters v. Commissioner,** 503 F.2d 359 (9th Cir. 1974)]

1) **Note**

On rare occasions, the IRS attacks as unreasonable the compensation of an employee other than a stockholder or a relative of a stockholder. These attacks have been upheld by the courts, even though the compensation in such cases could not be a constructive dividend. [**Harold's Club v. Commissioner,** 340 F.2d 861 (9th Cir. 1965); **Patton v. Commissioner,** 168 F.2d 28 (6th Cir. 1948)]

(b) **Determining "reasonableness" [§417]**

The main questions in such cases are the *value* of the services rendered to the business and what *similar businesses are paying* for like services. [Treas. Reg. §1.162-7]

1) **Salary based on percentage of income [§418]**

The fact that a salary is based on a percentage of income (or net profits) is suspicious, because of the resemblance to a dividend. However, in some cases, a percentage contract has been found *reasonable when entered into*; consequently, the salary payments were deductible even though in later years the percentage resulted in payment of more than the replacement value of the services. [**Rogers v. United States,** 340 F.2d 861 (9th Cir. 1965); Treas. Reg. §1.162-7(b)(2)] However, if the percentage contract was not the result of a "free bargain," it cannot be used to validate the reasonableness of large salary payments in later years. [**Harold's Club v. Commissioner,** *supra*—agreement between sons and their father, who was the "brains of the operation"]

2) **Independent investor test [§419]**

Several courts have employed an "independent investor" test rather than the vague multifactor balancing test. Under the "independent investor" approach, the amount of reasonable compensation is the amount that a hypothetical independent investor would choose to pay for the services, given the return on equity enjoyed by that investor after paying for the services. [**Exacto Spring Corp. v. Commissioner,** 196 F.3d 833 (7th Cir. 1999); **Dexsil Corp. v. Commissioner,** 147 F.3d 96 (2d Cir. 1998)] Thus, if the hypothetical independent investor is earning a very high rate of return on equity even after he pays very high salaries, the salaries are presumptively reasonable.

3) **Salary unrelated to value of services [§420]**

"Salary" payments that bear *no real relationship to value* of services have been disallowed. For example, an end-of-year discretionary bonus paid to a doctor-shareholder of a professional service association was held to be a "constructive dividend" where the total "salary" exceeded the *gross billings* for his services. [**Klamath Medical Service Bureau v. Commissioner,** 261 F.2d 842 (9th Cir. 1959)]

4) Agreement to return unreasonable salary [§421]

An agreement that the salary will be returned to the corporation if found to be unreasonable may suggest that the salary actually is unreasonable. [**Saia Electric Inc. v. Commissioner,** T.C.M. 1974-390] Under such an agreement, the employee is allowed to deduct salary repayments, if the agreement to return the salaries was made at or before the time the salary was paid. [**Oswald v. Commissioner,** 49 T.C. 645 (1968)] (*See infra*, §1076, for application of I.R.C. section 1341 to this situation.)

(c) Effect where salary represents distribution of profits [§422]

A few cases indicate that even though a salary is reasonable, a deduction will still be disallowed to the extent that the employee-shareholder *has not received a reasonable return* on his investment in stock of the corporation [**McCandless Tire Service v. United States,** 422 F.2d 1336 (Ct. Cl. 1970)], or that the payment otherwise resembles a dividend [**Nor-Cal Adjusters v. Commissioner,** *supra*].

(d) Salaries in excess of $1 million per year [§423]

A publicly held corporation cannot deduct remuneration (including most noncash compensation) in excess of $1 million per year to its chief executive officer or to one of its four most highly compensated executives. *Exception:* The employer can deduct such payments if they are payable on a commission basis on account of income generated by the employee or in certain other cases in which compensation is based on attainment of performance goals. [I.R.C. §162(m)] This performance-based compensation exception generally includes stock options and other stock-based compensation.

e. Public policy limitation [§424]

Although formerly a matter of case law, I.R.C. section 162 now specifically disallows the deduction of certain expense items because the deduction would be contrary to public policy. Below are the *only categories* of expenses that are disallowed; the courts cannot create new ones.

(1) Bribes to government employees [§425]

No deduction is allowed for any *illegal* bribe or kickback to any official or employee of *any government.* [I.R.C. §162(c)(1)] Additionally, no deduction is allowed for payments to a foreign official if the payment violates the Foreign Corrupt Practices Act of 1977. [15 U.S.C. §78]

(2) Other illegal payments [§426]

No deduction is allowed for any other *illegal* bribe, kickback, or other payment to anyone. The illegality can be established by a federal, state, or local *criminal law* or by a statute or rule that would subject the payor to *loss of license or privilege of doing business*. However, if a state statute or regulation (rather than a federal provision) is in issue, the IRS must prove by clear and convincing evidence that it is *generally enforced* before the deduction can be disallowed. [I.R.C. §162(c)(2); *see* **Boucher v. Commissioner,** 77 T.C. 214 (1981)—state law against insurance premium discounting was "generally enforced" even though there had been no prosecutions because of lack of aggressive law enforcement]

Example: An employment agency advertised for jobs and indicated sex preferences. Although this violated the Civil Rights Act of 1964, the cost was deductible because the statute does not provide for criminal penalties or the loss of license to engage in a trade or business for making payment to the newspaper. [Rev. Rul. 74-323, 1974-2 C.B. 66] (This point might have been decided differently under prior law (below), since the payments might have been viewed as frustrating sharply defined public policies.)

(a) Medical kickbacks [§427]

The Code provides for automatic nondeductibility of kickbacks or bribes by providers of services paid for under Medicare or Medicaid—whether or not they violate state law. [I.R.C. §162(c)(3)]

(b) Drug dealers [§428]

The Code also bars deductions or credits for any amount paid by illegal drug dealers. [I.R.C. §280E]

(c) Exception—reduction in sales price of goods [§429]

The disallowance of deductions for illegal payments does *not* apply to illegal rebates. As a result, a seller of goods or services who illegally rebates part of the purchase price back to the buyer can reduce gross income by the amount of the rebate. [**Sobel Liquors, Inc. v. Commissioner,** 628 F.2d 670 (9th Cir. 1980); Rev. Rul. 82-149, 1982-2 C.B. 56]

(d) Prior law [§430]

The prior law on illegal payments was confusing. Unethical kickbacks were allowed as deductions, even though contrary to good medical practice. [**Lilly v. Commissioner,** 343 U.S. 90 (1952)] Illegal rent payments by a bookie were also allowed. [**Commissioner v. Sullivan,** *supra,* §299] But more unsavory payments, such as bribes or kickbacks, were not allowed if they violated state law. [**Boyle, Flagg & Seaman, Inc. v. Commissioner,** 25 T.C. 43 (1955)]

(3) Fines [§431]

No deduction is allowed for any fine or similar penalty (criminal or civil) paid to a government for the violation of any law. [I.R.C. §162(f)] Note that this provision does not disallow deduction of a payment to a victim of crime rather than to the government. [*See* **Stephens v. Commissioner,** 905 F.2d 667 (2d Cir. 1990)—restitution payment to an embezzlement victim imposed as condition of probation deductible under section 162 since not paid to government] Note also that attorneys' fees incurred in resisting criminal sanctions related to an illegal business are deductible. [**Commissioner v. Tellier,** *supra,* §413]

(a) Prior law [§432]

The rule concerning fines was the same under prior law—it did not matter whether the violation was intentional or negligent, or whether the taxpayer had to commit the crime to stay in business. [**Tank Truck Rentals, Inc. v. Commissioner,** 356 U.S. 30 (1958)]

(4) Appearance with respect to legislation [§433]

In general, no deduction is allowed for any payments relating to the political campaign of a candidate for public office or to any attempt to influence the general public about legislative matters, elections, or referendums. [I.R.C. §162(e)(2); **Southern Pacific Transportation Co. v. Commissioner,** 90 T.C. 771 (1988)—no deduction for costs of seeking to influence voters on ballot propositions]

(a) Lobbying [§434]

Similarly, no deduction is allowed for any amount incurred to influence legislation, including the cost of direct communication with high officials of the federal executive branch intended to influence the official position of the officials. The ban on deducting lobbying expenses does not apply to attempts to influence local legislation (such as city or county government ordinances), but it does apply to attempts to influence state and federal legislation. The same ban applies to the deduction of an appropriate portion of dues paid to organizations engaged in lobbying. There is a de minimis provision for in-house expenditures up to $2,000 (in-house expenditures do not include payments to lobbyists or dues to lobbying organizations). [I.R.C. §162(e)]

(5) Damage payments [§435]

Civil penalties (such as double damage wage payments for violation of the Fair Labor Standards Act) paid to persons *other* than a government generally are deductible.

(a) Distinguish—antitrust violations [§436]

If a taxpayer is convicted of a criminal *antitrust violation* (or pleads nolo contendere), and later makes damage payments to the persons harmed by the antitrust violation, two-thirds of those payments are not deductible. [I.R.C. §162(g)]

2. "Nonbusiness" Expenses—Expenses for Production of Income

a. General rule [§437]

An *individual* taxpayer is entitled to deduct expenses paid or incurred [I.R.C. §212]:

(1) *For the production* or collection of income;

(2) *For the management, conservation, or maintenance of property* held for the production of income; or

(3) *In connection with the determination, collection, or refund of any tax.*

b. Effect of I.R.C. section 212 [§438]

This section makes available to the individual *investor* the same type of expense deduction available to business. Expenses deductible under section 212 are commonly referred to as "nonbusiness" or *investor expenses*. Thus, the costs of investing in stocks, bonds, and commodities are generally deductible under section 212 rather than section 162. [*See* **Moller v. United States**, *supra*, §354—person holding stocks for dividend income and long-term capital gains is not in trade or business] Similarly, certain real estate investments may fall under section 212 rather than 162 if very little work is required (*e.g.*, a factory is leased out to a tenant under a long-term net lease).

(1) Limited to individuals [§439]

This section authorizes deductions that may be claimed only by individual taxpayers—not by trusts or corporations. Trusts or corporations can deduct this type of expense under section 162 (trade or business expense) since they are automatically treated as being in business.

c. Similarity to I.R.C. section 162 [§440]

The scope of expenses deductible under section 212 is substantially the same as under section 162 (business expense). For example, the expense must be:

(i) *A "current" item*, as opposed to a capital outlay;

(ii) *"Ordinary and necessary"*;

(iii) *Not violative of public policy*; and

(iv) Incurred for *the production of income*, or *the management of income-producing property*, rather than for personal reasons.

However, for a variety of tax purposes, deductions under section 212 are less favorably treated than those under section 162. (*See supra*, §297.) In particular, section 212 expenses (other than those relating to the production of rent or royalties) are deductions from adjusted gross income ("below the line") and are subject to the rule that allows deduction of miscellaneous itemized deductions only in excess of 2% of adjusted gross income. [I.R.C. §§62(a)(4), 67; *see infra*, §§555-557, 562-564]

EXAM TIP — gilbert

For your exam, you should be careful to point out that deductions for "business expenses" and deductions for "expenses related to the production of income" fall *under separate I.R.C. provisions*, even though the requirements for taking the deductions are very similar. A *"business expense" falls under I.R.C. section 162*, while an *"expense related to the production of income" falls under I.R.C. section 212*.

---

d. Illustrations

(1) Proxy fight [§441]

Expenses incurred by a shareholder in connection with a proxy fight to obtain control of a corporation are deductible under I.R.C. section 212. Deduction of such expenses is allowed even to a minority shareholder who was not himself attempting to become a director, but who wished to replace management simply in the hope of making a greater profit on his shares. [**Surasky v. United States**, 325 F.2d 191 (5th Cir. 1963)]

(2) Stockholder's travel [§442]

A stockholder could possibly deduct travel costs incurred in attending stockholder meetings or visiting the factories of the companies whose stock he holds, but he would have to establish that the trip was rationally planned and the costs incurred were reasonable in relation to the amount of his investment and the value of information to be obtained. [**Kinney v. Commissioner**, 66 T.C. 122 (1976)] Note that no section 212 deduction is allowed for expenses allocable to a convention, seminar, or similar meeting. [I.R.C. §274(h)(7)]

(3) Litigation expenses related to property matters [§443]

The problem with litigation expenses is determining whether they were incurred for the "production or collection of income" (and hence deductible), or for the *acquisition* or *defense of title* to property (in which case they are capital items and not deductible).

(a) "Primary purpose" test [§444]

The key in these cases is the primary purpose of the litigation.

1) *If the primary purpose* of the litigation is to *establish or defend title or ownership* of some particular asset, the fees are

nondeductible capital expenditures. [Treas. Regs. §§1.263(a)-2(c); **Lark Sales Co. v. Commissioner,** 437 F.2d 1067 (7th Cir. 1971)—disallowing litigation costs relating to establishment of title to trademark "Dairy Queen"]

2) *If the primary purpose* of the litigation is to *recover profits or damages*, the legal fees and litigation expenses are deductible, even if issues as to title are incidentally involved.

Example: Taxpayer, a corporate director, was sued in a derivative suit for having usurped a corporate opportunity. Plaintiffs alleged that taxpayer's participation in another venture violated his fiduciary duties, and they sought to assert the corporation's title to the venture. The court held that the primary purpose of the litigation was defense of taxpayer's conduct as a fiduciary—and thus a business expense—not defense of title. [**Hochschild v. Commissioner,** 161 F.2d 817 (2d Cir. 1947); *but see* **Larchfield Corp. v. United States,** 373 F.2d 159 (2d Cir. 1967)—seems to be contrary]

(b) Acquisition costs [§445]

The Supreme Court declined to apply the primary purpose test to expenses relating to the *acquisition* of property. Under state law, majority shareholders had to buy out dissenting shareholders to prevent a corporate dissolution. They incurred litigation expenses in determining the value of the shares and argued that the primary purpose of the litigation was to fix the price of the stock, not to determine title. The Court held that this was irrelevant; all costs were referable to acquisition of the shares of the minority and hence not deductible. [**Woodward v. Commissioner,** *supra,* §391]

(4) Divorce and property settlement expenses [§446]

Attorneys' fees incurred in connection with divorce litigation are generally treated as nondeductible *personal* expenses arising from a family relationship, rather than any profitmaking activity.

(a) Property settlements [§447]

This is true even as to fees incurred (by either spouse) in connection with property settlements. The courts have consistently rejected the argument that the fees should be deductible as expenses for the "preservation of income-producing property." The *origin* of the dispute—*i.e.,* marital problems—controls. [**United States v. Gilmore,** *supra,* §340]

(b) Alimony [§448]

However, a spouse may, under section 212(1), deduct legal fees attributable to the production or collection of *alimony income*. [**Wild v. Commissioner**, 42 T.C. 706 (1965)]

(c) **Tax consequences of divorce [§449]**

Legal fees paid for advice on the *tax consequences* of divorce are deductible under I.R.C. section 212(3), which authorizes the deduction of "expenses incurred in connection with the determination, collection or refund of any tax." [**Carpenter v. United States**, 338 F.2d 366 (1964); *and see supra*, §341] But to be deductible, the tax advice must pertain to the *taxpayer's own tax problems*, not the spouse's. [**United States v. Davis**, *supra*, §294]

3. Depreciation [§450]

To measure the wearing out of an asset used in business or for investment, a taxpayer owning the asset deducts annually an arbitrary percentage of the cost of the asset. This deduction is known as *depreciation* (if the asset is an intangible such as a copyright, the deduction is known as *amortization*). For this purpose, "cost" is the unadjusted basis of the asset plus subsequent expenditures that were "capitalized." (*See supra*, §§365 *et seq.*) The depreciation rules are set forth in section 168, which for tangible assets replaces the previous rules in section 167. The system of depreciation under section 168 is called the "accelerated cost recovery system" ("ACRS").

a. Rationale

The traditional theory of depreciation required a taxpayer to allocate an asset's decline in value to the appropriate tax year, thereby matching the asset's decline in value against the income that it produces in any given year. However, the depreciation allowances under ACRS are much larger in the early years than in later years. Thus, *ACRS departs from the traditional theory* and is, in effect, a subsidy to business that encourages greater investment in plants and equipment.

b. Limitations on depreciation

(1) Passive loss rules [§451]

Deductions relating to passive activities cannot exceed income from those activities. [I.R.C. §469, *see infra*, §§543 *et seq.*] In many cases, the deductions disallowed by this provision consist largely of real estate depreciation.

(2) "At risk" limitation [§452]

The "at risk" limitation on deductions from certain investments is a significant limitation on depreciation (*see infra*, §538). Depreciation is based on cost, which frequently includes a nonpersonal liability obligation (*see infra*, §§730-732). But under section 465, depreciation (and other deductions) cannot exceed the amount of the taxpayer's actual investment and his personal liability obligations. Special at risk rules apply to real estate (*see infra*, §539).

(3) Property worth less than debt [§453]

If the property is worth less than the amount of the nonpersonal liability mortgage to which it is subject at the time of purchase, it has been held that the taxpayer *cannot* deduct depreciation on the property. [**Estate of Franklin v. Commissioner,** 544 F.2d 1045 (9th Cir. 1976); **Waddell v. Commissioner,** 86 T.C. 848 (1986), *aff'd*, 841 F.2d 264 (9th Cir. 1988)—no basis because promissory notes unlikely to be paid]

(4) Generic tax shelters [§454]

Many deals that give rise to large depreciation deductions are now treated as "generic tax shelters," and all deductions are disallowed under authority of section 183 or because the transaction lacked economic substance. [**Rose v. Commissioner,** *supra*, §323]

c. What property can be depreciated [§455]

All physical property (except land) that is used in a trade or business or held for production of income, and that has a *limited useful life*, may be depreciated.

(1) Intangibles [§456]

Intangible assets, including goodwill, that have a basis can be amortized over an arbitrary 15-year life. Contract rights, such as covenants not to compete, are also amortized over a 15-year life, regardless of the actual term of the covenant. [I.R.C. §197, *see infra*, §473]

(a) Prior law

Under prior law, goodwill could not be amortized. There was a large amount of case law struggling with the question of whether particular purchased intangibles had a determinable useful life so that they could be amortized. If a taxpayer could establish a determinable useful life for such intangibles, they could be amortized over that useful life. [**Newark Morning Ledger Co. v. United States,** 507 U.S. 546 (1993)] These cases are superseded, however, by I.R.C. section 197, which imposes a 15-year amortization period on such "customer-based" intangibles regardless of whether the taxpayer can establish a determinable useful life and regardless of the length of that life.

Example: Taxpayer purchased a newspaper, allocating $67 million to an intangible asset entitled "paid subscribers." The taxpayer amortized this asset, claiming that the list was a wasting asset because the subscribers would cancel their subscriptions over a determinable period. (The taxpayer presented strong expert testimony at the trial to this effect.) The Court held the asset was distinguishable from goodwill and could be amortized. [**Newark Morning Ledger Co. v. United States,** *supra*] Present law allows a 15-year amortization period regardless of whether the asset is goodwill.

(b) Books, films, sound recordings, software [§457]

The production costs of books, films, recordings, or other copyrighted items produced by the taxpayer are amortized over the period during which they are expected to produce income. Computer software produced by the taxpayer is depreciated over a 36-month period using the straight-line method, *i.e.*, one-third of the total depreciation is taken each year (*see infra*, §467). [I.R.C. §167(f)] If copyrights or software are purchased as part of the assets of an acquired trade or business, their cost is amortized over a 15-year period. [I.R.C. §197, *see infra*, §474]

e.g. **Example:** Suppose a film costs $1 million to produce and is expected to return $4 million in income. In the first tax year, it produces $800,000 in income (20% of the total expected). The taxpayer claims amortization of $200,000 (20% of the total cost). [*See* I.R.C. §167(g)—giving detailed rules and requiring that taxpayer estimate revenue from all markets for 10 years]

(2) Property having unlimited useful life [§458]

Assets other than intangibles that do not wear out (*e.g.*, works of art and land) cannot be depreciated. Thus, when a building is purchased, it is necessary to **allocate the cost between the building and the land** on which it is built, since only the building is depreciable.

(a) But note

The courts have allowed musicians to depreciate rare musical instruments, even though such instruments generally increase in value and last for hundreds of years, because they do suffer wear and tear with use. [**Liddle v. Commissioner,** 65 F.3d 329 (3d Cir. 1995)—17th century bass viol]

d. Who is entitled to depreciation deduction [§459]

The general rule is that the person who suffers the economic loss as a result of the decrease in value of the property due to depreciation is the one entitled to claim the deduction. Ordinarily, this is the person who owns, or at least has a capital investment in, the property. [**Helvering v. Lazarus,** 308 U.S. 252 (1939)]

(1) Landlord-tenant [§460]

When a lessor improves her land and then leases the property to a tenant, the lessor is entitled to the depreciation deductions.

(a) *However, if the tenant is required to maintain the property* so that when the property is returned, it will be of equivalent value, the lessor is not entitled to depreciation. [**Kem v. Commissioner**, 432 F.2d 961 (9th Cir. 1970)]

(b) *When the tenant leases unimproved land* and then constructs a building on the land, or constructs leasehold improvements in a leased building, the tenant is entitled to the depreciation deduction. However, the building or the improvement is depreciated over its normal recovery period (27.5 years or 39 years for the building) regardless of whether the term of the lease is shorter than the recovery period. If the lease terminates before the building or improvement is fully depreciated, the lessee would take a loss deduction at the time the lease terminates. [I.R.C. §168(i)(6)]

(c) *If the taxpayer purchases the lessor's interest* in leased property that has been improved by the tenant, the purchaser is entitled to depreciate the portion of his cost allocable to the improvements over their useful life. However, the purchaser is not entitled to allocate any amount of his purchase price to the lease, even if it calls for rentals above market value. [I.R.C. §167(c)(2)]

(2) Sale-leaseback [§461]

When the owner of a building "sells" it to an investor and then "leases" it back, the investor can claim depreciation only if he is treated as the *owner* of the building. If the investor is regarded as a mere *lender*, rather than a purchaser, he is not entitled to the depreciation deduction. [*See* **Frank Lyon Co. v. United States**, 435 U.S. 561 (1978)]

(a) Illustration

In *Frank Lyon Co.*, a bank constructed a building and sold it to Lyon. Lyon leased the building back to the bank, giving the bank the option to purchase. A third party ("NYLIC") had loaned Lyon the money to buy the building. The Court held that Lyon could depreciate the building because he was a true purchaser, not just a lender to the bank. The following factors were relevant:

(i) NYLIC loaned money to Lyon, not to the bank, and Lyon was primarily liable to repay this loan, no matter what happened to the bank or the building.

(ii) If the bank never exercised its option to buy the building, Lyon would own the building after 25 years.

Note: A factor that pointed toward treating Lyon's "purchase" as a mere loan was that the bank's payments to Lyon (both rental and on its option to purchase) exactly matched Lyon's obligations to NYLIC. Unless something unusual occurred, Lyon would simply make a 6% profit on its investment. For at least 25 years, Lyon's position was precisely the same economically as if it had merely loaned money to the bank.

(3) Purchaser [§462]

The purchaser under an executory sale contract may claim the depreciation deduction on the property after the burdens and benefits of ownership pass to him, even though the seller retains title for the purpose of securing the loan.

(4) Future interest holder [§463]

A life tenant is entitled to the deduction as if he were the absolute owner of the property. After the life tenant's death, the deduction is allowed to the remainderman or reversioner. [I.R.C. §167(h)]

(5) Trustee-beneficiary [§464]

In the case of property held in trust, the allowable deduction is apportioned between the income beneficiaries and the trustee on the basis of the percentage of trust income allocable to each (in the absence of anything to the contrary in the trust instrument). [I.R.C. §167(h)] Similar rules govern in the case of a decedent's estate.

e. Computation of depreciation

(1) Recovery periods [§465]

All assets are classified into a few brackets (which are generally intended to be considerably shorter than their actual economic lives). These "recovery periods" are:

(a) *For residential real property*, 27.5 years;

(b) *For nonresidential real property*, 39 years; and

(c) *For tangible personal property*, there are six possibilities: 3, 5, 7, 10, 15, and 20 years. The applicable recovery period for a particular asset depends on its "class life" as previously determined by the IRS. The majority of machinery and equipment items fall into the five-year class (because those are assets that have economically useful lives of five to nine years). Longer-lived equipment usually falls into the seven-year class. Cars and light-duty trucks fall into the five-year category, even though that period is probably longer than their economically useful lives in most cases. Rent-to-own property (such as furniture that consumers rent for relatively short periods, often with options to buy) qualifies for the three-year category. [I.R.C. §168(e)(3)(A), (i)(14)]

(2) Salvage value [§466]

Salvage value is the value that an asset is expected to have at the end of its useful life. Salvage value is ignored for purposes of ACRS depreciation.

(3) Methods of depreciation [§467]

ACRS provides for two kinds of depreciation: straight-line and accelerated. Straight-line depreciation provides for the same deduction every year during the recovery period. Accelerated depreciation provides for a greater deduction during the early years of ownership and a lower deduction in later years.

(4) Personal property—accelerated depreciation [§468]

A taxpayer may depreciate property in the three-year, five-year, and seven-year classes using the double-declining balance method of depreciation. In the 15-year and 20-year classes, 150%-declining balance depreciation may be used.

(a) Declining balance [§469]

To compute declining balance depreciation, first compute the straight-line rate. Then increase that rate by the appropriate factor (double or 150%). Apply that factor to the adjusted basis each year. Eventually, the basis will be reduced to the point that straight-line depreciation would provide a larger allowance. At that point, the taxpayer switches to straight line. [I.R.C. §168(b)]

(b) Half-year convention [§470]

Personal property is deemed to have been acquired and sold exactly halfway through the year, regardless of whether it was purchased or disposed of at the beginning or the end of the year. Therefore, the first year's depreciation will be half of a full year's depreciation. [I.R.C. §168(d)]

Example: A delivery truck is five-year property. Assume that a taxpayer purchases a delivery truck in January of Year 1 for $15,000. The straight-line rate would be 20% (for five-year property, straight-line depreciation is one-fifth of the total cost each year, or 20%). Since the truck is five-year property, the taxpayer may use the double-declining balance depreciation. That means that the depreciation rate is 40% (double 20%). Applying 40% to the adjusted basis each year would produce depreciation of $6,000 in Year 1, except that under the half-year convention the taxpayer can deduct only $3,000. In Year 2, the basis of the truck is reduced to $12,000. Thus, the depreciation available in Year 2 is 40% of $12,000 ($4,800). In Year 3, the basis of the truck is reduced to $7,200. Thus, the depreciation available in Year 3 is 40% of $7,200 ($2,880).

---

1) Exception

If more than 40% of the assets are bought during the last three months of the year, *all* assets acquired during the year are deemed to have been purchased in the middle of the *quarter* when they were purchased. [I.R.C. §168(d)(3)]

(c) Straight-line election [§471]

A taxpayer can elect to use straight-line depreciation instead of accelerated depreciation. [I.R.C. §168(a)(3)(C), (a)(5)] Thus, in the previous example, if the taxpayer elected straight-line depreciation, he would simply deduct 20% of the truck's original cost in each year (except for the first, in which he could take only half of 20%). Thus, in that example, the taxpayer would deduct $1,500 in Year 1, $3,000 in Year 2 to Year 5, and $1,500 in Year 6.

(5) Bonus depreciation—stimulus bill [§472]

In recent years, Congress has adopted provisions for additional first-year depreciation as a stimulus to the rebuilding of a region after disaster. Legislation adopted in 2002 was designed to provide such bonus depreciation for tangible personal property acquired between September 11, 2001, and January 1, 2005, but this was allowed to expire at the end of 2004. [I.R.C. §168(k)] Under the Gulf Opportunity Zone Act of 2005, another bonus depreciation provision was enacted, permitting deduction of 50% of the adjusted basis of new property investments made in the "Gulf Opportunity Zone" (created in the wake of Hurricane Katrina) for investments made after August 28, 2005, and placed in service by December 31, 2008, for real property, and December 31, 2007, for all other property. The adjusted basis is reduced by this bonus depreciation. The taxpayer then takes the normal depreciation for the year of acquisition, but computes it with regard to the reduced adjusted basis. (*See supra*, §470.)

Example: The punch press in Acme Corp.'s factory, located in New Orleans, was severely damaged by Hurricane Katrina. Acme Corp. purchases a replacement for $1 million on November 1, 2005, and immediately places it in service. The press is seven-year property. Acme should claim bonus depreciation of $300,000, which reduces the adjusted basis to $700,000. Assume Acme uses accelerated depreciation. The straight-line rate is 1/7. That figure is doubled to 2/7 and multiplied by the adjusted basis ($700,000 times 2/7 equals $200,000). This result is cut in half under the first-year convention—so ordinary depreciation is $100,000. Acme deducts a total depreciation of $400,000 in 2005 (bonus depreciation of $300,000 plus ordinary depreciation of $100,000). In 2006, the adjusted basis is $600,000, and Acme deducts approximately $170,000 ($600,000 times 2/7).

(6) Amortization of intangibles [§473]

Historically, although a taxpayer was not permitted to amortize purchased goodwill because it had no determinable useful life, courts permitted amortization of contract rights or of other purchased intangibles if the taxpayer met the burden of proving that the asset had a determinable useful life. [*See* **Newark Morning Ledger Co. v. United States**, *supra*, §456—allowing amortization of purchased subscription list of newspaper] The resulting confusion led Congress to provide a uniform system for the amortization of intangibles (including goodwill) over a 15-year period. [I.R.C. §197] Under this provision, some assets (such as a purchased three-year covenant not to compete) will have a much longer amortization period than under prior law; but some assets (such as goodwill) will be amortizable that were not amortizable under prior law.

(a) Section 197 intangibles [§474]

The 15-year amortization period under section 197 applies to the following intangibles:

1) Any of the following *purchased* (but not self-created) intangibles:

    a) *Goodwill;*

    b) *Going-concern value*;

    c) *Workforce* in place;

    d) *Business books and records,* and other information bases;

    e) *Patents, copyrights, formulas, and know-how* (when these assets were purchased together with other assets of a trade or business);

    f) *Customer-based intangibles* (*e.g.*, the subscription lists in *Newark Morning Ledger*); and

    g) *Supplier-based intangibles*;

2) Licenses, permits, or other *rights granted by government*;

3) A *covenant not to compete* entered into in connection with the acquisition of a trade or business; and

4) *A franchise, trademark, or trade name.*

(b) Intangibles not covered by section 197 [§475]

Section 197 does not apply to certain intangibles. These items either cannot be amortized at all or can be amortized only according to their proved useful lives. Examples of these types of intangibles are:

1)   An interest in a *corporation, partnership, trust, or estate* (not amortizable);

2)   Any interest in *land* (not amortizable);

3)   *Computer software* (amortizable over 36 months);

4)   *Professional sports franchise* (not amortizable); and

5)   An interest in a *film, sound recording, videotape, book, or similar property, or a patent or copyright that was self-created or purchased separately* (as opposed to being acquired as part of the assets of a trade or business). These intellectual-property-type assets are amortized under the income-forecast method described in §457, *supra*.

(7) Real property [§476]

Buildings can be depreciated only on the straight-line method. Nonresidential real property (*e.g.*, a factory) is depreciated over a 39-year life. Residential real property (*e.g.*, apartments) is depreciated over a 27.5-year life.

(a) Convention

Real property is depreciated on a mid-month convention. That means that depreciation is calculated on a monthly basis in the year that the property is purchased or constructed and in the year that it is disposed of. The property is deemed to have been acquired or disposed of in the middle of the month. [I.R.C. §168(d)(2), (d)(4)(B)]

Example: Acme Co. purchases a factory in November of Year 1 for $1 million. The straight-line rate is .0256 per year (*i.e.*, 1/39). Thus, in Year 2, Acme can deduct $25,600 in depreciation ($1 million × .0256). However, in Year 1, Acme can deduct depreciation only for December and half of November. That produces a deduction of $3,200 in Year 1 (*i.e.*, 1/12 of a year for December, 1/24 of a year for November).

---

f. Election to expense purchase price [§477]

The Code allows taxpayers to expense (*i.e.*, deduct immediately) a certain amount of the purchase price of tangible personal property used in business. [I.R.C. §179] In 2006, the maximum amount a taxpayer may elect to expense currently is $108,000. For every dollar of qualifying investment in excess of

$430,000, the maximum amount a taxpayer may elect to expense currently is reduced by one dollar. These figures are adjusted for inflation.

g. Limitations on deductions relating to consumer items [§478]

The Code imposes limitations on deductions (depreciation and rental expense) on "listed property." This category includes cars, cellular telephones, and home computers used for business. [I.R.C. §280F]

(1) ACRS depreciation [§479]

Unless the business use of listed property is more than 50% of its total use, only straight-line, not ACRS, depreciation can be used. [I.R.C. §280F(b)]

(a) Note

Of course, the percentage of business use determines the amount of depreciation available. For example, if the item is used 35% for business, only 35% of the depreciation is deductible.

(2) Limits on ACRS [§480]

During the first year after a car is purchased, no more than $2,560 can be claimed as depreciation (including the amount allowed under I.R.C. section 179—*see supra*, §477). No more than $4,100 can be claimed in the second year, $2,450 in the third year, and $1,475 for any succeeding year. These figures are indexed for inflation (starting from 1989). Thus, for example, it would take quite a few years to recover the full purchase price of a Mercedes acquired for business purposes. [I.R.C. §280F(a)]

(3) Employee use [§481]

No ACRS deductions, section 179 year-of-purchase deductions, or rental deductions are available to an employee for listed property purchased for use in her job unless the use is for the convenience of the employer and required as a condition of employment. [I.R.C. §280F(d)(3)] (For definitions of these terms, *see supra*, §§107 *et seq.*)

Example: Taxpayer, a law professor, buys a personal computer for working at home. Since her law school supplied a computer for her use at work, she cannot deduct depreciation. Nor could she deduct rental payments if she leased the computer. [*But see* **Cadwallader v. Commissioner,** 57 T.C.M. 1030 (1989)—allowing husband (a psychology professor) and wife (a state transportation planner) to deduct, under section 179, the cost of personal computers, which their employers did not require them to purchase but which were necessary for them to do their jobs, because no computers were available for them at work]

h. Caution—ultimate effect of deduction [§482]

The depreciation deduction taken each year *reduces the taxpayer's basis*. The result is that the more depreciation taken, the more gain (or less loss) there is when the property is ultimately sold.

(1) Note

In many cases, a gain will result from the fact that the depreciation exceeded the decline in value. Because of the "depreciation recapture" provision, such gains are often ordinary income rather than capital gain. [I.R.C. §1245, *see infra*, §§933-938]

4. Depletion [§483]

The owner of a wasting asset (*e.g.*, oil or minerals) is entitled to a reasonable annual allowance as compensation for the diminution of the asset. [I.R.C. §611] This depletion allowance thus provides to the owner of a wasting asset substantially what the depreciation deduction provides to the owner of a building.

a. Depletable property [§484]

Any "wasting asset" is depletable. This term covers not only oil, gas, and minerals, but also timber, gravel, certain deposits of groundwater, etc. Basically, any natural deposit that is consumed by use or exploitation may qualify. [Treas. Reg. §1.611-1]

b. Who is entitled to depletion deduction [§485]

The holder of the *"economic interest"* in the oil or other mineral is entitled to the deduction. [**Palmer v. Bender,** 287 U.S. 551 (1933)] To have an economic interest, the taxpayer must (i) have acquired, by investment, an interest in the mineral in place; and (ii) be entitled, by legal relationship, to a share in the income to be derived from the extraction of the mineral. [**Commissioner v. Southwest Exploration,** 350 U.S. 308 (1956)—owner of adjacent lands had sufficient economic interest where driller used the lands for slant drilling onto property from which oil was extracted, paying a percentage of profits for such use]

c. Methods of computing depletion

(1) Cost method [§486]

The cost or other basis of the wasting asset is divided by the estimated number of recoverable units (*e.g.,* tons of ore, barrels of oil, board feet of timber) to arrive at the "depletion unit." Then, the depletion allowable for each year is determined by multiplying the depletion unit by the number of units actually sold or withdrawn during the year. [I.R.C. §§611 - 612]

(2) Percentage method [§487]

Under this method (far more popular), the deduction is a fixed percentage of the *gross income* from the property during the taxable year. [I.R.C. §613] The percentage figure is set by Congress, and ranges from 5% (gravel deposits) to 15% (oil and gas) of gross receipts. [I.R.C. §613(b)]

(a) Limited application for oil and gas properties [§488]

Percentage depletion cannot be used for all oil and gas properties. It is available only to independent producers of gas and oil, and then only as to 1,000 barrels per day of oil or 6,000 cubic feet of gas per day. [I.R.C. §613A] The percentage depletion deduction cannot exceed 50% of the taxpayer's net income from the property.

Example: If the gross income from an oil well in the tax year is $100,000 and the various operating expenses are $80,000, the taxpayer's net income therefore is $20,000. Assuming that the taxpayer qualifies for percentage depletion, it would be $15,000 (15% of gross), but here it must be limited to $10,000 (50% of net).

(b) Tax advantages [§489]

Percentage depletion (particularly in the oil and gas industry) is especially attractive because:

1) *The greater the income, the greater the depletion deduction.* (*Contrast:* Depreciation and cost depletion are based on cost, not income; they stay the same regardless of the income produced from the property.)

2) *The deduction goes on indefinitely.* The percentage depletion allowance continues at the same rate *even after the entire cost of the property has been recovered tax free. But note:* Any percentage depletion claimed in excess of the taxpayer's cost of the property is subject to the minimum tax on *tax preferences.* [*See* I.R.C. §57(a)(8), *and see infra,* §§945 *et seq.*]

d. Drilling costs [§490]

In addition to depletion, the costs of production are deductible as *expenses* under I.R.C. section 162 (*see supra,* §§296 *et seq.*) or I.R.C. section 212 (*see supra,* §§437 *et seq.*).

(1) Oil and gas wells [§491]

In the case of oil and gas wells, the Code recognizes a borderline class of expenditures known as *intangible drilling and development expenses* (*e.g.,* wages, supplies, etc., in locating sites, preparing for production and drilling), which the taxpayer may *elect* to either deduct as current expenses, or capitalize and recover through subsequent depletion and depreciation deductions. [I.R.C. §263(c)]

(a) But note

If the property is sold at a gain, prior deductions for intangible expenses are *recaptured* as ordinary income. [I.R.C. §1254] Excess intangible drilling costs are a tax preference. [I.R.C. §57(a)(11)]

(2) Mineral deposits [§492]

Owners of other mineral deposits are afforded a similar option to expense, rather than capitalize, exploration and development costs. [I.R.C. §§615 - 616]

5. Losses [§493]

I.R.C. section 165 covers the deductibility of losses. To be deductible, a loss must qualify under section 165. As will be seen in the discussion below, deductibility depends on a number of factors, including the kind of taxpayer involved, the nature of the transaction out of which the claimed loss arose, and when the loss was sustained.

a. Definition of "loss" [§494]

A loss occurs when a transaction comes to an end and the taxpayer has not recovered her basis for the assets involved.

Example: Teri purchases a share of stock for $20. She could not deduct the $20—it is a capital outlay, not an expense. Therefore, she has a $20 basis for the asset. Later she sells the stock for $4. The transaction has come to an end and she has failed to recover her basis. She has a $16 loss. As will be discussed below, this loss is deductible since it arises in an investment activity, but only in the limited form of a "capital loss."

Compare: In the above example, suppose the stock had become *worthless* because the company was bankrupt. Again, the transaction has come to an end and the entire $20 will be a deductible loss. By statute, this is also treated as a capital loss. (*See infra*, §906.)

Example: Tina is an inventor and incurred $100,000 in costs developing a new bookbinding process. Under I.R.C. section 174, Tina has an option to either deduct these costs as expenses or capitalize them as part of the basis of the invention (*supra*, §401). If Tina deducts the costs, she will have a *zero basis* for the asset. If she then abandons work on the invention, *she would have no loss because she would have no basis*. If she elected to capitalize the costs, however, she would have a $100,000 basis; when she abandons the venture, she would have a $100,000 loss deduction. This would be deductible as a trade or business loss and would be an ordinary rather than a capital loss.

(1) Is there a "loss"? [§495]

The courts often scrutinize loss transactions closely to see whether a loss really occurred. *Illustration:* If a taxpayer sells a building at a substantial loss and then leases it back, it is possible that there would be no loss deduction if the rentals on the lease are below fair market rentals. If so, the taxpayer would have received not only cash for the building but also

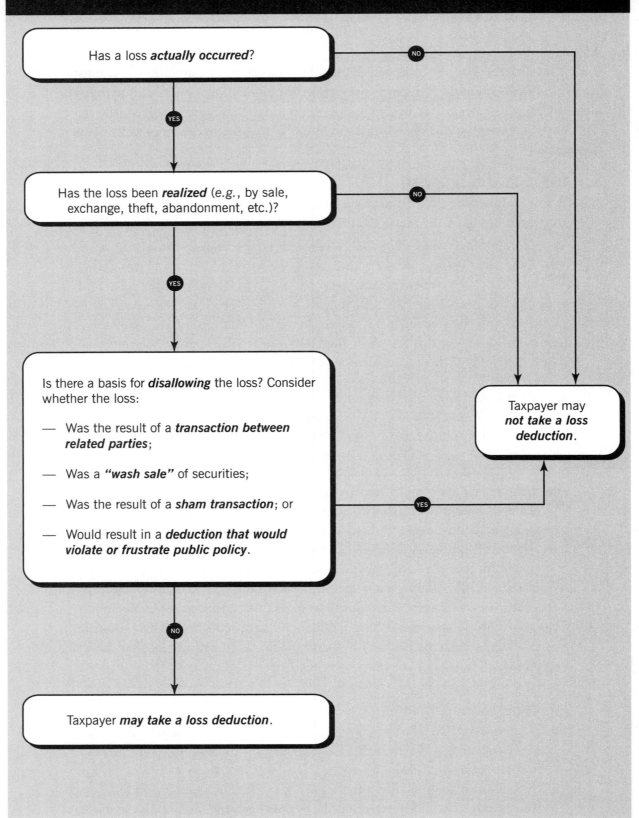

a discounted lease—and the sum of these items could be equal to or more than the taxpayer's basis. [*See* **Leslie Co. v. Commissioner,** 64 T.C. 247 (1975)] The loss could also be disallowed in this case if the transaction falls under I.R.C. section 1031 as a like kind exchange. (*See infra,* §§786 *et seq.*)

EXAM TIP — gilbert

Remember that courts will scrutinize a loss transaction to ensure that the taxpayer actually suffered a loss (vs. having structured a transaction to make it *appear* he has suffered a loss). If you encounter this problem on your exam, you should do the same—analyze the fact pattern in your question and discuss whether the *taxpayer has in fact suffered a loss*.

---

b. Types of losses allowed to individuals [§496]

A *corporate* taxpayer by its very nature is a business entity (and hence its losses are generally deductible as business losses). In the case of *individuals,* however, only certain types of losses are deductible.

(1) Losses incurred in trade or business [§497]

Any loss incurred in a trade or business is deductible. (*See supra,* §298, for definition of "trade or business.") [I.R.C. §165(c)(1)]

(2) Losses incurred in transactions entered into for profit [§498]

Losses incurred in transactions entered into for profit are deductible. This covers losses from the sale of securities or other *investments.* [I.R.C. §165(c)(2)]

(a) Personal residences [§499]

Since personal residences are not deemed held for profit, losses sustained on the sale of a personal residence are *not deductible.* [**Austin v. Commissioner,** 298 F.2d 583 (2d Cir. 1962)] *Note:* This is true even though a *gain* on sale or exchange of a residence is taxable unless it meets a statutory nonrecognition provision (*infra,* §§810-815).

1) Distinguish—conversion of residence to rental property [§500]

A taxpayer can convert her residence to an investment asset by renting it prior to sale. Then any decline in value that occurs after conversion to rental use would be deductible at the time of sale as a loss. [Treas. Reg. §1.165-9(b)] However, the conversion to rental use must be *bona fide,* and mere listing for rental is probably insufficient. [**Gevirtz v. Commissioner,** 123 F.2d 707 (2d Cir. 1941)]

(b) Wagering [§501]

Gambling is a profit-seeking activity, and hence wagering losses are deductible—but *only* to the extent of wagering gains. [I.R.C. §165(d)]

(c) Demolition losses [§502]

Loss is not allowed for demolition of a structure. The adjusted basis of the structure, and the cost of demolition, must be added to the basis of the underlying land. [I.R.C. §280B]

1) Exception—certain losses occurring before demolition [§503]

However, a loss may be deductible if incurred before the demolition occurs. For example, if a building is damaged by a casualty (such as a tornado), and then must be demolished, the casualty loss is deductible. It reduces the basis of the structure, and the remaining basis is then added to the basis of the land. [I.R.C. Notice 90-21, 1990-1 C.B. 332] Similarly, if the building is abandoned as the result of extraordinary obsolescence, then demolished, a loss deduction can be taken by reason of the abandonment. [**Cou v. Commissioner,** 103 T.C. 80 (1994)]

(3) Casualty losses

See infra, §§676-687.

DEODUCTIBILITY OF LOSSES—EXAMPLES	gilbert
LOSSES DEDUCTIBLE BY AN INDIVIDUAL:	**LOSSES *NOT* DEDUCTIBLE BY AN INDIVIDUAL:**
• Losses incurred in a trade or business • Losses incurred in a for-profit transaction • Gambling losses (but only to offset gambling earnings) • Casualty and theft losses	• Losses on sale of home • Most demolition costs

c. When loss allowable—"realization" [§504]

A loss is generally deductible only if "realized." This means it must be evidenced by a "closed and completed transaction" (*e.g.*, sale, exchange, theft, destruction, worthlessness, or abandonment) in the current tax year.

(1) Decline in value [§505]

A mere decline in value of property is not enough. [**Reporter Publishing v. Commissioner,** 201 F.2d 743 (10th Cir. 1953)—news service membership declining in value due to change in law not a deductible loss, since taxpayer continued to use news service in its business]

(2) Time of realization [§506]

Generally, the realization of loss on a *tangible asset* occurs in the year when there is *both* an intention to abandon the asset *and* an affirmative act of abandonment.

---

e.g. **Example:** A loss on a gold mine was realized when the directors resolved to abandon the mine and a contract to salvage the machinery and equipment was executed. [**A.J. Industries v. United States,** 503 F.2d 660 (9th Cir. 1974)]

(a) Treatment as "sale or exchange" [§507]

Whether a loss that is triggered by abandonment or worthlessness will be treated as a "sale or exchange" for the purpose of determining whether it is a capital loss or an ordinary loss is a complex question. (*See infra,* §§896-910.)

(3) Finality of loss [§508]

If there is a closed and completed transaction, the fact that there is a remote possibility of recoupment does not prevent deductibility. [**United States v. White Dental,** 274 U.S. 398 (1927)—property seized during war; possibility of reparation after war immaterial to deductibility] However, a reasonable possibility of recoupment would delay deduction of the loss until the possibility is exhausted (*e.g.,* fire loss to building that might be covered by insurance; no deduction until the insurance dispute is finally resolved).

(4) Exchanges [§509]

For loss to be realized by reason of an exchange of property, the property received must "differ materially either in kind or in extent" from the property transferred. [Treas. Reg. §1.1001-1(a)] Thus an exchange of a pool of mortgages secured by land in City A for a pool of mortgages secured by land in City B is a realization because the two pools of mortgages "differ materially" despite the fact that they have the same total principal amount, interest rate, and fair market value. The rates of default, prepayments, etc., are bound to differ in the future. Thus, loss on the exchange can be deducted. [**Cottage Savings Association v. Commissioner,** 499 U.S. 554 (1991)—loss deductible despite tax avoidance motive for exchange]

(5) Exceptions [§510]

There are a few exceptions to the rule requiring realization:

(a) *Theft losses* are deductible in the year in which the taxpayer *discovers* the loss. [I.R.C. §165(e)]

(b) *Casualty losses* in a natural disaster (proclaimed by the President) can be deducted either in the year the disaster occurs or on the tax return for the prior year. If the return for the prior year has already been filed, the taxpayer can obtain a refund of the prior year's tax. [I.R.C. §165(i)]

(c) ***Declines in value in inventory*** may be deducted in the year they occur since the Code permits an annual valuation of inventory (when the FIFO method of inventory costing is used) (*see infra*, §§1047 *et seq.*). [**Thor Power Tool Co. v. Commissioner,** 439 U.S. 522 (1979)—inventories cannot be valued below market value even if they will ultimately be scrapped]

(d) ***In the case of stock or securities***, the year of loss is the year in which they become worthless, which requires an analysis of all the facts and circumstances. [**Boehm v. Commissioner,** 326 U.S. 287 (1945)]

d. Disallowed losses

(1) Losses between related taxpayers [§511]
I.R.C. sections 1041 and 267 disallow loss deductions on certain sales between related taxpayers.

(a) Spouses [§512]
Under section 1041, neither gain nor loss can be recognized on a transfer between spouses or between former spouses incident to divorce. (*See infra*, §816.)

(b) Related parties [§513]
Under section 267, no loss deduction is allowed on a sale or exchange *"directly or indirectly"* between related taxpayers, even if the sale was at arm's length and the price was fair. Of course, ***gain*** on such sales is taxable.

(c) Who are relatives? [§514]
Taxpayers within the following categories are deemed "related" within the meaning of section 267:

1) ***Family members***—limited to taxpayer's siblings, ancestors, and lineal descendants. [I.R.C. §267(c)(4)]

2) ***Individual and a corporation*** in which the individual owns ***50%*** or more in value of the outstanding shares. [I.R.C. §267(b)(2)]

3) ***Trustor and trustee*** of same trust. [I.R.C. §267(b)(4)]

4) ***Trustee and beneficiary*** of same trust; or trustee of one trust

and beneficiary of another trust having the same trustor. [I.R.C. §267(b)(6), (7)]

5) *Individual and tax-exempt entity* that the individual or his family controls. [I.R.C. §267(b)(9)]

(d) Indirect sales [§515]

The courts have broadly construed the phrase "directly or indirectly."

> **Example:** A husband sold certain shares on one day, and claimed a loss from that sale. His wife purchased similar shares the same day. The Court held that the series of transactions were "indirectly" sales between related taxpayers, and the losses were disallowed. [**McWilliams v. Commissioner,** 331 U.S. 694 (1947); *and see* **Merritt v. Commissioner,** 400 F.2d 417 (5th Cir. 1968)—husband's assets sold at *forced sale* and wife was buyer]

(e) Relief provision for disallowed losses [§516]

If a loss has been disallowed under section 267, and the *transferee* later sells the property at a gain, she can offset against that gain whatever amount of loss was previously denied to the *transferor*. The effect is that the tax benefit of the loss deduction is shifted from the transferor to the transferee, and deferred until she can sell the property at a gain. [I.R.C. §267(d)]

> **Example:** Doug sells his farm, in which he has a basis of $100,000, to his son Kevin for $75,000. Doug cannot claim a $25,000 loss—it is *disallowed*. A couple of years later, Kevin sells the farm to a real estate development company (in which he has no interest) for $115,000. Kevin's gain ordinarily would be $40,000 ($115,000 minus $75,000); however, Kevin can take advantage of the previously disallowed loss of $25,000—thus, his recognized gain is $15,000 ($40,000 minus $25,000).

(2) Losses from "wash sales" of securities [§517]

When a taxpayer sells stocks or securities and buys the same (or substantially identical) assets within 30 days before or after the sale, the transaction is dubbed a "wash sale" and, in effect, ignored. I.R.C. section 1091 expressly provides that losses from wash sales are not deductible. The basis of the repurchased stock is its cost plus the disallowed loss.

> **Example:** Five years ago, Wiley purchased 1,000 shares of Acme, Inc. for $50 per share (or $50,000 in total). Recently, due to an accounting scandal, the price of Acme's shares declined to $5 per share.

To offset other gains from the sale of stock, Wiley decided to sell all of his shares of Acme, thus tentatively realizing a loss of $45,000. Three days later, Wiley has a change of heart and buys 1,000 shares of Acme for $4 per share ($4,000 in total). Wiley does not realize any loss on the sale of stock, and the basis of the repurchased stock is adjusted to $49,000 ($4,000 plus the $45,000 disallowed loss).

(3) Sham transactions [§518]

Even if a transaction does not fall within sections 1041, 267, or 1091, it can still be disallowed if it was a "sham"; *i.e.*, despite the appearance that a sale occurred, in reality there was no real interruption of the taxpayer's beneficial ownership. [**Higgins v. Smith,** 308 U.S. 473 (1940)]

(4) Public policy [§519]

Although the *judicially created* public policy theory has been repudiated as to deductions of ordinary business expenses under I.R.C. section 162 (*see supra*, §424), deductions of losses under I.R.C. section 165 can be disallowed if the court finds that allowing the loss deduction would immediately and severely frustrate a clearly defined public policy. [**Mazzei v. Commissioner,** 61 T.C. 497 (1974)] Moreover, if allowing a deduction would violate a public policy as defined by I.R.C. section 162, the deduction probably would not be allowed under I.R.C. section 165. [**Stephens v. Commissioner,** *supra,* §431—restitution to embezzlement victim imposed as condition of probation would not be considered a fine under I.R.C. section 162(f); thus, allowing a deduction under I.R.C. section 165 would not frustrate a clearly defined public policy]

e.g. Example: Two men showed Taxpayer a black box that purportedly could copy money to produce counterfeit bills. They demonstrated the machine with a $10 bill, but explained to Taxpayer that they needed a number of $100 bills to make the process worthwhile. After several more demonstrations, Taxpayer provided the men with $20,000 in $100 bills and the men absconded with the money. On his tax return, Taxpayer claimed a loss deduction for the theft. The deduction was *not* allowed because allowing a deduction under these circumstances would frustrate the federal policy against counterfeiting. [**Mazzei v. Commissioner,** *supra*]

EXAM TIP	gilbert

For your exam, remember that although *judicially created* public policy exceptions no longer exist as to deductions of ordinary business expenses under I.R.C. section 162, there still are *statutory* public policy exceptions under I.R.C. section 162 that the deduction cannot violate.

6. Bad Debts

a. "Bad debt" defined [§520]

A "bad debt" arises when an obligation owed to the taxpayer becomes un-collectible. It is simply one kind of loss. Like a loss, a bad debt is the end of a transaction in which the taxpayer fails to recover his basis in an asset (the debt owing to him). However, the Code provides special rules concerning the deduction of bad debts.

b. Requirements for deductibility

(1) Bona fide debt [§521]

First of all, there must be a valid debt owing to the taxpayer arising from a *debtor-creditor relationship*. This requires a showing that the taxpayer (creditor) made a loan to the debtor with the expectation that it would be repaid.

(a) Family loans [§522]

Alleged "loans" to family members or relatives are always closely scrutinized to determine the bona fides of the indebtedness. [**Smyth v. Barneson,** 181 F.2d 143 (9th Cir. 1950)]

(b) Guaranty [§523]

The loss on a guaranty is treated as a bad debt, because the guarantor (through subrogation) becomes the creditor when he is forced to pay his principal's debt. If the principal is insolvent, the debt is "bad" and a deduction is available. [**Putnam v. Commissioner,** 352 U.S. 82 (1956)]

(2) Worthlessness [§524]

It must appear that the debt became unenforceable or uncollectible *during the tax year* for which the deduction is claimed.

(a) Proof of "worthlessness" [§525]

"Worthlessness" requires a showing that something has happened that puts an end to any realistic hope of repayment, *e.g.*, bankruptcy of debtor.

(b) Debt became worthless in prior year [§526]

When the taxpayer finds out in a subsequent year that the debt became worthless in a prior year, his remedy is to recompute his income for the prior year, taking the deduction, and file a *claim for refund*. He can do so up to seven years after the return is filed, rather than the usual three-year period. [I.R.C. §6511(d)(1)]

EXAM TIP　　　　　　　　　　　　　　　　**gilbert**

For your exam, be sure to remember that in order for a bad debt to be deductible, the taxpayer must be able to show **both** that the debt was **bona fide** and that the debt became **worthless** (*i.e.,* unenforceable or uncollectible). Also note that if the debt became worthless in the prior year, the taxpayer must file an amended return for the prior year in order to benefit from the loss.

(c) Partially secured debt [§527]

A taxpayer holding a partially secured debt can postpone the "worthlessness" of the unsecured part (if desired for greater tax saving in a later year) by putting off liquidating the collateral. Until the collateral is liquidated, the unpaid balance of the note cannot be determined. [**Loewi v. Ryan,** 229 F.2d 627 (2d Cir. 1956)]

c. Business and nonbusiness bad debts

(1) Business bad debts [§528]

Bad debts incurred in connection with the taxpayer's trade or business are fully deductible. [I.R.C. §166(a)]

(a) And note

In the case of business bad debts, a deduction may be taken for *"partial worthlessness"* in the year in which part, but not all, of the debt becomes uncollectible. [I.R.C. §166(a)(2)]

(2) Nonbusiness bad debts [§529]

Nonbusiness bad debts are deductible as *short-term capital losses*. [I.R.C. §166(d)] (*See infra*, §826.)

(a) Family and investment loans [§530]

A nonbusiness bad debt might arise from a loan to a friend or family member (assuming that it is shown to be a bona fide debt). It might also arise in connection with *investment activities* since these must be distinguished from an active trade or business.

(b) Loans to corporations [§531]

Shareholder loans to corporations are usually treated as nonbusiness bad debts. The reason is that the shareholder, in making the loan, is treated as an *investor* in the corporation; consequently, he is not in a trade or business and does not have a business bad debt. [**Whipple v. Commissioner,** *supra*, §300]

1) Exceptions [§532]

There are some exceptions to the above rule:

a) The *Whipple* rule does not apply when the lender to a corporation can show that he is really trying to **protect his job**. Serving as a corporate employee is a trade or business, while investing is not. However, to prevail on this point, the taxpayer must prove that his **primary purpose** in making the loan was to keep his job, rather than protecting his stock investment. [**United States v. Generes,** 405 U.S. 93 (1972)]

b) Another exception to *Whipple* is the situation in which the taxpayer's purpose in making the loan to the corporation was to **promote some other distinct business** in which the taxpayer was also engaged. [**Maloney v. Spencer,** 172 F.2d 638 (9th Cir. 1949)—loans from the taxpayer (who the court found was "engaged in the business of acquiring, owning, expanding, equipping, and leasing food processing plants") to three corporations (in which taxpayer was the sole shareholder and which leased their plants from taxpayer) were made to promote the corporations' food packing businesses]

c) Similarly, a taxpayer can circumvent *Whipple* by showing that he is **in the trade or business** of buying, reviving, and selling corporations at a profit. However, this would require more than proof of many stock trades; the taxpayer would have to establish that he is actually a "promoter" of business enterprises. [**United States v. Clark,** 358 F.2d 892 (1st Cir. 1966)]

d. Amount deductible

(1) Limited to basis [§533]

The basis of the debt in the taxpayer's hands is the amount deductible. If the taxpayer lends money, the amount loaned is the basis. If the taxpayer purchases the debt from a third party (*e.g.,* Dealer sells Buyer a car in exchange for a $3,000 promissory note; Taxpayer Bank purchases the note from Dealer for $2,750), the purchase price is the basis.

(2) Accounts receivable [§534]

Whether an uncollectible account receivable can be deducted as a bad debt depends on whether the taxpayer is on the cash or accrual basis. (*See infra,* §§958 *et seq.*) If the taxpayer is on the accrual basis, she has previously taken the debt into income; this gives it a basis in her hands. When it becomes uncollectible, she deducts the amount of the basis. But if she is on the cash basis, she did not take the receivable into income;

consequently, it has a zero basis in her hands and its uncollectibility gives rise to no deduction. [**Alsop v. Commissioner,** 290 F.2d 726 (2d Cir. 1961)]

(3) Child support [§535]

Suppose Husband owes $10,000 in child support to Wife but fails to pay. The obligation is uncollectible and Wife gives up trying to collect it. Can Wife take a bad debt deduction? Answer: No, because the debt has no basis in her hands—not even to the extent that she has expended funds in support of the child. [**Diez-Arguelles v. Commissioner,** 48 T.C.M. 496 (1984)] This result is questionable because child support, when received, is tax free to the recipient. [I.R.C. §71(c), *and see supra*, §169] If, for example, Wife sold the $10,000 obligation (before it became uncollectible) to a third party for $7,000, the $7,000 should not be taxed to Wife (since it substitutes for a payment that would have been tax free). This result suggests that Wife indeed has a $10,000 basis in the debt and should receive a bad debt deduction. Similarly, Husband should have debt cancellation income when Wife fails to collect the $10,000 from him.

e. Recovery of bad debts [§536]

Bad debts taken as a deduction, but subsequently recovered, must be included in gross income in the year of recovery.

(1) Tax benefit rule [§537]

However, if all or any portion of the prior bad-debt deduction did not result in a *tax benefit* to the taxpayer (*i.e.*, it did not result in a reduction of taxes), then she may exclude a portion of the recovery to the extent the previous bad-debt deduction failed to effect a tax benefit. [I.R.C. §111] (*See infra*, §§1079-1084.)

7. "At Risk" Limitation on Tax Shelter Deductions [§538]

The Code sharply limits the current deduction of operating losses from certain investments to the amount that the taxpayer has "at risk" in the investment. [I.R.C. §465(a)]

a. Definition of "at risk" [§539]

The term "at risk" means the amount of the taxpayer's investment in the property, not counting loans the taxpayer has *no personal liability* to repay (a "nonrecourse" loan). Recourse loans from other investors in the activity or from relatives also do not count. [I.R.C. §465(b); *and see* **Waddell v. Commissioner,** *supra*, §453—loan agreement was structured in such a way as to make taxpayer/borrower liable for an interest payment of only $1,500 per year (and taxpayer/borrower could convert this liability to a nonrecourse liability after seven years for a fee of $1,000), with 50% of net profit greater than $1,500 used to reduce the principal; taxpayer/borrower was therefore only at risk in the amount of his original investment]

(1) Exception

In the case of *real estate investments* only, a taxpayer is at risk with respect to a nonrecourse loan from a *"qualified lender"*—meaning a lender such as a bank or thrift institution that is not the seller of the property or an investor in the property.

b. Activities covered [§540]

Section 465 applies to all business or investment activities. [I.R.C. §465(c)]

c. Definition of operating losses [§541]

"Losses" under section 465 are the excess of deductions from the activity over income from the activity during the year.

Example: Gina invests in producing a movie, using $50,000 of her own money and borrowing $550,000 from a studio. Gina has no personal liability to repay this loan and she is not personally involved in the actual production process. Gina uses the whole $600,000 to make the movie. In the first year of distribution, the movie brings in income of $160,000. However, the deductions allocable to the movie (mainly depreciation) are $400,000. Ordinarily, all of the $400,000 would be deductible. But, because of section 465, the excess of deductions over income ($240,000) can be deducted only to the extent Gina is "at risk"—$50,000. Consequently, she can deduct only $50,000. The remaining $190,000 is not deductible until some later year when the amount "at risk" rises above zero.

---

d. Relation to passive loss [§542]

Note that the "at risk" rules and the "passive loss" rules (below) can overlap. The movie deal just described would also produce a passive loss, so that the loss could be offset only against passive income. In such situations, the "at risk" rules should be applied first, limiting the amount of available loss to $50,000. Then that $50,000 could be deducted, but only against Gina's passive income, if any.

8. Passive Losses [§543]

A person engaged in a "passive activity" (individually or as a partner) cannot deduct the losses from such activities except against *income from passive activities*. [I.R.C. §469] This provision is intended to destroy tax shelters.

a. Definition [§544]

A passive activity is a business in which the taxpayer does not *"materially participate."* To materially participate, the taxpayer must be involved on a "regular, continuous, and substantial" basis. A limited partner never materially participates. A general partner may or may not materially participate.

(1) Objective tests [§545]

A taxpayer's participation in an activity is material if the taxpayer participates for more than 500 hours in the year. Even if the taxpayer cannot meet the 500-hour test, her participation will be deemed material if she participates in the activity for at least 100 hours and her participation is not less than that of any other individual (including nonowners). Married taxpayers can combine the work of both spouses to meet these tests. [Treas. Reg. §1.469-5T(a)(1), (a)(3), (f)(3)] The Regulations set forth a number of other mechanical tests based on hours worked.

(2) All facts and circumstances [§546]

Even if a taxpayer cannot meet the mechanical tests above, her participation is material if, "based on all of the facts and circumstances," the taxpayer "participates in the activity on a regular, continuous, and substantial basis" during the year. [Treas. Reg. §1.469-5T(a)(7)] An individual's management activities cannot be taken into account under the "facts and circumstances" test unless no person (other than the taxpayer) receives compensation for management services and no individual provides management services that exceed those of the taxpayer. [Treas. Reg. §1.469-5T(b)(2)(ii)] This provision is designed to prevent passive investors in an activity from claiming that they were involved in management even though there is a paid manager.

EXAM TIP   **gilbert**

The passive activity rule is likely to show up on your exam. Be sure to remember that a taxpayer can deduct losses from passive activities **only against income from passive activities**. Remember also that what is "passive" is determined by three tests—(i) whether the taxpayer spent **more than 500 hours in a year** on the activity; (ii) whether the taxpayer spent **at least 100 hours in a year** on the activity, and the taxpayer's participation **was not less than that of any other individual;** or (iii) whether the taxpayer was involved in the activity **on a regular, continuous, and substantial basis**.

---

b. Disallowed loss [§547]

Passive loss that exceeds passive income in a given year is *carried forward* and can be used against passive income in future years. On a fully taxable disposition of an activity, all previously suspended passive losses from that activity are deductible.

 Example: Todd is a general partner in F Partnership, which owns a money-losing farm. Todd occasionally visits the farm and discusses its management with Farmer Brown, the other partner, who lives on the farm and manages it on a day-to-day basis. For Todd, the farm is a passive activity. For Farmer Brown, it is not a passive activity. Assume that Todd's share of the farm's loss is $20,000. Todd has income from his law practice and also has income of $30,000 from interest and dividends. Todd cannot currently deduct his share of the farm's loss. Neither income from an active business (law practice) nor income from investments (*e.g.*, interest and dividends) can be offset by passive losses. He can deduct the $20,000 only against future income from the

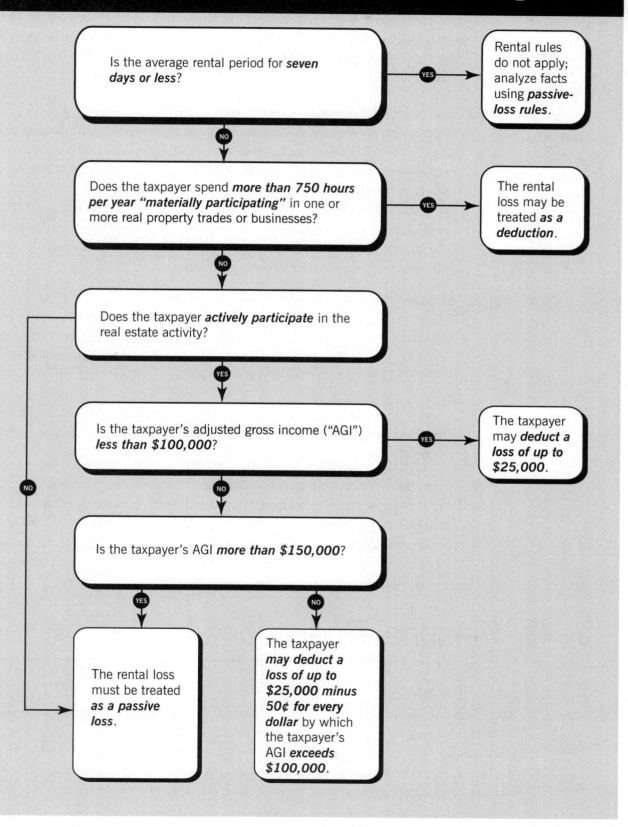

Is the average rental period for **seven days or less**?

YES → Rental rules do not apply; analyze facts using **passive-loss rules**.

NO ↓

Does the taxpayer spend **more than 750 hours per year "materially participating"** in one or more real property trades or businesses?

YES → The rental loss may be treated **as a deduction**.

NO ↓

Does the taxpayer **actively participate** in the real estate activity?

YES ↓

Is the taxpayer's adjusted gross income ("AGI") **less than $100,000**?

YES → The taxpayer may **deduct a loss of up to $25,000**.

NO ↓

Is the taxpayer's AGI **more than $150,000**?

YES ↓

The rental loss must be treated **as a passive loss**.

NO ↓

The taxpayer **may deduct a loss of up to $25,000 minus 50¢ for every dollar** by which the taxpayer's AGI **exceeds $100,000**.

farm (or other passive activity) or when the farm is sold in a taxable disposition. However, Farmer Brown can fully deduct his share of the farm's losses because it is not a passive activity for Farmer Brown.

c. Rentals [§548]

All rental activity is passive regardless of whether the taxpayer meets the material participation standard.

(1) Exception for moderate income lessors [§549]

A taxpayer (as individual or general partner) is allowed to deduct currently up to $25,000 in losses from real estate rental activity if the taxpayer *"actively participates"* (*e.g.*, by finding tenants, arranging for repairs, etc.). However, this exception applies only to taxpayers with adjusted gross income under $100,000. If adjusted gross income exceeds $100,000, the $25,000 figure is phased out at the rate of 50 cents for each dollar by which adjusted gross income exceeds $100,000. The exception for real property rental is not available to a limited partner.

(2) Exception for real estate professionals [§550]

Rental real estate can be excluded from the passive loss rules (and the losses are deductible in full) if the taxpayer spends more than 750 hours per year materially participating in one or more real property trades or businesses. A real property trade or business includes real property development, construction, acquisition, conversion, rental, management, or brokerage. The taxpayer's services in real property trades or businesses must be more than one-half of her total personal services rendered during the taxable year. [I.R.C. §469(c)(7)]

(3) Exception for short-term rentals [§551]

An activity is not treated as a "rental activity" if the average period of customer use is seven days or less. [Treas. Reg. §1.469-1T(e)(3)(ii); **Pohoski v. Commissioner**, T.C. Memo. 1998-17—average rental period for condo was less than seven days; owners materially participated in its management, making losses deductible under passive-loss rules]

C. Personal Deductions

1. Introduction [§552]

The Code specifies a limited number of items that are deductible even though they have no connection to business or investment. The rationale may be that certain items probably diminished the taxpayer's ability to pay taxes (*e.g.*, extraordinary medical expense or casualty loss), it was difficult to separate business and personal elements (*e.g.*, moving expense), or there is a desire to encourage certain kinds of behavior (*e.g.*, charitable contributions).

2. Definitions [§553]

A deduction is *either* from gross income or adjusted gross income ("AGI").

a. "Adjusted gross income" [§554]

AGI is defined as gross income less certain deductions. [I.R.C. §62]

(1) Deductions from gross income [§555]

The following deductions are *from gross income* (sometimes called "above the line"). All other deductions are *from AGI* (sometimes called "below the line").

(a) *Trade or business deductions* (except trade or business deductions of employees). [I.R.C. §62(a)(1)]

(b) *Reimbursed expenses of employees* (*e.g.*, travel and transportation expenses, union dues, etc.). The reimbursement is included in income, and the expense is deducted from gross income. [I.R.C. §62(a)(2)(A)] If the employee is required to account precisely for her reimbursed expenditures, however, she is permitted to exclude both the reimbursement from income and the expenditures from deductions. The reimbursed expenditure is simply dropped from the tax return entirely.

    1) The expenses of certain *"qualified performing artists"* are deductible from gross income. A "qualified performing artist" is a person who performed services in the performing arts for at least two employers during the year, who did not have AGI in excess of $16,000, and whose deductions exceeded 10% of gross income attributable to performance of such services. [I.R.C. §62(a)(2)(B), (b)]

    2) In legislation enacted in 2002, up to $250 of expenses of kindergarten, elementary, middle, and secondary school teachers incurred in 2002 or 2003 were deductible from gross income. This provision, which was designed to benefit teachers (as well as counselors, principals, and aides) who pay for classroom material out of their own pockets, was extended through 2005 in legislation enacted in 2004. [I.R.C. §62(a)(2)(D)] It remains to be seen whether this deduction will be extended for years beyond 2005.

(c) *Deduction for capital losses or other losses from the sale or exchange of property.* [I.R.C. §62(a)(3), (4)] Note that if such losses are capital, they may not be fully deductible. [I.R.C. §1211; *see infra*, §826]

(d) *Expenses deductible under I.R.C. section 212* applicable to rent and royalty income only. Other section 212 expenses (such as the cost of a safe deposit box to hold stock certificates) are deductible from AGI (*supra*, §437). [I.R.C. §62(a)(4)]

(e) *Alimony*. [I.R.C. §62(a)(10)]

(f) *Moving expenses* allowed by I.R.C. section 217 (*supra*, §325). [I.R.C. §62(a)(5)]

(g) *Interest on education loans* (*see infra* §§596-600). [I.R.C. §62(a)(17)]

(2) Significance of distinction [§556]

It is almost always preferable to have deductions from gross income ("above the line") than from AGI ("below the line") because:

(a) Below-the-line deductions must exceed standard deduction [§557]

If a taxpayer's below-the-line deductions are less than the standard deduction (*see infra*, §566), the taxpayer can use the standard deduction *and* claim above-the-line deductions. But to such a taxpayer, below-the-line deductions (except for personal exemptions—*see infra*, §§667 *et seq.*) are useless.

(b) Medical expenses [§558]

Medical expenses are deductible only to the extent that they exceed 7.5% of AGI (*see infra*, §§653, 665). Therefore, the lower the AGI is, the more medical expenses can be deducted.

(c) Child care credit [§559]

The child care credit is greater if AGI is lower (*see infra*, §§704-708).

(d) Distinguish—charitable contributions [§560]

Limitations on charitable contribution deductions are based on a percentage of AGI (*see infra*, §619). Thus, the higher AGI is, the more charitable contributions can be deducted. However, very few taxpayers encounter this limitation.

(e) Two percent floor and phaseout [§561]

As discussed in the next section, some below-the-line expenses are subject to a 2% floor. If an item is an above-the-line deduction, it cannot be subjected to the 2% floor. Moreover, some below-the-line deductions are phased out at the rate of 3% of the excess of AGI over a particular threshold (*infra*, §565). Thus, the higher the AGI, the greater the phaseout.

(3) Miscellaneous itemized deductions [§562]

Many, but not all, itemized deductions (*i.e.*, deductions from AGI) are subject to a 2% floor. Such items are deductible only to the extent that, in total, they exceed 2% of AGI. [I.R.C. §67]

(a) **Deductions not subject to the floor [§563]**

The more important itemized deductions that are *not* subject to the 2% floor are:

1) *Interest*;

2) *Taxes*;

3) *Casualty losses*;

4) *Charitable contributions*; and

5) *Medical expenses*.

(b) **Deductions subject to the floor [§564]**

This leaves many important below-the-line deductions subject to the 2% floor. For example, unreimbursed employee business expenses (*e.g.*, for union dues, transportation, travel, entertainment); the cost of preparing tax returns; and the costs of obtaining income from investments (other than rents or royalties).

---

e.g. **Example:** Tony's AGI is $100,000. His itemized deductions include qualified residence interest of $4,000, charitable contributions of $5,000, unreimbursed costs of working as an associate in a law firm (telephone, transportation, attending continuing education lectures) of $3,500, and the cost of $300 for having his tax return prepared. Tony can deduct his qualified residence interest and charitable contributions in full. However, the remaining $3,800 in itemized deductions are subject to the 2% floor. Two percent of his AGI is $2,000. Thus, only $1,800 of his unreimbursed employee business expenses and tax return preparation costs is deductible.

DEDUCTIONS—EXAMPLES **gilbert**

NOT SUBJECT TO THE 2% FLOOR	SUBJECT TO THE 2% FLOOR
• Interest	• Unreimbursed employee business expenses (for union dues, travel, entertainment, etc.)
• Taxes	
• Casualty losses	• Cost of preparing tax returns
• Charitable contributions	• Costs of obtaining income from investments (other than from rents or royalties)
• Medical expenses	

(4) Phaseout of itemized deductions [§565]

Itemized deductions are reduced by 3% of the excess of AGI over the applicable amount (adjusted for inflation to $150,500 for singles, and $75,250 for married filing separately, in 2006). [I.R.C. §68] However, no more than 80% of itemized deductions are wiped out by this provision.

(a) Exceptions

This provision does not apply to *medical expenses, investment interest, or casualty losses.* But it does apply, for example, to charitable deductions and qualified residence interest.

(b) Effect of other provisions

This provision is applied *after* all other deduction-limitation provisions, such as the 2% rule (*supra*, §§562, 564).

Example: Ed's AGI is $250,500 in 2006. His itemized deductions (exclusive of medical deductions, investment interest expense, and casualty losses) total $28,000. His AGI is $100,000 in excess of the applicable amount ($150,500). Thus, Ed's itemized deductions are reduced by 3% of $100,000, or $3,000. He can deduct only $25,000 instead of $28,000.

(c) Future phaseout

The provision reducing personal itemized deductions is scheduled to be phased out between 2006 and 2009 and eliminated in 2010. [I.R.C. §68(f)(2)]

b. Standard deduction [§566]

The standard deduction is a substitute for deducting below-the-line deductions. If a taxpayer's itemized deductions are less than the standard deduction, he simply takes the standard deduction instead. [I.R.C. §63]

(1) Amount of deduction [§567]

In 2006, the standard deduction is $10,300 on a joint return, $7,550 for a head of household, and $5,150 for singles and married persons filing separately. These amounts are adjusted for inflation. [I.R.C. §63(c)(4)]

(a) Reduction of the marriage penalty [§568]

The standard deduction for married taxpayers filing jointly and surviving spouses has been increased to twice the standard deduction for single filers. This provision is designed to reduce the so-called marriage penalty (*see supra*, §232). [I.R.C. §63(c)(2)(A)]

(2) Additional standard deduction for elderly and blind taxpayers [§569]

The Code provides an "additional standard deduction" for taxpayers who turn 65 years of age before year-end or who are blind. This additional deduction is adjusted for inflation—in 2006, the additional standard deduction is $1,250 for an unmarried taxpayer and $1,000 *per taxpayer* for a married taxpayer. These deductions are also cumulative—*i.e.*, a taxpayer may claim an additional standard deduction for being over age 65 *and* for being blind. [I.R.C. §63(c)(3), (f)]

e.g. **Example:** Tomas Taxpayer, who is 70 years old and blind, is married to Tina Taxpayer, who turned 65 during the tax year but who is not blind. The couple may claim an additional standard deduction of $3,000—$1,000 for Tomas being over 65, $1,000 for Tomas being blind, and $1,000 for Tina being over 65.

EXAM TIP **gilbert**

Note that there is a "marriage penalty" at work in the additional deductions for elderly and blind taxpayers. Two *unmarried* elderly taxpayers would be able to deduct $2,500, whereas two *married* elderly taxpayers would be able to deduct only $2,000.

---

(3) Dependents [§570]

If a taxpayer is claimed as a dependent on another's return, the dependent's standard deduction in 2006 is limited to the *greater* of $850 or $300 plus the individual's earned income. The $850 figure will be adjusted for future inflation. [I.R.C. §63(c)(5)]

(4) Effect of standard deduction [§571]

A taxpayer who does not itemize deductions from AGI, but takes advantage of the standard deduction instead, also receives the benefit of deductions *from gross income* and the deduction for personal exemptions. (*See infra,* §§667 *et seq.*)

3. Interest [§572]

Interest on personal debts (other than qualified residence interest and some student loan interest) is *not* deductible. Interest on investment or business debts is deductible, but with numerous limitations.

a. Requirements for deductibility

(1) Debt of taxpayer [§573]

The indebtedness must be owed by the taxpayer, not someone else. However, interest is deductible even though there is *no personal liability* on the loan. [Treas. Reg. §1.163-1(b)]

e.g. **Example:** Karen has a first and second mortgage on her house but has no personal liability on either one. She is in default in paying interest on the first mortgage. To prevent foreclosure of the first mortgage, Sam, the second mortgagee, pays the delinquent interest. The interest paid by Sam is probably deductible *by Karen* (on the theory that, in substance, Sam loaned the money to Karen and Karen paid it to the first mortgagee). Note that Karen receives this deduction even though she did not make the payment and was not personally liable to do so. [*See* Rev. Rul. 76-75, 1976-1 C.B. 14] Sam cannot deduct the payment, since he is not the debtor. Instead, he must add the payment to the basis for the debt owed to him by Karen.

(2) Bona fide debt [§574]

Courts disallow interest deductions in cases where the debt was a sham or the transaction lacked economic substance.

(a) Shams [§575]

If there was no real debt, interest payments are not deductible.

e.g. Example: Tess purports to purchase treasury notes with borrowed money. But the "lender" never had any money to loan and the notes are bought and resold the same day. Despite paperwork purporting to show a loan and an investment, the loan was nonexistent and the interest is not deductible. [**Goodstein v. Commissioner,** 267 F.2d 127 (1st Cir. 1959); Rev. Rul. 82-94, 1982-1 C.B. 31—purported loan from parent to child and immediate loan of same amount from child to parent]

(b) No economic substance [§576]

Even though the lender has money to loan, interest is not deductible if the transaction has no reasonable possibility of producing an economic gain or loss apart from the tax savings.

e.g. Example: Taxpayer buys a single-premium annuity policy from Insco (a reputable insurance company), but borrows both the premiums due on the policy and the increasing cash value of the policy from Insco each year. As a result, the annuity ultimately payable will be a mere pittance. Moreover, the interest rate on the loans from Insco is more than the interest rate at which the policy gains in value. Consequently, there is no "substance" to the transaction because it does not affect Taxpayer's "beneficial interest" (except taxwise), and the interest is not deductible. [**Knetsch v. United States,** 364 U.S. 361 (1960); **Winn-Dixie Stores, Inc. v. Commissioner,** 254 F.3d 1313 (11th Cir. 2001)]

1) Enactment of I.R.C. section 264 [§577]

Today, the interest deduction in the above example would be barred by I.R.C. section 264 (*see infra*, §603). However, the Court refused to interpret the later enactment of I.R.C. section

264 as implied approval of single-premium annuity schemes entered into before its effective date. [**Knetsch v. United States**, *supra*]

2) Application when property worth less than debt [§578]

When property is purchased with a nonpersonal liability loan, and the property is worth less than the amount of the loan, the debtor probably cannot take an interest deduction on any part of the loan. However, some authority indicates that interest may be deductible on that portion of the loan that equals the value of the property. The theory for denial of any deduction is similar to that of *Knetsch; i.e.*, the transaction lacks economic substance. [**Estate of Franklin v. Commissioner**, *supra*, §453—deduction disallowed; *compare* **Pleasant Summit Land Corp. v. Commissioner**, 863 F.2d 263 (3d Cir. 1988), *cert. denied sub nom.*, **C.I.R. v. Prussin**, 493 U.S. 901 (1989)—loan treated as valid to extent of value of property]

(c) Business purpose [§579]

Even if the debt is not a sham, and there is a definite possibility of gain or loss, interest is not deductible unless the taxpayer had *some purpose other than tax saving* in incurring the debt. Mixed motives (*i.e.*, tax saving plus some other economic purpose) would be sufficient. [**Goldstein v. Commissioner**, 364 F.2d 734 (2d Cir.), *cert. denied*, 385 U.S. 1005 (1966)]

1) Rationale

I.R.C. section 163 was intended to equalize the positions of people who borrow and people who use their own capital to enter into transactions having some economic purpose—not to induce transactions that lack any such purpose.

Example: Taxpayer won $140,000 in the Irish Sweepstakes. She then borrowed $1 million from a bank at 4% interest to purchase a like amount of Treasury notes bearing interest of 2%. Although gains or losses on this transaction were possible, because the price of the notes could fluctuate, Taxpayer was not concerned with anything but tax saving; hence, no deduction was allowed. [**Goldstein v. Commissioner**, *supra*]

---

2) Note—current rule

Both *Knetsch* and *Goldstein* involved attempts to write off large amounts of *prepaid* interest. As discussed *infra*, §605, immediate deduction is no longer allowed for prepaid interest, regardless of the bona fides of the indebtedness.

3) "Generic tax shelters" [§580]

The theories of *Knetsch* and *Goldstein* (*i.e.*, no economic substance and requirement of business purpose) were the basis for the concept of the "generic tax shelter" described in *Rose* (*supra*, §454). *Rose* describes a class of heavily tax-motivated "investments," lacking in any economic substance, that do not give rise to tax deductions.

(d) Family loans [§581]

While interest on a debt owed to a family member or relative is not *per se* disallowed as a deduction, courts scrutinize such transactions carefully to make sure there is a bona fide debt, *i.e.*, a contract backed by consideration and an expectation of repayment. [*See* **Brown v. Commissioner,** 241 F.2d 827 (8th Cir. 1957)]

(e) Loans to controlled corporation [§582]

A corporation can deduct interest paid, even where the lender is the controlling shareholder. But if the "loan" is reclassified as "equity," the "interest" payments are **constructive dividends** to the shareholder. (This problem is fully discussed in the Taxation of Business Entities Summary.)

b. Identifying interest [§583]

Payments for the *use* of borrowed money are interest and deductible as such. But payments for the lender's *services* are *not* interest.

(1) Service charges [§584]

Lenders frequently charge a fee for such services as appraisal of the collateral or investigation of the debtor's credit. Such charges are not deductible as interest. [Rev. Rul. 67-297, 1967-2 C.B. 87] However, a business or investment borrower could capitalize such charges as part of the cost of obtaining the loan and amortize them over the period the loan is outstanding. [**Lovejoy v. Commissioner,** 18 B.T.A. 1179 (1930)]

(2) "Points" [§585]

Many lenders charge "points," *i.e.*, additional amounts paid when the loan is obtained. These constitute additional interest. [Rev. Rul. 69-188, 1969-1 C.B. 54] (*See infra*, §606, for discussion of timing of the deduction for "points.")

(3) Imputed interest [§586]

In several situations, interest income and deductions are "imputed." That means that the borrower is treated as having paid interest, and the lender has interest income even though the contract called for no interest or for a lesser rate of interest.

(a) Loans [§587]

If a loan agreement calls for interest below the "applicable federal rate" (as periodically established by the IRS), interest is imputed. [I.R.C. §7872—*see supra*, §§239 *et seq.*] This provision applies especially to gift loans, to employer-employee loans, and to corporate-shareholder loans.

(b) Sales of property [§588]

If there is a sale of property in exchange for deferred payments, and the agreement calls for interest that is less than the applicable federal rate, interest is imputed. [I.R.C. §§483, 1274—*see infra*, §§923 *et seq.*]

(4) Tracing [§589]

Because some types of interest (*e.g.*, trade or business interest) are deductible, some types are not deductible (*e.g.*, personal loans), and some types may or may not be deductible (*e.g.*, interest on a loan incurred to purchase a passive activity), it is necessary to trace borrowed money into its actual use. A taxpayer who borrows money and commingles it with other funds in a single bank account and then uses the loan proceeds for various purposes may encounter serious difficulty in meeting her burden of proof as to how the borrowed funds were used. Separate bank accounts for each different use of the borrowed funds would be a good idea. [*See* Treas. Reg. §1.163-8T—stating general rule that debt proceeds are spent before any unborrowed amounts and before any later deposits into the account]

c. Exceptions—interest disallowed [§590]

In several situations, interest deductions are disallowed by statute.

(1) Personal interest [§591]

Generally, no deduction is allowed for interest incurred on debts arising out of the taxpayer's personal life. This includes interest other than interest incurred on debt arising out of a trade or business, an investment, or a passive activity (*see supra*, §543). Thus interest payments on credit card loans or personal car loans are not deductible. However, interest on certain education loans and qualified residence interest are deductible even though these arise out of personal life.

(a) Exception—qualified residence loans [§592]

A taxpayer can deduct interest on a loan *secured* by a qualified residence if it is either acquisition indebtedness or home equity indebtedness. [I.R.C. §163(h)(3), (4)]

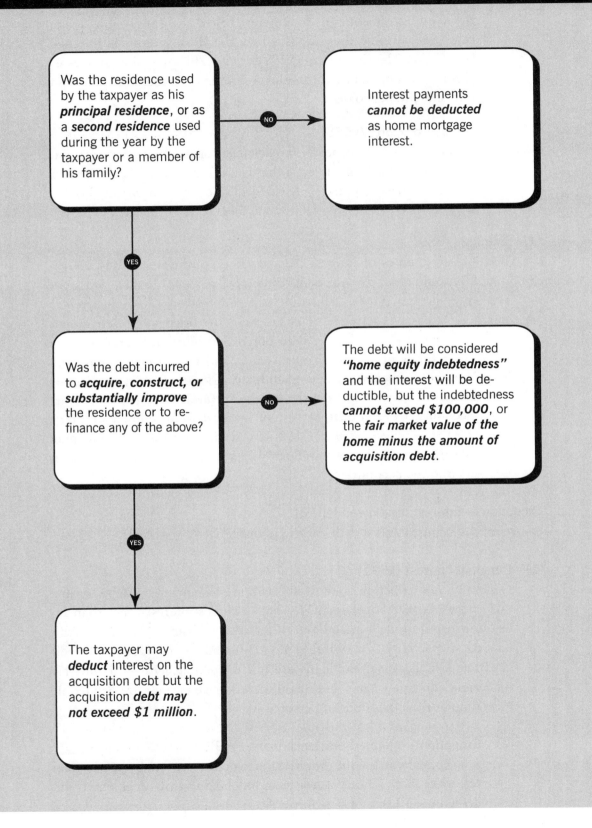

Was the residence used by the taxpayer as his *principal residence*, or as a *second residence* used during the year by the taxpayer or a member of his family?

NO → Interest payments *cannot be deducted* as home mortgage interest.

YES

Was the debt incurred to *acquire, construct, or substantially improve* the residence or to refinance any of the above?

NO → The debt will be considered *"home equity indebtedness"* and the interest will be deductible, but the indebtedness *cannot exceed $100,000*, or the *fair market value of the home minus the amount of acquisition debt*.

YES

The taxpayer may *deduct* interest on the acquisition debt but the acquisition *debt may not exceed $1 million*.

1) Acquisition indebtedness [§593]

"Acquisition indebtedness" is debt incurred to acquire, construct, or substantially improve a qualified residence. However, the aggregate amount of acquisition debt cannot exceed $1 million. If a taxpayer refinances an acquisition debt, the refinanced debt remains acquisition debt—but only to the extent of the amount of the original acquisition debt. [I.R.C. §163(h)(3)(B)]

2) Home equity indebtedness [§594]

"Home equity indebtedness" means any debt (other than acquisition debt) secured by a qualified residence. However, home equity indebtedness cannot exceed $100,000. Also, it cannot exceed the fair market value of the residence reduced by the amount of acquisition debt on the residence. [I.R.C. §163(h)(4)(C)]

3) Qualified residence [§595]

A "qualified residence" is either the taxpayer's principal residence or a second residence used during the year by a taxpayer or a member of the taxpayer's family as a residence. [I.R.C. §§163(h)(4)(A), 280A(d)(1); *see supra*, §358]

(b) Exception—interest on education loans [§596]

A taxpayer can deduct interest on qualified education loans but the amount of interest that can be deducted is quite limited. In addition, the ability to deduct education loans is phased out as income rises. [I.R.C. §221]

1) Amount deductible [§597]

The amount of education interest that can be deducted is $2,500. This figure is *not* indexed for inflation.

2) Income phaseout [§598]

If AGI exceeds $50,000 ($105,000 on a joint return), the amount deductible is phased out. Interest becomes completely nondeductible if AGI equals or exceeds $65,000 ($135,000 on a joint return). These phaseout levels will be adjusted for inflation.

3) Definitions [§599]

A qualified education loan is a debt incurred to pay higher education expenses incurred on behalf of the taxpayer, the taxpayer's spouse, or any dependent of the taxpayer. The student must be a degree candidate and carrying at least half the normal load. The taxpayer claiming the deduction may not be claimed as the dependent of another taxpayer. The creditor cannot be a party related to the borrower (*e.g.*, the student's grandmother).

4) Above the line [§600]

The deduction for interest on education loans is "above the line," meaning that it is a deduction from gross income. [I.R.C. §62(a)(17)] As a result, a student who pays interest on an education loan receives a tax benefit even if the student takes the standard deduction.

EXAM TIP   **gilbert**

For your exam, remember the only two instances where a taxpayer may deduct personal interest are *interest on a qualified residence* and *student loan interest*. *But note:* The interest on a qualified residence is *below the line*, while student loan interest is *above the line*.

---

(2) Expenses allocable to exempt income [§601]

The Code disallows any expense, including interest or attorneys' fees, attributable to producing income (other than interest income) that is tax-exempt. [I.R.C. §265(a)(1)] *Rationale:* Allowing such deductions would give an unwarranted double tax benefit.

Example: Because personal injury damages are excludible from income [I.R.C. §104(a)(2), discussed *supra*, §§89-99], the attorneys' fees incurred in recovering such damages cannot be deducted. However, if a lawsuit resulted in the recovery of damages that were partly taxable and partly nontaxable, a pro rata portion of the attorneys' fees would be deductible. [**Church v. Commissioner,** 80 T.C. 1104 (1983)]

---

(3) Tax-exempt interest [§602]

Interest on debts incurred to purchase or carry tax-exempt state and municipal bonds cannot be deducted. [I.R.C. §265(a)(2)]

(a) Note

It is not enough that the taxpayer simply borrows money at the same time he owns tax-exempt bonds—some "purposive connection" between the two is required. But the case law is quite strict in finding such connections. [**Wisconsin Cheeseman v. United States,** 388 F.2d 420 (7th Cir. 1968)]

(b) Connection

A "connection" between the debt and the tax-exempt bonds is obvious if the taxpayer either uses the proceeds to buy the bond or uses the bond as security for the debt. A borrowing in connection with an active business would not usually be connected to a tax-exempt bond that the taxpayer also owns (unless the borrowing was in excess of business needs). However, if a taxpayer borrows money, owns portfolio investments (*i.e.*, stock and taxable bonds), and also owns tax-exempt bonds, the IRS will disallow the interest because the taxpayer could have sold the portfolio investments to raise money to purchase or carry the tax-exempt bonds, rather than borrowing the money. [Rev. Proc. 72-18, 1972-1 C.B. 740]

(4) Loans to purchase insurance [§603]

No interest deduction is allowed on a debt incurred to buy "single-premium" life insurance, endowment, or annuity contracts (including those in which substantially all premiums are paid within four years). Similarly, an interest deduction is disallowed on loans made as part of a *systematic plan* of financing insurance premiums (generally by borrowing against increases in cash values under the policy). [I.R.C. §264(a)(2), (3)]

(a) Rationale

Since the interest element in life insurance is not taxed (*i.e.*, it becomes part of the tax-exempt life insurance proceeds payable at death), it is not fair for the interest incurred to purchase the insurance to be deductible.

(b) Exceptions

The disallowance rule of section 264(a)(3) does not apply if no part of four of the first seven premiums is borrowed. Also, it does not apply if the amount disallowed would be less than $100, if the borrowing occurred because of unforeseen financial problems, or if the borrowing was incurred in connection with trade or business. [I.R.C. §264(c)]

(5) Accrued interest owed to "related" cash basis taxpayer [§604]

Also nondeductible until paid is unpaid interest (or any other deductible expense) owed by a debtor on the *accrual basis* to a creditor on the *cash basis* who is *related* to or *controlled* by the debtor (*see infra*, §§1044 *et seq.*).

(6) Prepaid interest [§605]

Prepaid interest is not immediately deductible. It must be capitalized and deducted in the years the underlying loan is outstanding. [*See* I.R.C. §461(g)]

(a) Exception—"points" [§606]

Payment of "points" incurred to purchase the taxpayer's *principal residence* is immediately deductible if the payment of points is an established business practice in the area and the amount does not exceed that generally charged. [I.R.C. §461(g)(2)] *But note:* Points paid on refinancing a home are not immediately deductible. They must be deducted over the years the loan is outstanding.

(7) Excess investment interest [§607]

To further discourage uneconomic, tax-motivated transactions, if interest deductions on investments exceed the net investment income, the excess is *disallowed*. [I.R.C. §163(d)] But disallowed interest can be *carried forward* and deducted against investment income in future years.

(a) "Net investment income" [§608]

"Net investment income" is gross income from the investment, less all expenses directly connected to the investment, including depreciation at *straight-line* rates (*see supra*, §467). Dividends are not included in investment income if the taxpayer elects to have them taxed as a capital gain. (*See infra*, §822.) However, if the taxpayer chooses to forgo capital gain treatment for the dividends, they will be treated as investment income. [I.R.C. §§1(h)(11)(D)(i), 163(d)(4)(B)]

(b) Additional exception for corporations [§609]

A limitation, applicable to *corporate* taxpayers, disallows interest deductions in excess of $5 million on certain debts convertible into stock incurred in connection with corporate acquisitions. [I.R.C. §279]

(8) Passive activity [§610]

As noted above, losses on passive activities are not deductible in excess of income from such activities. [I.R.C. §469; *see supra*, §543] A large part of passive loss that is disallowed under this provision consists of interest incurred to purchase or to operate the passive activity.

4. Taxes [§611]

A tax may be either deductible as such, deductible only as a business or investment expense, or not deductible at all.

a. Taxes deductible as such [§612]

Every taxpayer is entitled to deduct *state and local* real or personal property taxes and state and local income taxes. [I.R.C. §164]

(1) Deduction of property taxes as between purchaser and seller [§613]

The portion of the property tax allocable to that part of the year *preceding* the date of the sale is considered imposed on the seller and she is entitled to a deduction in that amount. The balance is considered imposed on the buyer. [I.R.C. §164(d)]

(2) Disability insurance tax [§614]

A state payroll tax, used to finance a state disability insurance fund, is considered an income tax. Consequently, it is deductible as a tax. [**Trujillo v. Commissioner,** 68 T.C. 670 (1977)]

(3) Deduction of general sales tax in lieu of state income tax [§615]

Under legislation enacted in 2004, taxpayers may elect to take an itemized deduction for state and local general sales taxes in lieu of such a deduction for state and local income taxes. [I.R.C. §164(b)(5)] This is particularly valuable in states that impose sales taxes but not income taxes (Alaska, Florida, Nevada, South Dakota, Texas, Washington, and Wyoming). The election expired as of January 1, 2006, but legislation has been introduced to extend the deduction for future years.

b. Taxes deductible only as business or investment expense [§616]

A taxpayer engaged in trade or business, or holding property for the production of income, is entitled to deduct, *in addition* to the taxes enumerated in the previous paragraphs, all other taxes incurred *in connection with his business* or his property held for income production. [I.R.C. §§162(a), 212] For example, excise tax, federal import duties, federal Social Security tax on employers, state sales tax, and gasoline taxes may be deducted.

c. Taxes entirely nondeductible [§617]

Certain taxes are not deductible under any circumstances: federal income taxes, Social Security tax imposed on employees, excess profits taxes, federal estate and gift taxes, and state and local inheritance taxes. [*See* I.R.C. §§275, 164(b)]

5. Charitable Contributions [§618]

Taxpayers may deduct contributions to *recognized* charities—basically, to the *government* or any entity organized and operated *predominantly* for *charitable, religious, scientific, literary, or educational purposes.* [*See* I.R.C. §170(c)] No deductions are allowable for contributions to educational institutions practicing racial discrimination. [**Bob Jones University v. United States,** *supra,* §175]

a. Limitations

(1) Individuals [§619]

Individual taxpayers are entitled to deduct up to 50% of their *adjusted gross income* (*see supra,* §554) for gifts to most charities. [I.R.C. §170(b)(1)] Gifts to "nonoperating" private foundations and gifts of appreciated capital assets are subject to a 30% ceiling.

(a) Carryover

However, if an individual's contributions exceed the 50% or 30% ceiling, she can carry over and deduct the excess in the five succeeding taxable years. [I.R.C. §170(d)]

(2) Corporations [§620]

Corporations can deduct gifts only up to *10%* of their taxable income (although again contributions in excess of that amount can be carried over to the next five years). [I.R.C. §170(b)(2)]

(3) Estates and trusts [§621]

There is no limit on the amount an estate or trust may deduct for charitable contributions. [I.R.C. §642(c)]

(4) Recipient [§622]

The gift must be "to or for the use of" a recognized charity. The term "for the use of" means in trust for the charity. [**Davis v. United States,** 495 U.S. 472 (1990)—no deduction for parent's payment of child's expenses as a Mormon missionary since the transfer was not to the church or a trust for the church]

(5) Substantiation [§623]

All charitable gifts of $250 or more must be substantiated by a contemporaneous written acknowledgment from the donee organization. The donee organization must also state whether it provided any goods or services in consideration for any gift, and it must describe and value such goods or services. The value of such goods and services is *not* deductible and must be subtracted from the value of the donation. If the goods or services consist solely of intangible religious benefits, there must be a statement to that effect. [I.R.C. §170(f)(8); *and see infra,* §638—additional appraisal requirement]

b. Gifts in kind [§624]

A taxpayer may deduct the *fair market value* of contributions of property. [**Campbell v. Prothro,** 209 F.2d 331 (5th Cir. 1954)] Thus, for example, a taxpayer may deduct the value (not the basis) of stocks donated to a charity. However, there are several important *limitations* to consider where property, rather than cash, is donated.

(1) Fractional and future interests

(a) Residence or farm [§625]

Gifts of a fractional or future interest in the donor's *personal residence or farm* are deductible in the amount of the value of the interest at the time of the gift, taking into account depreciation and depletion of such property by reason of the donor's continued use of the property. [I.R.C. §170(f)(3)]

***

e.g. Example: Martha conveys her farm to United Way, reserving a life estate for herself. The farm is currently worth $100,000. Martha can deduct the $100,000, minus the cost of depreciation and depletion of the farm over her lifetime, and subject to the limitation based on her adjusted gross income (*see supra*, §619).

(b) Other real property and gifts to trusts [§626]

Gifts of *remainder* interests in *real property* (other than a personal residence or farm) or gifts to a *trust* (*e.g.*, "to B for life, remainder to Benevolent Charity") are deductible only if made in the form of a "*fixed annuity trust*" (which pays no more than a fixed dollar amount to the income beneficiary), a "*unitrust*" (which pays the beneficiary a fixed percentage of the value of the property), or a "*pooled income fund*" (a fund contributed to by many donors). (*See* detailed rules in I.R.C. section 170(f)(2) and discussion in the Estate and Gift Tax Summary.)

(c) Tangible personal property [§627]

A gift of a *future* interest in tangible personal property is *not* deductible at all when made. It becomes deductible only when the charity's interest becomes *possessory*. [I.R.C. §170(a)(3)]

e.g. **Example:** Paul has a valuable painting, an original "Dogs Playing Cards," which he gives to an art museum, reserving a life estate. He is allowed no current deduction. When Paul dies, either he (on his final return) or his estate will get the deduction.

(d) Income trusts [§628]

A deduction is also not allowed for a charitable gift of an *income* interest in a trust or other property, unless the income remains *taxable* to the donor (*see supra*, §§253-276), and the income interest is in the form of either a fixed annuity or a fixed percentage of the value of the property determined annually. [I.R.C. §170(f)(2)(B)]

(2) Gifts of appreciated property [§629]

Prior to 1969, a deduction was allowed for the *fair market value* of *any* property gifted to charity (rather than its cost to the taxpayer). This encouraged taxpayers to make gifts of appreciated property because they could *deduct* the present value of the property without realizing the gain or loss they would otherwise incur if they sold the property and donated the proceeds.

(a) Code provision limits former rule [§630]

This is still permitted when the donated property would (if sold) produce a *long-term capital gain*, *and* it is donated to a *public* charity. However, the amount of the deduction is limited to *30%* of the donor's AGI (instead of the regular *50%*). [I.R.C. §170(b)(1)(D)]

Example: Teri owns stock that cost her $2,000 when she bought it three years ago, but is now worth $10,000. Her adjusted gross income is $35,000. If she gives it to a public charity, she can deduct the full $10,000—the $8,000 long-term capital gain goes untaxed.

(b) Deduction reduced further in three situations [§631]

Even if the property would have produced long-term capital gain, the amount deductible is reduced by *the amount of that gain* in the following cases:

1) Private foundation [§632]

When the gift is to a private foundation (*i.e.*, a charity supported by only one or a few donors), the amount deductible is reduced by the amount of appreciation. However, this limitation does not apply if the foundation is an *operating foundation*— meaning it is directly engaged in doing charitable work as opposed to merely funneling money to other charities. [*See* I.R.C. §170(e)(1)(B)(i)] The limitation also does not apply to gifts of corporate stock for which market quotations are readily available. [I.R.C. §170(e)(5)]

2) Unrelated tangible personal property [§633]

When the gift is of tangible personal property unrelated to the charity's charitable purpose or function, the deduction is reduced by the amount of potential gain. [I.R.C. §170(e)(1)(B)(ii)]

Example: Paul's valuable painting (worth $10,000 and having a basis of $7,000) is given to an art museum. The *entire* $10,000 could be deducted because the painting is *related* to the charitable function.

Compare: If Paul instead gives the painting to a public charity that *operates a medical research clinic*, the amount deducted must be reduced by the amount by which the value exceeds Paul's basis (*i.e.*, only $7,000 could be deducted— $10,000 reduced by $3,000).

3) Patents, copyrights, and other intellectual property [§634]

When the gift is of a patent, copyright (other than self-created copyrights), trademark, trade name, trade secret, know-how, certain software, or similar property, or applications or registration of such property, the deduction is reduced by the long-term capital gain appreciation of such property. [I.R.C. §170(e)(1)(B)(iii)]

(c) Gifts that would not produce long-term capital gain [§635]

If the donated property would, if sold, produce short-term capital gain or *ordinary income*, then the amount deductible is reduced by the amount that would not have been long-term capital gain if the property had been sold. The effect of this reduction is generally that only the *amount of the donor's basis* is deductible—and *not* its higher fair market value. [I.R.C. §170(e)(1)(A)] This rule applies regardless of whether the donee charity is public or private, and it applies both to individual and corporate donors.

1) Application

Thus, charitable gifts of all noncapital assets (*e.g.*, farm products or inventories), or capital assets held for one year or less, are deductible only at the donor's basis.

---

e.g. Example: An artist donates her painting to a museum. Her basis is $100 and the value is $10,000. If the painting were sold, it would produce $9,900 of ordinary income. Only $100 is deductible (*i.e.*, $10,000 less $9,900).

---

2) Recapture of depreciation [§636]

If depreciation would have been recaptured had the property been sold (*see infra*, §§933-938), the amount deductible must be reduced by the amount that would have been ordinary income because of recapture.

3) Exception—certain contributions of inventory or equipment [§637]

A deduction is allowed to corporate donors for an amount in excess of basis for gifts of inventory to a public charity to be used solely for the care of the ill, the needy, or infants; however, the charity cannot resell the property. The amount deductible is the value of the inventory, less 50% of the amount of ordinary income that would have been realized if it had been sold. In addition, the deduction cannot exceed twice the donor's basis. A similar provision allows deductions for gifts of scientific equipment to educational institutions. [I.R.C. §170(e)(3), (4)]

(3) Property description and qualified appraisals [§638]

Taxpayers must submit property descriptions for contributions of more than $500 and qualified appraisals (as determined by the Secretary of the Treasury) for contributions of more than $5,000. This rule does not apply in the case of readily valued property such as publicly traded stock or securities. [I.R.C. §170(f)(11)]

(4) Contributions of used cars, boats, and airplanes [§639]

In the case of a contribution of a used car, boat, or airplane with a value in excess of $500, the taxpayer must receive a contemporaneous written acknowledgment that contains the vehicle identification number. If the charity subsequently sells the vehicle without any significant intervening use or material improvement, the taxpayer's deduction is limited to the amount of the gross proceeds from the sale. [I.R.C. §170(f)(12)]

c. Bargain sales [§640]

When a taxpayer *sells* property to a charity for a price *below* fair market value, the difference (the bargain element) is deductible as a charitable contribution.

(1) Calculation of gain [§641]

The transaction is treated as part sale and part gift, and the bargain seller is required to *apportion his basis* between the gift part and the sale part. This will increase the gain recognized by the donor. [I.R.C. §170(e)(2)]

Example: Teri sells shares of stock (held for more than one year) to a public charity at her cost ($12,000) although the stock is presently worth $20,000. Teri is entitled to an $8,000 charitable contribution deduction. But her basis in the stock at time of sale is deemed to be only 12/20th of cost—*i.e.*, $7,200 instead of $12,000—so that she realizes a $4,800 gain. Of course, if she sold the stock on the open market and donated the proceeds of the sale to the charity, she would have a $20,000 charitable contribution deduction and an $8,000 gain.

---

d. Contribution of services or use of property [§642]

There is no deduction allowed for a contribution of the taxpayer's services or use of his property.

(1) Personal services [§643]

The value of personal services donated to a charity (*e.g.*, movie star entertains at a charity ball) is not deductible by the donor. [Treas. Reg. §1.170A-1(g)] Similarly, the IRS has ruled that a blood donation is not deductible because it is analogous to a transfer of services. [Rev. Rul. 53-162, 1953-2 C.B. 127]

(a) Distinguish—out-of-pocket expenses [§644]

The taxpayer-donor *can* deduct any out-of-pocket expenses incurred in rendering services (*e.g.*, transportation costs). [Treas. Reg. §1.170A-1(g)]

1) Automobile expenses [§645]

A taxpayer who uses her own car to render services to a charity can deduct 14 cents per mile. [I.R.C. §170(i)] In addition, the taxpayer can deduct out-of-pocket costs, such as parking, but not general repair expenses or depreciation on her car.

2) Only taxpayer's own expenses [§646]

A taxpayer can deduct the expenses only of *her own* service to charity, not the costs of a third party's service. [**Davis v. United States**, *supra*, §622—parent cannot deduct child's outlays while serving as Mormon missionary]

(2) Use of property [§647]

Likewise, a taxpayer who donates to a charity the use of his property (*e.g.*, free rent in his office building) cannot take a charitable deduction for the value of such use. [I.R.C. §170(f)(3)]

e. No deduction if taxpayer benefits [§648]

Contributions made with the anticipation of economic benefit rather than from "detached and disinterested generosity" are not deductible as charitable contributions. [**Winters v. Commissioner**, 468 F.2d 778 (2d Cir. 1972)]

Example: A church operated a school that charged no tuition. The parents of the students, however, were encouraged to contribute to the school, and realized that they had to do so in order to keep the school operating. Under these circumstances, no deduction was available; payments were treated as costs of education from which an economic benefit was anticipated. [**Winters v. Commissioner**, *supra*]

Example: The Church of Scientology requires payment of a fixed amount for "auditing" sessions. The Church regards auditing as a religious experience designed to promote spiritual awareness. Because the taxpayer was required to pay for an identifiable benefit, the payment is not deductible. Denial of a deduction did not violate either the Establishment Clause or Free Exercise Clause of the Constitution. [**Hernandez v. Commissioner**, 490 U.S. 680 (1989)] In a similar case, the Ninth Circuit rejected an argument by Orthodox Jews that the portion of their private school yeshiva tuition attributable to religious education should be deductible, noting that a requirement that the IRS conduct an inquiry into the proportion of the school day that was religious rather than secular would risk violating the Establishment Clause. [**Sklar v. Commissioner**, 282 F.3d 310 (9th Cir. 2002)]

Example: Corporation donates part of a large parcel of land to build a school. However, it expected that the school district would build a road that would make Corporation's remaining property much more valuable. The deduction was denied because the taxpayer will extract a benefit greater than that which would inure to the general public. [**Ottawa Silica Co. v. United States,** 699 F.2d 1124 (Fed. Cir. 1983)]

(1) Right to purchase season tickets with donation to college or university [§649]

If a taxpayer makes a contribution to a college or university, and the contribution entitles her to purchase season tickets to athletic events, 80% of the contribution is deductible. Of course, the actual cost of the tickets is not deductible. [I.R.C. §170(l)]

Example: Bluto Blutarsky contributes $1,000 to Faber College, which entitles Bluto to purchase season football and basketball tickets for $750. Bluto may deduct 80% of the $1,000 contribution ($800), but he may not deduct the season ticket costs of $750.

(2) Part gift, part purchase [§650]

If a taxpayer intentionally purchases property or services from a charity at a price in excess of value, the difference qualifies as a charitable contribution. [**United States v. American Bar Endowment,** *supra*, §176]

Example: The American Bar Association ("ABA") offers to sell life insurance to lawyers at a price exceeding the market value of the insurance. If the lawyer can prove (i) the difference between the amount she pays and the market value, *and* (ii) that she knew about the difference and intended to make a gift to the ABA, she can deduct the difference as a charitable contribution. [**United States v. American Bar Endowment,** *supra*]

(a) Disclosure requirement [§651]

A payment made partly as a contribution and partly in consideration for goods or services provided by the charity to the donee is known as "a quid pro quo contribution." A charity that receives a quid pro quo contribution in excess of $75 must provide a written statement (at the time of solicitation or receipt of the contribution) that informs the donor that the charitable contribution is limited to the excess of the payment over the value of the goods or services received. The charity is subject to a penalty of $10 for every quid pro quo contribution it receives as to which it failed to make the required disclosure (with a limit of $5,000 for a particular fundraising event or mailing). [I.R.C. §§6115, 6714]

EXAM TIP   gilbert

Be alert for signs that a taxpayer in an exam question is *receiving consideration* in exchange for his charitable contribution. A taxpayer cannot receive value in return for a gift unless he can show that the value of what he contributed clearly exceeds the value of what he received (in which case, the *excess is deductible*).

---

(3) Travel [§652]

No outlay for traveling expenses (including meals and lodging) while away from home can be deducted as a charitable contribution unless there is no significant element of personal pleasure, recreation, or vacation in the travel. [I.R.C. §170(j)]

6. Medical Expenses [§653]

I.R.C. section 213 provides a limited deduction for medical expenses of the taxpayer and her dependents. In the case of divorced parents, a child will be considered the dependent of both parents for purposes of the medical expense deduction. Thus, if a father is entitled to claim the exemption for a child living with her mother (*see infra*, §§672-673), the mother can still deduct any medical expenses she pays for the child. [I.R.C. §213(d)(3)]

a. Items specifically deductible under the Code [§654]

Certain medical expenses are specifically listed in the Code as appropriate deductions. [I.R.C. §213] Taxpayers may deduct:

(1) *Any amount paid "for the diagnosis, cure, mitigation, treatment, or prevention of disease,* or for the purpose of affecting any structure or function of the body." [I.R.C. §213(d)(1)(A)] However, the cost of cosmetic surgery is not deductible unless necessary to ameliorate a deformity arising from a congenital abnormality, a personal injury, or a disfiguring disease. [I.R.C. §213(d)(9)]

(2) *Payments for transportation* that is essential to medical care. [I.R.C. §213(d)(1)(B)]

(3) *Amounts paid for medical insurance* (including Medicare insurance premiums) are deductible, but disability insurance premiums are not. The medical insurance premium must be separately stated. [I.R.C. §213(e)(1)(C), (e)(2)]

(4) *The cost of prescription drugs or insulin.* [I.R.C. §213(b), (d)(2)]

b. Borderline expenses [§655]

Many borderline expenses have required litigation to establish whether they are proximately related to health needs.

(1) Nonhospital living expenses [§656]

Amounts paid for lodging (although not in a hospital) are amounts paid for medical care if care is provided by a physician in a licensed hospital (or medical facility related to a hospital) and there is no significant element of personal pleasure, recreation, or vacation in the travel. The amount deductible cannot exceed $50 per individual per night, and the payments cannot be lavish or extravagant under the circumstances. [I.R.C. §213(d)(2);

and see **Commissioner v. Bilder,** 369 U.S. 499 (1962)—disallowing hotel costs of heart patient recuperating in Florida (before enactment of §213(d)(2))]

(a) Distinguish—some special diet foods [§657]

Costs of special diet foods may be deducted as a medical expense when prescribed by a doctor as a *supplement* to, rather than a substitute for, the taxpayer's regular diet (which would be a nondeductible living expense). [**Harris v. Commissioner,** 46 T.C. 672 (1966)]

(2) Long-term care costs [§658]

Long-term care ("LTC") costs incurred by chronically ill individuals are deductible as medical expenses. [I.R.C. §§213(d)(1)(C), 7702B] "Chronically ill" means the taxpayer is certified by a licensed health care practitioner as unable to perform, without substantial assistance, at least two activities of daily living due to a loss of functional capacity. The activities of daily living are eating, toileting, transferring, bathing, dressing, and continence. The costs of care in a nursing home or other LTC facility, or of a caretaker in the taxpayer's home, are deductible LTC costs. Within limits, the costs of LTC insurance are deductible as medical expenses. If an employer pays for such insurance for employees, it is a tax-free fringe benefit subject to the same limits. Receipt of the proceeds of such insurance is not taxable up to certain limits.

(3) Child care expenses [§659]

Child care expenses incurred while a mother is ill are *not* deductible as medical expenses because they are not sufficiently related to the mother's health. [**Ochs v. Commissioner,** 195 F.2d 692 (2d Cir.), *cert. denied,* 344 U.S. 827 (1952)]

(4) Legal expenses [§660]

Expenses incurred in establishing a guardianship for the taxpayer's mentally ill wife have been held deductible as "medical" expenses—where she refused voluntary hospitalization and the guardianship was necessary to have her committed for treatment. [**Gerstacker v. Commissioner,** 414 F.2d 448 (6th Cir. 1969)]

(5) Cost of a capital improvement [§661]

A capital improvement prescribed by a physician for medical reasons (*e.g.,* air conditioner, elevator, etc., for heart patient) is *deductible* as a medical expense, but the deduction is limited in *amount* to the excess of the cost of the improvement over any increase in the value of the property by reason of the improvement. [**Riach v. Frank,** 302 F.2d 374 (9th Cir. 1962)]

(6) Depreciation [§662]

Depreciation on a car used for medical transportation is not deductible since it is not considered an "amount paid" for medical expenses. [**Weary v. Commissioner,** 510 F.2d 435 (10th Cir.), *cert. denied,* 423 U.S. 838 (1975); *but see* **Commissioner v. Idaho Power Co.,** *supra,* §383—depreciation on construction machinery had to be treated as a "payment," which added to the basis of the building constructed, a result not altogether consistent with *Weary*]

c. Health savings accounts [§663]

In an attempt to reduce health care costs by encouraging a move away from health insurance that covers relatively modest expenses, Congress in 2003 created the Health Savings Account ("HSA"). This allows individuals with high deductible health plans to deduct contributions made to such accounts, the money from which is then available to reimburse the individual for his medical expenses. [I.R.C. §223] In 2006, a high deductible health plan is defined as a health plan with an annual deductible that is at least $1,050 for individuals ($2,100 for families) and not more than $5,250 for individuals ($10,500 for families). The monthly limit on deductible contributions to HSAs is 1/12 of the lesser of the annual deductible and $2,700 for individuals ($5,450 for families). Any amounts in the HSA that are not spent at the end of the year carry over to the next year.

d. Effect of insurance [§664]

Medical expenses are not deductible if compensated by insurance or otherwise.

e. Limitations on deductible amount [§665]

A taxpayer may deduct medical expenses only in excess of 7.5% of AGI. [I.R.C. §213(a)]

f. Self-employed persons [§666]

Self-employed persons are entitled to deduct their medical insurance premiums (assuming they are not entitled to participate in any subsidized health plan maintained by an employer) as business expenses. The deduction is 100% of the premiums. [I.R.C. §162(l)]

7. Personal and Dependency Exemptions and Child Tax Credits

a. Personal exemptions [§667]

A taxpayer is entitled to an exemption for himself. If spouses file a joint return, each claims an exemption. The exemption amount is $3,300 in 2006, and is adjusted for inflation. Exemptions are below-the-line deductions (*i.e.,* deducted from AGI). However, they can be deducted in addition to the standard deduction (*see supra,* §557). Exemptions are not subject to the 2% floor on miscellaneous itemized deductions (*see supra,* §562) or the deduction phaseout (*see supra,* §565).

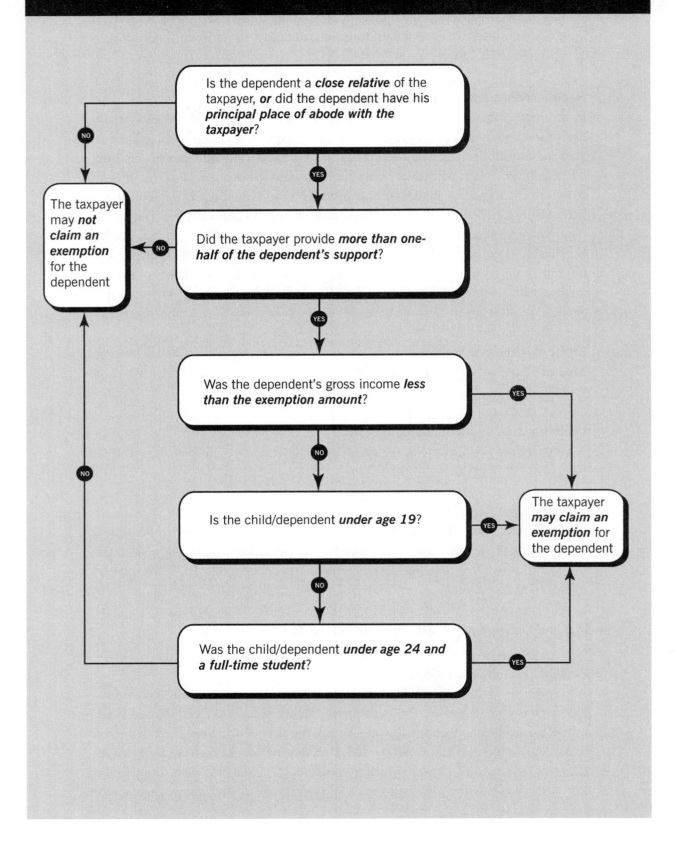

Is the dependent a **close relative** of the taxpayer, **or** did the dependent have his **principal place of abode with the taxpayer**?

NO

YES

The taxpayer may **not claim an exemption** for the dependent

Did the taxpayer provide **more than one-half of the dependent's support**?

NO

YES

Was the dependent's gross income **less than the exemption amount**?

YES

NO

The taxpayer **may claim an exemption** for the dependent

Is the child/dependent **under age 19**?

YES

NO

Was the child/dependent **under age 24 and a full-time student**?

YES

NO

b. Exemptions for dependents [§668]

An additional exemption is also provided for each "dependent." However, an individual cannot claim a personal exemption for himself if he is eligible to be claimed as a dependent on another taxpayer's return. A person is a dependent if the following conditions are met:

(1) *His gross income is less than the exemption amount.* However, if the individual is a *child of the taxpayer and is either under age 19 or a full-time student under age 24*, this rule is waived. It is also waived for gross income of disabled persons in sheltered workshops. [I.R.C. §151(c)]

(2) *The taxpayer supplies over one-half of the support* of the dependent. [I.R.C. §152(a)]

(3) *The dependent is either a close relative of the taxpayer or has his principal place of abode with the taxpayer.* [I.R.C. §152(a)] In the latter situation, their relationship must not violate local law. [I.R.C. §152(b)(5)]

c. Special rules concerning dependents

(1) Support in kind [§669]

In determining whether the taxpayer supplied over one-half of the dependent's support, items provided *in kind*, such as housing and food, are included—but not the value of services provided to the dependent.

(a) Note

Welfare payments for a child are treated as support provided by the *state*, not by the parent. Therefore, if the state provides more than one-half of the total support costs, the parent cannot claim an exemption. [**Lutter v. Commissioner**, 61 T.C. 685 (1974)]

(2) Multiple support agreement [§670]

If several people all contribute to the dependent's support (*e.g.*, four children each contributing 25% of their mother's support), any one of them can claim the exemption pursuant to a *multiple support agreement*. Such an agreement will allocate the exemption to one of the contributors, often rotating it from year to year. [I.R.C. §152(c)]

(3) Scholarships [§671]

In determining whether a taxpayer supplied over one-half of the dependent's support, a scholarship received by a dependent is ignored.

(4) Divorced parents [§672]

A frequent problem is determining which of the divorced parents is entitled to exemptions for the children. As a general rule, the exemption is given to the parent who *has custody* for the larger part of the taxable year. [I.R.C. §152(e)(1)]

(a) Exception—release of claim [§673]

The noncustodial parent gets the exemption if the custodial parent signs a written release of her right to claim the exemption for the current year. [I.R.C. §152(e)(2)] The noncustodial parent must attach this declaration, executed by using IRS Form 8332, to his return. This provision permits the parents to negotiate over who gets the exemption and to compensate the parent who does not claim it. The custodial spouse can waive her right to the exemption for all future years or can waive the right one year at a time. [*See* **King v. Commissioner,** 121 T.C. No. 12 (2003)—exemption provided to noncustodial parent on the strength of Form 8332 that released the exemption for 1987 "and all years thereafter."] However, the exemption cannot be shifted unless the custodial spouse actually signs the waiver. [*See* **Miller v. Commissioner,** 114 T.C. 184 (2000)—exemption not shifted when spouse attached a court order awarding him the exemption, and not a signed waiver by his ex-wife]

d. Phaseout of personal exemption [§674]

Personal exemptions are phased out at the rate of two percentage points for each $2,500 (or fraction thereof) by which the taxpayer's "AGI" exceeds the threshold amount. However, the personal exemption phaseouts themselves are scheduled to be phased out between 2006 and 2009. [I.R.C. §151(d)(3)] For 2006 and 2007, the reduction in the personal exemption is two-thirds of what it would otherwise be, and in 2008 and 2009, the reduction in the personal exemption is only one-third of what it would otherwise be in the absence of the gradual termination of the phaseout. [I.R.C. §151(d)(3)(E)] The phaseout is complete after 2009.

(1) Threshold amount [§675]

The threshold amount is adjusted annually for inflation. In 2006, the threshold amounts are: $150,500 on a single return, $225,750 on a joint return, $188,150 on a head of household return, and $112,875 on the return of a married person filing separately. The exemption is completely phased out when AGI exceeds $348,250 on a joint return, $310,650 on head of household, $273,000 for singles, and $174,125 for marrieds filing separately.

Example: Gloria, who is single, is entitled to three personal exemptions. Her 2006 AGI is $165,500, which is $15,000 more than the threshold amount. In the absence of the phaseout, her exemptions would be reduced by 12% ($15,000 ÷ $2,500 = 6; 6 × 2 = 12). Because personal exemptions are $3,300 each in 2006 ($9,900 for Gloria's three personal exemptions), she must reduce her exemptions by 12% of $9,900 or $1,188. Because this is 2006, though, her personal exemption must be reduced by two-thirds of that amount, or $792. Thus, Gloria's exemptions are worth $9,108 instead of $9,900.

---

8. Casualty and Theft Losses [§676]

Individuals can deduct losses arising from "fire, storm, shipwreck, or other casualty, or from theft" even though not connected to business or investment. [I.R.C. §165(c)(3)] However, each such loss is deductible only to the extent it **exceeds $100,** and the total of casualty and theft losses is deductible only to the extent it **exceeds 10% of AGI.** [I.R.C. §165(h)(1)] A business or investment casualty loss, however, is not limited either by the $100 or 10% provisions. [I.R.C. §165(c)(1), (2)]

a. Casualties [§677]

To be deductible as a casualty, there must be an element of **suddenness** about the event.

---

e.g. **Example:** Damage to the taxpayer's own car from an auto accident is deductible even when the taxpayer was negligent. (But damage to the other car involved in the accident, the cost of which is the taxpayer's responsibility, is not deductible; *see infra,* §682.)

---

(1) Inclusion in statute not required [§678]

Other sorts of disasters beyond those specifically mentioned in the statute are deductible if sufficiently sudden and unusual.

---

e.g. **Example:** A taxpayer was allowed to deduct the loss of a diamond when a car door was slammed on her finger and the diamond popped out of the ring and vanished. [**White v. Commissioner,** 48 T.C. 430 (1967)]

---

(2) Nonphysical causes [§679]

However, declines in value resulting from nonphysical causes are not deductible as casualty losses even though they may meet the requirement of suddenness. [**Chamales v. Commissioner,** T.C. Memo. 2000-33—property owner, whose property was besieged by media and tourists because it was located next to O.J. Simpson's home, could not claim a casualty loss]

(3) Anticipated physical losses [§680]

Mere decline in value of the property caused by apprehension of **future** disasters is not deductible as a casualty. [**Pulvers v. Commissioner,** 407 F.2d 838 (9th Cir. 1969)—decline in value due to nearby landslide that caused no physical damage to taxpayer's property not deductible; *but see* **Finkbohner v. United States,** 788 F.2d 723 (11th Cir. 1986)—allowing casualty loss deduction because of decline in the property's value due to the fact that it was adjacent to properties that were abandoned and torn down because of the threat of flooding]

b. Thefts [§681]

The taxpayer must prove actual criminal theft of property **as defined under local law,** not merely that the property was lost or that it mysteriously disappeared.

Example: In **Paine v. Commissioner,** 63 T.C. 736 (1975), corporate officials engaged in various fraudulent acts that violated federal securities laws, eventually resulting in taxpayer's stock declining in value. The taxpayer was not allowed to deduct the loss in value as a theft loss. *Rationale*: Breaches of fiduciary duty by the corporate officials may have wiped out the value of stock, but this was not a theft loss to the taxpayer because the taxpayer failed to prove that the actions of the corporate officials were criminal under state law. Instead, when the stock became worthless, the stockholders could take a capital loss deduction.

(1) Note

Similarly, an act of a foreign state cannot be treated as a theft loss. [**Billman v. Commissioner,** 73 T.C. 139 (1979)—worthlessness of Vietnamese currency]

c. Limited to taxpayer's property [§682]

Taxpayer can deduct casualty losses only for damages to her *own* property.

Example: Taxpayer drove her car into someone else's house. She could not deduct the damages to the house as a casualty loss since such losses are limited to damages to one's own property. Note, however, that if the accident had occurred in connection with taxpayer's trade or business, the costs would have been deductible as business expenses under section 162. [**Dosher v. United States,** 730 F.2d 375 (5th Cir. 1984)]

d. Amount deductible [§683]

A taxpayer can deduct the *lesser* of:

(i) *The adjusted basis* of the property; *or*

(ii) *The difference between the value of the property before and after* the casualty.

Note: For *personal* casualty and theft losses, *each* must be reduced by $100, and the *total* of personal casualty and theft losses is deductible only to the extent it exceeds 10% of AGI.

(1) Cost of repair [§684]

Repair costs are considered good evidence of decline in value occurring by reason of the casualty if the property is restored to its original condition.

Example: Alice's car (not used for business) had a basis of $1,200 and a value of $800 when it was damaged in a collision. Repair costs were $250. After repair, the car was in the same shape it had been before the accident. Alice had no insurance. Assuming that repair costs fairly measure the decline in value from the collision, she can potentially deduct $150: the lesser of $1,200 or $250, less $100 (since it is a personal casualty loss). Alice's adjusted gross income is $8,200; she also has a $900 theft loss ($1,000 less $100). Her total casualties are $1,050. She can deduct only the excess over 10% of AGI or $230 ($1,050 less $820).

(2) Insurance [§685]

Any insurance recoveries reduce casualty losses. If a taxpayer fails to file a claim with her insurance company (fearing that the policy might be canceled), the loss deduction is wiped out. [I.R.C. §165(h)(4)]

e.g. **Example:** Betty owned a valuable painting, which was held for investment and was stolen. Her basis was $8,000 but the value of the painting was $19,000. She recovered $5,000 of insurance. Her casualty loss is $3,000: the lesser of $8,000 or $19,000, reduced by the insurance recovery. Since the painting was held for investment, and not personal use, the casualty loss is *not reduced* by $100 and it is *not limited* to the excess over 10% of AGI.

e. Personal casualty gains and losses in the same year

(1) Gains exceed losses [§686]

If a taxpayer has both personal casualty or theft losses and gains in the same year, the gains and losses are netted. If the gains exceed the losses, all of the gains are treated as capital gains and all of the losses (in excess of $100 per loss) are deductible, but they are treated as capital losses. "Personal" means a loss of property that is used neither for business nor investment. (Casualty gains usually arise from insurance payments that exceed the basis of the damaged asset—note that these gains are unrecognized if the taxpayer appropriately reinvests the insurance proceeds.) [I.R.C. §165(h)(2)(B)—for discussion of nonrecognition of gain from involuntary conversions, *see infra*, §§803-807; for discussion of capital gains and losses, *see infra*, §§821 *et seq.*]

(2) Losses exceed gains [§687]

If personal casualty losses exceed casualty gains, the two figures are netted. Both gains and losses are ordinary rather than capital. The losses after subtracting $100 from each loss are deductible to the extent of the gains, but only so much of the excess over the gains as exceeds 10% of AGI is deductible. [I.R.C. §165(h)(2)(A)]

9. Other Personal Deductions

a. Nonbusiness bad debts [§688]

As discussed previously (*see supra*, §529), any debt not incurred in connection with a trade or business is treated as a nonbusiness bad debt and is deductible only as a short-term capital loss.

b. Alimony payments [§689]

A payor-spouse is entitled to deduct alimony payments, which constitute taxable income to the payee-spouse. Conversely, payments such as child support, which do not constitute taxable income to the payee, are not deductible by the payor (*see supra*, §§161-170). [I.R.C. §§71, 215] Note that alimony is deductible from gross income ("above the line"). [I.R.C. §62(a)(10)]

c. Contributions to retirement plans [§690]

A taxpayer may establish a traditional "individual retirement account" ("IRA") and contribute and deduct up to $4,000 per year ($5,000 for taxpayers who are age 50 and older). [I.R.C. §219(b)(5), (f)(1)] This deduction is "above the line" (*i.e.*, from gross income). [I.R.C. §62(a)(7)] Investment gains in the IRA are not currently taxed. Generally, the taxpayer *may* start taking distributions from the funds in an IRA when he reaches age 59½ and *must* start taking distributions from the funds at age 70½. ***Distributions from a traditional IRA are taxable.***

(1) Limitation [§691]

An IRA contribution can be made only to the extent that the taxpayer has "earned income." Moreover, *no* deduction for IRA contributions may be taken if the taxpayer (or her spouse) is an active participant in an employer's qualified pension or profit-sharing plan [I.R.C. §219(g)], with the exception that the full $4,000 deduction (or $5,000 for taxpayers who are age 50 and older) is available if the taxpayer's 2006 adjusted gross income is $50,000 or less (for single taxpayers) or $75,000 (for married taxpayers). These figures rise in subsequent years. Part of the maximum deduction is available if the taxpayer's adjusted gross income exceeds the applicable figure by less than $10,000 ($20,000 after December 31, 2006). Note that if the taxpayer or taxpayer's spouse is not covered by a qualified employer-maintained pension or profit-sharing plan, he can contribute and deduct the maximum amount per year to an IRA regardless of income.

(2) Roth IRAs [§692]

Contributions to Roth IRAs are not currently deductible. However, investment income is not taxable and ***none of the distributions from the Roth IRA are taxable*** if made after the taxpayer reaches age 59½ and more than five years after the first contribution to the Roth IRA. As a result, a very large amount of investment income can be sheltered from income tax since distributions need not begin by age 70½ and can be made to the taxpayer's heirs after death. Contributions to regular IRAs plus Roth IRAs cannot exceed $4,000 per year, but the income limitations on Roth IRAs are much higher than for regular IRAs. The amount is $150,000 for a taxpayer filing a joint return (with the total permitted contribution phasing out at $160,000) or $95,000 for a taxpayer filing a separate return (with the total permitted contribution phasing out at $110,000). These limitations apply whether or not the taxpayer is covered by an employer-maintained retirement plan. [I.R.C. §408A]

(3) Coverdell education savings accounts [§693]

A taxpayer can contribute up to $2,000 per year to a Coverdell education savings account for a beneficiary under 18. The contributions are not deductible, but investment income is not taxed and distributions are not taxable. The funds in an education IRA may be used to pay qualified post-secondary educational expenses—tuition, fees, books, supplies, and equipment at any educational institution—whether public, private, or religious. [I.R.C. §530] There are income limitations and phaseouts for these savings accounts that are the same as for Roth IRAs (*supra*).

DEDUCTIONS—ABOVE THE LINE VS. BELOW THE LINE — gilbert

FROM GROSS INCOME (*i.e.,* "ABOVE THE LINE")	FROM ADJUSTED GROSS INCOME (*i.e.,* "BELOW THE LINE")
• Trade or business deductions	• Standard deduction
• Reimbursed expenses of employees	**OR**
• Capital losses	• Medical expenses
• Deduction from sale or exchange of property	• Charitable contributions
• Deductible "nonbusiness" expenses related to rent or royalty income (*see supra*, §440)	• Casualty and theft losses
	• "Nonbusiness" expenses for property held for the production of income
• Alimony	• "Nonbusiness" expenses—expenses of a tax-related matter
• Moving expenses	• Other "miscellaneous itemized deductions"
• Interest on educational loans	
• Contributions to IRAs (but not Roth IRAs)	• Home mortgage interest

---

D. Tax Rates

1. **Return Category [§694]**

Once taxable income is determined, the tax is computed. The rates are set forth in I.R.C. section 1 and depend on whether the taxpayer is married or single. Most married taxpayers file a joint return. Single persons may qualify as a head of household (with lower rates than for other single people). (*See supra*, §238.)

2. Tax Rates [§695]

There are six tax brackets for 2006: 10%, 15%, 25%, 28%, 33%, and 35%. [I.R.C. §1(a) - (d), (i)] The levels at which the brackets change are adjusted for inflation. [I.R.C. §1(f)]

E. Credits

1. In General [§696]

After the amount of tax has been determined, the taxpayer may be entitled to certain *credits*. These reduce the actual tax payable on a *dollar-for-dollar* basis.

2. Credit for Taxes Withheld and Prepaid [§697]

The taxpayer is entitled to a credit against taxes payable for all sums withheld from wages for payment of taxes [I.R.C. §31]; and for all amounts prepaid in connection with declarations of estimated tax [I.R.C. §6315].

3. Foreign Tax Credit [§698]

In lieu of a deduction from income, the taxpayer may elect to take as a credit against tax the amount of income and similar taxes paid or accrued during the year to foreign countries or possessions of the United States. The amount of the credit is limited to that proportion of the tax that the taxable income from sources within the foreign country bears to the entire taxable income of the individual. [I.R.C. §§27, 901 - 905] Note that the taxpayer has the *option* to treat foreign taxes as a credit or a deduction from gross income, whichever is the most advantageous to the taxpayer.

4. Credit for the Elderly [§699]

Taxpayers who are age 65 or over receive a credit of 15% of their "section 22 amount." [I.R.C. §22]

a. "Section 22 amount" [§700]

The "section 22 amount" is $5,000 for a single individual, $7,500 in case of a joint return where both spouses are eligible, or $3,750 in the case of a married person filing a separate return.

b. Reductions from "section 22 amount" [§701]

The taxpayer must reduce the "section 22 amount" by Social Security received or other amounts excluded from gross income. (The "section 22 amount" does not have to be reduced by life insurance, annuities, compensation for personal injuries or sickness, or amounts received under accident or health plans.)

(1) And note

If AGI exceeds $7,500, the "section 22 amount" is further reduced by one-half of the excess over $7,500. (This figure is $10,000 in the case of a joint return, $5,000 in the case of a married person filing a separate return.)

c.   Disabled persons [§702]

The credit also applies to disability income received by a taxpayer under age 65 who is retired due to a permanent and total disability.

5. Welfare Employees and Work Incentive Credit [§703]

The Code allows for a credit of 50% of the wages paid to a person who is a member of a disadvantaged class (such as a welfare recipient or economically disadvantaged youth). The 50% credit applies to the first $6,000 of wages during the employee's first year; during the second year, the credit is 25% of the employee's wages. [I.R.C. §§38(b), 51]

6. Child or Dependent Care Credit [§704]

To enable themselves to work, many parents incur child care costs. Traditionally, the courts did not permit taxpayers to take such costs as a business expense deduction. [**Smith v. Commissioner**, 40 B.T.A. 1038 (1939), *aff'd*, 113 F.2d 114 (2d Cir. 1940)] Eventually, however, Congress provided a limited deduction, then broadened the deduction, and finally switched to a credit. [I.R.C. §21]

a.   Who is entitled to the credit [§705]

The child care credit is available to a taxpayer who incurs "employment-related expenses" in order to be gainfully employed. "Employment-related expenses" are those for household services and for care of a qualifying individual. A "qualifying individual" is a dependent under age 13 for whom the taxpayer is entitled to claim the exemption, or a dependent of the taxpayer (or the taxpayer's spouse) who is unable to care for himself. [I.R.C. §21(b)]

(1) Transportation costs excluded [§706]

The cost of transporting a child to a day-care center does not qualify for the credit even though the cost of the center itself does qualify. [**Warner v. Commissioner**, 69 T.C. 995 (1978)] The cost of summer camp likewise does not qualify for the credit.

(2) Taxpayer identification numbers required [§707]

The name, address, and Social Security number of the care provider must be provided on the return (unless the care provider is a tax-exempt organization, in which case only the name and address must be provided). [I.R.C. §21(e)(9)]

b.   Amount of credit [§708]

The amount of the credit is equal to a percentage of the child care costs that the taxpayer incurs. The percentage varies depending on income. The percentage is 35% if the taxpayer's AGI is $15,000 or less. The applicable percentage is decreased by one percentage point (but not below 20%) for each $2,000 (or fraction thereof) by which AGI exceeds $15,000.

Example: Andre and Babette, a married couple, have AGI of $22,200 in 2006. Their AGI exceeds $15,000 by $7,200—which is three whole $2,000 units and a fraction of a fourth. Thus, the applicable percentage (35%) must be reduced by four percentage points, making their applicable credit 31%.

---

c. Dollar limit [§709]

The amount of expenses for which a credit can be taken cannot exceed $3,000 for one qualifying individual and $6,000 for two or more qualifying individuals. [I.R.C. §21(c)]

(1) Earned income limitation [§710]

Child care expenses cannot exceed earned income. In the case of a married couple, the expenses cannot exceed the earned income of the spouse with the *lower* earned income. (There is a special rule for spouses who are students or disabled; they are treated as if they had monthly earned income of $250 if there is one qualifying individual or $500 if there is more than one.) [I.R.C. §21(d)(2)]

Example: In 2006, Natasha and Boris, whose applicable percentage is 33%, have one child, nine-year-old Rocky. Assume that child care costs for Rocky are $3,200, that Natasha's earned income is $18,000, and that Boris's earned income is $1,200. Ordinarily, $3,000 could be taken into account (since they have one child and the limit in 2006 is $3,000). However, this limit is capped by the lower-earning spouse's earned income (Boris's earned income of $1,200). Thus, the child care credit is 33% of $1,200, or $396.

---

d. Divorced parents included [§711]

Even if a custodial parent is not entitled to claim an exemption, she can take the child care credit. [I.R.C. §21(e)(5)]

7. Child Tax Credit [§712]

If a taxpayer is entitled to claim a *child under age 17 as a dependent*, the taxpayer is also entitled to a child tax *credit* of $1,000 per qualifying child. [I.R.C. §24] The child cannot have attained the age of 17 by the end of the calendar year. *Note:* A credit reduces tax dollar for dollar—so a $1,000 credit reduces tax liability by $1,000.

a. Phaseouts [§713]

The child tax credit is reduced by $50 for each $1,000 (or fraction thereof) by which the taxpayer's AGI exceeds the threshold amount. For this purpose, the threshold amount is $110,000 on a joint return, $75,000 on a single return, and $55,000 for a married individual filing a separate return. [I.R.C. §24(b)] Neither the amount of the credit nor the threshold amounts are indexed for inflation.

b. Definition of qualifying child [§714]

In recent years, Congress has attempted to standardize the definition of "child" in the Code to reduce the confusion that existed when different sections relied on different definitions. For purposes of the credit, a "qualifying child" includes the taxpayer's son, daughter, or other dependent (which includes a brother, sister, stepbrother, stepsister, or descendent of such relative) or a descendent of such son, daughter, or other dependent. To be a qualifying child, the individual (i) must have the same principal place of residence as the taxpayer for more than half the taxable year, (ii) must not have attained the age of 17 as of the close of the taxable year (or be a student who has not attained the age of 24 by the close of the taxable year), and (iii) must not have provided more than half of such individual's own support during the taxable year. [I.R.C. §§24(c)(1), 152(c)] The child must also be a United States citizen or resident.

(1) Special rule for disabled "child" [§715]

An individual of any age who is permanently and totally disabled is treated as a qualifying child as long as such individual otherwise meets the non-age requirements. [I.R.C. §152(c)(3)]

c. Refundability [§716]

The child tax credit is usually *refundable*, meaning that it can produce a refund even though it exceeds an individual's tax liability for the year. The credit is refundable to the extent of 15% of earned income in excess of $10,000. [I.R.C. §24(d)] The earned income level is adjusted for inflation. In 2006, the value of earned income used for determining the refundable amount of the credit is $11,300.

---

e.g. **Example:** In 2006, Tony Taxpayer has two children who qualify as dependents, and has earned income of $23,000. Tony does not have any tax liability. Tony is entitled to a refund of $1,755 ([$23,000 - $11,300] × 15% = $1,755).

---

d. Divorced parents [§717]

The rules for shifting child tax credits between divorced parents are the same as the rules for shifting dependency exemptions. (*See supra*, §672.) Thus, as a general rule, a custodial parent is entitled to the child tax credit as well as the exemption, but the credit can be shifted to the noncustodial parent if the custodial parent signs a written release of the right to claim the credit.

8. **Earned Income Credit [§718]**

   The Code provides a credit against tax for lower income taxpayers. This credit is quite valuable because it is refundable—if the credit exceeds the tax due, the taxpayer gets a refund. [I.R.C. §32] The earned income credit is an important anti-poverty device that has been significantly expanded in recent years.

   a. **Amount of credit for taxpayers with qualifying children [§719]**

      For 2006, a taxpayer with one child under age 19 (or under age 24 and a full-time student) may claim a credit of 34% of earned income up to $8,080 (or a maximum of $2,747). If the taxpayer has two or more children, the credit is 40% of earned income up to $11,340 (or a maximum of $4,536). The credit is reduced by 15.98% of earned income in excess of $14,810 ($16,810 on a joint return). Thus, for a taxpayer with one child, the earned income credit is completely phased out when the taxpayer has earned income of $32,001 (single taxpayer) or $34,001 (joint return). For a taxpayer with two or more children, the earned income credit is reduced by 21.06% of earned income in excess of $14,810 ($16,810 on a joint return). These amounts are adjusted annually for inflation.

   b. **Amount of credit for taxpayers without qualifying children [§720]**

      For 2006, a taxpayer who does not have qualifying children may claim a credit of 7.65% of earned income up to $5,380 (or a maximum of $412). The credit is phased out at the rate of 7.65% for earned income in excess of $6,740 ($8,740 on a joint return). Thus, the earned income credit is completely phased out at $12,120 (single return) or $14,120 (joint return). These amounts are adjusted annually for inflation.

9. **Adoption Tax Credit [§721]**

   A taxpayer can claim a credit for adoption expenses up to $10,000 per child. If the taxpayer's AGI exceeds $150,000, the amount allowable is phased out. (These amounts are indexed for inflation, so that in 2006, the maximum credit is $10,960 per child and it begins to phase out as the taxpayer's AGI exceeds $164,410. [I.R.C. §24(h)]) It is completely phased out at AGI of $190,000. The expenses for which a credit can be claimed are for the legal adoption of a child under age 18 (or a person over age 18 who is physically or mentally incapable of caring for herself). The expenses cannot be incurred in carrying out a surrogate parenting arrangement. [I.R.C. §23]

10. **Education Credits [§722]**

    Several tax credits are provided for the higher education costs of low- or moderate-income taxpayers. These credits are nonrefundable. They apply to tuition payments for the taxpayer, the taxpayer's spouse, or the taxpayer's dependent. [I.R.C. §25A]

    a. **HOPE scholarship credit [§723]**

       In 2006, the HOPE credit provides a maximum allowable credit of $1,650 per year for each of the first two years of post-secondary education. This consists of 100% of the first $1,100 of tuition and related expenses and 50% of the second $1,100 of tuition and related expenses. This credit is allowed per student; thus, a parent with several children in college could claim several HOPE credits.

b.   Lifetime learning credit [§724]

The lifetime learning credit provides a credit for 20% of qualified tuition expenses in any year when the HOPE credit is not claimed. The credit is 20% of tuition and related expenses paid on the first $10,000 of such tuition and related expenses. These limits are per taxpayer; thus they do not increase if the taxpayer is paying for several children.

c.   Phaseouts [§725]

Both credits begin to be phased out if AGI exceeds $45,000 on a single return and $90,000 on a joint return. They are completely phased out when AGI reaches $55,000 on a single return and $110,000 on a joint return.

COMPARISON OF DEDUCTIONS, EXEMPTIONS, AND CREDITS		**gilbert**
	EFFECT	**EXAMPLES**
ABOVE-THE-LINE DEDUCTION	Deducted *from gross income* to arrive at adjusted gross income ("AGI")	Ordinary and necessary business expenses (except of employees); alimony payments; some IRA contributions; capital losses
BELOW-THE-LINE DEDUCTION	Deducted *from AGI only if exceeds the standard deduction*; some subject to a floor	Qualified interest on residence; state and local income and property taxes; charitable contributions (up to 50% of AGI); medical expenses exceeding 7.5% of AGI; ordinary and necessary business expenses of employees
PERSONAL AND DEPENDENCY EXEMPTIONS	Deducted *from AGI to determine taxable income even if standard deduction is used*; phases out at high income levels	Exemption for taxpayer; exemption for dependents
CREDITS	*Reduces tax due dollar for dollar*	Child tax credit; credit for the elderly; welfare employees and work incentive credit; child care credit; earned income credit; adoption tax credit; education credits

Chapter Four:
Gain or Loss on Sale or Exchange of Property

CONTENTS

Chapter Approach

Chapter Approach

This chapter considers the tax consequences of transfers of property. An exam question concerning a property transfer will usually require *computation of the amount of gain or loss* and will often involve issues of *realization and recognition*.

1. **Basis**

    To calculate the gain or loss from the disposition of property, it is first necessary to *ascertain the basis* of the property. In most cases, that basis must be "adjusted" for various items (such as depreciation). Analyze issues of basis as follows:

    (i)   If basis is *cost*, what was the cost? Be sure to include purchase-money debt.

    (ii) If the property was received by *gift*, apply the carryover basis rules.

    (iii) If the property was *inherited*, use the date of death value (unless it was income in respect of a decedent).

    (iv) If the property was received as *compensation*, use the amount included in income.

    (v)   If the property was received as a result of a *nonrecognition provision*, use the carryover basis with appropriate adjustments.

    Then *adjust basis* by *depreciation* (including depreciation that could have been but was not claimed), *capitalized expenditures, casualty losses, etc.*

2. **Amount Realized**

    The transaction in which the property is disposed of must be analyzed. To tax the gain (or deduct the loss) on disposition, the transaction must be treated as a "*realization*." It is necessary to compute the amount realized in the transaction in order to compute the gain or loss and to properly apply any nonrecognition provision (below). When discussing realization on an exam, keep in mind the following points:

    a. The amount realized includes all *debts* from which the transferor is relieved (even if property is worth less than a nonrecourse debt).

    b. If the amount is *not ascertainable*, you should argue both the open and closed transaction methods.

    c. If the property received is of *indeterminate value*, it is presumed equal in value to the property given up.

d. Gifts are not ordinarily realizations, but watch for a *discharge of debt coupled with a gift*.

3. **Nonrecognition of Gain or Loss**

    The taxation of gain (or deduction of loss) may be deferred if a *"nonrecognition"* section of the Code is applicable. The nonrecognition issue should be analyzed as follows:

    a. Determine whether there was an *exchange* qualifying under section 1031 by asking:

        (1) Does the property received meet the *"like kind"* test?

        (2) Was there a *triangle* exchange or *deferred* exchange?

        (3) Was *boot* received? If so, figure recognized gain and adjust basis. Note that if boot was transferred, gain or loss is recognized on the transferred boot and it also increases the taxpayer's basis in the new property. Watch for related party rules, which require recognition if the related party disposes of the property within two years.

    b. Determine whether there was an *involuntary conversion* qualifying under section 1033 by asking:

        (1) Was the property involuntarily converted by *condemnation or casualty*?

        (2) Was it *replaced by similar property* within two years?

        (3) Was there an *election* not to recognize gain?

        (4) Was the full amount received *reinvested*? If not, adjust basis.

    c. Determine whether there was a gain on the *sale of a principal residence* qualifying for exclusion by asking:

        (1) Was the dwelling the taxpayer's *principal residence* for *two* or more of the *five years* preceding the sale?

        (2) Has the taxpayer excluded gain on the sale of a principal residence within the past *two years*?

        (3) The taxpayer may exclude up to $250,000 of gain; a married couple, each of whom meets the two- and five-year qualifications, may exclude up to a $500,000 gain if they file a joint return.

    d. Determine whether there was a *transfer between spouses* or former spouses incident to divorce. Gain or loss is not recognized and basis stays the same.

4. Character of Gain or Loss

After all of the above is done, the character of the gain or loss must be analyzed to see whether it is *capital or ordinary*. (This material is discussed in the next chapter, along with the alternative minimum tax on tax preferences.)

A. Computation of Basis, Gain, or Loss

---

1. Computation Formula [§726]

To determine gain or loss on the disposition of property, adjusted basis must first be calculated using the following formula:

$$\textit{adjusted basis} = \text{unadjusted basis} + \text{additions} - \text{reductions}$$

If the amount realized on disposition of the property is greater than the adjusted basis, the difference is a gain, but if the amount realized is less than the adjusted basis, the difference is a loss, or mathematically:

$$\textit{gain} = \text{amount realized} - \text{adjusted basis}$$

$$\textit{loss} = \text{adjusted basis} - \text{amount realized}$$

2. Basis [§727]

Basis must be known both for computation of gain or loss and also for computing depreciation (*see supra,* §§465 *et seq.*).

a. Unadjusted basis [§728]

Unadjusted basis is usually cost. However, there are special rules for *gifts, inherited property, and tax-free exchanges*. [I.R.C. §§1020 - 1023]

(1) Cost basis [§729]

Generally the basis of property is the cost of the property. [I.R.C. §1012] Cost includes the cash or other property paid to obtain the asset.

(a) Mortgages [§730]

Cost also includes any purchase-money mortgage or trust deed on the property, regardless of whether the taxpayer is personally liable on the mortgage or assumes or takes subject to existing mortgages. [*See* **Commissioner v. Tufts**, 461 U.S. 300 (1983)]

1) Depreciation [§731]

Because the basis of property includes purchase-money debt, a taxpayer frequently will have a high basis for purchased property even though she has not expended much cash of her own. This means that the property will generate high depreciation deductions (if it is held in a trade or business or for the production of income). Note, however, that the ability to deduct losses on such property may be sharply limited by the "at risk" rules (*see supra,* §§538-542) if the debt is nonrecourse, and by the passive activity loss rules (*see supra,* §§543-551) if the property is held for rental or other passive activity.

(b) Contingent liabilities [§732]

If the liability is contingent and might never have to be paid, the basis of the property does *not* include the debt. [**Albany Car Wheel Co. v. Commissioner,** 40 T.C. 831 (1963), *aff'd,* 333 F.2d 653 (2d Cir. 1964)] Similarly, if the property is worth significantly less than the amount of a nonrecourse liability, it is likely that no part of the debt is included in basis. [**Estate of Franklin v. Commissioner,** 544 F.2d 1045 (9th Cir. 1976)] However, it is possible that part of the debt will be included in basis to the extent of the fair market value of the property. [**Pleasant Summit Land Corp. v. Commissioner,** *supra,* §578] This issue remains unresolved.

(c) Long-term obligations [§733]

A court will examine all the realities of a transaction to determine whether the property is actually worth more than the debt and whether the debtor is really the owner of the property. If the risks of gain or loss are on the lender, rather than on the borrower, the lender is treated as the real investor, and the borrower cannot treat the loan as part of her basis. [**Carnegie Productions, Inc. v. Commissioner,** 59 T.C. 642 (1973)]

Example: In **Mayerson v. Commissioner,** 47 T.C. 340 (1966), although a building's purchase price of $332,500 was financed with $5,000 down, $5,000 payable in one year, and $322,500 payable in 99 years ("interest only" payments were required to that time), the Tax Court allowed a purchaser to include in basis the entire debt. The building in question was old, and it needed a number of repairs—both to attract tenants and to correct numerous building code violations. As a result of the building's age and condition, a traditional mortgage was unavailable. The parties agreed that the buyer would renovate the building and correct any building code violations. The parties also contemplated that traditional mortgage financing would be procured as soon as practicable, which would enable the taxpayer to retire the note before the end of the 99-year term. This in fact occurred. Furthermore, it was the taxpayer's responsibility to determine the most profitable use of the building and to find tenants. Finally, the parties had no prior contact with each other prior to the transaction in question. Thus, the debt was treated as realistic and not a sham.

(d) Purchase expense [§734]

Expenses of acquisition, such as broker's or attorneys' fees, are added to basis.

(e) Option cost [§735]

If the property was purchased through exercise of an option, any amount paid for the option (if not already credited to the purchase price) is added to the purchaser's cost basis.

(f) "Tax-detriment" rule [§736]

"Cost" also includes any income charged to the taxpayer in acquiring the property. For example, if Taxpayer pays $10 for stock in her employer's corporation that is really worth $30, the "bargain purchase" being a form of additional compensation to Taxpayer, Taxpayer has $20 worth of income (*see supra*, §41). This $20 becomes part of Taxpayer's "cost basis" on the stock; *i.e.*, her basis is $30, not $10.

EXAM TIP   **gilbert**

In exam questions, be on the lookout for noncash sources of basis. Cost basis of property *includes more than the cash that was exchanged* between the parties. Cost also includes *debts incurred* to purchase the property (*e.g.*, a purchase-money mortgage), *purchase expenses* (*e.g.*, a broker's fee), amounts paid for *options* (if the amount is not credited to the purchase price), and *any income charged* to the taxpayer *as a result of the transaction*.

---

(2) Inter vivos gifts [§737]

For purposes of computing *gain* (as well as for depreciation purposes), the donee takes the donor's basis on property acquired as a gift. However, for purposes of computing *loss*, the donee's basis is the *fair market value* at the time of gift, *or* the donor's basis, whichever is *lower*. [I.R.C. §1015]

 Example: Alex gives Becky land that originally cost $10,000, but is worth $12,000 at the time of gift. Becky's basis for the land is $10,000 for all purposes.

 Example: If, however, the land in the example above was only worth $8,000 at the time of the gift, and Becky later sold it for $7,500,

Becky's basis for determining *loss* would be $8,000 (not $10,000), and Becky's loss would be only $500.

---

e.g. **Example:** If the land in the example above was worth $8,000 at the time of the gift and Becky sold it for $9,000, there would be *neither gain nor loss:* no gain, because basis for determining gain is $10,000, and no loss, because basis for determining loss is $8,000. [Treas. Reg. §1.1015-1(a)(2)]

(a) Increase by gift tax paid [§738]

The donee can increase her basis by a portion of the gift tax paid by the donor. The portion of the gift tax that can be used to increase basis is the amount determined by a fraction—the net appreciation in value of the gift over the amount of the gift—multiplied by the total gift tax paid. In other words, "increase in basis" is to "gift tax paid" as "appreciation" is to "amount of gift." [I.R.C. §1015(d)(6)]

---

e.g. **Example:** On Alice's gift of stock to Trudy, Alice pays a gift tax of $10,600. Alice's basis for the stock was $40,000, and the stock was worth $50,000 at time of transfer to Trudy. Therefore, the net appreciation is $10,000. The net appreciation ($10,000) over the amount of the gift ($50,000) is 20%. Twenty percent of the gift tax ($10,600) is $2,120. Thus, Trudy's basis is $42,120 ($40,000 + $2,120).

---

1) Limitation—ceiling on increase

Gift taxes paid can never increase basis to an amount in excess of the property's value at the date of the gift. Thus, there would be no increase in basis for the gift tax in the second and third examples above (*supra,* §737).

(3) Tax-free exchanges [§739]

The basis of property acquired in a tax-free exchange is that of the property transferred. However, it must be adjusted for any nonqualifying consideration paid or received (*see infra,* §§784 *et seq.*).

(4) Inherited property [§740]

The basis of inherited property in the hands of a decedent's estate or in the hands of the person inheriting it is its value at the date of decedent's death. [I.R.C. §1014] If the estate elected to use the "alternate valuation date" for the estate tax purposes, the income tax basis of the property would be its value six months after the date of death.

(a) Note—carryover basis after 2010 [§741]

Under legislation passed in 2001, the treatment of inherited property is scheduled to change in 2010. Taxpayers who die in or after 2010 will not receive the "stepped up" basis provided for in the present version of section 1014. Instead, beginning in 2010, the basis of inherited property will be *the lesser* of the decedent's basis or the fair market value of the property on the date of death. [I.R.C. §1022] However, executors will be able to increase the basis of property in the estate in aggregate by up to $1.3 million (or $3 million for property passing to a surviving spouse). This new provision is extremely complex and will, in all likelihood, be amended before it goes into effect.

 Example: Axhi bought stock for $2,000 in 1947. It was worth $100,000 when he died in 2006. Axhi left the stock to Bella. Bella's basis is $100,000; the $98,000 appreciation in the stock is *never* subjected to income tax.

(b) Form in which property is held [§742]

When property is owned by more than one person, the basis may be affected on the death of one owner. The effect depends on the form in which the property was held.

1) Community property [§743]

If a decedent and her surviving spouse owned the property as community property, both halves receive a new basis. [I.R.C. §1014(b)(6)]

Example: Harold and Wanda, a husband and wife, owned real estate as community property. Its basis was $150,000 and it was worth $600,000 when Wanda died. Wanda left her community interest to Sally. Sally's basis is $300,000. Harold's basis for his retained half is also increased to $300,000.

2) Tenants in common [§744]

When a married couple owns property as tenants in common rather than as community property, the surviving spouse's half interest does not receive a new basis, but the deceased spouse's half does.

Example: Harold and Wanda, a husband and wife, owned a home as tenants in common. The property's basis is

$150,000. The property was worth $600,000 when Wanda died. Wanda left her interest in the property to Sally. Sally's basis would be $300,000, but Harold's basis would still be $75,000.

3) Joint tenancy [§745]

If two people owned the property as joint tenants, the portion of the property that was includible in the decedent's gross estate for estate tax purposes under I.R.C. section 2040 receives a new basis and the balance of the property retains its basis. In the case of married joint tenants, half of the value of the property is subject to estate tax on the death of the first tenant; consequently, the result would be the same as that described for tenancy in common in the preceding paragraph. [I.R.C. §1014(b)(9)]

 Example: Fred and Wilma own Blackrock as joint tenants. Blackrock's basis is $100,000. The property was worth $1 million when Fred died. Wilma's basis would be $550,000—$500,000 for Fred's interest and $50,000 for Wilma's interest. If Fred and Wilma were married, the value of half of Blackrock would be subject to estate tax.

(c) Term interests [§746]

Special rules apply to "term interests" received by gift or bequest. "Term interests" include a life estate, a term for years, or an income interest in a trust. In such cases, the recipient of the term interest has a basis for her interest but, in most situations, is not allowed to make any use of it.

Example: Homer gives property to Marge for life, remainder to Bart. Assume that, considering Homer's basis and actuarial tables for Marge's life, the life estate has a basis of $7,500 in Marge's hands. Marge cannot amortize this basis. As a result, the entire amount of income that Marge receives annually is taxed, without any reduction to measure the decline in value of her interest as she gets older.

1) Sale of term interest [§747]

The seller of a term interest is treated as if her basis was zero. [I.R.C. §1001(e)(2)] *Rationale:* The term interest is treated as a capital asset under **McAllister v. Commissioner** (*see infra*, §857). The Code denies the seller a basis in order to make such sales less attractive to the seller.

Example: Same facts as above, except now Marge decides to sell her life estate to Montgomery for $12,000. She cannot offset the sale price with any of her $7,500 basis—the entire $12,000 is taxed as a capital gain. Note that this result would *not* change even if Marge were to sell her life estate to Bart.

2) Exception [§748]

If both the holder of the remainder and the holder of the term interest sell their interests to a third party, each of them is entitled to use his basis. [I.R.C. §1001(e)(3)]

Example: Same facts as in the example at §746, *supra*, except now both Marge and Bart agree to sell their respective interests to Montgomery. Now, Marge *is allowed* a basis recovery. Assuming that she receives $12,000 for her interest, her capital gain would be $4,500.

3) Amortization [§749]

The holder of a term interest cannot reduce the income received by a deduction for the decline in value of her interest that occurs with time (*e.g.*, a 10-year term is worth more in the first year than in the last year). [I.R.C. §§102(b)(2), 273]

4) Not always applicable [§750]

These rules denying the use of basis to holders of term interests apply only to interests received by gift or bequest—not to purchased interests.

(d) Income in respect of a decedent [§751]

Certain items inherited from a decedent do not receive a basis adjustment to fair market value by reason of I.R.C. section 1014. These items are known as "income in respect of a decedent." They involve situations in which income was not taxed to the decedent even though most of the events leading to the realization of income occurred before the decedent's death. [I.R.C. §§1014(c), 691]

Example: Decedent, a salesperson, negotiated a sale for which she was entitled to receive a commission. However, the money was not paid until after her death. Because she used the cash basis of accounting, the $10,000 was not taxed to her while she was alive. This is income in respect of a decedent.

DETERMINING UNADJUSTED BASIS AFTER "NONSALE" TRANSFERS OF PROPERTY

gilbert

METHOD OF TRANSFER	RESULT
INTER VIVOS GIFT	*Gain:* Donee's basis is **donor's basis** plus a portion of any gift tax that the donor paid. *Loss:* Donee's basis is the **lower** of the property's **fair market value** at the time of the gift **or** the **donor's basis** plus a portion of the gift tax paid.
TAX-FREE EXCHANGE	The basis in the new property is the **basis of the transferred property** plus adjustments for any nonqualifying consideration paid or received.
INHERITANCE	*In general:* Legatee's basis is the property's **value at the time of decedent's death** (or alternatively six months thereafter). *Community property:* Legatee's and/or surviving spouse's basis in property is its **value at the time of decedent's death**; both halves receive a new basis. *Tenancy in common or joint tenancy:* Legatee's basis in property is its **value at the time of decedent's death**, but **surviving spouse's basis** in property **does not change**.
GIFT OR BEQUEST OF TERM INTEREST (*e.g.,* life estate, income interest in trust)	The holder of the term interest has a **basis of zero**. If the holder and remainderman combine their interests and sell to a third party, the basis of the term interest would be calculated by using the donor's basis and actuarial tables.

Example: A bonus was paid after the decedent's death attributable to services rendered before death. However, the exact amount was not determined until after death and, consequently, it could not have been income to the decedent before death even under the accrual method of accounting. Still, it was held to be income in respect of a decedent since it was traceable to pre-death services. **[O'Daniel's Estate v. Commissioner,** 173 F.2d 966 (2d Cir. 1949)]

Example: Decedent was a farmer who turned over grapes to a marketing co-op, but the price had not been fixed at that time and payment was not made until after decedent's death. It was held immaterial whether decedent had sold the grapes to the co-op or merely entrusted the grapes. In either case, the proceeds were attributable to a transaction entered into during life and thus were income in respect of a decedent. **[Commissioner v. Linde,** 213 F.2d 1 (9th Cir. 1954)]

1) Distinguish—services not completed at time of death [§752]

If significant services remained to be rendered at the time of death and before payment was due, the item would **not** be income in respect of a decedent. **[Commissioner v. Peterson,** 667 F.2d 675 (8th Cir. 1981)—decedent made contract for future sale of calves that had to be cared for before payment was due; gain is not income in respect of decedent]

2) Taxed to recipient [§753]

Whoever receives income in respect of a decedent (decedent's estate or legatee) is taxed on it to the same extent the decedent would have been taxed. If the item would have been capital gain to the decedent, it is capital gain in the hands of the recipient.

3) Deduction for estate tax [§754]

If the item of income in respect of a decedent was also subject to estate tax in the decedent's estate, the recipient is allowed to treat the estate tax as a deduction from income. [I.R.C. §691(c)]

b. Adjusted basis [§755]

Adjusted basis is determined by *adding* to the unadjusted basis all subsequent expenditures chargeable to the asset that were not deductible as current expenses, *i.e.,* items properly capitalized (*see supra,* §§365-406). From this sum is subtracted (i) receipts, losses, or other items properly chargeable to the capital account; and (ii) depreciation, depletion, amortization, or obsolescence allowed (or allowable) on the capital asset. [I.R.C. §1016]

HOW TO CALCULATE BASIS AND ADJUSTED BASIS
gilbert

STEP ONE: UNADJUSTED BASIS

Cost of property

+ Debt to purchase property

+ Purchase expenses

+ Amounts paid for options

+ Any income to taxpayer as a result of transaction

= **UNADJUSTED BASIS**

STEP TWO: ADJUSTED BASIS

Unadjusted basis

+ Items properly capitalized

− Receipts, losses, or other items properly chargeable to the capital account

− Depreciation, depletion, amortization, or obsolescence allowed or allowable

= **ADJUSTED BASIS**

(1) Treatment of depreciation [§756]

If a taxpayer failed to claim as much depreciation as was "allowable," the full amount *allowable* reduces the basis anyway. However, if the taxpayer deducted and was allowed more than the amount that was legally allowable (*e.g.*, due to mistake, aggressive tax practices, etc.), the full amount *actually allowed* reduces the basis.

Example: Taxpayer bought a building for $100,000 and deducted depreciation of $40,000 on it. However, $45,000 was the amount legally allowable. He built interior walls to create office space; this cost $8,000. One room was rendered unusable by an explosion; Taxpayer deducted a loss of $16,000 and did not repair this part of the building. His basis is now $47,000. This figure is computed by starting with $100,000 and adding the capitalized improvement ($8,000) and deducting depreciation allowable ($45,000) and the casualty loss ($16,000).

(a) Tax benefit limitation [§757]

If the taxpayer claimed more than the legally allowable amount, but did not receive any tax benefit from the excess, he does not reduce the basis by the excess. [I.R.C. §1016(a)(2)(B)]

(2) Tenant's improvements [§758]

A lessor has no income by reason of the lessee's construction of improvements on the leased property—either at the time of construction or at the termination of the lease. [I.R.C. §109; *and see supra*, §127] However, if the improvements are intended as a substitute for the payment of rent, they are taxable when built. The lessor is not entitled to increase the basis of the property for the tenant's improvements *unless they were in fact treated as rent* and taxed to him when built. [I.R.C. §1019]

c. Allocation of basis

(1) Partial sale [§759]

When the taxpayer sells or exchanges only a *part* of his asset, he must allocate basis between the part sold and the part retained "in some reasonable manner." [Treas. Reg. §1.61-6(a)]

(a) But note

If this cannot be done conveniently, then the amount received is simply applied against the basis of the part retained. For example, Taxpayer sold an easement to divert foreign waters into a nearby river that formed part of the property. Because the basis of the easement as compared to that of the remaining property was uncertain, the amount received by Taxpayer was held to reduce Taxpayer's basis on the retained property. [**Inaja Land Co. v. Commissioner,** 9 T.C. 727 (1947)]

(2) Lump sum purchase of several assets [§760]

Likewise, when a taxpayer purchases a number of different assets for a lump sum (*e.g.,* purchase of a going business), he must allocate the purchase price to the various assets involved in accordance with their relative values.

B. The Requirement of Realization

1. In General [§761]

Before any increase in net worth becomes taxable (or a decline in value can be deducted as a loss), a *realization* must occur. This means that a crystallizing event has taken place that makes it reasonable and convenient to compute gain or loss. [**Cottage Savings Association v. Commissioner**, 499 U.S. 554 (1991)]

EXAM TIP   **gilbert**

For your exam, be sure to remember that a gain or loss must be *both realized and recognized* before it would be taxable. (*See infra,* §§784 *et seq.*)

---

a. Note

The requirement that income be realized has been held to be a *constitutional limitation* on the government's power to tax. [**Eisner v. Macomber,** *supra,* §22—however, few believe that this case would be followed today]

2. Realization in Property Transactions [§762]

The owner of property realizes gain or loss only on the *sale or other disposition* of property. [I.R.C. §1001] In other words, the disposition is deemed the most appropriate time for computing the owner's gain or loss.

a. Mortgages [§763]

Mortgaging is *not* a realizing transaction—even when the taxpayer-owner borrows more than the basis of the property. [**Woodsam Associates, Inc. v. Commissioner,** 198 F.2d 357 (2d Cir. 1952)]

b. Transfers as payments of debt [§764]

The transfer of appreciated property by a taxpayer in satisfaction of a claim against him is a realization—it is the equivalent of an *exchange*.

---

e.g. **Example:** Taxpayer owes Lender $1,000. Taxpayer transfers to Lender property worth $1,000, but on which Taxpayer's basis is only $400. There is a realization of a $600 gain to Taxpayer. [**United States v. Davis,** 370 U.S. 65 (1962)]

---

(1) Mortgage plus gift [§765]

A gift of property is not a realization (*see supra*, §196), just as mortgaging is not. However, if the two transactions are **combined**, the result may be a realization.

---

e.g. **Example:** Taxpayer had property with a basis of $100 and a value of $400. He mortgaged the property, borrowing $250; there was no personal liability. Then Taxpayer gave the property to a trust for his children subject to the mortgage. *Held:* Because the effect of the transaction was to relieve Taxpayer of the debt, he is deemed to realize the amount of the debt. Thus, Taxpayer realized a gain of $150 on the gift ($250 liability minus $100 basis). [Treas. Reg. §1.1001-2(a)(4)(iii); **Johnson v. Commissioner,** 495 F.2d 1079 (6th Cir. 1974)]

---

(2) Effect of donee's gift tax payment [§766]

If the donor makes the gift conditional on the donee's payment of gift tax, the donor realizes a gain if the gift tax liability exceeds his basis. According to the Supreme Court, the donee's payment of the donor's gift tax produces an immediate economic benefit to the donor equal to the excess of the gift tax over the donor's basis. [**Diedrich v. Commissioner,** 454 U.S. 813 (1982)]

(3) Mortgage foreclosure [§767]

Foreclosure of a mortgage is also a realization—it is treated as a sale by the debtor-mortgagor to the creditor-mortgagee. [*See* **Parker v. Delaney,** 186 F.2d 455 (1st Cir. 1950)]

c. Exchanges [§768]

An exchange is a realization of gain or loss if the property received "differs materially either in kind or in extent" from the property given up. [Treas. Reg. §1.1001-1(a)] Thus, a swap of a pool of mortgages secured by homes in City A for a pool of mortgages secured by land in City B is a realization. This is so even if the swap is done purely for tax avoidance reasons (to recognize a loss) and even if the mortgages in each pool have the same total principal amount, interest rate, and fair market value and are viewed by banking regulators as economically identical. For tax purposes, the mortgages are different because they are secured by different real property; thus, the rates of default or prepayment will vary in the future. The mortgages, therefore, "differ materially" under the regulation. [**Cottage Savings Association v. Commissioner,** *supra*, §761]

EXAM TIP   **gilbert**

On your exam, be sure you are able to identify **when a realization occurs**. Realization does not only occur by sale—it can take many forms, including by sale, by payment of debt, by mortgage foreclosure, and by exchange for property that is materially different.

---

3. Amount Realized [§769]

The amount realized is the sum of the money, plus the fair market value of any other property, received by the taxpayer in a realizing transaction—*i.e.,* on the sale or other disposition of the asset. [I.R.C. §1001(b)]

a. Mortgaged property [§770]

Upon disposing of mortgaged property, a taxpayer's "amount realized" is the sum of the câsh received *plus* the amount of any debt secured by the property for which the taxpayer is no longer liable.

(1) *Crane* rule [§771]

In **Crane v. Commissioner,** 331 U.S. 1 (1947), a leading case in the area, a taxpayer inherited an apartment building from her husband. The building was appraised for federal estate tax purposes at $262,042.50, an amount that was exactly equal to an outstanding mortgage on the building ($255,000) plus the interest then in default ($7,042.50). The taxpayer agreed with the mortgagee to continue to operate the building—collecting rents, paying for operating expenses, etc.—and to pay the mortgagee any net rentals. This relationship continued for seven years, during which time the taxpayer reported the rents as gross income and claimed (and was allowed) deductions for taxes, operating expenses, interest, and depreciation. The interest in default, however, continued to increase. The taxpayer then sold the building to a third party for $3,000 and an agreement to assume the mortgage. The taxpayer claimed that her equity in the building when she acquired it was zero. The Court disagreed, holding that the seller realized the full amount of the outstanding note even though she had no personal obligation to pay it and received only a token amount of cash from the buyer.

(2) Significance [§772]

In many real estate deals, the buyer of property (such as an apartment house) acquires it with a small down payment and borrows the balance using a nonrecourse loan (*i.e.,* a loan for which the borrower has no personal liability). For purposes of claiming depreciation on the building, the taxpayer's basis includes not only the down payment but also the full amount of the nonrecourse loan (*see supra*, §730). However, when the property is disposed of—whether by sale or foreclosure—the taxpayer must treat as an amount realized not only the cash received, but also the full amount of the outstanding loan. Often, this treatment produces a substantial gain because the taxpayer claimed depreciation that exceeded the actual decline in value of the property.

Example: Taxpayer bought Blackacre in Year 1 for $20 down and $140 of nonrecourse debt, making his basis $160. For Years 1 to 6, Taxpayer correctly claimed a total depreciation amount of $45, making Taxpayer's adjusted basis of the property $115. During Year 6, Taxpayer sold Blackacre for $135. Taxpayer's depreciation ($45) exceeded the decline in value of the property ($25). Therefore, Taxpayer has a gain on the sale of $20.

(3) Property worth less than nonrecourse loan [§773]

Suppose that property that secures a nonrecourse loan is worth less than the amount of the loan. The taxpayer might sell the property subject to the loan or the loan may be foreclosed by the lender. Since the loan is nonrecourse, the lender cannot collect the deficiency. Nevertheless, the taxpayer still is treated as realizing the full amount of the mortgage then outstanding. Any other treatment would be inconsistent with allowing her to include the nonrecourse loan in her basis when she acquired the property. [**Commissioner v. Tufts**, 461 U.S. 300 (1983); I.R.C. §7701(g)]

(a) When transferor realizes amount of mortgage [§774]

Property is considered to be disposed of, so the transferor realizes the full amount of the mortgage, when the property is given away, when the mortgage is foreclosed, or when the property is held by a grantor trust and the trust is converted to a nongrantor trust. [Treas. Reg. §1.1001-2; *see supra*, §§765-767; on grantor trusts, *see supra*, §§249-276]

(4) Nonrecourse vs. recourse debt [§775]

The rules relating to recourse debts are not entirely the same as those relating to nonrecourse debts.

(a) Disposition of property under nonrecourse debt [§776]

In the case of a nonrecourse debt, a taxpayer realizes the full amount of the debt when he disposes of the property. The debt is simply treated as part of the sale price of the property. Consequently, if the property was a capital asset, the resulting gain is capital gain (except to the extent it is turned to ordinary income by the depreciation recapture rules). [**Commissioner v. Tufts**, *supra*]

(b) Recourse debt [§777]

Suppose that a creditor under a recourse debt forecloses his mortgage. Since the property is worth less than the mortgage, the creditor could collect a deficiency judgment from the borrower. However, the creditor fails to do so. The amount forgiven by the failure to collect the deficiency is treated as debt cancellation income to the borrower. Debt cancellation income is ordinary income, not capital gain, although there are a number of exceptions to the rule that such income is immediately taxable. [Treas. Reg. §1.1001-2; **Aizawa v. Commissioner**, 99 T.C. 197 (1992), *aff'd*, 29 F.3d 630 (9th Cir. 1994)—taxpayer realizes bid price at foreclosure sale, since bid was equal to value of property, *not* full amount of debt; **Frazier v. Commissioner,** 111 T.C. 243 (1998)—fair market value of property much less than bid price; Rev. Rul. 90-16, 1990-1 C.B. 12] For a discussion of debt cancellation income, *see supra,* §§125-139.

---

e.g. **Example:** Taxpayer owns Blackacre, which has a basis of $4,000. Blackacre is subject to a mortgage of $9,000, but it is only worth $8,100. Taxpayer transfers the property, either to the lender or to a third party. *If the debt is nonrecourse,* Taxpayer has a capital gain of $5,000 because she is treated as having realized the amount of the debt. *If the debt is recourse,* Taxpayer has a capital gain of $4,100 and debt cancellation income of $900 if the creditor does not collect the $900 deficiency. Debt cancellation income is ordinary, not capital. However, if Taxpayer were insolvent, Taxpayer could exclude the debt cancellation income. (*See supra,* §143.)

---

b. Sale for future payments [§778]

Property is frequently sold in exchange for a down payment plus additional payments in the future. (Note that the deferred payment obligation must call for interest at or above the applicable federal rate or interest will be imputed; *see infra,* §§923 *et seq.*)

(1) Installment method [§779]

Normally in this situation, the seller will use the installment method of taxation, under which the income will be recognized as payments are made. (*See infra,* §§1055 *et seq.*) If the seller elects not to use the installment method (or does not qualify for it), the amount realized on the sale and the timing of income recognition depends on several factors.

(2) Cash method [§780]

If the sale price is a fixed amount and the seller uses the cash method of accounting, the seller treats the fair market value of the consideration received (cash and installment obligation) as the amount realized. In no event will the value of the consideration received be less than the value of the property given up. [Treas. Reg. §15.453-1(d)(2)(ii); **Philadelphia Park Amusement Co. v. United States,** 126 F. Supp. 184 (Ct. Cl. 1954)—property received presumed equal in value to property given up] If the amount is a contingent payment obligation, the normal rule is that the obligation must be assigned a valuation; only in rare and extraordinary cases in which the market value of neither the property surrendered nor the obligation received can be determined can the open transaction method (*see* below) be used. [Treas. Reg. §15.453-1(d)(1)(2)(iii)]

(3) Accrual method [§781]

If the sale price is a fixed amount and the seller uses the accrual method of accounting, the seller treats the full sale price as the amount realized, regardless of the market value of the obligation. [Treas. Reg. §15.453-1(d)(2)(ii)] If the sale price is contingent, an accrual method taxpayer includes the market value of the obligation in income unless it cannot be valued. [Treas. Reg. §15.453-1(d)(1)(2)(iii)]

(4) Open transaction method [§782]

In rare and extraordinary cases in which neither the obligation received nor the property surrendered can be valued, taxpayers can use the open transaction method. Under this method, gain is reported only after the payments have exhausted the seller's basis; the buyer's obligation is treated as having no present value. [**Burnet v. Logan,** 283 U.S. 404 (1931)] Even in such cases, the installment method can be (and normally is) used. (*See infra,* §§1060 *et seq.*)

(a) IRS opposition [§783]

The IRS opposes the open transaction method because it defers tax on the seller's income until after the entire basis has been recovered. Such deferral of tax is quite valuable. Moreover, once basis is exhausted, the gain is entirely capital gain. However, if the installment method is not used and the transaction is closed by valuing the obligation and including that value in income, any subsequent income (*i.e.,* amounts received in excess of the valuation) is taxed as ordinary income. [**Waring v. Commissioner,** 412 F.2d 800 (3d Cir. 1969)]

---

e.g. **Example:** Taxpayer owns Acme Co. stock, having a basis of $40. Taxpayer sells it to Buyer for $15 down and an annual payment for the next five years of 20% of Acme Co.'s profits. Taxpayer elects out of the installment method. Under **Burnet v. Logan,** *supra,* this might well be considered an "open transaction." The $15 down payment would not be taxed but would reduce Taxpayer's basis to $25. The next $25 would also be tax-free and would reduce the basis to zero. All subsequent payments would be taxable as capital gain.

---

e.g. **Example:** Suppose in the preceding example that it is held that the stream of payments has a present value of $110. The transaction is "closed." Consequently, Taxpayer would realize a capital gain of $85 in the year of sale (amount realized of $110 plus $15, less basis of $40). The contract right would have a basis of $110 in Taxpayer's hands. Recovery on the contract right would be allocated between tax-free recovery of the $110 basis and profit. The profit would be ordinary income because there is no sale or exchange when a debt is collected (*see infra,* §907).

C. Nonrecognition of Gain or Loss

1. In General [§784]

I.R.C. section 1001(c) provides that the gain or loss realized on the sale or exchange of an asset is *recognized* (taxed) only to the extent provided in I.R.C. section 1002. Section 1002 states that all gain or loss is recognized subject to certain exceptions—the "nonrecognition" provisions discussed immediately below. Thus, the "nonrecognition" statutes are a second line of defense: Gain or loss must be both *realized* and *recognized*.

2. Nonrecognition Provisions [§785]

The Code provides many exceptions to the general rule that all gain or loss is recognized at the time of a sale or exchange. However, there is a price for nonrecognition: The basis of the property received by the taxpayer is the basis of the property transferred (a substituted basis; *see supra*, §739). Therefore, the gain or loss is simply *deferred* until the acquired property is ultimately sold.

a. Like kind exchanges [§786]

No *gain or loss* is recognized on an exchange where property held either for investment or for use in business is exchanged solely for property of *like kind*. [I.R.C. §1031(a)]

(1) Like kind defined [§787]

Like kind refers to the *general nature or character* of the property, not to its grade or quality. For example, real estate held for business use or investment is of like kind with any other business or investment real estate—and this is true even though one parcel is improved and the other is unimproved (*e.g.*, a ranch held for investment traded for a hotel used in business). However, property within the United States and property outside of the United States are not of like kind. [I.R.C. §1031(h)]

(a) Personal property [§788]

The definition of like kind is stricter for personal property. For example, coins that are valuable for collecting purposes are not of like kind with foreign currency. [**California Federal Life Insurance Co. v. Commissioner**, 680 F.2d 85 (9th Cir. 1982)] Indeed, the IRS asserts that gold bullion and silver bullion are not of like kind since silver is used primarily as an industrial commodity while gold is primarily an investment. [Rev. Rul. 82-166, 1982-2 C.B. 190]

(2) Coverage limited to tangible property other than inventory [§789]

I.R.C. section 1031 does *not* apply to stocks and bonds or partnership interests; neither does it apply to stock in trade, inventory, or other property held for *sale* to customers in the ordinary course of a trade or business.

(*See infra*, §§831 *et seq.*) It covers only real or tangible property held for investment or for use in business, *e.g.*, buildings, machinery, fixtures, etc.

EXAM TIP   **gilbert**

On your exam, it is very important to remember that the nonrecognition provision [I.R.C. §1031] for like kind exchanges is very narrow: It applies only to *real or tangible personal property* held for investment or for use in business. Don't be fooled by facts telling you, *e.g.*, that an insurance company exchanged 100,000 shares of Kohl's stock that it was holding as an investment for 100,000 shares of Sears stock; such an exchange does not qualify as a like kind exchange.

---

(3) "Triangle exchanges" [§790]

A three-way exchange may qualify under the statute. For example, suppose Taxpayer wants to sell his ranch property to Purch for $100,000, but wants to defer the tax. Taxpayer intends to reinvest the proceeds in an apartment house anyhow, so he has Purch buy the apartment house for $100,000 and then Purch and Taxpayer exchange properties. This qualifies as a like kind exchange for purposes of I.R.C. section 1031. [**Alderson v. Commissioner,** 317 F.2d 790 (9th Cir. 1963)—the fact that property is acquired solely for the purpose of making the exchange held immaterial]

(a) Deferred exchanges [§791]

Suppose that Taxpayer has not yet selected the apartment house that is to be exchanged for his ranch. It is possible to have a deferred exchange in which Taxpayer transfers his ranch to Purch, and Purch agrees to purchase an apartment house (when Taxpayer selects it) and transfer it to Taxpayer. If Taxpayer fails to select an apartment house within five years, Purch will pay Taxpayer cash for the ranch. An apartment house was selected within the five-year period, and the court held that Taxpayer was entitled to nonrecognition of gain. [**Starker v. United States,** 602 F.2d 1341 (9th Cir. 1979)]

(b) Statutory limit [§792]

The rule in *Starker* has been limited by a subsequent statute. Although a deferred exchange is still permitted, the replacement property must be "identified" within 45 days after the taxpayer transfers the property to the purchaser, and the replacement property must be actually received by the taxpayer within 180 days after he transfers his property (or, if earlier, the due date of the tax return for the year in which the taxpayer transferred the property). The Regulations set forth a number of methods to avoid being in actual or constructive receipt of the boot property, the most common of which involves the use of qualified intermediaries. [*See* I.R.C. §1031(a)(3); Treas. Reg. §1.1031(k)—detailed definitions and examples of deferred exchanges]

(4) Sale and leaseback [§793]

Suppose Taxpayer sells his building to Purch for a price substantially less than his basis in the property and then leases it back from Purch on a long-term lease. Can Taxpayer claim a loss on the transaction, or is this an exchange of like kind properties within I.R.C. section 1031, so that no loss is recognized?

(a) IRS position [§794]

If the lease is for *more than 30 years*, the IRS deems it the equivalent of a fee interest [Treas. Reg. §1.1031(a)], so the "like kind" requirement is met, and the loss is not recognized.

(b) Judicial approach [§795]

Although an earlier case upheld the IRS position [**Century Electric Co. v. Commissioner**, 192 F.2d 155 (8th Cir. 1952)], the trend of judicial opinion is that a sale and leaseback cannot be treated as an "exchange"—so section 1031 is not applicable. [**Jordan Marsh Co. v. Commissioner**, 269 F.2d 453 (2d Cir. 1959); **Leslie Co. v. Commissioner**, 64 T.C. 247 (1975), *aff'd*, 539 F.2d 943 (3d Cir. 1976)]

(5) Effect of "boot" [§796]

If a taxpayer receives both like kind and non-like kind property in a section 1031 exchange, the non-like kind property is called "boot." *Realized gain is recognized* to the extent of the boot. [I.R.C. §1031(b)]

Example: Taxpayer owns a hotel with a basis of $30,000 and a value of $100,000. She exchanges it for an apartment building having a value of $85,000, together with $15,000 in cash. The cash is boot. Her realized gain is $70,000. The recognized gain is $15,000.

Example: Same as previous example except that Taxpayer's basis is $90,000. Her realized gain is $10,000. All of it is recognized. Although the boot was equal to $15,000, the taxpayer *never recognizes more than her realized gain.*

Example: Same as the first example except that Taxpayer's basis for the hotel was $110,000. She has a realized loss of $10,000. None of it is recognized. The presence of boot in a section 1031 exchange *does not permit recognition of loss.* [I.R.C. §1031(c)]

(a) Transfer of boot [§797]

A taxpayer does not recognize any gain on the *like kind* property if she *transfers* boot to the other party, rather than receiving it. However, if the boot transferred by the taxpayer consists of property other than money, and this property is worth more or less than its basis, the taxpayer *must recognize gain or loss on the boot.*

---

e.g. **Example:** Taxpayer exchanges land with a basis of $60,000 and a value of $180,000 for land worth $200,000, and to equalize the deal, also transfers IBM stock having a basis of $8,000 and a value of $20,000. Taxpayer does not recognize any of the gain on the land because he did not receive any boot. But Taxpayer must recognize the $12,000 gain on the stock.

(b) Adjustment to basis [§798]

The presence of boot requires adjustments to basis of the acquired property. The formula is:

New basis = old basis + gain recognized − money received.

Thus, in the three examples in §796, *supra*, the basis of the new apartment house would be $30,000, $85,000, and $95,000, respectively. [*See* I.R.C. §1031(d), *and see* additional examples in Treas. Reg. §1.1031(d)-1]

1) If the boot received is in a form other than money, part of the basis must be allocated to the boot. Thus, in the first example (*supra,* §796) suppose that Taxpayer received stock worth $15,000 instead of $15,000 in cash. The basis of the apartment building plus the stock would be $45,000 (old basis + gain recognized − money received). Of the $45,000 basis, $15,000 is allocated to the stock (its fair market value). That leaves $30,000 for the apartment house.

2) If a taxpayer pays boot (rather than receives it), the basis of the new property is *increased* by the amount of cash paid, the basis of the property paid, and gain recognized on the boot; it is reduced by loss recognized on the boot. Recall the example in §797, where Taxpayer exchanges land with a basis of $60,000 and a value of $180,000 for land worth $200,000 and Taxpayer also transfers IBM stock with a basis of $8,000 and a value of $20,000. Taxpayer's basis for the new land is $80,000: old basis ($60,000) + basis of property paid ($8,000) + gain recognized ($12,000) = $80,000.

(6) Effect of mortgages [§799]

Most real property that is exchanged is subject to outstanding mortgages. Usually, the property will remain subject to the mortgage in the hands of the person acquiring it. For tax purposes, this is treated the same as if the acquiring party paid cash.

(a) Illustration [§800]

Alex owns land with a basis of $65,000 and value of $100,000. It is subject to a mortgage of $40,000. Alex exchanges it for Becky's land, which is worth $85,000 and is subject to a mortgage of $25,000.

(i) The effect of Alex and Becky's each taking subject to the other's mortgage is that each is treated as having paid cash to the other. Thus, Becky has, in effect, paid Alex $40,000; Alex has effectively paid Becky $25,000. These amounts are then netted out—so that the only boot payment is the difference—$15,000 to Alex.

(ii) Alex's realized gain is $35,000 (value of $100,000 less basis of $65,000). Of this amount, $15,000 is recognized—the boot received.

(iii) Alex's basis for the new land is $65,000: old basis ($65,000) + boot paid ($25,000) + gain recognized ($15,000) – cash received ($40,000) = $65,000.

[*See* Treas. Reg. §1.1031(d)-2—additional examples]

(7) Exchanges between related persons [§801]

If a taxpayer exchanges property under section 1031 with a related person, and the related person disposes of the property within two years of the exchange, the taxpayer must recognize gain or loss on the original exchange. The same thing happens if the taxpayer disposes of the property acquired in the exchange within two years of the exchange. [I.R.C. §1031(f)(1)] The gain or loss is recognized in the year the related party disposes of the property. The definition of related person is supplied by I.R.C. section 267(b) (*see supra,* §514).

(a) Exceptions [§802]

Certain dispositions by the related party will not trigger recognition of gain or loss. These include dispositions after the death of either the taxpayer or the related person, an involuntary conversion of the property (*see* below), or a transaction with respect to which the IRS is satisfied that neither the exchange nor the disposition had tax avoidance as one of its principal purposes. [I.R.C. §1031(f)(2)]

Example: In 2004, Stocker and Bigco engage in a swap. Stocker transfers Blackacre to Bigco, and Bigco transfers Whiteacre to Stocker. Bigco is a corporation, and Stocker owns 60% of Bigco's stock. Thus, Stocker and Bigco are related parties. [I.R.C. §267(b)(2)] In 2005, Bigco sells Blackacre. This sale requires Stocker to recognize in 2005 the gain on Blackacre that was not recognized in 2004, when the swap occurred. Moreover, Bigco's disposition of Blackacre requires Bigco to recognize in 2005 its gain on Whiteacre, which it did not recognize in 2004, when the swap occurred.

b. Involuntary conversion [§803]

Gain is frequently realized when a taxpayer's property is condemned and she receives an eminent domain award from the government. Similarly, gain is often realized when property is destroyed or stolen and the taxpayer recovers insurance proceeds. These transactions are called "involuntary conversions." Since by definition the realization was involuntary and probably undesired, the Code allows the taxpayer to elect not to recognize the gains.

(1) Code provision [§804]

I.R.C. section 1033 provides that if the taxpayer replaces the property "involuntarily converted" *within two years* after the close of the tax year in which she receives the proceeds from the conversion, with other property *"similar or related in service or use"* to the property converted, realized gain will be recognized only to the extent that the amount realized from the conversion exceeds the cost of replacement.

Example: Taxpayer's factory had a value of $100,000 and an adjusted basis of $60,000. It was totally destroyed by fire, and Taxpayer received $100,000 in insurance proceeds. She invested $86,000 in a new factory within two years and elected to take advantage of section 1033. Her realized gain was $40,000, and her recognized gain is $14,000 (*i.e.,* the proceeds that were not reinvested).

(a) Method of replacement [§805]

The replacement may be made by actually purchasing property "similar or related in service or use" to the converted property, or by acquiring at least 80% of the voting stock of a corporation owning such property. [I.R.C. §1033(a)]

(b) Section is elective [§806]

Unlike the other nonrecognition provisions, nonrecognition under I.R.C. section 1033 is *elective*, not mandatory. A taxpayer can recognize the gain if she wishes to do so. Also, I.R.C. section 1033 applies only to nonrecognition of gain—not loss. Realized losses on involuntary conversion must be recognized.

(c) Moving expenses related to condemnation of property [§807]

Amounts received from the state for the expenses of moving to a new factory after the old one is condemned are eligible for nonrecognition under section 1033. Similarly, severance damages are eligible (they are damages paid by the state to reflect the decline in value of the retained portion of condemned land). [**Graphic Press Inc. v. Commissioner**, 523 F.2d 585 (9th Cir. 1975)]

(2) Distinguish—section 1031 (like kind exchanges) [§808]

The "similar or related in service or use" test of section 1033 is considerably stricter than the "like kind" test of section 1031 (especially as applied to real property). Under the section 1033 test, the end uses of the property must be similar; *e.g.,* a drill press used by taxpayer in a factory would not be similar to equipment that the taxpayer leases to others. Nor would the fixtures in a retail grocery be similar to a drill press in a factory. However, if the taxpayer was the lessor of the original property and also of the replacement property, I.R.C. section 1033 applies even though the use by the tenants is different. [**Liant Record Inc. v. Commissioner,** 303 F.2d 326 (2d Cir. 1962)]

(a) Special rules for condemnation of business real property [§809]

A special rule applies to condemnations of business real property (or sales of such property under threat of condemnation). No gain is recognized if the proceeds are reinvested in like kind property, whether *or not* the property is "similar or related in service or use" to the property condemned. Thus, the more generous test of I.R.C. section 1031 is used rather than the stricter section 1033 test. Moreover, three years is allowed as the replacement period instead of the usual two. [I.R.C. §1033(g)]

COMPARISON OF LIKE KIND EXCHANGES, INVOLUNTARY CONVERSIONS, AND CONDEMNATIONS OF BUSINESS REAL PROPERTY	**gilbert**		
	LIKE KIND EXCHANGES	**INVOLUNTARY CONVERSIONS**	**CONDEMNATIONS OF BUSINESS REAL PROPERTY**
SITUATION	Voluntary exchange of property	Exchange due to casualty, loss, condemnation, or theft	Condemnation of business real property only
TYPE OF REPLACEMENT PROPERTY	Same general nature or character; stricter similarity requirement for personal property	Similar or related in service or use	Any real property used for business
ELECTIVE/NOT ELECTIVE	Not elective	Elective	Elective
REPLACEMENT PERIOD	Replacement property must be identified within 45 days of transfer and must be actually received within 180 days	Two years	Three years

c. Nonrecognition of gain on sale of principal residence [§810]

No loss can be recognized on the sale of a personal residence (*see supra*, §499).

In most cases, gain from the sale of a principal residence is not recognized. However, gains on the sale of a residence in excess of $250,000 (or $500,000 on a joint return) are taxable as capital gain. [I.R.C. §121] Prior law, which allowed nonrecognition of gain of any amount, but only if taxpayer reinvested the sales price in a new home, has been repealed. [Former I.R.C. §1034]

(1) Requirements for section 121 [§811]

To qualify for exclusion of gain ($250,000 or $500,000), the taxpayer must have *owned and used* the dwelling as a *principal residence* for periods aggregating *two years or more in the five-year period* ending on the date of the sale or exchange. [I.R.C. §121(a)] If the taxpayer acquired the property in a like kind exchange under section 1031 and converted it to personal residence use, the taxpayer must hold the property for five years from the date of its acquisition to qualify for the exclusion. [I.R.C. §121(d)(10)]

(2) Once every two years [§812]

The exclusion is not available if during the two-year period ending on the date of the sale or exchange there was *any other sale or exchange to which section 121 applied.* [I.R.C. §121(b)(3)]

(3) Married couples [§813]

To qualify for the $500,000 exclusion, a married couple must file a joint return for the year in which the sale or exchange occurs. To file a joint return, the couple must still be married on the last day of the taxable year. Either spouse can be the record owner of the house, but *both* spouses must meet the two-year use and two-year prior sale requirements. [I.R.C. §121(b)(2)] The $250,000 exclusion is available on a joint return if *either* spouse (but not both spouses) meets the ownership, use, and prior-sale requirements. [I.R.C. §121(d)(1)]

---

e.g. Example: Jack owns a condominium, which he bought in 1999 and for which his basis is $150,000. In 2005, he marries Kate and has her added as a record owner of the condo. They live happily thereafter in the condo. In early 2006, they decide to move into a larger house in the suburbs in order to start a family, and they sell the condo for $500,000 in the same year. Only $250,000 of the $350,000 gain may be excluded because Kate has not lived in the condo for more than two years.

EXAM TIP **gilbert**

A question regarding the sale of a taxpayer's residence may come up on your exam. Remember the test—if the taxpayer (i) owned and used the house as a *principal residence for at least two of the past five years* and (ii) has *not used the exclusion in the past two years*, he may exclude from income $250,000 of the gain ($500,000 for married couples, assuming *both* spouses meet the above test).

(4) Marital dissolution rules

(a) Marital property divisions [§814]

If a spouse or former spouse receives a residence in a marital property division described in I.R.C. section 1041 (*see infra*, §816), the period that the spouse or former spouse owns the property *includes the period that the transferor owned the property*. [I.R.C. §121(d)(3)(A)]

(b) Out spouse rule [§815]

Frequently in marital dissolution situations, one spouse ("in spouse") is allowed to remain in the house but the house continues to be owned by both spouses. Later the house is sold and the proceeds are divided between the in spouse and the out spouse. The out spouse is treated as using the property as a principal residence during the period that the in spouse is granted use of the property *under a divorce or separation instrument*. [I.R.C. §121(d)(3)(B); *see supra*, §163, for discussion of the phrase "divorce or separation instrument"]

d. Sales between spouses [§816]

No gain or loss is recognized on *sales or other transfers* between spouses or between former spouses if the sale is *incident to a divorce*. [I.R.C. §1041]

(1) Prior law [§817]

Under prior law, property settlements in divorce frequently were taxable. [**United States v. Davis**, 370 U.S. 65 (1962)—Husband's transfer of appreciated stock to Wife in discharge of Wife's marital property rights produced gain to Husband] This created serious problems in negotiating property divisions and resulted in enactment of section 1041, which makes all such transfers nontaxable events.

(2) Recipient's basis [§818]

The recipient's basis remains the same as the transferor's basis—whether the property was appreciated or depreciated and regardless of whether the acquiring party paid for the property. [I.R.C. §1041(b)(2)]

(3) Incident to divorce [§819]

Even if a property division occurs after divorce, it still falls under the nonrecognition rule if it occurs within one year after the marriage ceases or (even if after one year) it is "related to the cessation of the marriage." [I.R.C. §1041(c); *see* Treas. Reg. §1.041-1T—transfer within six years of divorce and required by divorce instrument presumed to be related to cessation of marriage]

Example: Husband and Wife own property accumulated during their marriage worth $500,000. The property is in Husband's name. As part of a property division ordered by the family court, an asset worth

$250,000 is conveyed to Wife. Husband's adjusted basis for this asset was $60,000. Under section 1041, Husband recognizes no gain on this transfer. Wife's basis for the asset is $60,000. Under prior law, the transfer would have produced $190,000 in gain to Husband, and Wife's basis would have been $250,000. The result is the same whether Husband and Wife live in a community property or noncommunity property state.

e. Mortgage repossessions [§820]

In the past, sellers of property who financed the purchase with a mortgage were taxed when they foreclosed on the property and took it back. Under the current rule, however, the gain is not recognized in this situation, and the seller does not get a bad debt deduction. [I.R.C. §1038]

NONRECOGNITION CHECKLIST   gilbert

GAINS FROM THE FOLLOWING EVENTS GENERALLY ARE NOT RECOGNIZED AND THEREFORE MAY NOT BE CURRENTLY TAXABLE

☑ *Like kind exchanges*—When *real property* held for investment or business purposes is replaced with similar real property, no gain or loss is recognized. When *tangible personal property* held for investment or business purposes is replaced with other property having the same character, gain or loss is not recognized. If the taxpayer receives "*boot,*" gain but not loss is recognized. "Transfers" include replacement property identified within 45 days of transfer and actually received within 180 days of the original transfer.

☑ *Involuntary conversion*—A gain on property that was involuntarily converted need not be recognized if replaced with property "*similar or related in service or use*" within two years of conversion.

☑ *Sale of principal residence*—*Gain* of up to $250,000 on the sale of a taxpayer's principal residence is not recognized, *provided* that the taxpayer (i) owned and used the "*principal residence*" for periods aggregating *two years or more during the past five years*; and (ii) the taxpayer has *not used this provision during the past two years*. *Losses* on a principal residence *cannot* be recognized.

☑ *Sales between spouses*—*No gain or loss* is recognized on sales or other transfers between spouses or former spouses *when the transfer is incident to divorce*.

☑ *Mortgage repossessions*—A seller who financed a sale with a mortgage does not recognize a gain if he forecloses on the property. Note, however, that he also does not receive a bad debt deduction.

Chapter Five: What Kind of Income Is It? Capital Gains and Losses and Tax Preferences

CONTENTS

Chapter Approach

Chapter Approach

This section deals with items of income or deduction that are specially treated. Most of the chapter concerns capital gains and losses, which arise on the sale or exchange of certain kinds of property ("capital assets"). Capital gain is taxed at a lower rate than ordinary income, but the deduction of capital losses is restricted. The chapter also covers the alternative minimum tax on tax preferences, which imposes a special tax on certain deductions and items of income.

1. **Capital Gains and Losses**

   Long-term capital gain is taxed at a maximum rate of 15%, while ordinary income can be taxed at rates up to 35%. Capital losses are fully deductible against capital gains, and deductible up to $3,000 against ordinary income. If a possible capital gain or loss issue arises on your exam, analyze it as follows:

   a. Determine whether the asset is a *capital asset*. All assets are capital unless they fall within a statutory exception (dealer property, taxpayer-produced copyrights, etc.) or within a case law exception (sales of rights to income, contract rights to render personal services, and certain personal rights).

      (1) Be sure to *fragment assets* if the question involves the sale of a business. This allows for a separate examination of each asset to determine gain or loss.

      (2) Real property and depreciable personal property held for one year or more and used in a trade or business are *quasi-capital assets* under I.R.C. section 1231. If there is a net gain, all transactions are capital. If there is a net loss, all transactions are ordinary.

   b. Determine whether there was a *sale or exchange*. Note that a foreclosure of mortgaged property is a sale or exchange. On the other hand, some cases hold that a transfer of contract rights to the other party to the contract is not a sale or exchange.

   c. Determine whether any *special restrictions* apply:

      (1) In a sale for deferred payments, where a contract fails to charge the applicable rate, *interest is imputed*. Thus, the buyer may have an unexpected interest deduction, and the seller may have interest income rather than capital gain.

      (2) All *depreciation* (up to the realized gain) on personal property is *recaptured* and thus treated as ordinary income. For buildings, the depreciation

is not recaptured as ordinary income, but it is taxable at a higher rate than the balance of the gain.

(3) Losses in *transactions between family members* or between an individual and a corporation that he controls are not deductible.

2. Alternative Minimum Tax

For any exam question that asks you to compute the amount of tax owed, consider whether the alternative minimum tax applies. The tax is arrived at by adding back certain tax preferences, making certain deductions, subtracting an exemption, and applying a 26% or 28% rate. If the result exceeds the taxpayer's regular tax, he *must pay* the alternative minimum tax instead.

A. Introductory Material

TAX ON CAPITAL GAINS		**gilbert**
LENGTH OF HOLDING	**TYPE OF GAIN**	**TAX RATE**
12 months or less	short-term capital gain	taxpayer's normal rate
more than 12 months	long-term capital gain	5% for taxpayer in the 15% bracket 15% for other taxpayers

1. Capital Gain [§821]

Long-term capital gain is taxed at a lower rate than ordinary income.

a. General rule [§822]

The tax on an individual's net capital gain is 15%, except that for an individual in the 15% bracket, the tax on net capital gain is only 5%. [I.R.C. §1(h)] Net capital gain means the excess of net long-term capital gain over net short-term capital loss. [I.R.C. §1222(11)] For this purpose, "long term" means a holding period of more than 12 months. These rates, enacted in 2003 and extended in 2006, are temporary and scheduled to expire on December 31, 2010. At that time, the long-term capital gain rates will revert to their pre-2003 levels of 10% for taxpayers in the 15% bracket and 20% for other taxpayers.

b. Sales of real estate [§823]

Gain on depreciable real estate is recaptured to the extent of depreciation on the property. The maximum tax on the recaptured portion of the gain is 25%. The maximum tax on additional gain, if any, is 15%. [I.R.C. §1(h)(6)]

c. Dividends [§824]

Qualified dividend income, defined as income from dividends received from domestic corporations or certain qualified foreign corporations, is added to net long-term capital gains for purposes of computing the tax. Thus, while such dividends are not technically capital gains, they are subject to tax at the same rate as net long-term capital gains (15% or 5%). [I.R.C. §1(h)(11)—for further discussion of qualified dividend income, *see* Taxation of Business Entities Summary]

d. Collectibles [§825]

Collectibles, such as stamps, most coins, antiques, gems, etc., do not qualify for the low capital gain rates (15% or 5%). Such items are taxed at a maximum rate of 28%. [I.R.C. §§1(h)(4)(A), 408(m)]

2. Capital Loss [§826]

Capital loss can be deducted against capital gain for the year (long-term or short-term) plus $3,000. If capital loss exceeds capital gain plus $3,000, the excess can be carried forward to future years and offset against capital gains in those years plus $3,000. [I.R.C. §§1211(b), 1212]

Example: Taxpayer has long-term capital gain of $140,000 and short-term capital loss of $12,000. The loss is fully deductible. Net capital gain is $128,000.

Example: Taxpayer has short-term capital gain of $60,000 and long-term capital loss of $220,000. Of this loss, $60,000 is deductible against the capital gain and an additional $3,000 is deductible against ordinary income. The balance of the loss ($157,000) is carried forward to future years.

EXAM TIP   gilbert

On your exam, you may encounter a fact pattern in which the taxpayer will attempt to *treat a gain differently than is provided in the Code*. For example, such a fact pattern could arise when a taxpayer has a large ordinary loss in a given year, thereby providing the taxpayer with a motive to improperly treat a capital gain as an ordinary gain in order to take full advantage of his ordinary loss, even though the tax rate is higher for an ordinary gain. Don't be fooled by this type of fact pattern—just follow the approach *infra*, §828.

3. Other Implications of Capital Asset Treatment [§827]

The capital versus ordinary distinction must be drawn for numerous other purposes under the Code. For example, a charitable contribution deduction is reduced by the amount of gain that would have been either ordinary income or short-term capital gain had the asset been sold. [I.R.C. §170(e)(1)(A)]

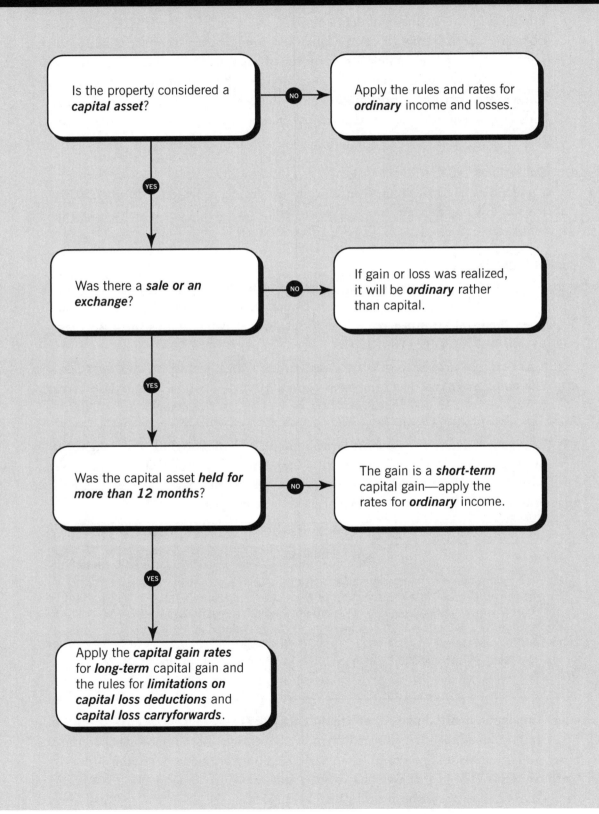

Is the property considered a *capital asset*?

—**NO**→ Apply the rules and rates for *ordinary* income and losses.

YES

Was there a *sale or an exchange*?

—**NO**→ If gain or loss was realized, it will be *ordinary* rather than capital.

YES

Was the capital asset *held for more than 12 months*?

—**NO**→ The gain is a *short-term* capital gain—apply the rates for *ordinary* income.

YES

Apply the *capital gain rates* for *long-term* capital gain and the rules for *limitations on capital loss deductions* and *capital loss carryforwards*.

4. Approach [§828]

To classify a particular gain or loss arising from the disposition of property, ask the following questions:

(i)   Is the property involved a *"capital asset"*?

(ii) Was there a *"sale* or *exchange"*?

(iii) Is the gain or loss *long-term* or *short-term*?

If the gain or loss is long-term, apply the rules for limitation of *capital loss deductions* and *capital loss carryforwards*. Otherwise, apply the rates for ordinary income.

B. Is It a Capital Asset?

1. General Rule [§829]

I.R.C. section 1221 states that *all* property held by the taxpayer is a capital asset—except the specific types of property discussed in the following paragraphs.

a. Note—judicial interpretation

In spite of the broad language of I.R.C. section 1221 ("all property . . . except"), the courts have held that the statute does not mean what it says; *i.e.,* the statutory exceptions below are *not* exclusive.

2. Statutory Exceptions [§830]

I.R.C. section 1221 specifically states that the following types of property are *not* capital assets (and hence any gain or loss on disposition of the property is treated as "ordinary" income or loss):

a. Property held for sale [§831]

Inventory and property held for *sale to customers in the ordinary course of business* are not capital assets. [I.R.C. §1221(a)(1)]

 Example: Shoes in the hands of a shoe manufacturer or in the stockroom of a shoe store are inventory and thus are not capital assets.

(1) Real estate [§832]

Most of the problems in applying this section arise in connection with real estate. Although land and buildings can be held for investment, this is frequently not the case. When a taxpayer buys a large parcel of land and splits it into smaller lots, which she then sells to individual customers, the lots generally will not be capital assets since the lots are held "primarily for sale to customers in the ordinary course of business." The same result follows if the taxpayer builds and sells many houses. The problem is in deciding whether the taxpayer is an investor or a "dealer" (someone who holds the property for sale to customers).

(a) Determinative factors [§833]

These cases are decided by considering all the particular circumstances. The most important factor is the number and continuity of the sales. If only isolated sales have been made, it is likely that the taxpayer is an investor. But if there is a steady flow of sales, the taxpayer will probably be considered a dealer. Another important factor is the extent to which the taxpayer improved or subdivided the property. If the taxpayer merely buys a parcel of land and sells it intact, the land is probably a capital asset. If the taxpayer subdivides it or builds on it, it is more likely held for sale. Other relevant factors are the purpose for which the property was purchased and used (*e.g.*, a farm field purchased for farming is probably a capital asset; a farm field purchased and subdivided for sale is probably not a capital asset) and the extent to which the taxpayer made efforts (through advertising, etc.) to sell the property. [*See* **Biedenharn Realty Co. v. United States,** 526 F.2d 409 (5th Cir.), *cert. denied,* 429 U.S. 819 (1976)]

(b) Liquidating investments [§834]

According to some cases, when property is purchased and held for investment or farming, and then is liquidated through many piecemeal sales, and the taxpayer does not reinvest the proceeds in real estate, the sales give rise to capital gain. [**Curtis Co. v. Commissioner,** 232 F.2d 167 (3d Cir. 1956)] The prevailing view, however, is that large-scale sales activity changes the taxpayer's purpose into holding for sale in the ordinary course of business—and thus the sales produce ordinary income, unless the change in purpose was induced by unanticipated, external factors such as acts of God. [**Biedenharn Realty Co. v. United States,** *supra*]

(c) Undecided or dual purpose [§835]

Sometimes property will be held for several purposes. In that case, the property is a capital asset unless sale to customers is the *most important purpose*. [**Malat v. Riddell,** 383 U.S. 569 (1966)—defining the word "primarily" in section 1221(a)(1)] Indeed, a taxpayer who is a real estate dealer as to some parcels can be an investor as to other parcels. [**Malat v. Riddell,** *supra*]

(d) Exception—real property subdivided for sale [§836]

One rather narrow statutory provision is sometimes of assistance in classifying these transactions. Under I.R.C. section 1237, a parcel of land will be treated as *not* being held primarily for sale to customers in the ordinary course of business if:

(i) *The taxpayer holds no other real estate for sale*;

(ii) *The taxpayer made no substantial improvement* in the land, such as installing sewers; and

(iii) *The land was held for five years.*

In addition, after *five or more lots from a single tract* are sold, the taxpayer must treat an amount equal to 5% of the selling price as ordinary income; the balance of the gain, if any, would be capital gain.

(2) Securities [§837]

Unlike real property, securities are generally treated as capital assets, regardless of the extent and continuity of the taxpayer's dealings with them. This was Congress's intent when it added "to customers" to I.R.C. section 1221(a)(1). [**Bielfeldt v. Commissioner,** 231 F.3d 1035 (7th Cir. 2000); **Van Suetendael v. Commissioner,** 152 F.2d 654 (2d Cir. 1946)]

(a) "Dealers" and "traders" of securities [§838]

However, if a taxpayer is classified as a "dealer" in securities, the securities are not treated as capital assets. To be considered a dealer, the taxpayer must do more than buy and sell large amounts of securities in an attempt to make a profit on price fluctuations. Instead, the taxpayer must also render some form of service.

---

e.g. **Example:** A stockbroker who owns shares that he sells to his customers at market price plus a commission would be a "dealer," as would a floor specialist on one of the stock exchanges. (A floor specialist is a person or entity that maintains an inventory in a particular stock, and that agrees to buy and sell that stock under certain conditions in order to ensure that there is always a market for the stock.) [**Bielfeldt v. Commissioner,** *supra*—taxpayer who lost hundreds of millions of dollars speculating in government bonds is not a dealer and thus has a capital loss rather than an ordinary loss]

---

1) Mark-to-market accounting [§839]

Dealers in securities *must value securities they are holding at year-end* (called "mark to market"). This means that all gains and losses at year-end are taken into income even though the securities have not been sold. [I.R.C. §475(a)] This is an important exception to the realization requirement. (*See supra,* §§761 *et seq.*, for a discussion of the realization requirement.) All gains and losses on securities that are marked to market are *ordinary* and not capital. [I.R.C. §475(d)(3)]

2) Traders [§840]

Individuals who are "engaged in a trade or business as a trader in securities" can elect to use mark-to-market accounting and thus treat all transactions as ordinary rather than capital. [I.R.C. §475(f)] A trader (as opposed to an investor) engages in a *continued series of short-term speculations*; he does not hold securities for the long term or in order to make a profit on dividends or interest. [*See* **Moller v. United States**, *supra*, §438] Had section 475(f) been in effect at the time, the taxpayer in *Bielfeldt*, *supra*, probably could have claimed that he was "engaged in a trade or business as a trader" in government bonds, and he probably could have elected mark-to-market treatment and received an ordinary loss.

EXAM TIP   gilbert

These cases highlight why an individual would (or would not) want to treat a gain or loss as capital or ordinary—and they can be used to help you remember the effects of different treatment for your exam. A trader would prefer the mark-to-market accounting method when he has large amounts of *losses* in order to have the losses be *treated as "ordinary,"* which in turn could enable him to offset many other types of ordinary income. Equally as important, however, is the fact that mark-to-market accounting is often *disadvantageous* for a dealer, because that accounting method requires him to treat securities *gains as ordinary income*. If the stock market is performing well, he may have a large "gain" as ordinary income, which has a higher tax rate than a capital gain.

---

(3) Hedging transactions [§841]

Assets acquired in a "hedging transaction," which are so identified on the date acquired, are not capital assets. [I.R.C. §1221(a)(7)] A hedging transaction is a transaction entered into in the normal course of trade or business to manage risk of price, currency, or interest rate fluctuations (*e.g.*, a breadmaker may purchase wheat "futures"—contracts calling for future delivery at a fixed price—in order to stabilize its manufacturing costs). [I.R.C. §1221(b)(2)]

(a) Prior law [§842]

Prior law relating to hedging transactions was very confused. Generally, gains and losses from the sale of commodity futures contracts that were an integral part of a business's inventory purchase system were ordinary, not capital. [**Corn Products Co. v. Commissioner**, 350 U.S. 46 (1955)]

1) *Corn Products* case

In the *Corn Products* case, a manufacturer of products made from corn bought corn "futures" to protect itself against a sharp increase in the price of corn. The Supreme Court held that the futures were an "integral part" of the taxpayer's business and therefore could not be capital assets.

(b) Current regulations [§843]

Corn Products was superseded by regulations. [Treas. Reg. §1.1221-2(a)] These regulations provide that the term "capital assets" does *not* include property that is "part of a hedging transaction." Thus, since the taxpayer's corn futures in *Corn Products* were purchased as an attempt to protect the taxpayer against a sudden price increase, the futures were "part of a hedging transaction" and would not be capital assets. The regulations have not yet been amended to take account of section 1221(a)(7), *supra*.

1) Non-hedging transactions

Under the regulations, assets that are acquired for business (not investment) purposes, but that are not part of a hedging transaction, may be treated as capital assets if that treatment is not excluded for some other reason. The regulations provide: "gain or loss from the [non-hedging] transaction is not made ordinary on the grounds that the property involved in the transaction is a surrogate for a noncapital asset, that the transaction serves as insurance against a business risk, that the transaction serves a hedging function, or that the transaction serves a similar function or purpose." This regulation is consistent with a Supreme Court decision that limited *Corn Products* to its facts. Note that *Corn Products* does not cover investments in corporate stock, even if the "investments" were made to protect the taxpayer's business rather than for investment purposes. [**Arkansas Best Corp. v. Commissioner**, 485 U.S. 212 (1988)]

b. Receivables [§844]

An *account receivable or note* acquired in the ordinary course of business in *payment for services rendered* by the taxpayer, or on sale of an *inventory item*, is not a capital asset. [I.R.C. §1221(a)(4)]

c. Depreciable property and realty [§845]

Depreciable property and any real property (depreciable or not) *used in a trade or business* are not capital assets.

(1) Note

Actually, such assets if held more than one year are treated as *"quasi-capital assets"* under I.R.C. section 1231 (*see infra,* §§881 *et seq.*) with *very favorable tax treatment*. Generally speaking, losses on sales of such assets are treated as ordinary losses (*i.e.,* fully deductible), while gains are capital gains.

d. Copyrights [§846]

Generally, copyrights and other literary or artistic property are *not* capital assets in the hands of the taxpayer whose **personal effort created them** (or any donee). [I.R.C. §1221(a)(3)—*but see* I.R.C. §1221(b)(3), providing a limited exception for musical property through 2010]

(1) Letters [§847]

Letters or memoranda are not capital assets in the hands of the creator or the person for whom they were produced.

(2) Purchasers distinguished [§848]

An investor who *purchases* artwork or other copyrightable works from the creator may be entitled to treat them as capital assets (unless he is a dealer and purchased them primarily for resale in the ordinary course of his business, in which case they would fall under section 1221(a)(1)).

e. Patents [§849]

I.R.C. section 1235 provides that a patent is a *capital asset* in the hands of the *inventor* or anyone who *financed* the invention (other than a relative or employer of the inventor). Hence, monies derived from the sale or transfer of a patent are capital gains—even the monies that are payable to a person in the business of inventing or financing patents.

(1) Note

This is true even where the royalty payments are made payable over a period coterminous with the transferee's use of the patent, or contingent on the productivity of the patent. [I.R.C. §1235(a)]

(2) But note

To qualify for the capital gains treatment, there must be a bona fide transfer of all *substantial* rights under the patent. However, in such cases, transfers between related taxpayers or to a corporation in which the inventor owns 25% or more of the stock do *not* qualify. [I.R.C. §1235(d)]

STATUTORY TREATMENT OF CERTAIN ASSETS AS CAPITAL OR NONCAPITAL	**gilbert**
CAPITAL ASSETS	**NONCAPITAL ASSETS**
• Real estate not held for sale	• Real estate held for sale
• Securities in the hands of an "average" investor or in the hands of a "trader" when the trader does not elect mark-to-market accounting	• Securities in the hands of a "dealer" or in the hands of a "trader" when the trader elects mark-to-market accounting
• Copyrights held by purchaser	• Copyrights in the creator's hands
• Patents in the hands of the inventor or person who financed the invention	• Assets held in a "hedging transaction"

f. Options [§850]

If optioned property would be, if acquired, a capital asset in the hands of the option holder, then the option itself is a capital asset, and its sale will yield capital gain or loss. [I.R.C. §1234]

(1) Distinguish—ordinary income property [§851]

However, if the option relates to a *noncapital* asset (*e.g.,* inventory, personal services, etc.), any gain or loss is ordinary income.

EXAM TIP   **gilbert**

For exam questions asking you whether the gain or loss on the sale of an option is capital or ordinary, you need only look **at the optioned property**. If the underlying property would be considered a **capital asset** in the hands of the purchaser (*e.g.,* option for a copyright), then a gain or a loss on the sale of that option would be considered capital. The converse is also true—if the asset on which the taxpayer holds an option would be considered a **noncapital asset** in the hands of a taxpayer (*e.g.,* option to buy inventory), the sale of that option would produce an ordinary gain or loss.

---

(2) Effect of failure to exercise [§852]

If the optionee fails to exercise the option, the amounts paid by him for the option are deductible only as a capital loss (assuming the option relates to a capital asset). [I.R.C. §1234]

(a) Distinguish

But such payments are *ordinary income to the optionor* since he has not sold or exchanged the underlying property. If the option had been exercised, any payments under the option attributable to the purchase price would be entitled to capital gains treatment if the underlying asset was a capital asset.

3. Exceptions Developed in Case Law [§853]

As noted above, the courts have developed additional categories of items that are not capital assets. Generally, they have done so when the property or the transaction seems to fall outside of the purposes for granting the favored capital gain treatment. These purposes are to provide a form of *income averaging* for gains that are likely to have occurred over a long period of time and to *remove the disincentives* against sale of appreciated property. Generally, the courts try to distinguish between items that are *investments* (which qualify for capital gain) and mere *substitutes for ordinary income* (which produce ordinary income).

a. Rights to income [§854]

As discussed in detail earlier in this Summary (*see supra,* §§191, 201), income is chargeable to the person either rendering the services for which the income is paid or owning the property from which the income is earned.

(1) Sale of right to income [§855]

The above principles and cases are also relevant with respect to *sales* of the right to income. Thus, if the taxpayer sells (rather than gives away) the right to future income from her property, while retaining the underlying property, the sales proceeds—*being a "substitute" for the income*—are taxable to her as ordinary income, not capital gains. Moreover, none of the taxpayer's basis in the property is allocated to the income right.

---

e.g. **Example:** Taxpayer is entitled to future cash dividends of $122,820 from Champion Spark Plug Company. To offset a large deduction in the current tax year, Taxpayer needs to produce a large amount of current income. Taxpayer agrees to sell his right to receive the future dividends—some of which extend into the next tax year—to his son for $115,000 (representing the discounted present value of $122,820). Taxpayer retains ownership of the stock. The payment of $115,000 is ordinary income to Taxpayer. [**Stranahan's Estate v. Commissioner,** 472 F.2d 867 (6th Cir. 1973)]

---

e.g. **Example:** Taxpayer owns certain oil lands. She sells her rights to the next $10,500 of royalties to Bob Buyer for $10,000. Since Taxpayer retained the oil lands while merely anticipating some of the ordinary income, the $10,000 is ordinary income. None of the basis for the land is allocated to the income right. [**Commissioner v. P.G. Lake,** *supra,* §195]

---

e.g. **Example:** Taxpayer wins the lottery, which entitles him to 20 annual payments of $450,000. After the fifth payment, Taxpayer sells the rights to the remaining payments for a lump sum payment of $3.95 million. The lump sum payment is ordinary income. [**United States v. Maginnis,** 356 F.3d 1179 (9th Cir. 2004)]

---

(2) Distinguish—sale of source of income [§856]

The result would be different if the taxpayer had sold her *entire interest* in the *property* from which the right to income springs (*e.g.,* the shares of stock or the entire oil deposit). In such a case, the sales proceeds would be *capital gain*, rather than ordinary income. The same result would occur if the taxpayer sold an undivided fractional interest in the entire property (such as a one-third interest in the stock or in all the oil).

(a) Sale of life estates [§857]

A close case occurs where the *life beneficiary of a trust* sells her interest in the trust (or a portion thereof lasting for her lifetime). It could be argued that her "interest" is nothing more than the right to receive income during her life, and hence the proceeds of sale should be ordinary income. However, the courts have held the opposite, treating the sale as the sale of an *interest in property* (rather than merely as assignment of income), so that capital gains treatment can be obtained. The key point is that the seller disposes of the interest for the entire time it will exist (*i.e.,* her lifetime), as opposed to selling a few years of income but retaining the right to subsequent income. [**McAllister v. Commissioner,** *supra,* §747]

1) No basis recovery

Under present law, the seller of the income interest is denied any basis recovery on the sale. [I.R.C. §1001(e); *see supra,* §746]

b. Contract rights [§858]

Classifying the proceeds from the sale of contract rights as either capital gain or ordinary income has caused considerable difficulty.

(1) Is it "protectable in equity"? [§859]

According to one notable decision, a possible standard for analyzing whether a contract right is "property" for purposes of capital gains taxation is whether it is "protectable in equity." [**Commissioner v. Ferrer,** 304 F.2d 125 (2d Cir. 1962)]

---

e.g. **Example:** In *Ferrer,* the court held that the sale of an exclusive right to produce a particular play and a right to prevent a particular story from being made into a movie were both protectable in equity and thus capital assets. However, a right to a percentage of the proceeds from a particular movie was held not protectable in equity and thus its sale gave rise to ordinary income. (The latter determination is inconsistent with some other cases in the area.)

(a) Note

The *Ferrer* result requires an allocation of a lump sum purchase price into its various component parts, some of which are capital gains and some of which are ordinary income.

(2) Leases [§860]

A lease is an interest in property and hence amounts paid *to the lessee* for an *assignment* of the lease are capital gains.

(a) Payment by lessor [§861]

Likewise, amounts paid *by the lessor* to the lessee for a *cancellation* or *change in terms* of the lease are treated as capital gains. [Rev. Rul. 56-531, 1956-2 C.B. 983]

(b) Distinguish—payment for release [§862]

But an amount paid *by the lessee* to the lessor for a *release* from the lease is not capital gain. *Rationale:* The lessor is not really selling a contract right; he is compromising a rent obligation while retaining the reversion. [**Hort v. Commissioner,** 313 U.S. 28 (1941)]

(c) Sublease distinguished [§863]

The above discussion applies to assignments of the entire leasehold (a complete transfer of the lessee's interest). If the transfer is only a sublease (*i.e.*, a reversion of some sort is retained by the master tenant), the income received by the master tenant is ordinary income, like any other rents.

(3) Personal services [§864]

A sale of one's contractual rights to render personal services produces ordinary income.

---

e.g. **Examples:** Taxpayer, a noted celebrity, contracts to render future services for XYZ Corp., for which XYZ Corp. agrees to pay her a stipulated amount. Taxpayer then sells her rights to payment from XYZ Corp. to Bob Buyer. The sale proceeds received by Taxpayer are clearly ordinary income—just as the payments from XYZ Corp. would have been. [**McFall v. Commissioner,** 34 B.T.A. 108 (1936)] Similarly, amounts paid to a theatrical agent to transfer her contract for exclusive rights to represent a singer produced ordinary income. [**General Artists Corp. v. Commissioner,** 205 F.2d 360 (2d Cir. 1953)]

---

e.g. **Example:** As a result of rendering services, Taxpayer, a real estate broker, received the right to 25% of the profits when the buyer of land ultimately resold it. When Taxpayer finally received his interest in the profits, it was treated as ordinary income since it was originally referable to his services. [**Pounds v. United States,** 372 F.2d 342 (5th Cir. 1967)]

(a) Distinguish—consideration in property and services [§865]

But when, in addition to services, the seller transfers other consideration in the nature of "property" (*e.g.*, patent rights), there must be an *allocation* of any "package" compensation paid—*i.e.*, a value assigned to "each stick in the bundle," and the compensation treated as ordinary income and capital gain proportionately. [**Commissioner v. Ferrer,** *supra*, §859]

(4) Insurance policies [§866]

An insurance policy is basically a contract, and amounts received for assignments of beneficial interests in insurance policies are therefore usually capital gains.

(a) Distinguish—annuities and endowments [§867]

A group of cases has held that if a taxpayer who owns an *annuity or endowment* policy sells his contract to a third person shortly before it matures, the monies received from the buyer are taxable to the seller as ordinary income. *Rationale:* The sale proceeds are merely substitutes for amounts receivable upon a maturity or surrender of the contract, which would be ordinary income. [**Commissioner v. Phillips,** 275 F.2d 33 (4th Cir. 1960)]

c. **"Personal rights" [§868]**

Although I.R.C. section 1221 states that "all property" held by the taxpayer (other than the enumerated exceptions) are capital assets, it appears that personal rights are *not* "property" within this definition. Hence, income from "personal rights" is ordinary income, not capital gain.

---

e.g. **Example:** Glenn Miller's widow sold the "right" to make a movie based on Glenn Miller's life. *Held:* The sale was not the sale of a capital asset. [**Miller v. Commissioner,** 299 F.2d 706 (2d Cir. 1962)—"not everything which commands a payment may be regarded as property"]

---

(1) Note

Similar holdings are encountered with regard to compensation paid for invasion of the "right" of privacy, sale of the "right" to use one's name or picture for commercial purposes, etc. [Rev. Rul. 65-261, 1965-2 C.B. 281]

d. **Classification through correlation with related transaction [§869]**

In a number of situations, transactions have been classified as capital or ordinary because they are deemed to be part of a related transaction.

(1) Illustration—tax benefit rule [§870]

Alex holds certain notes of Becky, which he deducts as bad debts. Later, the debts prove to have value. If Alex had collected the debts, he would have had ordinary income (*see* discussion of I.R.C. section 111, *supra,* §§536-537). If he sells the debts to others, he has ordinary income, not capital gain, because the prior bad debt deductions offset ordinary income. [**Merchants National Bank v. Commissioner,** 199 F.2d 657 (5th Cir. 1952)]

(2) Illustration—lookback rule [§871]

Taxpayer sells stock and treats it as capital gain. Later, the buyer claims there was fraud and Taxpayer returns part of the money, attempting to treat the repayment as producing an ordinary loss. However, the repayment produces capital loss, because the prior sale of stock resulted in a capital gain and thus the sale or exchange involved a capital asset. [**Arrowsmith v. Commissioner,** 344 U.S. 6 (1952)]

(a) Application to insiders' profits [§872]

A corporate employee who is an "insider" makes a "short-swing" profit by selling his shares in the corporation, then buying them back in a short time period when the share price falls. The "profit" must be returned to the corporation under section 16(b) of the Securities Exchange Act. Several decisions hold that this creates a capital loss under *Arrowsmith*. [**Commissioner v. Cummings,** 506 F.2d 449 (2d Cir. 1974)]

4. Sale of Business Interests

a. Sole proprietorships—fragmentation theory [§873]

A sole proprietorship business is not regarded as an entity. Rather, it is an aggregate of the various assets of the business. Therefore, in determining gain or loss, as well as in distinguishing capital gain from ordinary income, each asset must be examined separately. Then, the basis, gain, or loss on each capital asset must be computed separately. This is the so-called fragmentation theory. [**Williams v. McGowan,** 152 F.2d 570 (2d Cir. 1945)]

(1) Allocations [§874]

If the parties make a reasonable *allocation* of price to each asset, it will be respected. Otherwise, the IRS will make the allocation, which will be upheld by the courts unless shown to be arbitrary. Some courts have held that if the sale agreement makes an allocation, the parties are *bound* by it, but the IRS is not. [**Commissioner v. Danielson,** 378 F.2d 771 (3d Cir.), *cert. denied,* 389 U.S. 858 (1967)]

(2) Goodwill [§875]

Goodwill is treated as a capital asset. It is depreciable by the buyer over a 15-year period. [I.R.C. §197; *see supra,* §§473-474]

(a) Note

The practice of a single professional—*e.g.,* doctor, lawyer, or accountant—can contain goodwill. Thus, when the professional sells all or a part of the practice, there may be a goodwill element entitled to capital gains treatment. However, the facts will be closely scrutinized to make sure that there really is goodwill. [Rev. Rul. 70-45, 1970-1 C.B. 17]

(3) Covenant not to compete [§876]

On the other hand, money paid to the seller in consideration of his promise not to compete in the future is treated as ordinary income to the seller (a substitute for income). As a corollary, the amount paid is an asset to the buyer, which he can amortize over a 15-year period regardless of the actual term of the covenant. [**Hamlin's Trust v. Commissioner,** 209 F.2d 761 (10th Cir. 1954); I.R.C. §197]

(4) Allocations to assets, goodwill [§877]

Because goodwill is depreciable over a 15-year term, taxpayers often try to allocate the purchase price of a business to assets depreciable over shorter periods, leaving very little to be allocated to goodwill. However, the rule is that taxpayers cannot allocate to tangible assets more than the value of those assets; all residual value must be allocated to goodwill. [I.R.C. §1060, Treas. Reg. §1.1060-1T(d), (e)]

b. Partnerships and corporations [§878]

The treatment of the sale of a partnership or a corporation differs from the treatment of the sale of a proprietorship.

(1) Sale of assets [§879]

If either a partnership or corporation *sells its assets*, the result is the same as in a sale of assets by a proprietorship—*i.e.,* the consideration paid is fragmented between the various assets.

(2) Sale of interest [§880]

But if a partnership *interest* is sold, it is treated as a capital asset, except that the amount referable to "unrealized receivables" or "substantially appreciated inventory" is ordinary income. [I.R.C. §§741, 751] Similarly, corporate stock is treated as a single capital asset unless it is a "collapsible corporation." [I.R.C. §341] (The treatment of sales of partnerships and corporations is discussed in detail in the Taxation of Business Entities Summary.)

5. Assets Used in Trade or Business—Quasi-Capital Assets [§881]

I.R.C. section 1221(a)(2) provides that certain assets *used in a trade or business* and *held for more than one year* are not capital assets. These assets are specifically provided for in I.R.C. section 1231. They are sometimes called "quasi-capital" assets and are treated more favorably than any other kind of asset. In addition, "supplies of a type regularly used or consumed by the taxpayer in the ordinary course of a trade or business of the taxpayer" are not capital assets. [I.R.C. §1221(a)(8)]

a. Coverage [§882]

Quasi-capital assets described in section 1231 are those held more than one year and used in a trade or business.

(1) Property used in a trade or business [§883]

Quasi-capital assets are real property used in a trade or business (whether or not depreciable) and personal property used in a trade or business that is subject to depreciation under section 167 (*e.g.,* machines or trucks). Assets such as goodwill, which are amortized under section 197 (not section 167), are not treated as quasi-capital assets. (*See supra,* §§473-474.)

(2) Other section 1231 assets [§884]

Section 1231 assets also include the following:

(a) *Unharvested crops sold with the land*;

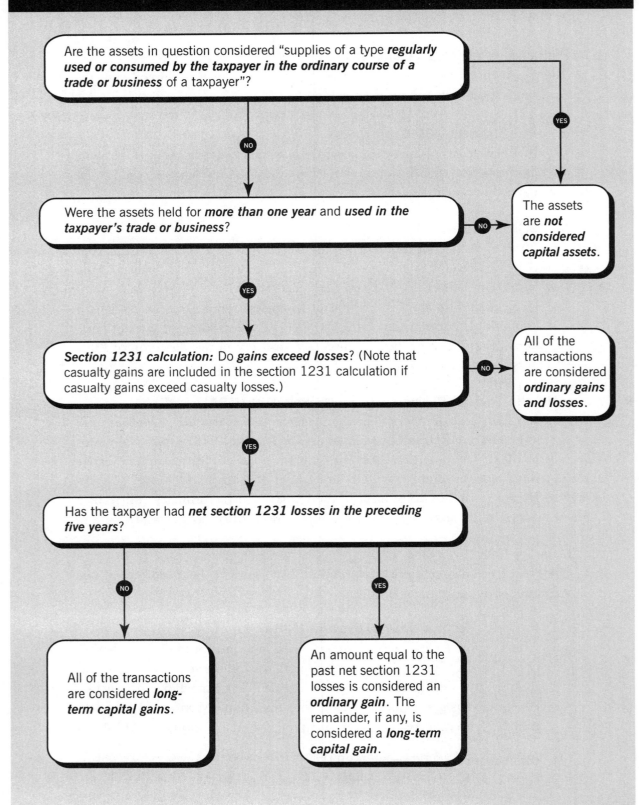

Are the assets in question considered "supplies of a type *regularly used or consumed by the taxpayer in the ordinary course of a trade or business* of a taxpayer"?

NO

YES

Were the assets held for *more than one year* and *used in the taxpayer's trade or business*?

NO

YES

The assets are *not considered capital assets*.

Section 1231 calculation: Do *gains exceed losses*? (Note that casualty gains are included in the section 1231 calculation if casualty gains exceed casualty losses.)

NO

YES

All of the transactions are considered *ordinary gains and losses*.

Has the taxpayer had *net section 1231 losses in the preceding five years*?

NO

YES

All of the transactions are considered *long-term capital gains*.

An amount equal to the past net section 1231 losses is considered an *ordinary gain*. The remainder, if any, is considered a *long-term capital gain*.

(b) *Herds of livestock* held at least 24 months for draft, breeding, sporting, or dairy purposes (but not poultry); and

(c) *Coal, timber, and minerals* in certain cases. [*See* I.R.C. §1231(b) for details]

(3) Exclusions [§885]

However, section 1231 does *not* include inventories, stock in trade, property *held primarily for sale* in the ordinary course of a taxpayer's trade or business, or *copyrights in the hands of the creator.* (*See supra,* §§830 *et seq.*)

---

e.g. **Example:** Machinery that a taxpayer generally leases to customers, but sells if the customer insists, is held primarily for sale. Consequently, the assets are not section 1231 assets and the gain is ordinary income—even though sales, as opposed to leasing, yield only about 2% of the taxpayer's income. The theory is that the sales are "accepted and predictable." [**International Shoe Machinery Co. v. United States**, 491 F.2d 157 (1st Cir.), *cert. denied,* 419 U.S. 834 (1974)]

---

b. Computation [§886]

All the gains and losses on section 1231 assets are grouped together. If the gains exceed the losses, all the transactions are *long-term capital transactions.* (Thus, the gains are long-term capital gains and the losses are long-term capital losses.) But if the losses exceed the gains, all the transactions are *ordinary* (*i.e.,* ordinary income and ordinary loss).

(1) Recapture of losses [§887]

If a taxpayer has a net gain on section 1231 assets (ordinarily long-term capital gain), but had net section 1231 losses within the preceding five years, the gain will be treated as ordinary income to the extent of previously unrecaptured losses. [I.R.C. §1231(c)]

c. Special rules for casualties [§888]

Taxpayers must aggregate all recognized gains and losses arising from casualties of assets used in the trade or business or for investment. If the gains exceed the losses, *all* transactions are included within the section 1231 calculation. If the losses exceed the gains, *none* of the gains or losses are included in the section 1231 calculation. [I.R.C. §1231(a)(4)(C)]

(1) Casualty gains [§889]

A casualty can produce a gain if the insurance proceeds exceed the taxpayer's basis. In many cases, however, gains from casualties or government condemnations are not recognized because the proceeds are *reinvested in qualifying property.* [*See* I.R.C. §1033; *and see supra,* §§803-809]

(a) Note

The reason for inclusion of casualties under section 1231 is that otherwise they would not be capital gains or losses because of the absence of a "sale or exchange." (*See infra, §910.*)

(2) Distinguish—personal casualty gains or losses [§890]

Gains or losses on personal assets (such as one's personal car or residence) are not included under section 1231. If personal casualty gains exceed personal casualty losses, both gains and losses are treated as capital. [I.R.C. §165(h)(2)(B)] If personal casualty losses exceed personal casualty gains, the losses are deductible to the extent of the gains, but the excess is not deductible except to the extent it exceeds 10% of AGI. [I.R.C. §165(h)(2)(A)] Recall that personal casualty losses are always first reduced by $100 (*see supra, §676*).

d. Limitation—recapture of depreciation [§891]

The provisions requiring recapture of depreciation *supersede* section 1231 and turn capital gain into ordinary income. Only the excess of gain over the amount of recaptured depreciation is treated as a section 1231 gain (*see infra, §§933-938*).

e. Illustration of section 1231 [§892]

Belle owns a health club and has many investments. Consider the following items of loss and gain:

(i) *Condemnations*

Gain on condemnation of Oregon land held as investment $ 4,000

(ii) *Casualties*

Loss on theft of painting held as investment   − 9,000

(iii) *Sale of assets used in business (and held more than one year)*

Gain on sale of land used for parking lot	3,000
Loss on sale of gym equipment	−17,000

The casualty loss is not included in the section 1231 calculation (because casualty losses exceed casualty gains). The net of the other items (condemnation of investment property, sale or exchange of business property) shows a $10,000 loss. Therefore, the condemnation and the gain and loss on the sale of business assets are all *ordinary* items.

f. Exception as to sales between "related" taxpayers (I.R.C. section 1239) [§893]

The preferential tax treatment accorded to depreciable property used in a trade or business is subject to a limitation—capital gains treatment is *not* allowed if the sale or exchange is between the taxpayer and a *controlled corporation*, or between two controlled corporations. In such a case, any gain is ordinary income. [I.R.C. §1239]

(1) Treatment of losses [§894]

Loss in such a transaction is *not* deductible at all (*see* discussion of "losses among related taxpayers"; *see supra,* §§511-514).

(2) Coverage [§895]

I.R.C. section 1239 applies to gain on *any depreciable property*, which means that it is not limited to section 1231 assets (used in a trade or business), but also covers "nonbusiness" assets (used for production of income). It is *not* applicable to certain important types of property, *e.g.,* securities and land.

C. Was There a "Sale or Exchange"?

1. In General [§896]

Ordinarily, there must be a "sale or exchange" of a capital asset for the transaction to be taxed as a capital gain or loss. Case law and statutes have clarified some borderline situations.

a. Aborted sales [§897]

Difficult problems often arise when a sale of property falls through and the seller retains the buyer's money. If a "sale" occurred and the seller repossessed the property because of failure to pay the entire price, the amount that the seller keeps is entitled to capital gains treatment. But if the sale never occurred (*i.e.,* the seller retained the benefits and burdens of ownership), the amount the seller keeps is viewed as liquidated damages and taxed as ordinary income. [**Handelman v. Commissioner,** 509 F.2d 1067 (2d Cir. 1975)]

b. Transfer of mineral interest [§898]

A mineral interest is a capital asset, and therefore an outright sale or assignment thereof will ordinarily produce capital gains. However, if the seller retains an *economic interest*, he is treated as not having sold the minerals. His receipts are ordinary income (but he can deduct *depletion*; *see supra,* §§483-485). [**Wood v. United States,** 377 F.2d 300 (5th Cir. 1967)]

c. Transfers of franchises, trademarks, and trade names [§899]

Capital gains treatment is possible for transfers of franchises, trademarks, and trade names, but *only if* the transferor did *not* retain "any significant power, right, or continuing interest" with respect to the subject matter of the franchise, trademark, or trade name. [I.R.C. §1253(a)]

(1) Application

Thus, in the usual commercial franchise (in which the franchisor imposes

strict controls on operation by franchisee, reserves the right of termination, etc.), payments received from a franchisee are ordinary income to
the franchisor.

(2) Exception—sports franchises [§900]

Franchises to engage in professional sports do not fall within the above
rule and hence are entitled to capital gains treatment in spite of "strings"
or "controls" retained by the transferor. [I.R.C. §1253(e)]

d. Contract rights [§901]

As discussed previously (*see supra*, §§858-867), the courts have classified many
contract rights as capital assets. However, according to a minority view, when
the contract right is transferred from *one party to the contract to the other*,
there is no sale or exchange. [**Commissioner v. Pittston Co.**, 252 F.2d 344 (2d
Cir. 1958)] Under that view, the contract right would have to be transferred to
some *third party* to produce capital gain. However, the better view is that a
sale or exchange occurs even in a transfer to the other contracting party. [**Commissioner v. Ferrer**, *supra*, §865]

(1) Legislative clarification [§902]

To some extent, this problem has been clarified by legislation:

(a) Amounts received by a lessee for cancellation of a lease, or by a distributor of goods for the cancellation of a distributor's agreement (if
the distributor has a substantial capital investment), are treated as received in exchange for the lease or agreement. [I.R.C. §1241]

(b) The amount lost on expiration of an option contract is treated as if
the option were sold for zero dollars; thus, the expiration produces a
capital loss if the option was to acquire a capital asset. [I.R.C. §1234;
see supra, §§850-852]

(c) Gains or losses on the cancellation, lapse, expiration, or other termination of any right or obligation, including securities futures, are
treated as capital rather than ordinary. [I.R.C. §1234A]

e. Foreclosure [§903]

When a creditor forecloses and takes back property that secured a debt, this is
treated as a sale or exchange by the debtor. Consequently, the debtor's gain or
loss is capital. [**Helvering v. Hammel**, 311 U.S. 504 (1941)]

f. Abandonment [§904]

If property becomes worthless or is abandoned, there is no sale or exchange,
and the taxpayer has an ordinary (vs. capital) loss. [**Matz v. Commissioner**,
T.C. Memo. 1998-334—abandonment of worthless mineral rights; **Citron v.
Commissioner**, 97 T.C. 200 (1991)—worthless partnership interest; *see infra*,

§906, for discussion involving a special rule for worthless bad debts or securities]

2. **Special Situations in Which "Sale or Exchange" Deemed to Occur [§905]**
There are certain transactions that do not fall within the ordinary meaning of "sale or exchange," but are nevertheless considered to be such for tax purposes.

a. **Worthless debts and securities [§906]**
Nonbusiness *bad debts* (*see supra*, §529) and *worthless securities*, although not actually sold or exchanged, are deductible only as capital losses in the year they become "worthless." [I.R.C. §§182 - 183]

b. **Payments to creditors**

(1) **General rule [§907]**
Ordinarily, a creditor who collects a debt has neither a gain nor a loss on collection (except for interest) because he has a basis equal to the amount of the debt. However, if a creditor has a gain or loss on the collection of a debt, an issue arises whether the collection can be treated as a "sale or exchange." The courts have held that collection of a debt is not a sale or exchange. [**Fairbanks v. United States,** 306 U.S. 436 (1939); **Nahey v. Commissioner,** 196 F.3d 866 (7th Cir. 1999)—no sale or exchange where taxpayer acquired rights to a lawsuit and settled the case for $6 million]

(a) **Note**
A statutory change has partially superseded the rule that collection of a debt is not a sale or exchange. By statute, the collection of a "debt instrument," such as a bond or a promissory note, is treated as a sale or exchange by the creditor. [I.R.C. §1271(a)(1), (b)(1)]

(b) **Legislative change [§908]**
The rule of *Fairbanks* has been changed by legislation described above. Since the debt involved was a "debt instrument," its sale by the creditor would be treated as a sale or exchange. However, the result in *Nahey, supra*, is not changed by section 1271—the right to collect money from a lawsuit for breach of contract is not a "debt instrument."

> **e.g.** **Example:** In Year 1, Acme Corp. borrowed $5,000 from George in exchange for a promissory note bearing 6% interest due in Year 4. The interest is payable each year and it is currently paid in Years 1 to 4. (The interest is ignored in this example.) In Year 2, George sells this note to Dick for $3,700. George has a $1,300 capital loss on this sale. In Year 4, Acme Corp. pays Dick $5,000.

The note is a "debt instrument," and Dick has a capital gain of $1,300.

(2) Exception—original issue discount [§909]

The Code requires imputation of interest on discount debts (such as bonds or other obligations). For example, X Corp. might borrow $10,000 in Year 1 from Taxpayer and promise to repay $12,000 in Year 6. The debt might carry interest at only 3%, even though the prevailing market rate of interest is 7%. The $2,000 discount on the debt occurred because the bond pays a low interest rate. The $2,000 discount is called "original issue discount" and it is taxed to the creditor as ordinary income during the period the debt is outstanding. Thus, Taxpayer cannot claim the $2,000 profit he makes in Year 6 as a capital gain because it has already been taxed to him as ordinary income. X Corp. receives a corresponding deduction for interest during the period the debt is outstanding. [I.R.C. §§1272 - 1275] (For more information on imputed interest, see infra, §§923 et seq.)

c. Involuntary conversion [§910]

Involuntary conversion of property (e.g., receipt of insurance proceeds after a fire) and cutting of timber are treated as the equivalent of a "sale or exchange" and included within the section 1231 calculation (see supra, §888).

3. Validity of "Sale or Exchange" Not Affected by Seller's Retention of Control [§911]

If there is a complete transfer of title of a business for a fair consideration, the "sale" will probably be upheld—even where the purchase price is made payable out of income to be earned from the assets transferred (so that buyer assumed no financial risk) and seller retains control of the business.

Example: Taxpayer sold his business to a charity on an installment purchase contract, with a nominal down payment. To avoid any taxable income to itself, the charity dissolved the business and leased the assets to an operating company (managed but not owned by Taxpayer) at a high rental fee (equal to substantially all of the profits from the business). The rental income was tax-exempt to the charity (under former law), and it used the tax-exempt income (i.e., the operating profits) to pay off the purchase price of the business. The "sale" was upheld, and Taxpayer was thus entitled to capital gain on the payments received from the charity, even though the charity had assumed no real risk and Taxpayer retained operating control of the business. The business profits that would otherwise have been taxable to Taxpayer as ordinary income were taxable to him only at capital gains rates, as payments on the "purchase price." [**Commissioner v. Brown**, 380 U.S. 563 (1965)]

a. Treatment of excess price [§912]

When the purchase price is more than the value of the assets sold, the excessive part is taxed as ordinary income, but the balance is taxed as capital gain. [**Berenson v. Commissioner,** 507 F.2d 262 (2d Cir. 1974)]

b. Effect of I.R.C. section 514 [§913]

The tax dodge sanctioned in *Brown* is no more. I.R.C. section 514 now provides that a charity, otherwise tax-exempt, is *taxable* on income from debt-financed property unrelated to its charitable purposes. However, the principle enunciated by the Court—that the validity of a "sale or exchange" is not affected by the seller's retention of control—seems unimpaired.

c. Distinguish—grantor trust rules [§914]

The *Clifford* rules (*see supra,* §277) apparently do not apply in determining the validity of a "sale or exchange" for capital gains purposes.

D. Was There a Sufficient "Holding Period"?

1. In General [§915]

To qualify as *long-term* capital gain, the capital asset must have been held by the taxpayer for *more than 12 months* before the "sale or exchange." (*See supra,* §§821-822.)

a. Calculating the holding period [§916]

The holding period is measured from the time the property is acquired until it is transferred. If an escrow is involved, the date the escrow closes is regarded as the acquisition (or transfer) date. However, if all conditions of sale have been satisfied, the transfer would be deemed to occur even if the escrow were kept open. [*See* **Dyke v. Commissioner,** 6 T.C. 1134 (1946)] Moreover, the day of acquisition is excluded and the date of disposition is included in measuring the one-year period. [Rev. Rul. 66-7, 1966-1 C.B. 188]

2. "Tacking" of Holding Period Where Substituted Basis [§917]

A holding period commences only on a *change in basis* on the property. If there is no change in basis (as in the so-called tax-free exchanges; *see supra,* §§784 *et seq.*), there is no new holding period. In such cases, the taxpayer acquires the holding period of his transferor and can "tack" it on to the time he holds the property.

e.g. **Example:** When Nicholas makes a *gift* of an asset to Tina, Tina's basis for the property is a "substituted basis" (*see supra,* §737), and hence there is no new holding period. Tina is allowed to "tack" Nicholas's holding period on to her own.

E. Gains on Small Business Stock

1. General Rule [§918]

A taxpayer (other than a corporation) can exclude from income 50% of the gain on the sale of qualified small business stock. The stock must have been held at least five years. [I.R.C. §1202(a)] This benefit is much more favorable than treating the gain as a long-term capital gain.

2. Limit [§919]

The amount of gain subject to the 50% exclusion may not exceed the *greater* of:

(i)   *$10 million* (in the taxable year and prior taxable years); or

(ii) *Ten times the adjusted basis* of the stock being disposed of.

[I.R.C. §1202(b)(1)]

Example: Taxpayer has a basis of $4 million in his Mom-and-Pop Co. stock. The stock is qualified small business stock. He sells the stock for $28 million. Taxpayer can exclude $12 million from income (50% of the total gain). Although the gain exceeded $10 million, it did not exceed 10 times the adjusted basis of the Mom-and-Pop Co. stock.

3. Qualified Small Business Stock [§920]

In addition to being held for at least five years, to constitute qualified small business stock: (i) the stock must have been *issued after August 1993*; (ii) the taxpayer must be the *original purchaser* of the stock from the corporation; and (iii) the corporation must conduct an *active business* (excluding most service and real estate businesses) and have *assets after the stock issuance not exceeding $50 million*. [I.R.C. §1202(c) - (e)]

4. Minimum Tax [§921]

Seven percent of the excluded gain from the sale of qualified small business stock acquired after December 31, 2000, is treated as a tax preference under the alternative minimum tax. [I.R.C. §57(a)(7); *see infra,* §§945 *et seq.,* for discussion of the alternative minimum tax]

F. Special Computations

1. In General [§922]

In addition to the normal computations above, special rules either turn capital gain into ordinary income or require deferral of certain losses.

2. Imputed Interest [§923]

Interest on deferred payments is ordinary income to the seller of property, deductible by the purchaser (unless the interest deduction is disallowed). However, sometimes taxpayers sell property for deferred payments without providing for any interest (or for interest at below market rate) and correspondingly increase the sales price. This converts the seller's ordinary income to capital gain on the sale of the property (but of course it also decreases the buyer's interest deduction and increases his basis for the property). To prevent this sort of manipulation, the Code provides for imputing interest—turning some of the payments labeled as "principal" into interest. This gives the seller ordinary income and gives the buyer an interest deduction (if the interest is the type that is deductible—*see supra*, §§572 *et seq.*). [I.R.C. §§483, 1274]

a. Imputed interest rate [§924]

Sections 483 and 1274 both require comparison of the interest rate in a transaction to the "applicable federal rate" ("AFR"). AFR is the rate the federal government pays on its debt of various maturities: up to three years (short-term), three to nine years (mid-term), and over nine years (long-term). These rates are periodically announced by the IRS.

b. Section 483 [§925]

Section 483 uses a different computation method from section 1274. Section 483 applies to sales of farms (if the sale price does not exceed $1 million), to sales of a principal residence, and to any sale for less than $250,000 in principal and interest payments. [I.R.C. §1274(c)(3)]

c. Computation [§926]

Assume the AFR is 7% but that a particular deal calls for only 3% interest. Figure the present value of the principal and interest payments due under the contract using the AFR and an actuarial table. This is called the "imputed principal" amount. The imputed principal amount is the buyer's basis and the seller's amount realized. The difference between the stated principal and the imputed principal is original issue discount ("OID"). OID is included in the seller's income (in addition to the 3% stated interest) and is treated as interest paid by the buyer (in addition to the 3% stated interest).

Example: In Year 1, Sue sells Blackacre for $1 million to Bob. Bob is to pay nothing down and $200,000 per year for five years plus interest at 3%. The AFR is 7%. The stated principal amount is $1 million, but the imputed principal is only $855,000. Thus, Bob's basis and Sue's amount realized are both $855,000. The difference between the two amounts ($145,000) is OID, which will be taxed as interest income to Sue and will be treated as an interest payment by Bob (deductible if Bob meets the various tests for deductibility).

---

d. Timing [§927]

Under section 483, interest imputation occurs as payments are made. Part of each principal payment will be treated as interest rather than principal. Under section 1274, an accrual method is used. Each year, part of the OID is treated as interest regardless of whether any principal payments are made.

(1) OID accrual [§928]

Under section 1274, multiply the imputed principal amount plus OID taken into income in prior years times the difference between the AFR and the stated interest (4% in the example). Thus in Year 1, the interest payment is $34,200 ($855,000 × 4%). In Year 2, the interest payment is $35,568 ($855,000 + $34,200 × 4%).

e. Exceptions [§929]

There are a number of total and partial exceptions to the imputed interest rules of I.R.C. section 483.

(1) De minimis rule [§930]

Section 483 does not apply if the selling price is $3,000 or less. [I.R.C. §483(d)(2)]

(2) Intrafamily real estate deals [§931]

The imputed interest rate cannot exceed 7% with respect to land sales between family members (up to $500,000 per sale). [I.R.C. §483(e)]

(3) Personal use property [§932]

Finally, in the case of "personal use property," the imputed interest rules do not apply to the buyer (thus giving him no deductions for imputed interest)—only to the seller. For this purpose, "personal use property" means property that the buyer will not use in business or for investment. [I.R.C. §1275(b)]

3. Recapture of Depreciation [§933]

Special provisions require taxpayers to report as *ordinary income* (rather than as capital gain) certain portions of any gain attributable to prior depreciation. In addition, recapture amounts do not qualify for deferral under the installment method of accounting. (*See infra*, §1059.) Recapture amounts also reduce charitable contribution deductions. (*See supra*, §636.)

a. Personal property [§934]

Recognized gain on depreciable personal property is treated as ordinary to the extent of all depreciation taken. It does not matter whether the depreciation was straight-line or accelerated.

(1) Application [§935]

This provision applies to all tangible personal property (such as machinery) and also to fixtures (*e.g.*, a furnace that is attached to a building). [I.R.C. §1245(a)]

(2) Statutory scheme [§936]

"Recomputed basis" means the adjusted basis plus all depreciation. Amounts deducted in the year of purchase under section 179 must also be added (*see supra,* §477). The amount by which the lesser of recomputed basis or the amount realized exceeds adjusted basis is treated as ordinary income. [I.R.C. §1245(a)(1), (2)]

---

e.g. **Example:** Assume Tina buys a printing press in Year 1 for $25,000. From Year 1 to Year 3, she deducts straight-line depreciation of $18,000. Assume she sells the press in Year 3 for $11,000. Her adjusted basis is $7,000 (*i.e.,* $25,000 - $18,000). Her recomputed basis is $25,000 (*i.e.,* $7,000 + $18,000). Ordinary income is calculated by subtracting the adjusted basis ($7,000) from the lesser of the amount realized ($11,000) or recomputed basis ($25,000). Thus, the ordinary income is $4,000 (the entire realized gain).

---

cf. **Compare:** However, if Tina sells the press for $28,000, her ordinary income is $18,000 (*i.e.,* $25,000 - $7,000). The remaining $3,000 is section 1231 gain.

---

cf. **Compare:** Assume now that Tina sells the press for $4,000. Her loss is $3,000 (*i.e.,* $4,000 - $7,000), and it is a section 1231 loss. There is no recapture since section 1245 does not apply to losses.

---

(3) Summary

Section 1245 can be summarized as follows: The realized gain is turned into ordinary income to the extent of depreciation previously claimed.

b. Real property (buildings) [§937]

I.R.C. section 1250 recaptures "additional" depreciation deductions taken with respect to *buildings.* "Additional" depreciation is any depreciation in excess of the straight-line rate. Since only straight-line depreciation can now be deducted on buildings, section 1250 is of diminishing importance.

c. Certain transfers not subject to depreciation recapture [§938]

Depreciation is recaptured on any sale or other disposition of property except as specifically provided in I.R.C. sections 1245(b) and 1250(d). Among the more important exceptions are:

(1) *Transfers by reason of death or gifts.*

(2) *Nonrecognition transfers,* such as those under I.R.C. sections 1031 and 1033 (*see supra,* §§785-809). However, if those transfers become partially taxable because of the presence of boot, the gain will become ordinary income to the extent of the recapturable depreciation.

(3) *In case of a gift*, the donee keeps the donor's basis (*see supra*, §737) and, if the donee sells the property, depreciation recapture is applicable to him, as it would have been to the donor. *In case of a nonrecognition transfer*, the new property derives its basis from the old property, and on sale of the new property, depreciation would be recaptured.

4. Disallowed Losses [§939]

It is well to recall at this point that certain types of losses (be they "ordinary" or "capital") are disallowed entirely. These issues have been discussed previously and are mentioned here only for review.

a. Losses between related taxpayers [§940]

As discussed previously (*see supra*, §§511-514), losses in transactions between members of the same family, between an individual and a corporation he controls, etc., are *not* deductible. This is true irrespective of the bona fides of the transaction, and even though *gain* in transactions between related taxpayers is recognized and taxed. [I.R.C. §267]

b. Personal losses [§941]

As discussed previously (*see supra*, §§496 *et seq.*), personal expenses or losses not connected with a trade or business are generally not deductible. This covers losses on sales of personal residences. [I.R.C. §262]

(1) Distinguish

Net casualty losses are deductible only to the extent that they exceed 10% of AGI. [I.R.C. §165(c)]

c. Losses on "wash sales" [§942]

Losses on "wash sales" also are not recognized and cannot be deducted in computing tax liability. [I.R.C. §1091; *see supra*, §517]

d. Passive losses [§943]

Loss on a passive activity is deductible only to the extent of income from the activity. [I.R.C. §469; *and see supra*, §547]

e. "At risk" rules [§944]

For certain investments, annual operating losses are limited to amounts "at risk." [I.R.C. §465; *see supra*, §538]

G. Alternative Minimum Tax

1. Introduction [§945]

Once taxable income is calculated by reducing gross income and adjusted gross income by the deductions to which the taxpayer is entitled (including deductions arising from capital gains and losses), the percentage tax rates [I.R.C. §1] are applied to determine the tax payable. However, an "alternative minimum tax" may apply. [I.R.C. §55]

2. Computation [§946]

To compute alternative minimum tax ("AMT"), start by computing "alternative minimum taxable income" ("AMTI"). This consists of taxable income plus certain tax preferences and disallowed deductions. Then subtract an exemption. As of 2006, the exemption is $62,550 on a joint return and $42,500 on a single return (from 2001 - 2006, Congress has permitted this exemption amount to temporarily increase; unless new legislation is passed in 2007, the exemption amounts will return to year 2000 levels in 2007). Then compute the AMT on the balance at the rate of 26% on AMTI up to $175,000 and 28% on AMTI in excess of $175,000. If the AMT exceeds the taxpayer's regular income tax, the taxpayer must pay the AMT instead of the regular tax.

a. Phaseout [§947]

The exemption amounts are phased out as AMTI rises over designated amounts. These amounts are $150,000 (joint return) and $112,500 (single return). The phaseout is at the rate of 25% of the excess over these levels.

---

e.g. **Example:** Suppose Taxpayer is single and has AMTI of $118,500. This is $6,000 over the phaseout amount for a single person. Therefore, Taxpayer's minimum tax exemption is only $41,000 instead of $42,500 (it was decreased by $1,500—an amount equal to 25% of the excess of AMTI over $112,500). [I.R.C. §55(d)(3)]

---

b. Capital gains [§948]

The AMT on net capital gain is computed separately from the AMT on ordinary income. The AMT on net capital gain is at the same rate as for regular tax purposes. Thus the reduced capital gain rates payable under the regular tax will not have the effect of triggering additional AMT. [I.R.C. §55(b)(3)]

3. Disallowed Deductions Under the AMT [§949]

Certain regular income tax deductions are not allowable under the AMT. The disallowed amounts must be added to taxable income to compute AMTI.

a. Medical deductions [§950]

The AMT allows deduction of medical expenses in excess of 10% of AGI (whereas the regular income tax allows deduction of medical expenses in excess of 7.5% of AGI). [I.R.C. §56(b)(1)(B)]

b. Depreciation [§951]

For AMT purposes, a taxpayer must use 150% declining balance depreciation instead of 200% on nonreal business property (such as trucks or machines). Thus, depreciation on nonreal business property must be recomputed for AMT purposes. [I.R.C. §56(a)(1)]

c. Miscellaneous itemized deductions [§952]

Miscellaneous itemized deductions under the regular tax are not deductible for

AMT purposes. [I.R.C. §56(b)(1)(A)(i); *see supra*, §§562 *et seq.*, for discussion of miscellaneous itemized deductions under I.R.C. §67(b)] Thus, taxpayers with large employee business expenses or expenses of earning income may find themselves subject to significant AMT liability. [**Prosman v. Commissioner**, T.C. Memo. 1999-87—employee business expenses; **Kenseth v. Commissioner**, 259 F.3d 881 (7th Cir. 2001)—attorneys' fees in bringing successful age discrimination suit]

d. State and local taxes [§953]

The deduction from AGI for state, local, and foreign taxes (such as income tax and real property tax) is not allowed for AMT purposes. [I.R.C. §56(b)(1)(A)(ii)]

e. Standard deduction and personal exemptions [§954]

These are not available under the AMT. [I.R.C. §56(b)(1)(E)] On the other hand, the overall limit on itemized deductions which applies on the regular tax does not apply to the AMT. [I.R.C. §56(b)(1)(F); *see supra*, §565, for a discussion of the limits on itemized deductions under I.R.C. §68]

f. Qualified residence interest [§955]

Only interest incurred in acquiring, constructing, or improving a qualified residence is deductible under the AMT. In other words, interest on a home equity loan is not deductible. [I.R.C. §56(b)(1)(C), (e); *see supra*, §§592-595 for discussion of qualified residence interest]

4. Tax Preferences [§956]

The tax preferences subject to the alternative minimum tax include [I.R.C. §57]:

a. *The bargain element of an incentive stock option when exercised* (*see infra*, §998);

b. *The excess of percentage depletion over adjusted basis of a mine or oil and gas well* (*see supra*, §487);

c. *Intangible drilling costs* on oil and gas wells (less the amount of such costs that would be recovered through straight-line depreciation) in excess of 65% of the net income from oil and gas (*see supra*, §490);

d. *Interest on certain private activity municipal bonds* (*see supra*, §75); and

e. *Seven percent of the excluded gain from the sale of qualified small business stock* acquired after December 31, 2000 (*see supra*, §§918-921).

5. Illustration [§957]

Tom Taxpayer is unmarried and has taxable income under the regular tax of $250,000. He deducted and paid state income and property taxes of $20,000 and interest on a home equity loan of $12,000. He exercised an incentive stock option, paying $4,000 for stock worth $84,000. Assume Tom's regular income tax was $80,000. Must Tom pay AMT?

Computation:

Taxable income		$250,000

Plus Adjustments:

State taxes	20,000	
Home equity loan	12,000	
Incentive stock option	80,000	
Total adjustments:		112,000
AMTI		362,000

Less Exemption: $42,500 minus 25% of the excess AMTI over $112,500. Since the excess AMTI here is $249,500 ($362,000 - 112,500), and 25% of $249,500 = $62,375, the exemption is reduced to zero   <0>

Subject to AMT (excess over exemption)	$362,000

AMT

26% on $175,000	45,500	
28% on excess over $175,000	52,360	
Total tax:		$ 97,860

Since the taxpayer's regular tax was $80,000, he must pay the AMT of $97,860 instead—an additional amount of $17,860.

EXAM TIP   **gilbert**

AMT was originally imposed to ensure that wealthy people and corporations do not use tax loopholes to avoid paying their "fair share" of taxes. However, unlike many other tax provisions, AMT is not adjusted for inflation and therefore it can now reach middle-class taxpayers as well as the wealthy. Thus, if an exam question involves a taxpayer with a *large amount of deductions* or *income over the AMTI exemption phaseout thresholds*, be sure to at least mention the possibility that the taxpayer might owe AMT.

Chapter Six:
Tax Accounting
Problems

CONTENTS

Chapter Approach

Chapter Approach

The problems to be covered in this chapter include the determination of *when* income becomes taxable (or a deductible item becomes deductible), and special rules governing how various items of income or deductions may be reported for best tax advantage. Accounting issues are frequently tested because timing questions are critical in tax law.

1. **Accounting Method**

   The primary accounting methods are cash and accrual, but you also need to know how to apply the installment method.

   a. **Cash method**

      Under the cash method of accounting, an item is income when cash (or its equivalent) is received. An item is deductible when cash (or its equivalent) is paid. When solving a problem with a cash method taxpayer, be prepared to confront the following issues:

      (1) **Constructive receipt**

          If the taxpayer has *both the right and the power* to receive the income, she has "constructively received" it; the income cannot be delayed.

      (2) **Timing rule**

          If an employer uses property as compensation and the property is subject to a *substantial risk of forfeiture* and is *nontransferable*, taxation is deferred until the property becomes nonforfeitable or transferable. If the property must be sold at a formula price, and the restriction never lapses, the formula determines the amount included in income.

      (3) **Claim of right doctrine**

          If a taxpayer receives money or property under a claim of right, it is *income* even though it may have to be returned.

      (4) **Prepaid income and expenses**

          Prepayments are generally income when received. Deposits are more like loans and thus are not income. Prepaid expenses are *not deductible*; they must be capitalized and amortized.

   b. **Accrual method**

      Under the accrual method of accounting, an item is income when earned and is deductible when the obligation to pay arises. In both cases the test is whether *all events* have occurred that establish a legal right to receive or make payment. The following issues may arise in connection with an accrual method taxpayer:

(1) Prepaid income

The Supreme Court has held that prepaid income is *taxable when received* even though it is unearned. Watch for statutory and regulatory exceptions to this rule (*e.g.,* automobile clubs, magazine publishers).

(2) Contingent liabilities

There is *no deduction* for contingent liabilities, estimates, or disputed items.

(3) Economic performance rule

Economic performance does not occur, and no deduction is allowed, until property or services are *received* by the taxpayer (or provided by the taxpayer), or in the case of tort liability, until payment is made. [I.R.C. §461(h)]

(4) Inventories

You should be familiar with the *FIFO* (first in, first out) and *LIFO* (last in, first out) methods of computing inventories.

c. Installment method

The installment method automatically applies when a seller receives payment on a deferred basis, unless the seller-taxpayer elects out of it. Under this method, income is recognized pro rata *as payments are received*. When dealing with a problem concerning an installment method taxpayer, the following rules are important:

(1) *Depreciation recapture* is taxed in the year of the sale.

(2) Special calculations are required when *mortgaged property* is sold.

(3) Under the *related party rule*, if a related buyer resells within two years, the seller must recognize income.

(4) *Dealers* cannot use this method.

(5) If *outstanding debt exceeds $5 million*, a special rule requires payment of interest.

2. Annual Accounting Period

Our system is primarily annual—the income and deductions of each year are reported separately, regardless of what happened in earlier or later years. However, there are important exceptions:

a. Repayment of amount previously received

When an amount previously received under a claim of right is repaid, the taxpayer may choose the brackets of the income or the repayment year.

b. Tax benefit rule

A taxpayer must include the recovery of an item previously deducted in income in the brackets of the recovery year.

c. Net operating loss deduction

If a taxpayer's business deductions exceed her income, she has a net operating loss. These losses can be carried back two years, forward 20 years.

A. Accounting Method—When Is an Item Taxable or Deductible?

1. Introduction [§958]

I.R.C. section 446 authorizes taxpayers to use whatever method of accounting that they ordinarily use in keeping their books. However, in practice, the methods expressly recognized in the Code [I.R.C. §446(c)], and discussed below, are the most frequently encountered. Taxpayers cannot change their accounting method without prior approval of the government, even from a wrong method to a correct method. [**Witte v. Commissioner,** 513 F.2d 391 (D.C. Cir. 1975)] The Commissioner, on the other hand, may change the taxpayer's method if the method being used does not "clearly reflect income." [I.R.C. §446(b)]

2. Cash Receipts and Disbursements Method [§959]

Under the cash receipts and disbursements method, items of income are includible in the year in which *cash* (or cash equivalent) is *received*. Deductions are taken in the year in which *payment is made*.

a. Cash equivalents [§960]

An item is income even if paid in a medium other than cash.

(1) Stock [§961]

If an employer pays an employee in corporate stock or other property, the fair market value of the property is income when received. However, if the property is forfeitable, special rules apply. (*See infra,* §§984 *et seq.*)

(2) Promissory notes [§962]

If a taxpayer receives a promissory note or other deferred payment obligation in exchange for property, the fair market value of the obligation is normally treated as the equivalent of cash. The obligation is normally valued at the value of the property surrendered (less any cash down payment). (*See supra,* §780.)

b. Constructive receipt doctrine [§963]

If a cash basis taxpayer has an *unqualified right* to a sum of money or property, plus the power to obtain it, she has "constructively received" it. Thus, it is income currently even though she has not actually received it. [Treas. Reg. §1.451-2(a)]

EXAM TIP   **gilbert**

Don't oversimplify the *cash receipt and disbursement method*. Although income is generally included in the year it is received, you must also remember that a taxpayer *must* include income once the taxpayer has an unqualified right to receive it. This is called the *constructive receipt doctrine*.

---

(1) Rationale

The main purpose of this doctrine is to prevent cash basis taxpayers from avoiding taxes by putting off actual receipt of income until their tax circumstances are more favorable.

(2) Illustrations of constructive receipt doctrine

(a) Uncashed checks [§964]

A taxpayer who receives a check in December of Year 1, but fails to cash it until January of Year 2, is in constructive receipt in Year 1 of the funds called for in the check. [*See* **Lavery v. Commissioner**, 158 F.2d 859 (7th Cir. 1946)]

(b) Interest not withdrawn [§965]

Interest on a savings account is taxable to the taxpayer in the year in which the account is credited, even though not actually withdrawn in that year. Similarly, maturing bond coupons are income to the bondholder in the year of maturity, even though not cashed until a later year. [Treas. Reg. §1.451-2(a), (b)]

(c) Unpaid corporate salaries [§966]

A taxpayer who has *voting control* of a corporation that *owes* him salaries or other taxable funds may be treated as in constructive receipt of such income—provided the corporation has authorized the payment and the funds are available. This is particularly true if the corporation has accrued an expense payment for the money owed. [**Benes v. Commissioner**, 355 F.2d 929 (5th Cir. 1966)]

1) But note

The taxpayer must have both *a right and a power* to receive payment to be in constructive receipt.

> **Example:** Assume Taxpayer owns all of the stock of Acme Corp., and that the corporation declares a dividend in Year 1 "payable January 1, Year 2." Taxpayer will **not** be taxed on this dividend until Year 2. She has no **right** to the money until that time, and it makes no difference that she had the **power** to declare it payable at an earlier date.

(d) Difficulty in obtaining check [§967]

In a questionable decision, a taxpayer was held not in constructive receipt of a check that he could have picked up on December 31 (a weekend day). He would have had to drive 40 miles to obtain it. Moreover, he could not have cashed it at a bank until January 2. The day, the distance, and the futility of the trip were "substantial barriers" to asserting control over the check. [**Baxter v. Commissioner,** 816 F.2d 493 (9th Cir. 1987)]

(3) Mandatory application [§968]

The constructive receipt doctrine must be applied even where it **aids the taxpayer.**

> **Example:** Suppose Taxpayer fails to report certain income in Year 1, although he constructively received it. He actually receives the income in Year 2, when his tax bracket is higher. The government can only assess a deficiency for the **earlier** tax year. [**Ross v. Commissioner,** 169 F.2d 483 (1st Cir. 1948)]

(4) Deferred compensation [§969]

If, before services are rendered, the employer and employee agree that payment will be deferred until a year after that in which the work is done (*e.g.,* at retirement), the money is not constructively received. It is not taxed until actually paid. [Rev. Rul. 60-31, 1960-1 C.B. 174; **Robinson v. Commissioner,** 44 T.C. 20 (1965)] It does not matter that the employer would have been willing to pay the employee currently; the terms of the contract are controlling. [**Amend v. Commissioner,** 13 T.C. 178 (1949)] However, the agreement can be evidenced only by the employer's **unsecured** promise to pay.

(a) When agreement made [§970]

The IRS says that a deferred compensation agreement must be made **before the services** are rendered. [Rev. Rul. 69-650, 1969-2 C.B. 106] However, case law indicates that if the agreement to defer is made after the work is done **but before payment is due,** deferral will still be permitted. [**Veit v. Commissioner,** 8 T.C.M. 919 (1949)]

For your exam, remember that if a cash basis taxpayer agrees to receive income for current services in later years, the payments will not be currently taxable *if* (i) the agreement to delay payment is made *before the services are rendered* (according to the IRS) or made *before payment is due* (according to case law), and (ii) the contract *does not confer an economic benefit* (*e.g.,* does not provide security for payment) on the taxpayer.

(b) Employer's deduction [§971]

The timing of the employer's deduction is matched with the employee's income. The employer cannot deduct deferred compensation until it is actually paid, even if the employer uses the accrual method. [I.R.C. §404(a)(5)]

(c) Economic benefit [§972]

Even if deferred compensation is not constructively received, it is currently taxable to the employee if paid in a form that confers an "economic benefit" on the employee. Sometimes, the same idea is expressed by saying that the deferred compensation is "the equivalent of cash" ("equivalent of cash" and "economic benefit" mean the same thing).

1) Security [§973]

If the employer's promise is secured (*e.g.,* by a mortgage), the promise confers an economic benefit on the employee.

2) Payment to a trust [§974]

Deferred compensation that is paid to a trust for the employee's benefit is an economic benefit to the employee if the assets of the trust are beyond the reach of the employer's creditors. [**Minor v. United States,** 772 F.2d 1472 (9th Cir. 1985)] However, if the assets in the trust can be reached by the employer's creditors, the payment to the trust does not confer an economic benefit on the employee.

3) Forfeitability [§975]

If deferred compensation paid to a trust is subject to a *substantial risk of forfeiture* and is also nontransferable, it is not considered an economic benefit. [I.R.C. §402(b)(1)] The principles of I.R.C. section 83 (*see infra,* §§983-984) are followed in making this determination. For example, if an employee is required to render substantial future services in order to receive the deferred compensation in the trust, the benefit would probably be considered forfeitable. It would not be taxed to the employee until the forfeitability conditions were removed or until the interest became transferable. [**Minor v. United States,** *supra*]

---

e.g. **Example:** A medical partnership rendered services and received deferred compensation, which was placed into a trust. The interest of each doctor in the trust was forfeitable, but the interest of the *partnership as a whole was nonforfeitable.* The Court held that the partnership realized income in the year the payment was made to the trust. This meant that each partner was currently taxed on his pro rata share—even though his own interest in the plan was forfeitable. [**Basye v. United States,** 410 U.S. 441 (1973)]

---

cf. **Compare:** Attorneys settled a personal injury suit. In payment of their contingent fee, they received an annuity from the defendant's insurance company. The insurance company promised to pay them a certain amount per year for 12 years. The annuity was not treated as an economic benefit because it was a mere unsecured promise to pay and was not protected from claims of the insurance company's creditors. [**Childs v. Commissioner,** 103 T.C. 634 (1994), *aff'd,* 89 F.3d 356 (11th Cir. 1996)]

---

4) **Annuity contracts [§976]**

If the employer funds deferred compensation by purchasing a nonforfeitable annuity contract for the employee, the employee is currently taxed—even though he cannot collect under the annuity contract until retirement. [**United States v. Drescher,** 179 F.2d 863 (2d Cir. 1950)—employee received "present economic benefit"]

c. **Qualified pension and profit-sharing plans [§977]**

I.R.C. sections 401 through 407 permit the deferral of an employer's contributions to "qualified" pension and profit-sharing plans for its employees. The employer can immediately *deduct* the contributions. [I.R.C. §404] Even if employees' interests are nonforfeitable, they do not realize income until the funds are actually distributed to them—usually after retirement, when the employees are in a lower tax bracket. [I.R.C. §402(a)]

(1) **Income not currently taxed [§978]**

Another major tax advantage is that income earned by such plans (interest, dividends, etc.) is not currently taxable to the employee. It is taxed only at the time of distribution. Moreover, the trust that holds and invests the money is a tax-exempt entity, so it pays no tax.

(2) Tax treatment on retirement [§979]

At retirement, the employee gets back her *own* contributions paid into the plan as a return of capital (tax free, of course); the part equal to her *employer's* contributions is then taxed to the employee as ordinary income.

(3) Plan must be nondiscriminatory [§980]

To "qualify" for this favorable tax treatment, a plan must have broad employee coverage. This requirement is designed to head off plans that benefit only officers or key employees. [I.R.C. §§401(a)(4), (5); 410]

(4) Limits on contributions and benefits [§981]

There are limitations on the amount of contributions that can be made in any one year to a "defined contribution" plan such as a profit-sharing plan or money-purchase pension plan. The limit is not more than 15% of salary and not more than $44,000 in 2006 (adjusted annually for inflation). Also, the benefits payable from a "defined benefit" plan such as a traditional pension plan cannot exceed $175,000 in 2006 (adjusted annually for inflation). [I.R.C. §§404(a)(3), 415]

(5) Application to noncorporate employers ("Keogh plans") [§982]

Partnerships and proprietorships also can have qualified pension and profit-sharing plans. They can provide the same benefits as a corporate plan.

d. Property transferred in connection with performance of services—"timing rule" of section 83 [§983]

I.R.C. section 83 sets forth ground rules for the "timing" of an employee's income (and the employer's deduction) when the employer uses property (including stock) as compensation. As a general rule, the property is taxed to the employee when she receives it, at its fair market value, without taking into account any restrictions on the property.

(1) Effect of forfeitability [§984]

However, if the property is *both* subject to a substantial risk of forfeiture *and* is nontransferable, taxation is *deferred*. The employee is not taxed until the first year in which the property is *either* nonforfeitable or transferable. The amount includible in income is thus the value of the property in that later year.

---

e.g. **Example:** In Year 1, Erin Employee is allowed to purchase stock in her employer (Acme Corp.) for $6 per share. The stock is then worth $20 per share and is nontransferable. In addition, Erin is required to resell the stock to Acme Corp. for $6 per share if she resigns or is fired, but this restriction will terminate in Year 5. In Year 5, the stock is worth $100 per share. Assuming Erin still works for Acme Corp. in Year

5, she is taxed for the first time that year on $94 per share ($100 per share value less $6 per share purchase price). Her basis is now $100 per share.

(a) Employer's deduction [§985]

As a general rule, the employer takes a deduction arising out of the transfer of property to an employee in the same year that the employee is required to include the transfer in income. [I.R.C. §83(h)] However, the employer loses the deduction unless the employee actually includes the value of the stock in income. [**Venture Funding Ltd. v. Commissioner,** 110 T.C. 236 (1998), *aff'd in unpublished opinion*, 198 F.3d 248 (6th Cir. 1999)] The employer can guard against losing the deduction by filing an information return that alerts the IRS that the employee has received compensation through a transfer of property. [Treas. Reg. §1.83-6(a)(2)]

e.g. Example: Same facts as above. Assume also that Acme filed an information return indicating that Erin received compensation through a transfer of property, and that Erin correctly claimed the transaction as income. Acme should take a deduction of $94 per share in Year 5.

(2) Nonlapse restrictions [§986]

If the property is subject to a restriction that will never lapse, so that it must be resold at a formula price, the price set by the formula determines the amount to be included in income. [I.R.C. §83(d)]

e.g. Example: In Year 1, Eric Employee purchases stock from his employer (Acme Corp.) for $6 per share when its book value (*i.e.,* value determined according to financial statements) is $9 per share. However, a restriction is imposed that if Eric ever wants to sell the stock, he must first offer it to Acme Corp., which will have the right to buy it at book value. The value of Acme stock on the stock exchange in Year 1 is $13 per share. Eric is taxed only on $3 per share (the $9 per share book value less the $6 per share purchase price), not $7 per share (market value less purchase price).

(3) Distinguish—other restrictions ignored [§987]

Restrictions on the property not amounting to substantial risks of forfeiture or formula-price limitations that will never lapse are ignored in valuing the property.

(a) Constitutionality [§988]

This rule has been upheld as constitutional, despite the fact that it requires taxpayers to pay tax on income they have not yet realized. [**Sakol v. Commissioner,** 574 F.2d 694 (2d Cir.), *cert. denied,* 439 U.S. 859 (1978)]

(b) Exception [§989]

If profit on the stock would be payable to the corporation under section 16(b) of the Securities Exchange Act of 1934 (*see supra,* §872), the stock is considered to be both forfeitable and nontransferable until the six-month period of section 16(b) expires. [I.R.C. §83(c)(3)]

(4) Employee election [§990]

A taxpayer may elect to include the value of the property in income when received, even though it is nontransferable and subject to a substantial risk of forfeiture. [I.R.C. §83(b)]

(5) Proper taxpayer [§991]

The Code makes it clear that the employee is taxed, even if the property is transferred to someone else (*e.g.,* his children). [I.R.C. §83(a)] Similarly, the person for whom the services were performed gets the deduction, even if the transfer is made by someone else (*e.g.,* stockholder of employer). [I.R.C. §83(h)]

e. Employee's stock options [§992]

An increasingly common form of compensation to employees is the issuance of stock or stock options by the employer company. Several issues arise from such transactions: Are the stock options taxable as income, or excludible? If taxable, at what value? When are they taxable? And, if the stock has increased in value, is the increase capital gain?

(1) General rule [§993]

Stock or an option to buy stock, issued by an employer to an employee, is in the nature of compensation for services rendered (or to be rendered). As such, the option or the stock is taxed as *ordinary income* to the employee, despite the argument that it was granted to give the employee a stake in the business rather than to compensate him. [**Commissioner v. LoBue,** 351 U.S. 423 (1956)]

(2) Timing of income [§994]

Generally, the *exercise* of the option is the taxable event.

(a) Grant not taxed [§995]

Since the option by itself usually lacks an ascertainable market value, the grant of the option is generally not the taxable event. However, if the option does have an ascertainable value (*i.e.,* there is an established market for it), it can be included in income when received.

(b) Tax treatment upon exercise [§996]

If an option was not taxed when it was granted, its exercise is the taxable event. The difference between the current market price and the option price is treated as ordinary income to the employee, and the basis of the stock will be the option price plus the amount included in income. Any subsequent gain would be capital gain.

---

e.g. Example: In Year 1, Acme Company issues an option with no ascertainable market value to Elmer Employee to purchase one share of its stock for $10 anytime for the next five years. Acme Company stock was selling for $11 when the option was issued. Assume further that Elmer exercises the option in Year 3 when the share is worth $19. Elmer has $9 of ordinary income in Year 3 and a basis of $19 for the share.

---

1) But note

If the stock is subject to a substantial risk of forfeiture and is nontransferable, the income would be deferred under I.R.C. section 83 (*see supra*, §§983-984) until either of those restrictions ceased to apply.

(3) Employer's deduction [§997]

The employer gets a deduction at the same time the employee has income. Thus, in the example above, Acme Company has a $9 deduction in Year 3.

(4) Incentive stock options [§998]

If a stock option qualifies as an "incentive stock option," there is no tax on either the grant or the exercise of the option. The employee is not taxed until he sells the stock, and then the sale is taxed as a capital gain or loss. The employer receives no deduction at any time. [I.R.C. §422] Requirements for incentive stock options are that:

(i) *The employee may not dispose of the stock for a period* extending two years after the option was granted and one year after exercising the option. (These requirements are waived if employee dies.)

(ii) *The option price must equal or exceed the value of the stock* when the option is granted.

(iii) *The term of the option must not exceed 10 years*, and the option must be *nontransferable*.

(iv) *The employee cannot own more than 10% of the employer's stock* when the option is granted (although this requirement is waived if

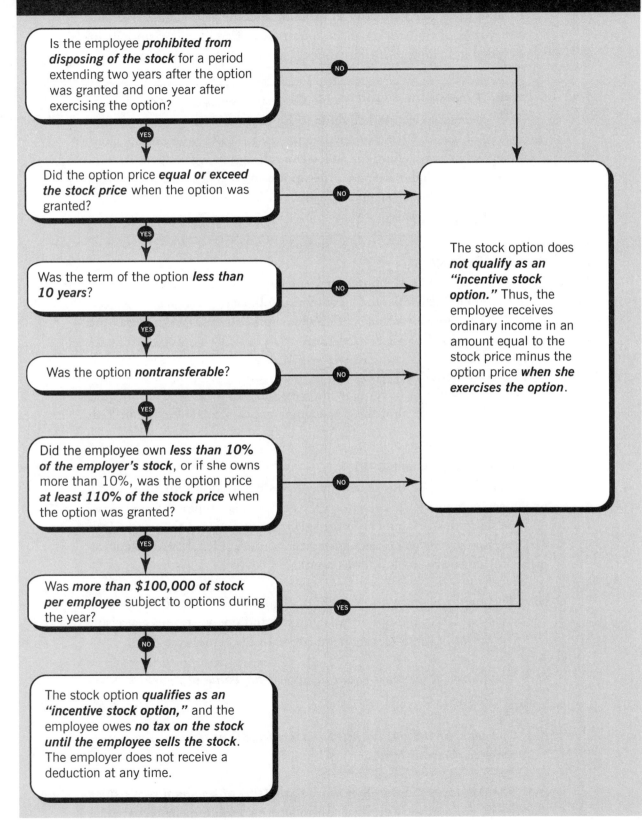

Is the employee **prohibited from disposing of the stock** for a period extending two years after the option was granted and one year after exercising the option?

— NO →

Did the option price **equal or exceed the stock price** when the option was granted?

— NO →

Was the term of the option **less than 10 years**?

— NO →

Was the option **nontransferable**?

— NO →

Did the employee own **less than 10% of the employer's stock**, or if she owns more than 10%, was the option price **at least 110% of the stock price** when the option was granted?

— NO →

Was **more than $100,000 of stock per employee** subject to options during the year?

— YES →

The stock option does **not qualify as an "incentive stock option."** Thus, the employee receives ordinary income in an amount equal to the stock price minus the option price **when she exercises the option**.

NO ↓

The stock option **qualifies as an "incentive stock option,"** and the employee owes **no tax on the stock until the employee sells the stock**. The employer does not receive a deduction at any time.

the option price is at least 110% of the value of the stock when granted).

(v) *Not more than $100,000 of stock per year per employee can be subject to options.*

(a) Note

The exercise value of an incentive stock option is a tax preference subject to the alternative minimum tax. (*See supra,* §§945 *et seq.*)

f. Claim of right doctrine [§999]

If a taxpayer receives money or property and claims he is entitled to it, and he can freely dispose of it, it is immediately taxable. The fact that he might have to give it back is disregarded. [**North American Oil Consolidated v. Burnet,** 286 U.S. 417 (1932)] This rule is equally applicable whether taxpayer is on the cash or the accrual basis.

(1) Rationale—"administrative convenience" [§1000]

Although it would make sense to delay taxation until the taxpayer's entitlement to the money has been confirmed, this might not be administratively feasible. The taxpayer might "forget" to take the money into income in the later year. Besides, his power to use the money as he likes means that immediate taxation is not unjust.

---

e.g. **Example:** *Amounts received by mistake* are taxable when received even though they may have to be repaid. [**United States v. Lewis,** 340 U.S. 590 (1951)—employee received $22,000 bonus in 1944 that was incorrectly calculated; state court order required him to pay back a portion of bonus in 1946]

---

e.g. **Example:** *Money received because of a favorable trial court judgment* is income when received, despite the possibility that it will have to be returned should an appeal be successful. [**North American Oil Consolidated v. Burnet,** *supra*—company won right to funds in receivership in 1917; final appeal dismissed in 1922]

---

e.g. **Example:** *Embezzled money* is immediately income to the embezzler, even though he is under duty to repay. [**James v. United States,** *supra,* §158]

---

(2) Treatment upon repayment [§1001]

The taxpayer receives a deduction in the later year when he repays money received under a claim of right. As to some (but not all) such repayments, he is entitled to figure the deduction at the tax bracket of either the year of receipt or the year of repayment. [I.R.C. §1341; *see infra,* §1076]

g. Prepaid income [§1002]

Since income under the cash method is tied to the receipt of cash, rather than the time the money is earned, prepayments are income when received (*e.g.,* prepaid interest or rent).

(1) Deposits [§1003]

If a customer makes an advance payment for goods and services to the seller, the amount received is currently taxable to the seller, even though the goods or services are furnished in a later year. Similarly, an advance payment of rent is taxable to the lessor when received. However, a security deposit is not currently taxable to the seller or lessor because such a deposit is more like a loan than an advance payment. [**Commissioner v. Indianapolis Power & Light Co.,** 493 U.S. 203 (1990)—deposit by utility customer treated as loan]

(a) Explanation

In *Indianapolis Power,* the Supreme Court analogized the security deposits to loans which, of course, are not taxable to the borrower, rather than to advance payments. The utility paid interest to the customers on the deposits, which made them seem like loans. More important, however, was the fact that the customer controlled whether the deposit would be applied to utility bills or whether the deposit would be returned to the customer (after service was terminated or after the customer established that he was a reliable billpayer). Because the utility had no guarantee that it would be able to keep the funds, it was more like a borrower than the recipient of an advance payment. In the case of an advance payment, the recipient is entitled to keep the funds if it honors its contractual commitments. [**Commissioner v. Indianapolis Power & Light Co.,** *supra*]

h. Prepaid expenses [§1004]

Ordinarily, a cash basis taxpayer is entitled to deduct expense items in the year paid. However, according to most cases, this rule does not apply to amounts prepaid for goods or services to be received in later tax years.

(1) Rationale—preventing tax avoidance [§1005]

To allow a cash basis taxpayer to deduct prepaid expenses currently would allow her to **distort** her income and to reduce taxes in years of high income. Also, the prepayment can be considered the purchase of an asset— a future benefit—which must be **capitalized.** Thus, generally, no current deduction is allowed for amounts expended by a cash basis taxpayer during the year for rents, salaries, or other expenses attributable to future tax years.

(2) Effect—capitalization and amortization [§1006]

The deduction is not lost. Rather, the prepaid expense must be *capitalized* (treated as the acquisition of an asset in the year of payment), and then deducted ratably (amortized) in the future tax year. (Amortization is discussed *supra*, §§456, 473-475.)

(a) Prepaid rent [§1007]

Prepaid rent on business property must be capitalized in the *year paid*, and then *amortized* over the years to which the prepayment applies.

(b) Prepaid insurance [§1008]

Likewise, prepaid insurance on investment property is treated as an asset, to be deducted ratably over the period covered by the insurance. [**Commissioner v. Boylston Marketing Association**, 131 F.2d 966 (1st Cir. 1942); *but see* **Waldheim Realty v. Commissioner**, 245 F.2d 823 (8th Cir. 1957)]

(c) One-year prepayments [§1009]

A prepayment of an expense for a period that does not exceed one year need not be capitalized, even though the year extends beyond the end of the taxable period in which the payment is made. [**Zaninovich v. Commissioner**, 616 F.2d 429 (9th Cir. 1980); **U.S. Freightways Corp. v. Commissioner**, *supra*, §407—same rule for accrual method taxpayer] However, a taxpayer cannot deduct a prepayment for less than one year if no payment was yet due under the taxpayer's contract with the payee. [**Bonaire Development Co. v. Commissioner**, 679 F.2d 159 (9th Cir. 1982)]

EXAM TIP   **gilbert**

On your exam, don't apply the general rule that a cash basis taxpayer must take a deduction for an expense in the year it was paid too liberally. Many types of *prepayments* require the expense to be *capitalized and amortized*.

---

(3) Application

(a) Prepaid interest [§1010]

Prepaid interest can be deducted only over the period of the underlying loan. [I.R.C. §461(g)]

1) Distinguish—"points"

"Points" paid on purchase money loans secured by a taxpayer's principal residence are currently deductible. [I.R.C. §461(g)(2)]

(b) Farming [§1011]

Traditionally, farmers could deduct planting costs and farming supplies immediately. However, there are now some limitations.

1) *"Farming syndicates"* cannot deduct feed, seed, or fertilizer until it is used. [I.R.C. §464]

2) *Farmers* cannot deduct planting costs of *fruit trees*. [I.R.C. §278]

3) *Corporations* must capitalize all pre-production expenses—although there are exceptions for small businesses and family farms. [I.R.C. §447]

(c) Property taxes [§1012]

Prepaid property taxes are deductible. [**Glassell v. Commissioner,** 12 T.C. 232 (1949)]

i. Payment with credit cards [§1013]

If any deductible item is paid by a credit card, the deduction is taken when the item is charged—not when the bill is later paid to the issuer of the credit card. [Rev. Rul. 78-38, 1978-1 C.B. 68; 78-39, 1978-1 C.B. 73]

3. Accrual Method [§1014]

Under the accrual method, the taxpayer reports income in whatever tax year it is *earned*—even though not paid or payable until a later year. Likewise, a taxpayer deducts expenses in the tax year in which the expenses are *incurred*, even though not yet actually paid out. Under this method, the *right to receive* income and the *duty to pay* the various items of deduction are the elements by which the tax is computed. This method is more complex than the cash method, but it is economically sounder.

a. Accrual method required [§1015]

In some circumstances, a taxpayer is required to adopt (or switch to) the accrual method rather than use the cash method.

(1) Income-producing inventories [§1016]

Generally, if inventories are a material income-producing factor for a taxpayer, the accrual method must be used. [Treas. Reg. §1.446-l(c)(2)] (For discussion of inventories, *see infra,* §§1047-1053.) However, the IRS has modified this principle by several administrative decisions. First, a taxpayer with average annual gross receipts of less than $1 million is not required to account for inventories (*see infra,* §§1047 *et seq.*) or use the accrual method. [Rev. Proc. 2001-10, 2001-2 C.B. 272] Second, the IRS will permit certain small service businesses with annual gross receipts of more than $1 million but less than $10 million to use the cash method, even though the business sells goods and would otherwise be required to account for inventories. This decision covers primarily service businesses that also sell goods (*e.g.*, plumbers, auto mechanics). It does not cover businesses engaged in manufacturing or wholesale or retail trade. [Rev. Proc. 2002-28, 2002-18 I.R.B. 875]

(2) Corporations, some partnerships, tax shelters [§1017]

Corporations, partnerships that have a corporate partner, and tax shelters must use the accrual method. [I.R.C. §448]

(a) Exceptions

There are some important exceptions to this rule:

1) An *S corporation* is one that has elected to be taxed in a manner similar to partnerships (*i.e.*, the corporation is not separately taxed; its profits and losses flow directly through to the returns of its shareholders). S corporations are not required to use the accrual method, nor are partnerships that have an S corporation as a partner.

2) A corporation or partnership (with a corporate partner) need not use the accrual method if its *annual gross receipts average less than $5 million*. [I.R.C. §448(b)(3), (c)]

3) A corporation or partnership need not use the accrual method if it is a "*qualified personal service corporation.*" This means that substantially all of its activities involve performance of services in the fields of health, law, engineering, architecture, accounting, actuarial science, performing arts, or consulting. In addition, substantially all of its stock must be held by employees performing the services (or retired employees or the estate of deceased employees or persons who inherited the stock within the previous two years). [I.R.C. §448(d)(2)]

4) *Farming businesses* need not use the accrual method. [I.R.C. §448(b)(1), (d)(l)]

(b) Note

Tax shelters are required to use the accrual method because much of the tax avoidance potential of such enterprises arises from use of the cash method. For this purpose, a tax shelter is any publicly offered partnership, any partnership where at least 35% of the losses are allocated to limited partners, or any other plan whose principal purpose is tax avoidance. [I.R.C. §§448(d)(3), 461(i)(3), 1256(b)(3)(B), 6661(b)(2)(C)(ii)]

b. Special problems with income under accrual method

(1) Deferred income [§1018]

As indicated, the income of an accrual basis taxpayer includes all amounts that the taxpayer has a *fixed* right to receive. The test is whether *all the events that establish a right to income have occurred* and whether the *amount of the income is reasonably determinable.*

(a) When income accrues [§1019]

A seller of goods accrues income when all events have occurred that establish the buyer's obligation to pay. However, sellers have some latitude about whether the critical event is the shipment of goods or the passage of title. Either approach clearly reflects income if used consistently. [**Hallmark Cards Inc. v. Commissioner,** 90 T.C. 26 (1988)—Valentine cards shipped in December but contract provides that title and risk of loss remain with seller until January 1; income does not accrue until January 1]

(b) Time payment is due [§1020]

The fact that the debtor has to have a positive cash flow before it is obligated to pay is not a contingency that allows the creditor to postpone accrual of income. Similarly, the fact that the debt to the creditor is subordinated to other debts would not prevent accrual. Both of these contractual provisions relate only to the time when payment must be made, not to the debtor's liability to make the payment. [**Harmont Plaza, Inc. v. Commissioner,** 64 T.C. 632 (1976), *aff'd,* 549 F.2d 414 (6th Cir. 1977)]

(c) Insolvent debtor [§1021]

If the debtor is insolvent, however, the income need not be accrued. [**H. Liebes & Co. v. Commissioner,** 90 F.2d 932 (9th Cir. 1937)]

1) Proof of insolvency [§1022]

The taxpayer must make a strong showing to establish doubts about collectibility. [*See* **Georgia School Book Depository v. Commissioner,** 1 T.C. 463 (1943)—taxpayer required to accrue commissions earned on sale to state, even though payment was to be made only from a special fund, which had no assets at the time, but which ultimately was likely to be funded]

(2) Prepaid income [§1023]

A problem exists where an accrual basis taxpayer is paid in the current tax year for services to be rendered, or goods to be supplied, in future tax years. The issue is whether the income should all be taxable in the year of receipt or whether it can be spread out over the tax years in which the services or goods are to be provided.

(a) Court position—taxed when received [§1024]

The Supreme Court cases (all dealing with prepayments for services, but apparently applicable to prepayments for goods as well) hold that prepaid income is taxable **when received**. Although this is contrary to proper accounting practice, the Court felt that Congress had mandated this result because it repealed legislation that would have allowed accrual basis taxpayers to defer prepaid income. [**American Automobile Association v. United States,** 367 U.S. 687 (1961)—dealing with prepaid dues to automobile club; **Schlude v. Commissioner,** 372 U.S. 128 (1963)—dealing with prepaid dance lesson fees]

1) Majority rule

Since the Supreme Court cases, the lower court cases have generally held that an accrual basis taxpayer cannot defer prepaid income from goods or services. [*See* **Hagen Advertising Displays v. Commissioner,** 407 F.2d 1105 (6th Cir. 1969)—dealing with prepayments for goods]

2) Minority rule

A few cases have held that taxpayers who make a strong showing can avoid the rule that prepayments are always included in income when received. These cases seem to be of dubious validity as long as the Supreme Court sticks to *American Automobile* and *Schlude.*

 Example: A professional *baseball team* can defer prepaid season ticket income since it can predict precisely when the games will be played. [**Artnell Co. v. Commissioner,** 400 F.2d 981 (7th Cir. 1968)]

 Example: A taxpayer who is prepaid for *some* engineering jobs, but is paid after rendering services for other jobs, was allowed to defer inclusion of the prepayments. The IRS wanted the taxpayer to include prepayments when received and also to accrue income on the other jobs before payment. The court thought that this was an improper hybrid method of accounting. [**Boise Cascade Corp. v. United States,** 530 F.2d 1367 (Ct. Cl.), *cert. denied,* 429 U.S. 867 (1976)]

(b) Statutory relief in certain situations [§1025]

Congress enacted special remedial legislation to allow deferral of *certain* types of prepaid income. (I.R.C. section 456 allows automobile clubs to spread their membership income over the period in which they are obligated to render services to their members; and I.R.C.

section 455 allows newspaper and magazine publishers to spread subscription income over the period of the subscription.)

(c) IRS position—deferral allowed [§1026]

More recently, the IRS has reversed itself. It now permits an accrual basis taxpayer to defer advance payments from the sale of goods. It also permits a *limited* deferral of advance payments for services.

1) Goods [§1027]

An accrual basis taxpayer now has the *choice* of reporting advance payments for goods in the year of *receipt, or whenever properly accruable* under her regular method of accounting. However, advance payments for goods held in *inventory* cannot be deferred past the second taxable year following receipt. [Treas. Reg. §1.451-5]

2) Services [§1028]

Advance payments for services, however, must still be reported in the year of receipt, with this exception: If the services are to be *completed by the end of the following year*, the taxpayer can *defer to the following year* whatever portion of the advance payment is attributable to that year's services. [Rev. Proc. 71-21, 1971-2 C.B. 549] But prepaid *rent* must be reported in the year received.

(3) Dividends [§1029]

Since a dividend becomes a fixed obligation of the corporation when declared, it would seem that accrual basis shareholders should report income from dividends as of the date of declaration. However, due to administrative considerations (particularly, the difficulty of determining the date of declaration in every case), the taxpayer is treated as having no income from dividends until actually received—the same as if he were on the cash basis. [**Commissioner v. American Light & Traction**, 156 F.2d 398 (7th Cir. 1946); Treas. Reg. §1.301-1(b)]

(4) Increasing rents [§1030]

Under certain leases, both the lessor and lessee must account consistently for the rents on the accrual basis, even if either or both of them normally use the cash method. This provision applies only to "section 467 rental agreements," which are leases calling for increasing payments with total rent payments in excess of $250,000. [I.R.C. §467]

(a) General rule [§1031]

If the lease allocates particular payments to particular periods, the parties must accrue income and deductions for that period.

> **Example:** If a five-year lease allocates $0 rent to Year 1 and $100,000 rent to Years 2 through 5, both the lessor and lessee accrue no income or deduction in Year 1 and accrue income or deduction of $100,000 in Years 2 through 5. [I.R.C. §467(b)(1)(A)]

(b) Exception [§1032]

In certain circumstances (*e.g.*, a lease calling for the payment of rent during a year after the year to which the rent applies), the Code calls for an accrual of a constant amount during each year of the lease computed according to present value principles. [I.R.C. §467(b), (e)(1)]

c. Deductions under the accrual method [§1033]

As indicated above, the criteria for deductibility are whether: (i) *all the events* have occurred that establish an *unconditional duty to pay*; (ii) *economic performance* has occurred; and (iii) the amount is *reasonably ascertainable*. [I.R.C. §461(h)(4); **United States v. Anderson,** 269 U.S. 422 (1926); Treas. Reg. §461(a)(2)] Note that the courts refuse to consider the likelihood of actual payment as a factor in determining deductibility. Thus, taxpayers who are insolvent have been allowed to deduct unpaid expenses even though in all probability these items will never be paid. [**Zimmerman Steel Co. v. Commissioner,** 130 F.2d 1011 (8th Cir. 1942)]

(1) Fixed duty to pay

(a) Contested liabilities [§1034]

If the taxpayer disputes its liability for an expense, the taxpayer recognizes no unconditional obligation and hence is not permitted to accrue the item as a deduction. [**Dixie Pine Products v. Commissioner,** 320 U.S. 516 (1944)]

1) *If the taxpayer transfers money to provide for satisfaction of the disputed liability,* she is entitled to deduct it. For example, she might make a payment under protest and immediately sue for recovery. [I.R.C. §461(f); **Chernin v. Commissioner,** 149 F.3d 805 (8th Cir. 1998)—"transfer" to creditor occurred when taxpayer's bank account was garnished]

2) *However, payment of the disputed amount into a trust* does not meet the requirements of section 461(f) where the other parties to the dispute were not parties to the trust agreement. [**Poirier & McLane Corp. v. Commissioner,** 547 F.2d 161 (2d Cir.), *cert. denied,* 431 U.S. 967 (1977)—trust assets would (and in fact did) revert to taxpayer if it was successful in the litigation; *but see* **Varied Investments Inc. v. United States,** 31 F.3d 651 (8th Cir.

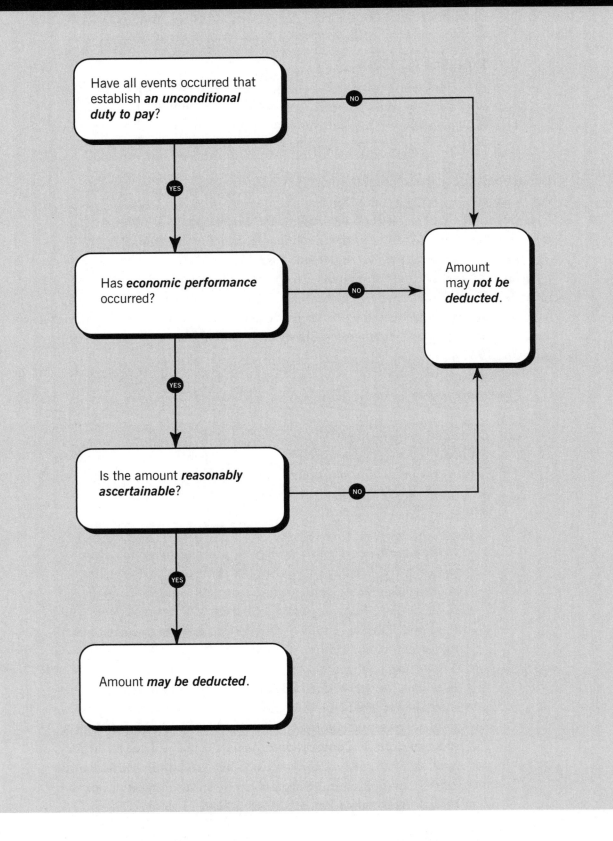

Have all events occurred that establish *an unconditional duty to pay*?

NO

YES

Has *economic performance* occurred?

NO

YES

Is the amount *reasonably ascertainable*?

NO

YES

Amount may *not be deducted*.

Amount *may be deducted*.

1994)—disagreeing with *Poirier & McLane* and allowing deduction for transfer of funds into an escrow account where claimant did not sign the escrow agreement]

(b) Contingent liabilities [§1035]

A deduction cannot be accrued if liability is contingent and the contingency has not occurred.

---

e.g. **Example:** An employer pays the medical expenses incurred by its employees. At the end of the year, some employees have received medical treatment but have not yet filed their claims. Although the employer can predict quite accurately the amount of claims that will ultimately be filed, it cannot deduct these costs. The filing of a claim is an "event" that has not yet occurred; until it does, the employer's obligation to pay remains contingent. Because some employees never do file the claims, the "event" is not an "extremely remote and speculative possibility." [**United States v. General Dynamics Corp.**, 481 U.S. 239 (1987)]

---

1) Recipient of payment [§1036]

However, a taxpayer can deduct an obligation to make payment when all the events have occurred to establish liability, even if the identity of the recipient cannot be ascertained.

---

e.g. **Example:** A gambling casino pays "progressive jackpots," meaning that the amount of a slot machine jackpot keeps rising until somebody finally wins it. At the end of the year, the jackpot has risen to $25,000. Casino can accrue a deduction for the jackpot because state law requires that it ultimately be paid—even though the recipient cannot be identified and it is not known when the jackpot will be won. [**United States v. Hughes Properties, Inc.**, 476 U.S. 593 (1986)] However, the result in this case has been reversed by the economic performance rules (*see infra*, §1038). [I.R.C. §461(h); Treas. Reg. §1.461-4(g)(8), example (4)]

(c) Very long-term obligations [§1037]

If an obligation is to be paid many years in the future, a conflict arises: The taxpayer wants to accrue the deduction immediately, thus producing an immediate tax saving, but the IRS wants to defer the deduction until the amount is actually paid. The case law is uncertain. In many situations, however, the economic performance rule will require deferral until the year of payment (*see, e.g., infra*, §1041).

Example: Mooney Aircraft, Inc., sold an airplane and promised to refund $1,000 to the owner of the plane when the plane was retired (called a "Mooney bond"). The IRS exercised its discretion to switch Mooney Aircraft to the cash method with respect to deducting the $1,000. The court held this was not an abuse of the IRS's discretion, because an immediate deduction would not clearly reflect income. The length of time before payment (20 to 30 years) was just too long. [**Mooney Aircraft, Inc. v. United States,** 420 F.2d 400 (5th Cir. 1969)] The same result (deduction deferred until year of payment) is now required by regulations adopted under the economic performance rule, discussed below. [Treas. Reg. §1.461-4(g)(3)]; *and see* **Ford Motor Co. v. Commissioner,** 71 F.3d 209 (6th Cir. 1995)—tort liabilities to be paid out over 58 years; accrual of entire amount of payment in single year does not clearly reflect income]

(2) Economic performance rule [§1038]

The "all events" test will not be met for purposes of deducting expenses any earlier than the time that "economic performance" occurs with respect to any item.

(a) Purchase of property or services [§1039]

If someone provides services or property to the taxpayer, economic performance does not occur until the services or property are actually provided or used by the taxpayer.

Example: Suppose that in Year 1 Taxpayer agrees to pay $5,000 for stationery to be delivered in Year 3. The cost of the stationery is not deductible until Year 3. [I.R.C. §461(h)(2)(A)]

(b) Sale of property or services [§1040]

When a taxpayer is obligated to provide services or property to someone else, economic performance does not occur until the services or property are actually provided. [I.R.C. §461(h)(2)(B)]

(c) Tort liability [§1041]

If the taxpayer is obligated through judgment or settlement agreement to make installment payments arising out of tort or workers' compensation liability, no deduction can be taken until the payments are actually made. [I.R.C. §461(h)(2)(C)] Prior to enactment of this section, there was authority for allowing the full deduction in the year the obligation became a fixed duty to pay, even if the installment payments were to be made over many years. [*See* **Burnham Corp. v. Commissioner,** 90 T.C. 953, *aff'd,* 878 F.2d 86 (2d Cir.

1989)—total estimated amount of monthly payments to be made for the balance of the plaintiff's life were immediately deductible in the year of the tort settlement] Even before enactment of section 461(h)(2), however, the IRS could reach the same result by switching the taxpayer to the cash method. [*See* **Ford Motor Co. v. Commissioner,** 102 T.C. No. 6 (1994)]

(d) Exception for recurring items [§1042]

To simplify accounting for recurring items, a deduction can be taken in the year before it would be permitted under the above rules if performance will occur within a reasonable time after the close of the year, or within eight and one-half months after the close of the year, whichever comes first. The item must be recurring in nature, consistently treated by the taxpayer, and either not material in amount or (if material) accrual in the earlier year would promote better matching of income and expenses. For this purpose, it helps the taxpayer's case if the item is deducted in the earlier year on its *financial statements*. [I.R.C. §461(h)(3)]

(3) Ascertainable amount [§1043]

Deduction is not permitted unless the amount of the item is reasonably ascertainable.

(4) Disallowance of deduction for amount owed to related taxpayer [§1044]

The Code disallows the accrual of deductions for any item owed to a related cash basis taxpayer until the item is *actually paid*. [I.R.C. §267(a)(2)]

(a) Related persons [§1045]

The above rule applies to a long list of relationships. [I.R.C. §267(b)] For example, it applies to payments between members of a family, and payments between an individual and a corporation of which the individual owns more than 50% of the stock (directly or indirectly). [I.R.C. §267(b)(1), (b)(2), (c)(4); *see supra,* §514]

---

e.g. **Example:** In December of Year 1, the directors of Widgets Corp. (an accrual method taxpayer) vote a bonus to Bernie (a 51% shareholder who uses the cash method). The bonus is paid on June 6 of Year 2. Although Widgets Corp. ordinarily could accrue the bonus in Year 1, it is prevented from doing so until actual payment in Year 2.

---

cf. **Compare:** Under these facts, Bernie might be found to be in constructive receipt of the bonus in Year 1 because he had both a right and power to collect it (*see supra,* §§963-968). If so, Widgets Corp. could deduct it in Year 1. [**Hyplains Dressed Beef Inc. v. Commissioner,** *56* T.C. 119 (1971)]

(b) Pass-thru entities [§1046]
A stricter rule applies to deductions claimed by pass-thru (so spelled in the Code) entities (S corporations or partnerships). If an amount is owed by an accrual method pass-thru entity to any cash method shareholder or partner (regardless of the percentage of that person's interest), the entity cannot deduct the item until actually paid. [I.R.C. §267(e)—pass-thru entities are discussed in detail in the Taxation of Business Entities Summary]

d. Inventories [§1047]
Whenever inventories are an income-producing factor of the business, the taxpayer *must* account for purchases by using an *inventory*. [Treas. Reg. §1.471-1] This means that the cost of goods sold deduction is increased by the merchandise on hand at the beginning of the tax year and decreased by the merchandise on hand at the end of the year. The basic effect is that the taxpayer cannot deduct the cost of goods or materials in the year he purchases them *unless he sells them that year.*

(1) Methods of computing inventory [§1048]
There are two primary methods by which the taxpayer may take his inventory.

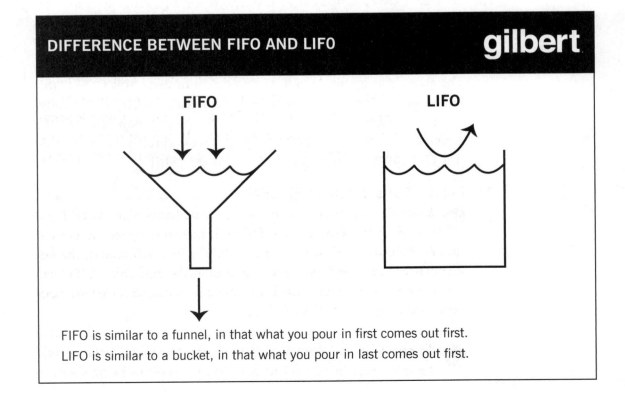

DIFFERENCE BETWEEN FIFO AND LIFO   **gilbert**

FIFO   **LIFO**

FIFO is similar to a funnel, in that what you pour in first comes out first.
LIFO is similar to a bucket, in that what you pour in last comes out first.

(a) First in, first out ("FIFO") [§1049]

If the same type of merchandise was purchased at various prices during the year, and so intermingled that the items cannot readily be identified, the "cost" (for inventory purposes) of the goods on hand at the close of the taxable year is the cost of the goods *last* purchased. The theory is that the *goods first acquired* were those that were *first sold*.

 Example: Athletic Co. sells running shoes. In its first year of operation, it buys 500 pairs of shoes for $20 per pair and later 300 pairs for $25 per pair (a total of $17,500). At the end of the year, it has only 100 pairs of shoes remaining. Under FIFO, the 100 shoes would be valued at $25 each (or $2,500), since it is assumed that Athletic Co. sold the shoes that it bought first, and the remaining shoes are part of the 300 bought for $25 per pair. Thus, cost of goods sold would be $15,000 (purchases of $17,500 less closing inventory of $2,500). The opening inventory for the next year would also be $2,500.

1) Valuation [§1050]

Taxpayers using FIFO can, if they wish, value the assets in inventory at cost or at market value, whichever is lower. [Treas. Reg. §§1.471-2, -4]

a) Exception [§1051]

For purposes of determining market value, the taxpayer is not permitted to follow generally accepted accounting principles by writing down its inventory arbitrarily. "Market" means the replacement value of the inventory unless management is offering it for sale at a lower price or unless it is damaged. [**Thor Power Tool Co. v. Commissioner,** *supra,* §510—spare parts cannot be written down to scrap value as long as they are still held for sale at normal prices]

(b) Last in, first out ("LIFO") [§1052]

Under LIFO, inventory is computed at cost, but the goods on hand at the end of the year are treated as if they had been the earliest items purchased or produced. [I.R.C. §472] (In other words, the last items placed in inventory are assumed to be the first sold.) LIFO can be used for tax purposes only if this method is also used for financial reporting purposes. [I.R.C. §472(c)]

 Example: In the preceding example, the closing inventory would be only $2,000 instead of $2,500. The 100 pairs of shoes in inventory would be considered to be from the *earliest* lot purchased (at $20 per pair). Thus, the cost of goods sold would be $15,500 instead of $15,000, and taxable income would be $500 lower than if FIFO were used.

1) Tax planning [§1053]

In a time of inflation, taxpayers prefer to use LIFO. As the example indicates, when prices are rising, LIFO will produce a lower taxable income. The reverse is true when prices are falling.

(2) Limitation on altering computation method [§1054]

A taxpayer cannot change his inventory method without the approval of the IRS.

EXAM TIP   **gilbert**

If you encounter a fact pattern on your exam in which the taxpayer has **switched (or wants to switch) inventory accounting** methods, be sure to check for the **required IRS approval**. Without IRS approval, a taxpayer may not switch inventory accounting methods.

---

4. Installment Method [§1055]

The installment method of taxation is intended to allow sellers of *property* who are receiving payment on a deferred basis to pay tax on their gain only as they receive cash from the sale. The basic idea is that the profit is recognized ratably as payments are made. The installment method can be used only for a sale of property, not services, and only if the sale produced a gain, not a loss. [I.R.C. §453]

a. Election [§1056]

No election is required to use the installment method. It is automatic. A taxpayer who wishes *not* to use the installment method must elect out of it on her tax return for the year in which the disposition occurred. [I.R.C. §453(d)] If an election out occurs, a cash method taxpayer would include in income all cash and the value of cash equivalents received. (*See supra,* §§960-962.) An accrual method taxpayer would include the entire gross profit in income.

b. Mechanics of installment method [§1057]

To use the installment method, compute a fraction: "gross profit" (selling price less basis) over "total contract price." Multiply that fraction times each payment to determine how much of that payment must be taken into income.

Example: Taxpayer sells stock of Omega Corp. with a basis of $30 and a value of $150 for $25 down and the balance of $125 in 10 payments of $12.50 each, plus interest on the unpaid balance of 9% per year. The fraction is gross profit of $120 over total contract price of $150, or 4/5. Therefore, 4/5 of the down payment is gross profit ($20) and 4/5 of each later principal payment will also be gross profit ($10).

---

(1) Interest separately treated [§1058]

Of course, payments of interest are separately treated. In the previous example, the interest element of each payment is entirely included in income. If the contract failed to provide for interest at the currently required rate, interest would be imputed under section 483 or 1274 (*see supra*, §923).

(2) Depreciation recapture [§1059]

Often, property sold on the installment method has been depreciated by the seller, and depreciation must be recaptured under section 1245 or 1250 (*supra*, §§933-938). The recapturable amount is ordinary income in the year of sale. It cannot be deferred even though the sale is accounted for under the installment method. The amount recaptured as ordinary income is added to the basis of the property for purposes of determining the fraction that will be used under the installment method. [I.R.C. §453(i)]

---

e.g. Example: Tom Taxpayer sells a truck, which he bought earlier for $1,000, for $2,500. The buyer pays Tom $500 down, with the balance paid in 10 payments of $200 each, plus interest of 9% on the unpaid balance. Assume that Tom must recapture $700 of depreciation. The $700 is ordinary income in the year of the sale. The basis of the property is increased from $1,000 to $1,700. The fraction is now $800/$2,500 (0.32). Therefore, only $160 of the down payment is taxable (probably as a gain under section 1231). Only $64 of each later payment of $200 is taxable.

---

c. Indeterminate sale price [§1060]

The installment method can be used even though the sale price is not fixed. [I.R.C. §453(j); Treas. Reg. §15A.453-l(c)] There are three possibilities:

(1) *The sale price is not fixed but will be payable over a defined period of time* (*e.g.,* five years). In this case, taxpayer recovers a pro rata portion of her basis equally over each year. [Treas. Reg. §15A.453-l(c)(3)]

---

e.g. Example: Suppose in the example *supra*, §1057, Taxpayer sells the stock for $25 down and an additional amount equal to 30% of the profits of Omega Corp. for five years. Under the installment method, Taxpayer recovers 1/5 of her basis each year ($6). Thus, in the year of the sale, she has income of $19 ($25 amount realized less $6 recovery of basis).

---

(2) *The sale price is not fixed, but there is a maximum amount that the buyer must pay.* In this case, the maximum amount is treated as the amount realized for purposes of measuring gross profit and total contract price.

---

e.g. Example: Suppose that in the previous example, Taxpayer sells the stock for $25 down and an additional amount equal to 30% of the profits of Omega Corp., but the sale price is capped at $125. The total contract price is $150 and the gross profit is $120. If in a later year it becomes clear that the maximum amount will never be paid, an appropriate adjustment is made in the formula. [Treas. Reg. §1.15A.453-1(c)(2), (7)]

---

(3) *The sale price is not fixed, and there is neither a fixed term nor a maximum amount.* The IRS will scrutinize such deals to make sure a sale really occurred. If it did, basis is recovered equally each year over an arbitrary period of 15 years unless the taxpayer persuades the IRS that a different period would be more appropriate. [Treas. Reg. §15A.453-1(c)(4), (7)]

d. Restrictions on use of installment method

(1) Debt payable on demand or readily transferable [§1061]
If, instead of an ordinary promissory note secured by a mortgage, the seller receives a debt instrument that is payable on demand, or is issued by a corporation or government and is readily tradable, such instrument is treated as a cash payment, thus preventing use of the installment method. [I.R.C. §453(f)(4), (5)]

(2) Sale to related person [§1062]
When the seller sells to a related person on a deferred payment basis, and the related person resells the property for cash within two years, the original seller is treated as if she received the cash for purposes of accounting under the installment method. Related persons include family members, related corporations, etc. [I.R.C. §453(e), (f)(1)]

(3) Dealer property [§1063]
The installment method does not apply to "dealer property." This means personal property in the hands of a person who regularly sells or otherwise disposes of the same type of property on the installment plan. It also means real property held by a taxpayer for sale to customers in the ordinary course of trade or business. [I.R.C. §453(b)(2), (1); *see supra*, §§831-836]

e. Interest on deferred income [§1064]
In the case of very large installment sales, the taxpayer is required to pay interest to the government on the deferred tax liability. [I.R.C. §453A]

(1) Sale price must exceed $150,000 [§1065]

The interest rule applies only to an installment sale where the sale price exceeds $150,000. In addition, the face amount of *all* such obligations held by the taxpayer that arose during, and are outstanding at the close of, the taxable year must exceed *$5 million.* [I.R.C. §453A(b)(2)]

(2) Computation of interest [§1066]

Compute the interest obligation as follows: The deferred tax liability is the amount of tax that would be due if all of the unrecognized gain on the obligations were recognized at the close of the year. The applicable percentage is the fraction determined by dividing the face amount of obligations outstanding in excess of $5 million by the aggregate face value of the obligations. The interest rate charged is the rate currently being charged on tax underpayments.

---

e.g. **Example:** During the year, Sam Seller made a single installment sale in which the sale price was $25 million. The deferred gain on the sale was $16 million. Assume Sam's tax bracket is 28%. The deferred tax liability would be 28% of $16 million, or $4,480,000. The applicable fraction is 4/5 ($20,000,000/$25,000,000). Four-fifths of $4,480,000 is $3,584,000. Assume an interest rate of 10%. Thus, Sam must pay the government $358,400.

---

(3) Pledges [§1067]

If an installment obligation falls under the rules of section 453A (*i.e.,* the sale price exceeds $150,000 and the total installment sales exceeded $5 million), and the taxpayer pledges the installment obligation as security for a loan, the pledge is treated as a disposition of the obligation and deferred gain is recognized under the disposition rules. (*See infra,* §1070.)

f. Mortgaged property [§1068]

Often a buyer will assume or take subject to a mortgage or trust deed on the property owing to a third party. The amount of this mortgage is always taken into account in determining the seller's gross profit, but it is not taken into account under section 453 for purposes of determining either payments received in the year of sale or total contract price. [Treas. Reg. §1.453-4(c)] As a result, the seller does not have to worry about when or whether the buyer makes payments on the debt to the third party.

(1) Illustration

Sue sells Blackacre to Barb for $10,000. The basis of Blackacre is $3,000, and it is subject to a $2,000 first mortgage in favor of Bank. Barb pays $1,000 down, takes subject to the mortgage to Bank, and gives Sue a note for $7,000, secured by a second mortgage on Blackacre, which provides for two payments in future years of $3,500, plus interest on the unpaid balance at the rate of 15%.

(2) Calculation

The gross profit is $7,000; both mortgages are taken into account in measuring gross profit. However, the first mortgage is ignored for purposes of measuring both payments and total contract price. Thus, the fraction is $7,000/$8,000, or 7/8. The only current payment is the $1,000 down payment, of which $875 is taxable. Of the $3,500 payments, $3,062.50 is taxable. Thus, the entire $7,000 gross profit will be taxed. [Treas. Reg. §1.453-4(c)]

(3) Exception [§1069]

If the first mortgage exceeds the basis, the excess is considered a payment received in the year of sale and is part of the total contract price.

---

e.g. **Example:** If the first mortgage in the previous problem were $5,000 (and the second mortgage was therefore reduced to $4,000), the current payments would be $3,000 (the $1,000 down payment plus the $2,000 excess of mortgage over basis) and the total contract price would be $7,000 (*i.e.*, the down payment, the excess of first mortgage over basis, and the second mortgage). The fraction would be $7,000/$7,000, or 1. Thus the entire $3,000 of payments in the year of sale (*i.e.*, the down payment plus the excess of mortgage over basis) would be taxable as would the entire amount of payments as they are made on the second mortgage.

---

g. Disposition of installment obligations [§1070]

Disposition of an installment obligation is a taxable event, whether the disposition is a sale or any other kind of disposition, including a gift. In the case of a disposition, the transferor is deemed to immediately receive the amount realized in the case of a sale (or a satisfaction of the debt by the debtor) and thus to immediately recognize part or all of the previously unrecognized gain. In the case of a gift, the transferor is deemed to receive the fair market value of the installment obligation. [I.R.C. §453B(a)]

(1) Exception—death of taxpayer [§1071]

If the taxpayer dies, the deferred gain is not recognized, and the estate or legatees are permitted to continue accounting for payments on the installment obligation. However, they do not get a stepped-up basis for the obligation since it is considered income in respect of a decedent. [I.R.C. §§453B(c), 691(a)(4), (5)]

(2) Exception—transfer between spouses [§1072]

Transfer of installment obligations between spouses (or former spouses if the transfer is incident to divorce) are excepted from the disposition rule. Suppose at the time of Harold and Wanda's divorce, Wanda transfers an installment obligation to Harold. Wanda does not recognize the deferred gain and Harold continues to account for collections by using the installment method. This rule does not apply to a transfer *in trust* for a spouse or former spouse—a transfer in trust is a disposition. [I.R.C. §453B(g)]

ACCOUNTING METHODS—SUMMARY	**gilbert**
CASH RECEIPT AND DISBURSEMENT METHOD	Income is included in the year in which the taxpayer *receives the equivalent of cash*; deductions are taken in the year in which *payment is made*.
ACCRUAL METHOD	Income is included in the year in which *it is earned*; deductions are taken in the year in which the *expense is incurred*.
INSTALLMENT METHOD	For *sales of property*, a taxpayer (whether he uses the *cash or accrual method*) must include a *percentage of the payments as gain* in the year in which he receives the payment. Note that the taxpayer may opt out of this method and that it *cannot be used for losses*.

B. The Annual Accounting Period

1. Introduction [§1073]

The determination of income and deductions is based on an annual, not a transactional, basis. Hence, even though a taxpayer is engaged in transactions stretching over several years, he ordinarily must pay a tax each year based on his income that year. Items of income and deductions are therefore allocated to a particular year, not to a particular transaction.

2. Selection of Taxable Year [§1074]

Most individual taxpayers report on a calendar year basis (January to December). Other entities (which previously could choose different reporting years) have been required to switch to the calendar year (unless they establish, to the satisfaction of the IRS, a business purpose for a different period). These include partnerships, S corporations (corporations that have elected to be taxed like partnerships), and personal service corporations. [I.R.C. §§443(i), 706(b)(1)(B), 1378] Corporations that are neither S corporations nor personal service corporations are entitled to elect to use a non-calendar year when they file their first returns; they cannot change that year without IRS approval. [I.R.C. §442]

3. **Repayment of Income Reported in Prior Year [§1075]**

As discussed above (*see supra,* §999), payments made to the taxpayer during the tax year that he receives under a "claim of right" are taxed as income to him that year, even though he may have to pay them back in a later tax year. A repayment in a later year does *not* reopen the tax computation for the year the income was received. Rather, *a deduction is allowed in the year repayment is made*. This results from the annual accounting concept. [*See* **United States v. Lewis,** *supra,* §1000—employee forced to repay portion of bonus paid in prior year]

a. **Choice of brackets [§1076]**

Of course, this could be quite unfair to the taxpayer if he were in a high bracket in the year in which the income was paid to him, but in a low bracket when he had to repay it. To ameliorate this, a special provision allows the taxpayer to deduct the amount at the tax bracket of *either* the current year or the earlier year in which the payment was received. [I.R.C. §1341] However, the amount repaid must be at least $3,000 to merit this special treatment.

Example: Tom Taxpayer is employed by Omega Corp. In Year 1, assume Tom is in a 30% tax bracket. He receives a large salary, but Tom's employment contract obligates him to return to Omega Corp. any portion of the salary that the IRS disallows as unreasonable compensation (*see supra,* §§415-423). In Year 3, Tom returns $30,000 to Omega Corp. Tom has negative income in Year 3. Tom can use section 1341 in Year 3 and thus receive a tax saving of $9,000 rather than zero (*i.e.,* 30% of $30,000 rather than no benefit). [**Van Cleave v. United States,** 718 F.2d 193 (6th Cir. 1983)]

---

(1) **Distinguish—reducing income in later years [§1077]**

Section 1341 generally applies only to situations in which the taxpayer is required to *repay* an amount previously reported. If the taxpayer is ordered to reduce its price to customers in later years because of its actions in prior tax years, section 1341 is not applicable. [**Wicor, Inc. v. United States,** 263 F.3d. 659 (7th Cir. 2001)]

Example: Gas Co. is regulated by the state public utility commission ("PUC"). In Year 1, Gas Co. was permitted to charge its customers $160,000 on the assumption that its federal taxes in Year 1 would be $40,000. However, the income tax rate for Year 1 was reduced; therefore, Gas Co. was required to pay federal taxes of only $32,000. As a result, PUC required Gas Co. to reduce its rates in Year 3 by $8,000. The Year 1 tax rates were also much higher than the Year 3 tax rates. The court held that section 1341 does not cover a mandated reduction of income in Year 3, only an actual repayment in Year 3. In other words, section 1341 would have applied if Gas Co. had refunded $8,000 to its customers, but it does not apply when Gas Co. is compelled to reduce its price to customers by $8,000. [**Wicor, Inc. v. United States,** *supra*]

b. Tax benefit offset [§1078]

If the taxpayer elects to claim a deduction in the year of repayment, he must *offset* any *tax benefit* he obtained in the year he reported the income.

Example: Skelly Oil Co. was a producer of natural gas and was ordered to refund to its customers overcharges it had made in prior years (and reported as income). It was entitled to deduct the refunds in the year made, *but* the deduction was reduced by the *depletion allowance* Skelly Oil Co. had claimed with respect to the income in the years of the overcharge. [**United States v. Skelly Oil Co.,** 394 U.S. 678 (1969)]

---

(1) Note

When the income was taxed as a capital gain in the earlier year, a taxpayer can deduct the repayment only as a capital loss. [**Arrowsmith v. Commissioner,** *supra,* §871] However, by using section 1341, a taxpayer can treat the capital loss as if it had occurred in the year of the capital gain.

4. Tax Benefit Rule [§1079]

When a deduction in an earlier year is followed by a recovery in a later year of the amount deducted, the taxpayer must include the amount previously deducted as income in the later year. [**Hillsboro National Bank v. Commissioner,** 457 U.S. 1103 (1983)] However, the recovery is *not* includible in income to the extent that the earlier deduction *did not reduce the amount of tax.* [I.R.C. §111(a)] This is referred to as the "tax benefit rule"—a recovery is not income unless the earlier outlay produced a tax benefit.

a. "Recovery" [§1080]

A "recovery" means an event *inconsistent* with the earlier deduction.

Example: Bruce Wayne gives a building to Gotham City as a charitable contribution and deducts its fair market value (which furnishes Bruce a tax benefit). However, the gift provides that the building must be used for a hospital. In a later year, the city decides not to convert the building into a hospital and returns the building to Bruce, an event inconsistent with the prior deduction. The return of the asset is treated as income in the year of return. [*See* **Alice Phelan Sullivan Corp. v. United States,** 381 F.2d 399 (Ct. Cl. 1967)]

Example: Tilly pays on December 15 of Year 1 (and deducts under I.R.C. section 162, thereby receiving a tax benefit) 90 days' rental on office space for her business. However, on January 5 of Year 2, she converts the space to her residence. The prepayment of rent was deductible in Year 1, because of its short term (*see supra,* §1009). However, the conversion to personal use was inconsistent with having deducted the item as a business expense. She must include in income in Year 2 the amount of the prepaid rent applicable to the period for which the space is not used for business. [**Hillsboro National Bank v. Commissioner,** *supra*—dictum]

Example: Ranch Corp. paid on December 15 of Year 1 (and correctly deducted in Year 1, thereby receiving a tax benefit) the cost of cattle feed that would not be used up until some time in Year 2. On January 20 of Year 2, Ranch Corp. was completely liquidated, and all assets (including the unconsumed portion of the feed) were distributed to Farmer Brown, the sole shareholder. Although I.R.C. section 336 (under prior law) provided that a corporation realized no gain on the transfer of its assets to shareholders in complete liquidation, the tax benefit rule requires that Ranch Corp. include as income in its final tax return for Year 2 the amount of unconsumed feed. The distribution to Farmer Brown is inconsistent with the assumptions that made the Year 1 deduction appropriate for Ranch Corp. Note that the tax benefit rule can even override explicit statutory nonrecognition provisions like section 336. [**Hillsboro National Bank v. Commissioner,** *supra*]

---

b. **Erroneous deduction [§1081]**

A recovery is income even if the amount deducted in the earlier year was not legally deductible. [**Unvert v. Commissioner,** 656 F.2d 483 (9th Cir. 1981); **Hughes & Luce v. Commissioner,** 70 F.3d 16 (5th Cir. 1995)]

c. **Measuring tax benefit [§1082]**

Under the tax benefit rule, it is necessary to see whether a prior deduction reduced income tax.

(1) **Carryforwards [§1083]**

In considering whether a deduction reduced income tax, it is necessary to take the unexpired net operating loss carryforwards or capital loss carryforwards into account. If the deduction created an unexpired carryforward, it is treated as having reduced tax. [I.R.C. §111(c)]

d. **Brackets [§1084]**

Suppose that the taxpayer is in the 15% bracket in Year 1, and she deducts a loss of $5,000. Her taxable income was $12,000; therefore, she received a tax benefit from the entire $5,000 deduction. In Year 5, she recovers the $5,000 item and is in the 30% bracket. The *amount* of tax saving in Year 1 is *irrelevant*; the entire item is taxed at the applicable bracket in Year 5, even though the result is that it will cost much more in taxes than was saved in Year 1. [**Alice Phelan Sullivan Corp. v. United States,** *supra,* §1080]

5. Net Operating Loss Deduction [§1085]

If all of the business deductions available to a taxpayer—expenses, depreciation, depletion, losses, and bad debts—exceed his income, he has a net operating loss ("NOL"). [I.R.C. §172]

a. Distinguish "loss" from NOL [§1086]

Note that this is a different meaning for the word "loss" than was previously employed. The word "loss" in tax parlance usually means a failure to recover basis when a transaction comes to an end. Here, the word "loss" means an excess of deductions over income.

b. Use of NOL [§1087]

The NOL can be *carried back* and used as a deduction for the two years preceding the loss year. The taxes for those years are then refigured, and the taxpayer is entitled to a refund. If some of the NOL has not been used up by the carryback, it is *carried forward* into the 20 years after the loss year and used as a deduction. It must be carried to the earliest of the 22 possible years before the balance can be used in any later year.

c. Amount of NOL [§1088]

The amount of an NOL that may be carried forward or back is equal to a negative taxable income figure adjusted as follows:

(1) *No deduction for capital losses in excess of capital gains* is allowed.

(2) *Personal exemptions* are disallowed.

(3) *Deductions not attributable to a trade or business* are allowed only to the extent of income that is not attributable to a trade or business. The result of this computation is to confine the NOL to trade or business rather than personal or investment losses.

Review Questions
and Answers

Review Questions

1. In Year 1, Angelo borrowed $100 from Bobbi, which Angelo used to go on a vacation. In Year 2, Angelo repaid the $100 to Bobbi, with $6 interest. The loan bears interest at a rate in excess of the applicable federal rate.

    a. Is anything included in Angelo's or Bobbi's gross income?   _____

    b. Does either Angelo or Bobbi have any deductions?   _____

2. Calvin, a theater critic, receives free tickets to plays and gives them to his friends. Must he include the value of the tickets in income?   _____

3. Don, an accountant, is getting divorced. Edna, an attorney, needs accounting services for her law practice. Edna agrees that she will represent Don; for each hour she spends on Don's case, Don will give Edna an hour-and-a-half of accounting services. Thereafter, Edna provides 30 hours of legal services for Don (worth $1,500) and Don provides 45 hours of accounting services for Edna (also worth $1,500).

    a. Do Don and Edna have income from these transactions?   _____

    b. Does either of them get any deductions?   _____

4. French has been George's valet for many years and they have become close personal friends. When French retires, George unexpectedly presents him with a check for $25,000.

    a. Is the $25,000 includible in French's income?   _____

    b. Can George deduct the $25,000?   _____

    c. Would French be taxed if George had left him $25,000 in his will?   _____

5. The Zero Manufacturing Co. has a custom of paying $8,000 to the widows or widowers of deceased employees. Horace died and Zero paid Iris, his widow, $8,000.

    a. Must Iris include the full $8,000 in income?   _____

    b. Can Zero deduct the $8,000?   _____

6. Home Magazine gives an annual $10,000 prize to persons who create the most ingenious new interior decorating scheme for their homes. It is necessary to submit a photograph of the rooms involved. Lem wins the prize this year.

a. Must Lem include the $10,000 in income? _____

b. If entering the contest cost Lem $100 for making photos and $40 as an entry fee, could he deduct the $140? _____

7. Mildred attends University. She received a $9,000 scholarship of which $4,200 was applied to her tuition and books. Is any amount of the scholarship taxable? _____

8. Norm takes out a life insurance policy on his life, naming Oona (his cousin) as the beneficiary. Norm pays premiums of $2,000 and Oona pays premiums of $3,500. When Norm dies, Oona collects $10,000.

a. Must Oona include anything in income? _____

b. Could Norm or Oona deduct the premiums they paid? _____

c. Would the answer to question a. have been different if Oona had purchased an existing policy from Norm for $2,000 and then paid $3,500 more in premiums? _____

9. Paul, the surviving spouse of Rhea, is the beneficiary of a $100,000 life insurance policy on her life. He elects to have the company pay out the proceeds in 10 annual payments of $15,000 each. Must Paul include any part of the $15,000 payment in income? _____

10. Steve purchases an annuity policy for $10,000 that will pay him annual payments of $1,000 per year beginning at age 65 until his death. His life expectancy at age 65 is 16 years.

a. How much of each annuity payment is taxable? _____

b. Steve dies at age 66 after receiving only one payment. Is he entitled to a loss deduction in the year of his death? _____

11. Tom buys a $20,000 bond issued by Dubuque, Iowa. He pays $1,000 down, promising to pay the additional $19,000 in the future. In Year 1, he pays $1,900 interest on his debt obligation. He also pays $20 for a safe deposit box to store the bond in. He receives $1,400 of interest income on the bond.

a. Is the $1,400 of interest income taxable? _____

b. Is either the $1,900 interest expense or the $20 for the safe deposit box deductible? _____

12. Indicate whether any of the following items received by Vera (who is single and whose adjusted gross income is $23,000) are taxable:

a. Social Security retirement benefits of $7,000. _____

b. Payments of Supplemental Security Income ("SSI") based on need amounting to $1,300. _____

13. The *San Francisco Chronicle* writes an article describing Silvio as a hired killer for the Mafia. Silvio sues for defamation, recovering $20,000 as actual damages (which include damages to his business as a babysitter) and $50,000 as punitive damages.

a. Is the $20,000 taxable to Silvio? _____

b. The $50,000? _____

c. Can the *Chronicle* deduct the payments? _____

14. Zero Manufacturing Corp. sued Scratch Electric Co. for antitrust violations, based on price fixing by Scratch of certain materials purchased by Zero. In previous years, Zero had deducted its payments to Scratch and received a tax benefit. The lawsuit was settled for $400,000: $150,000 allocated as damages to Zero's goodwill, $200,000 as damages for lost profits, and $50,000 as punitive damages. Zero had no basis for its goodwill, which had been completely destroyed. Scratch had previously been convicted of criminal antitrust violations by reason of the same conduct alleged in Zero's lawsuit.

a. Must Zero include the $150,000 in income? _____

b. Must Zero include the $200,000? _____

c. The $50,000? _____

d. Can Scratch deduct all of its payments to Zero? _____

15. Cowboy is given bunkhouse facilities and meals on the ranch so that Rancher can have him available for emergencies at all times. The annual value of the lodging is $1,200 and the annual value of the meals is $1,000. Must Cowboy include these amounts in income? _____

16. Alpha Manufacturing Co. owes $10,000 to Piedmont Corp. for services rendered. It offers to settle the debt for $6,000. Piedmont accepts because Alpha's financial condition is so poor that Piedmont does not think Alpha can ever pay the debt in full. Prior to the settlement, Alpha's assets were $34,000 and its liabilities were $37,000. Both Alpha and Piedmont use the accrual method of accounting; thus, Alpha had previously deducted the $10,000, and Piedmont had included it in income.

a. Does Alpha have gross income from this transaction? If so, how much? _____

b. Does Piedmont get a deduction? _____

17. Law Firm gives free legal services to any of its employees who need them. Joe (a paralegal) needs a new will. Carol (a young associate) drafts one for him free of charge. At Law Firm's usual rates, the will would have cost $500. Carol's salary for the time she spent on this job was $120.

   a.   Should Joe include the $500 in income?   _____

   b.   Assuming the $500 is includible, can Joe deduct it?   _____

18. The divorce agreement between H and W calls for H to pay W $40,000 per year for five years (terminable on W's death) plus $12,000 in child support per year.

   a.   How much can H deduct when he pays $52,000 in the first year?   _____

   b.   How much should W include in income?   _____

19. The divorce agreement between H and W calls for H to pay $40,000 per year for 10 years, terminable on W's death. In the first year, H pays the $40,000 but in the second and third years he pays nothing. What consequences to H in the third year?   _____

20. Diego owned a vegetable farm. He gave his son, Sam, the right to harvest and sell the vegetables on the farm. But Diego reserved the right to sell the land and keep the proceeds of sale (as it was located close to a city, it was very valuable real estate). This year, Sam harvests and sells artichokes worth $20,000. Is Sam taxed on the $20,000?   _____

21. Gordon set up a trust, giving the income to Kent for life, remainder to Wayne. Kent receives about $10,000 per year from this trust. In Year 1, Kent gave Lois one-half of his life estate. He also gave Jimmy the remaining one-half of the income for the next five years. In Year 2, Lois receives $5,000 and Jimmy receives $5,000.

   a.   Is Lois taxed on the $5,000 she received?   _____

   b.   Is Jimmy taxed on the $5,000 he received?   _____

22. Miguel, an attorney, tells his clients to pay legal fees to his child, Rafael. In that tax year, Rafael receives $21,000. Is he taxed on the $21,000?   _____

23. Luanne, an attorney, has been working for years on a big personal injury case; if she wins it, she will get one-third of the recovery. Needing cash, she sells her rights to the fee in Year 1 to Tex for $30,000, even though the case has not yet gone to trial. In Year 3, she tries and wins the case, getting a judgment for $300,000. However, before the judgment is collected, Tex gives his rights to the $100,000 contingent fee to his son, Jake. Shortly thereafter, Jake receives $100,000.

   a.   Does Luanne's sale result in her being entitled to capital gain?   _____

b.   Is the $100,000 taxed to Jake?   _____

24.   Jean owns a plastics molding factory. She transfers the factory to a partnership, making herself a general partner, and creates newly formed trusts for her children as limited partners. Independent trustees are used. Jean pays herself a reasonable $60,000 per year salary. After payment of the salary, the partnership has a profit of $100,000. Trust A, which has a 10% interest in the partnership, receives $10,000. Is Trust A taxed on the $10,000?   _____

25.   Paulie is a 10-year-old child movie star. By contract, his earnings are paid to his father, Phil, who completely controls the choice of movies Paulie works in and Paulie's working conditions. This year, Phil receives $50,000 from Paulie's earnings and spends $15,000 on such items as singing lessons for Paulie. Phil also keeps $5,000 for himself since his contract with Paulie entitles Phil to a 10% management fee.

a.   Is Paulie taxed on the $50,000?   _____

b.   Can Paulie deduct the $15,000 spent on singing lessons and the like?   _____

c.   Can Paulie deduct the $5,000 retained by Phil?   _____

26.   Harold and Wilma are husband and wife. They live in a community property state. This year, Wilma earns $28,000 of gross income, which is classified as community property over which she has the power of control. Wilma and Harold file separate returns. Must Wilma report $28,000 on her return?   _____

27.   On January 1 of Year 1, X Corp. loans $250,000 interest free to Enrique, its sole shareholder. Enrique uses the loan proceeds in his separate business as a photographer. The loan is repayable when X Corp. demands it. The applicable federal rate is 6%. (Assume only annual compounding is required.)

a.   What consequences to Enrique in Year 1?   _____

b.   What consequences to X Corp. in Year 1?   _____

28.   Giovanna puts some GM stock in trust with the income payable to her minor son Carlo for 12 years, reversion to Giovanna. Must Carlo include the dividends on the stocks in his income?   _____

29.   Ken places property in trust for Barbie and Teresa for life, remainder to Kelly. In each of the following cases, will Ken be taxed on the income from the trust?

a.   Ken, as the trustee, can invade corpus for either Barbie or Teresa if money is required for educational or medical needs.   _____

b.   Ken has power, as trustee, to apportion the income of the trust between Barbie and Teresa, depending on their medical and educational needs.   _____

c.   Matt, Ken's grandfather, will have the exclusive power as trustee to apportion income between Barbie and Teresa as required for educational and medical needs. _____

d.   The Bank of America and Matt (Ken's grandfather) have power to apportion income or principal among the beneficiaries in any manner that they wish. _____

e.   Ken is the trustee and has power either to distribute income currently to Barbie and Teresa or to accumulate the income. However, the accumulated income must be paid to Barbie or Teresa during their lifetimes or to their estates or appointees. _____

30.   Sam puts property in trust for Tom for life, remainder to Natalie. However, Sam can revoke the trust any time after one year.

a.   Will the income of the trust be taxed to Sam? _____

b.   Would the answer be different if Sam can revoke only with the consent of Tom? _____

31.   Aaron puts property in trust with the income to be accumulated during the life of his wife, Beth, remainder to Clem. The trustee is the Bank of America. It can pay any of the accumulated income to Beth if, in the Bank's discretion, she is in need of it.

a.   If Beth does not receive any income, is Aaron taxed on it? _____

b.   Suppose that the income could, in the Bank's discretion, be used only for the support of Aaron's minor son, Don. If Don does not receive any money, is the income taxed to Aaron? _____

32.   Ella puts property in trust, with the income to Fred for life, remainder to George. In the following cases, will the income from the trust be taxed to Ella?

a.   Jack, a business partner of Ella, has the power to borrow interest-free from the corpus of the trust. _____

b.   Ella, acting as a trustee in a fiduciary capacity, has the power to vote stock in the trust. _____

33.   Ivan sets up a trust with the income payable to Oleg for life, remainder to Igor. Nicolai has the power to assign the trust assets to himself at any time.

a.   Is Nicolai taxable on the trust income, even though he does not assign the corpus to himself? _____

b.   Suppose that Ivan had the power to distribute corpus to Oleg at any time before Nicolai assigns the trust to himself. Is Nicolai taxable on the income? _____

34. The terms of Trust A require that all income be currently distributed to the life beneficiary, Mary. However, capital gains are allocated to the corpus. This year the trust has ordinary taxable income of $25,000. However, the trustee did not distribute it to Mary. The trust also has a $12,000 long-term capital gain. Is the trust taxable on:

    a.   The $25,000?   _____

    b.   The $12,000?   _____

35. The beneficiaries of Trust B are Paul and Roy. Paul is entitled to receive $5,000 per year, or the entire income of the trust, whichever is less. The trustee can also distribute income to Roy in his discretion. This year the trust has $14,000 of income. The trustee distributed $5,000 to Paul and $15,000 to Roy. On what portion is Roy taxed?   _____

36. Are the following expenditures deductible to the person who pays them?

    a.   Arnie, a shareholder of Zero Corp., pays $250, which represents the salary Zero owed to one of its employees.   _____

    b.   Roger moves from Newark to Miami to take a new job as an engineer. The cost of moving his furniture and personal belongings is $1,000. He also incurs a $2,000 real estate broker's commission when selling his old house in Newark and has costs of $180 while searching for a new place to live in Miami. Are all of these costs deductible?   _____

37. Are any of the following costs of travel deductible?

    a.   Karen is a private duty nurse and works at the home of different patients every day, to whom she is referred by the nurse's registry. The distance from her house to the nurse's registry is one mile. She goes directly from her home to the home of Mathilda (20 miles).   _____

    b.   Ron is a bass player in the local symphony orchestra. He must transport his instrument with him when he goes to symphony hall to play a concert. But for the need to transport the bass, he would take the subway. Can Ron deduct his auto expenses?   _____

    c.   Tom is a self-employed attorney. He travels from New York to Washington. The primary purpose of the trip is business. However, he spent one of the three days in Washington as a tourist, visiting places of interest. The airfare to Washington is $80. His cost of meals in Washington is $180. His lodging cost is $360. How much, if anything, is deductible?   _____

    d.   Richard has no permanent residence. He is employed as an announcer in the Ringling Bros. Circus. He travels with the circus from place to place. He pays $2,000 for lodging.   _____

e.   George is a philosophy professor at UCLA. He takes a job teaching for one year at Michigan. His cost of meals and lodging while there is $8,000.   _____

38.   Ralph (a full-time veterinarian) has adjusted gross income of $118,000. He owns a house, which he rents to tenants. This year the income from the house was $12,000, but the total deductions were $30,000. He had no other investments except for some stocks that brought in dividend income of $21,000. What portion of the $30,000 is deductible?   _____

39.   Proceedings are brought by Paul's relatives to commit him to a mental institution. Paul knows that if this occurs, it would totally destroy his business as a salesman. Therefore, he incurs legal fees in an effort to resist the commitment. Are these costs deductible?   _____

40.   Are any of the following educational costs deductible?

a.   Wilhelm wishes to become a professional violinist and therefore attends the Juilliard School of Music.   _____

b.   Barbara, a professional pianist who is employed by the Boston Symphony, takes some additional piano lessons from a famous pianist.   _____

41.   Zero Manufacturing Co. has a group life insurance policy on which it pays the premiums. All of the employees of Zero participate in the plan, and they are allowed to name the beneficiaries of the policy. Arthur is an employee of Zero and has life insurance in the amount of $50,000 under the plan.

a.   Is Arthur taxable on the premiums Zero pays on his policy?   _____

b.   Can Zero deduct the premiums?   _____

42.   Ripoff Corp. engages in the following transactions this year. Is it entitled to current deductions?

a.   At a cost of $50,000, it grades and paves an empty lot to be used for employee parking.   _____

b.   Ripoff owns a bulldozer that it purchased in earlier years. The depreciation on the bulldozer allocable to the taxable year is $15,000. The bulldozer is used during the entire year by Ripoff in preparing sites for new factory buildings for its own operations.   _____

43.   Carol is an attorney who uses the cash basis. The lease on her new office is for five years at $40,000 per year. Carol prepays the five years' rent although the lease calls for payments each month. Lee is the landlord who uses the accrual basis.

a. Can Carol deduct her entire rent prepayment in this tax year? _____

b. Must Lee take the entire rent prepayment into income in this tax year? _____

44. For use in his accounting business, Zeke leases a used bookkeeping machine. Although the usual rent for this machine is $1,000 per year, Zeke's arrangement provides for rent of $1,400 per year. At the end of a five-year period, he has an option to purchase the machine by paying an additional $200. The amount of the rental payments, plus the option payment, is about 25% more than the value of the machine when Zeke signs the agreement. Can Zeke deduct his rental payments? _____

45. Are any of the following outlays deductible currently?

a. Amounts paid to an employment agency that fails to find the taxpayer (who is a salesperson) a new sales job? _____

b. The amounts paid to develop a new invention by someone who is not otherwise in business but hopes to make money from the invention? _____

c. The costs of searching for a city in which to locate a new law practice where no appropriate location is found? _____

46. Theda decided to take over a defunct advertising agency that had previously gone out of business with many unpaid debts. To recapture some of the previous clients, Theda began to pay off these debts. In Year 4, she pays $10,000. Larry was a creditor of the former advertising agency. The agency owed him $2,000, which Larry deducted as a bad debt in Year 1. This deduction resulted in a substantial tax saving to Larry. In Year 4, Larry receives $2,000 from Theda.

a. Can Theda deduct the $2,000 payment to Larry? _____

b. Must Larry include this repayment in his gross income? _____

47. Defco, a drug company, produced a new drug called R20. Paula took R20 to deal with allergies and was severely injured when R20 was discovered to cause permanent lung damage. Paula's lawsuit against Defco is settled by Defco's agreement to pay Paula $40,000 per year for the rest of her life without interest. Her life expectancy is estimated at 25 years. The case is settled in Year 1, and Defco makes the first payment in Year 1. Paula uses the cash method and Defco uses the accrual method.

a. Must Paula include any part of the $40,000 in income? _____

b. Can Defco deduct the entire obligation in Year 1? _____

48. Spinoff Recording Co. wishes to have certain songs by its artists played on a specific radio station. It pays the program director of the station $5,000 in return for his

promise to play certain songs during the year. This form of payment is illegal under state law but the law has apparently never been enforced.

a. Can Spinoff deduct these payments?

b. Is the $5,000 taxable to the program director?

49. Pierre, a personal injury attorney, pays $5,000 to nurses in the X Hospital to refer cases to him. This practice violates the rules of the applicable Bar Association and, if Pierre is caught, he is in danger of professional discipline. This disciplinary rule is frequently enforced. Can Pierre deduct the payments?

50. Acme slaughters and sells pork at a packing house. Because of unavoidable failures in equipment, the pork is often short-weighted—that is, a customer would be charged for more than he actually received. Department of Agriculture inspectors frequently discover that Acme has violated the statute against short-weighting. Acme has to pay many criminal fines of $50 each. This law is applicable even to unintentional violations.

a. Can Acme deduct these fines?

b. Can Acme deduct legal fees that it incurs in resisting these fines?

51. Raoul is a self-employed doctor who is very interested in trying to resist the passage of national health insurance legislation. Can Raoul deduct any of the following expenditures?

a. He gives $5,000 to the campaign of a candidate for the Senate who is opposed to such legislation.

b. He travels to Washington to make an appearance before a committee of the House of Representatives considering such legislation, in order to try to influence the legislative product.

52. Rex feels he was cheated by Sasha in their joint effort to locate and develop a tungsten mine. Although Rex found the right place to dig, Sasha recorded it in his own name and has been working the claim by himself. He refuses to let Rex have any part of the proceeds from the sale of the metal. Rex sues Sasha to establish his one-half interest in the mine and for damages to recover his part of $150,000 in ore already sold by Sasha.

a. Are attorneys' fees from this litigation deductible by Rex?

b. If Rex wins, is the $150,000 taxable to him?

53. Lloyd, an attorney, leases an office in a building owned by Red. Can Lloyd claim depreciation on the following assets?

a.   The building? _____

b.   Walls within the office suite which Lloyd builds to create separate offices for the different attorneys and secretaries? _____

c.   Paintings that he hangs on the wall? _____

54.   Ralph owns real property and leases it to Sara. The lease is for 25 years. Sara constructs an office building thereon with a useful life of 40 years.

a.   Does Ralph have income because of the construction of this building? _____

b.   Over what period of time should Sara depreciate the building? _____

c.   Ralph sells his interest in the land and building to Vic. Vic allocates $250,000 of this purchase price to the building, which was constructed by the tenant. Is Vic entitled to depreciate this portion of the purchase price? _____

55.   Bess acquires a photocopier for use in her law firm. It costs $24,000. She purchases it on December 1 of Year 1. For tax purposes, it is five-year property. Ignore the special allowance under section 179.

a.   If Bess uses the straight-line method of depreciation, how much can she deduct in Year 1? _____

b.   If she uses accelerated depreciation, how much can she deduct in Year 1? _____

c.   How much depreciation would Bess be entitled to in Year 2 under the straight-line method? _____

d.   Under the accelerated method? _____

e.   How much could Bess deduct under section 179 (assuming this is the only property she purchased in Year 1)? _____

56.   In Year 1, Jake purchased an oil well for $100,000. It was estimated to contain 100,000 barrels of oil. In Year 2, the oil well produced a gross income of $40,000. The various costs of operation of the well, including depreciation of physical facilities, totaled $30,000. The well produced 8,000 barrels of oil this year. (Assume Jake qualifies for percentage depletion.)

a.   How much cost depletion can Jake collect? _____

b.   How much would be available if percentage depletion is claimed? _____

c.   Assume that in Year 12, Jake would like to claim percentage depletion of $10,000 on his well. He has previously claimed depletion equal to the entire basis of the property. Is the percentage depletion nevertheless deductible? _____

d. Assume that Jake claims $10,000 of percentage depletion and basis has been exhausted. Is the amount claimed included as a "tax preference" for purposes of the alternative minimum tax on tax preferences? _____

57. David acquires a piece of land for $30,000, allocating $12,000 to the purchase of the land and $18,000 to a building on the land. Assume David planned to tear down the building to construct an office building on the property. When he tears down the building, can he deduct the $18,000 allocated to the building as a loss? _____

58. Floyd purchased a barber shop last year, allocating $30,000 of the purchase price to goodwill. This year, Floyd decides that the goodwill has declined in value to $0 since business is terrible. Can he claim a loss deduction? _____

59. Leon owned 500 shares of General Motors stock that he purchased 20 years ago for $50,000. At present, the stock is worth only $22,000, and so he sells it to his brother Julius for $22,000 in cash. Two months later, Leon repurchases the property from Julius for its then fair market value of $19,000. Can Leon deduct the $28,000 loss on the sale to Julius? _____

60. Mike wished to borrow $5,000 to purchase a car. Because of his poor credit, he could not get a loan. Therefore, Gloria guaranteed Mike's loan. Mike did not pay for the car, and Gloria had to make good on her guarantee in the amount of $5,000. Gloria and Mike were personal friends. In the year in which she makes the payment, can Gloria deduct the entire payment? _____

61. In the course of her banana business, Chiquita makes a $10,000 loan to Dole, one of her customers. In Year 2, it is determined that $6,000 of this debt is no longer collectible and it is realistic to expect Dole to repay only $4,000.

a. Can Chiquita deduct $6,000? _____

b. In Year 3, Chiquita accepts $4,000 from Dole in total satisfaction of the debt. Does Dole have income on this transaction? _____

62. Larry owns 20% of the stock of Zero Corp. He also loans $50,000 to the corporation. Larry works for the corporation and gets a salary. The other stockholders are members of Larry's close family. The debt is uncollectible. Is it deductible as a business bad debt? _____

63. Nhu is an accountant who uses the cash basis. She does $20,000 worth of work for John in Year 1. By Year 3, it has become clear that the debt is entirely uncollectible. Can Nhu deduct $20,000 in Year 3? _____

64. Rich (who is single) has gross income of $16,000. He has a short-term capital loss of $600 and alimony of $500, which are deductible. He has employee business expenses such as union dues and the cost of uniforms of $400. How much is Rich's adjusted gross income? _____

65. Jim is a successful lawyer. In Year 1, he has net investment income from stocks and bonds of $60,000. On January 2 of Year 1, he borrowed $500,000 for the purpose of buying bonds. He prepaid $400,000 of interest on the loan. This was interest for 10 years, and was the only interest he paid in Year 1. How much interest can he deduct in Year 1? _____

66. Ray (an attorney) owns a part interest in a restaurant. He works at the restaurant 296 hours during the year and his wife works another 207 hours. His share of the restaurant's losses were $60,000. Can he deduct this amount? _____

67. Are the following state or local taxes deductible to a taxpayer who is not in business?

 a. State gift tax? _____

 b. State gasoline tax? _____

 c. Federal import duties on imported merchandise? _____

 d. State sales tax? _____

68. Barbara gives her farm to her child, Carol, for life, remainder to the Red Cross.

 a. Is the actuarial value of the remainder deductible as a charitable contribution? _____

 b. Suppose instead that the gift was $100,000 in cash in a trust for Carol for life, remainder to the Red Cross. Is the remainder deductible? _____

69. Alison purchased General Motors stock for $10,000 on July 1 of Year 2. By September, the stock has gone up to $14,000 and she donates it to Public University. Her adjusted gross income is $100,000.

 a. How much of a deduction is Alison entitled to? _____

 b. Suppose that Alison had owned the stock for three years. Now how much would be deductible? _____

 c. How much would be deductible if Alison's gift to University was an antique automobile? Assume that the automobile was purchased for $10,000, it is now worth $14,000, and Alison has owned it for four years. _____

70. Glen bought stock for $5,000 which is now worth $25,000. He sells it to the University of Illinois for $5,000. He has held it for four years.

 a. How much is deductible? _____

 b. Does Glen have any capital gain on the sale? _____

71. Bruce has adjusted gross income of $22,000. During this year, he pays medical insurance premiums of $250. He has expenses for prescription drugs of $400 and doctor bills of $1,100. How much is his medical expense deduction? _____

72. Mike and Susan are married and file a joint return showing AGI of $37,000. They have two children, Bob and Carol. Bob is 17 years old and earned $4,600 this year. His parents applied $6,000 toward his support. Carol is age 24 and does not live with her parents. She is not a student. She earned $4,600 during the year, but her parents supplied $6,000 toward her support.

    a.   On Mike and Susan's joint return how many personal exemptions can be claimed? _____

    b.   Can Bob claim himself as an exemption on his own return? _____

73. Harold and Wanda are divorced. They have one child, Clarissa, who lives with Wanda. In this tax year, Harold supplied child support of $4,000. Wanda contributed $2,500 to Clarissa's support.

    a.   The divorce agreement contains no provision with respect to who receives the personal exemption. Can Wanda claim the exemption? _____

    b.   Suppose the family court judge allocated the exemption to Harold. Can he take the exemption? _____

74. Mary is an employed single parent with one child. In 2006, Mary's earned income and adjusted gross income are both $26,000. Mary pays $400 per month for nursery school to care for her child while she is at work. Is she entitled to any deduction or credit for her child care costs? _____

75. Morris purchased a used car for $1,000, which he used for nonbusiness purposes. At a time when the value of the car was $700, it was damaged in an accident. The car was a total loss. Morris's AGI was $4,000. How much can Morris deduct? _____

76. Rex owns a home having a basis of $150,000. The home is damaged by a volcanic eruption. Prior to the eruption, its value was $425,000. After the eruption, its value was $200,000. Rex collected insurance of $60,000. Rex's AGI was $60,000. How much is his casualty loss deduction? _____

77. Vladimir purchases an apartment house, paying $5,000 down and executing a mortgage for $95,000. He also pays a brokerage fee of $3,000 on this purchase. In addition, there is some pending litigation in which a tenant in the apartment house sued the previous owner for personal injuries incurred in the swimming pool. Vladimir promises to pay the judgment in that case, if there is one. The risk of such a judgment occurring is estimated at $12,000. What is Vladimir's basis for the apartment house after he buys it? _____

78.   Sarah purchased real property in 1975 for $10,000. This year, when its value is $100,000, she gives it to her daughter, Deborah. Deborah holds it for one month and sells it for $96,000. Assume that Sarah paid a $4,000 gift tax on the transfer to Deborah.

    a.   How should Deborah account for the sale?   _____

    b.   Assume in the previous transaction that the fair market value of the property was only $8,000 at the time of the gift, and that Deborah sells the property for $1,000. How should she account for this transaction?   _____

    c.   Assume that in the preceding example, Deborah sells the property for $9,250. How should she account for this transaction?   _____

79.   Zeke died this year. His sole asset was Blackacre, which had a basis of $200,000 and a value of $1 million. He left it to Kojak.

    a.   What is Kojak's basis for the property?   _____

    b.   Assume Zeke also owned furniture and clothing having a basis of $16,000. The value was $9,000. What is Kojak's basis for this property?   _____

80.   Aidan dies leaving property to John for life, remainder to Colin. The basis to John and Colin is $100,000. Based on actuarial calculations, John's interest is worth 40% and Colin's interest is worth 60%.

    a.   Can John amortize his basis for his life estate over his life expectancy?   _____

    b.   John sells his life estate for $41,000. How does he account for this transaction?   _____

    c.   Suppose that John and Colin together sell their interests, John receiving $41,000 therefor. How does John account for this transaction?   _____

    d.   Assume that in paragraph b., Alice was the person who purchased John's interest for $41,000. Can she amortize her basis over John's life?   _____

81.   Herbert and Wilma, who are married, live in California (which uses the community property system) and purchased property in 1968 for $50,000. When Herbert died this year, the property was worth $200,000. Assume that the property was purchased with community property funds so that Herbert and Wilma each contributed $25,000.

    a.   Assume that the property was held as community property. Assume further that Herbert left his share of the property to their children and Wilma still owns her community one-half. What is the basis of Wilma's one-half?   _____

    b.   Suppose instead that the property was held in joint tenancy. Under the applicable estate tax rules, one-half of the fair market value at the date of death is subject to estate tax in Herbert's estate. What is the basis for income tax purposes of Wilma's one-half?

c.   What will be the basis for income tax purposes, under the assumptions in paragraph b., of Herbert's one-half?

82. Tim was a movie star who was entitled to 10% of the gross box office receipts from a certain picture. He died on February 16 of Year 1. The amount payable for the six-month period ending June 30 of Year 1 was $15,000, and was paid to Tim's estate on July 6 of Year 1. The amount of these royalties was quite predictable, and the fair market value of the right to receive royalties for this period was $13,500 on the date of Tim's death.

a.   How much must the estate include in its gross income for Year 1?

b.   Assume that the estate tax attributable to this item is $2,000. How much should the estate include in income?

83. Pablo purchased a punch press for use in his factory for $19,500. He deducted $10,000 in depreciation on this property. The correct amount allowable was only $8,000. However, the statute of limitations has now run on the years in which excessive depreciation was claimed and the IRS cannot correct it. Pablo received a tax benefit for all depreciation he claimed.

a.   What is the basis of the punch press?

b.   Suppose in the preceding problem that only $3,000 in depreciation was claimed. Because the statute of limitations has run, the additional depreciation to which Pablo is entitled cannot now be deducted. What is the basis of the asset?

84. David purchased a building for $100,000. He sold the air rights over the building for $16,000. This enabled the purchaser who owned the parcels on both sides of David's property to connect his two buildings on top of David's building. Should David report income on the sale of the air rights?

85. Miriam purchases a factory building, paying $5,000 down and incurring a $95,000 nonrecourse purchase money mortgage. She is not personally liable on this mortgage. While she holds the property, she correctly deducts $18,000 of depreciation on it.

a.   Assume she made no payments on the mortgage and the mortgage is foreclosed. Does she have a gain on the mortgage foreclosure?

b.   Assume that instead of selling the property, Miriam borrows an additional $100,000, giving a second mortgage on the property. Does she have income on this transaction?

86. Winston owns all the shares of stock of Zero Corp. He sells them to Joan for $15,000 cash plus 25% of the profits earned by Zero Corp. in the next 10 years. After consulting with their accountants, Winston and Joan believe that this profit interest is worth $80,000. Winston had a $22,000 basis for his stock. If Winston elects out of the installment method, should he report gain on the sale to Joan? _____

87. Herbert and Wilma are getting divorced. Their marital property is worth $100,000.

   a. Assume that Herbert and Wilma live in a state in which the divorce court has discretionary power to award some of the marital property held in the name of one spouse to the other spouse. The court awards $20,000 to Wilma, which consists of their home. This house has a basis of $8,000 and is held in Herbert's name. Does Herbert have gain on the transfer of this house to Wilma? _____

   b. In the transaction described in paragraph a., does Wilma have income? _____

   c. What is Wilma's basis for the house? _____

88. Bob owns an apartment house having an adjusted basis of $200,000 and a fair market value of $350,000. He exchanges it for a factory building having a fair market value of $290,000. Joyce, the owner of the factory, pays Bob $60,000 in cash as part of the transaction.

   a. How much gain does Bob recognize on this transaction? _____

   b. Suppose that the adjusted basis of the apartment house was $330,000. How much gain would Bob recognize? _____

   c. Suppose that Bob's basis was $420,000 for the apartment house. How much loss can he recognize? _____

   d. What will be the basis for the factory building received in problem a.? _____

   e. What will be the basis for the factory building received in problem b.? _____

   f. What will be the basis for the factory building received in problem c.? _____

89. Lois owns a vacation cottage that has a basis of $4,000 and a value of $9,000. It is destroyed by a flood. Lois collects insurance proceeds of $9,000 and 20 months later purchases another cabin for $7,500.

   a. Must Lois recognize a $5,000 gain in the collection of the insurance proceeds? _____

   b. Suppose Lois invested the entire $9,000 proceeds in a new Ferrari. Must she recognize the entire gain? _____

90. Martha, who is single, owns a house that she has lived in for seven years. She purchased it for $75,000 and it is now worth $160,000. On February 9 of Year 1, she buys a new house for $220,000. On January 3 of Year 3, she sells her old house for $160,000.

    a.   What portion of the gain on sale of the old house is taxable to Martha?   ————

    b.   What is the basis of the new house?   ————

91. At the time of their divorce, Harry and Wanda had owned and used their home as a principal residence for one year. They bought it for $200,000 and took title as joint tenants. As provided by the divorce decree, Wanda stayed in the house. Harry moved out. The decree provided that when the house is sold, Harry and Wanda would split the proceeds. Five years later, Wanda sold the house for $1,400,000. Harry and Wanda each took $700,000. By this time, Harry had married Mary, and Harry and Mary filed a joint return.

    a.   How much gain should Wanda report in the year of sale?   ————

    b.   How much gain should Harry report in the year of sale?   ————

92. Over the years, Regis has purchased many large farms and subdivided them into lots suitable for building purposes. This year he sold 24 lots on three different farms. In each case, Regis had built roads and utility outlets on the property. He engaged in extensive advertising to sell the property. Are his gains on these properties capital gains?   ————

93. Luis acquired a piece of real estate in Texas four years ago, which he has held without any development activities. He feels the market is now ripe since a nearby town has expanded close to the property. He lists it for sale with a broker and it is sold. Is this gain treated as long-term capital gain?   ————

94. Vicky is a land developer who has held many parcels of property primarily for sale to customers. She acquires land suitable for a shopping center site. She intends to develop the property and rent it out. However, if the appropriate zoning cannot be obtained, she intends to sell the property. As feared, appropriate zoning is not available, and Vicky sells the property at a large gain. Is she entitled to capital gains treatment?   ————

95. Warren is heavily involved in the stock market. During the year, he purchases stocks and sells stocks on more than 300 occasions. He spends part of every day at his brokerage house watching the tape and subscribes to many different stock market journals.

    a.   Are his gains and losses on the sale of stock capital?   ————

    b.   Can Warren deduct the price of the investment advisories and newsletters to which he subscribes?   ————

96. Betty composes a folk song and sells all substantial rights in it to a publisher for $20,000. This is the first song she has ever sold.

    a.   Is Betty entitled to capital gains treatment on this sale?

    b.   Suppose instead that Betty had invented an improved amplification system for rock music. She sells it to a musical instrument manufacturing company. Is she entitled to capital gains treatment?

97. The President of the United States has many letters and memoranda written to and by him that are worth $500,000. He donates them to the National Archives (a branch of the United States government). Is he entitled to a charitable contribution deduction?

98. Zero Manufacturing Co. purchases all of the stock of a company that manufactures a particular copper part, which is essential for Zero's business. On many occasions, Zero has had difficulty obtaining these parts. Therefore, it purchases the stock exclusively for the purpose of ensuring itself of a source of supply of this vitally needed part. Later, it sells the stock at a loss because it has discovered other means of ensuring itself a source of supply. Is this a capital loss?

99. An investor in a stage play receives percentages of the gross box office receipts. The play is very successful. He sells his rights to the next $17,500 of box office receipts for $15,000. Is he entitled to capital gain?

100. Zahi has an interest for life in all of the profits of a farm. This was given to him by his grandfather. Zahi does not manage the farm; he simply receives the annual proceeds from the manager. He sells his entire right in these proceeds. Is he entitled to capital gain?

101. Allen owned a shopping center. One of the stores was leased to Leonard for use in selling tropical fish. The terms of this lease were unfavorable to the lessee and Leonard wanted to relocate his store.

    a.   Leonard pays Allen $10,000 to be released from the terms of the lease. Is this amount taxable to Allen as ordinary income?

    b.   Suppose instead that Allen wanted to use the store to lease to the May Co., which had adjoining space, and which would pay a high rent. Allen pays Leonard $10,000 to surrender his rights under the lease. Does Leonard have capital gain?

102. Bill wishes to sell the Fresno franchise of a professional football league. He is looking for a buyer. Fred, an attorney, comes to Bill and explains that a client of his (Del) is willing to buy the team. As compensation for his services in putting the deal together, Fred will be entitled to 1% of the gross receipts from the sale of season tickets during the next season. Before any money is received, Fred sells

his right to receive this percentage to Paul for $15,000. Is this amount taxed as capital gain? _____

103. Tess sold some shares of stock, correctly reporting a long-term capital loss of $90,000. Later, as the result of a class action, it was determined that there was a securities fraud occurring at the time of the sale. Tess receives $3,000 by way of damages. Is this taxable as a capital gain? _____

104. Dan wishes to purchase a piece of real property now held by Paul. It is a capital asset in the hands of both of them. Dan first purchases an option for $5,000, which provides that he can purchase the property at any time during the following six months. Paul has held the property for 10 years.

   a.   Assume Dan purchases the property, paying an additional $90,000. What is his basis for the property? _____

   b.   Assume that Dan decides not to purchase the property and lets the option lapse. Can Dan treat the $5,000 he paid for the option as an ordinary loss? _____

   c.   If the option lapsed, is the $5,000 treated as capital gain to Paul? _____

   d.   Assume that Dan sold his option to Ed for $12,000. Would the $7,000 gain be treated as a capital gain? _____

105. Donna is a lawyer who sells her practice for $28,000. The entire basis of the practice is $3,000. All of this basis is attributable to the furniture and law books. These were originally purchased for $12,000 and have been depreciated down to $3,000; they are now worth $5,000. The other assets sold are accounts receivable (zero basis, $12,000 value), goodwill (zero basis, $5,000 value), and a covenant not to compete ($6,000). Can Donna treat her $25,000 as a capital gain? _____

106. Thomas Manufacturing Co. sells two parcels of real property used in its trade or business in Year 4. Thomas obtained the two parcels in Year 1. One has a basis of $10,000 and a value of $4,000, and the second has a basis of $18,000 and a fair market value of $21,000. Is the gain on the second parcel taxed as capital gain? _____

107. Mary, a dentist, has the following transactions this year. She sells a dentist's chair and other dental equipment, having a basis of $9,000, for $5,000. During this year, a house held for investment (not personal use) burns down; the insurance proceeds exceeded her basis by $6,000. She also owned a small apartment building, which was condemned by the city of Newark; the proceeds from the condemnation were $9,000 less than her basis. She did not reinvest the proceeds from either the fire or the condemnation. Is her gain by reason of the fire taxed as a capital gain? (Assume that Mary held all assets for more than one year.) _____

108. Bob has a store that sells auto mufflers and shock absorbers. He decides to "franchise" the idea to others in other towns, using the same name. Bob retains the right to control such things as advertising, business hours, prices, and other aspects of the franchisee's operation. The franchisee pays Bob $15,000 for the franchise.

    a.   Is this capital gain to Bob? _____

    b.   Can the franchisee deduct any part of the $15,000? _____

109. Bill owes $100 evidenced by a promissory note. Roy acquires this note for $65 from Fred, who had previously loaned the $100 to Bill. Bill pays Roy $95 in full settlement of this debt. Both Fred and Roy can be treated as investors.

    a.   Does Fred have a capital loss when he sells the note to Roy? _____

    b.   Does Roy have a capital gain when Bill pays off the debt? _____

    c.   Does Bill have income when he pays off the debt? _____

110. Laura sells her trucking business to Arnold for $100,000. However, Laura will continue to operate the business and is entitled to all of the profits until the entire purchase price has been paid. Thereafter, Arnold can keep the profits. Does Laura have capital gain when she receives these profits? _____

111. In Year 1, which was after 2000, Jomo purchased stock for $200,000 in S Company, a new computer software venture with total assets of $5 million. In Year 6, Jomo sold the stock for $4 million. Does he receive any special tax benefit for this gain beyond the normal benefit for long-term capital gain? _____

112. Sanjay has taxable income of $10,000, apart from any capital transactions. He has long-term capital gain of $6,000 and short-term capital loss of $26,000. What is his taxable income? _____

113. Rory sells investment land to Ryan for $10,000. Ryan is to pay for it by cash payment due 18 months after the date of the sale. Rory does not elect out of the installment method. Assume that Rory's basis for the land is $1,000 and it is a capital asset. When Ryan makes her $10,000 payment, will Rory's entire gain be treated as capital gain? _____

114. In Year 6, Zeke, a farmer, sells a tractor he had purchased in Year 1. The original purchase price was $9,000. Zeke deducted depreciation of $8,000. He now sells it for $2,200.

    a.   Is Zeke's gain ordinary income? _____

    b.   Suppose that Zeke was able to sell the tractor for $11,000 because Zeke discovered the tractor was a rare model having value to collectors. Is his entire gain ordinary income? _____

c. Suppose that in paragraph a. Zeke sells the tractor for $400. Assume also that he has gains under I.R.C. section 1231 in the same year aggregating $10,000. Is his $600 loss ordinary loss? _____

d. Suppose that in paragraph a. the tractor was exchanged for a new plow also worth $2,200. Is there any ordinary income on this transaction? _____

115. Don is married and reported adjusted gross income of $200,000 on his joint return. He exercised an incentive stock option. The difference between the value of the stock and the amount he paid was $80,000. He paid income tax of $57,000. Does Don owe alternative minimum tax ("AMT")? _____

116. Paul owns Blackacre, having a basis of $1,000 and a value of $10,000. In Year 1, he sells it to Steve for $10,000. Steve furnishes his nonnegotiable promissory note due in Year 3, bearing 10% interest. Assume that the fair market value of this note is $8,500 and that 10% is above the applicable federal rate.

a. If Paul uses the cash basis of accounting and elects out of the installment method, does he have income in Year 1? _____

b. Suppose Paul was an accrual basis taxpayer and elects out of the installment method. Would he have income in Year 1? _____

c. Suppose Paul, who uses the cash method, received stock worth $10,000 instead of the promissory note. He does not sell the stock until Year 3. Does he have income in Year 1? _____

117. Cassie is a cash basis attorney who drafts a will for a client. The work is completed and a bill is sent out in October of Year 1. In November, the client comes in offering to pay the $200 fee. Cassie asks the client not to remit until January of Year 2.

a. Does Cassie have income in Year 1? _____

b. Assume that in the preceding problem, before drafting the will, Cassie and her client agreed that payment would not be made until Year 2. Nevertheless, the client was entirely willing to pay the money in Year 1. Is Cassie taxed in Year 1? _____

118. Suman is an employee of the Zero Manufacturing Co. In addition to his normal salary, it is agreed that he will receive $8,000 in Year 6 when he retires. He is concerned about the solvency of Zero and therefore insists that the $8,000 be placed in trust for his benefit beyond the reach of Zero's creditors, with the money in the trust to be distributed to him in Year 6. Is Suman taxed in Year 1 (the year the $8,000 is placed in trust)? _____

119. Zero Manufacturing Co. has a qualified pension plan. In Year 1, it pays $400 into the plan on behalf of Ling, an employee. Ling is entitled to a pension when

she retires. The $400 paid in that year is the amount necessary to fund the pension. Ling's rights are vested and nonforfeitable.

a. Must Ling include the $400 income in Year 1? _____

b. Can Zero Manufacturing Co. deduct the $400 in Year 1? _____

c. During Year 2, the pension plan trust earns $25,000 in interest and dividends. Must the plan pay tax on these amounts currently? _____

120. Acme Corp. has a stock option plan (which does not meet the requirements for an incentive stock option plan). In Year 1, Pete, an employee, receives an option to purchase 100 shares of Acme stock at $100 per share. The fair market value of Acme stock, on the day the option is granted, is $100. Although the fair market value of the option is estimated to be $2,500, the market value is not easily and clearly ascertainable. In Year 3, when the stock is worth $130 per share, Pete exercises his option.

a. Does Pete have income in Year 1? _____

b. In Year 3, does Pete have income? _____

c. In what year does Acme get a deduction? _____

d. What is Pete's basis for the shares he acquires in Year 3? _____

e. Assume that the stock which Pete received in Year 3 was nontransferable for five years. Furthermore, the stock would have to be resold back to Acme at its purchase price ($100 per share) for a five-year period if Pete was no longer employed at Acme during that five-year period. Is Pete taxed in Year 3? _____

f. Under the facts described in paragraph e., assume that in Year 4 the stock became transferable and the forfeiture provision was removed. At that time, the stock was worth $220 per share. Would Pete be taxed in Year 4? _____

121. Kendra, an attorney, hires Lloyd, another attorney, as her employee. Kendra is in a high tax bracket in Year 1 and, in December of that year, pays Lloyd both his December and January salaries. Both Kendra and Lloyd use the calendar year and the cash method.

a. Must Lloyd include the money in gross income in Year 1? _____

b. If Lloyd is an accrual basis taxpayer, must he include the payment in gross income in Year 1? _____

c. Suppose in this problem Kendra had paid Lloyd for three years of services in advance. Assuming that Lloyd is an accrual basis taxpayer, must he include the entire amount in gross income in Year 1? _____

122. R Corp. declares a dividend on December 1 of Year 1, payable on January 15 of Year 2, to holders of record on December 15. Jalisa is an accrual basis taxpayer who owns stock in the corporation. Must she include the dividend in gross income in Year 1?

_____

123. Paul, a contractor, is building a house for Roy. Paul uses the accrual method of accounting. In Year 1, Paul completes 90% of Roy's house. Assume that state law provides that even if Paul had stopped working, he could sue and receive 90% of the agreed compensation for building the house.

a. Must Paul include in gross income in Year 1, 90% of the total amount of compensation he is contractually entitled to receive?

_____

b. In Year 2, Paul finishes the house for Roy. However, it is then discovered that Roy is insolvent and his liabilities far exceed his assets. Must Paul accrue the compensation due him under the contract?

_____

124. Louis operates a travel service and uses the accrual method of accounting. In Year 1, a charter flight he had promoted strands 100 tourists in Europe. It seems very likely that Louis will be liable for damages for breach of contract to these tourists in the amount of about $25,000. He is resisting these claims, but feels that he has little chance of success. Can Louis deduct $25,000 in Year 1?

_____

125. Laura owns 80% of the stock of Zero Corp. She is also the president. Zero Corp. uses the accrual method of accounting; Laura uses the cash method. Both use the calendar year. In Year 1, Laura fails to collect her salary of $50,000, which is payable in December. The treasurer of the corporation does not write a check to her. This amount is finally paid in June of Year 2.

a. Must Laura include the unpaid salary in gross income in Year 1?

_____

b. Can Zero Corp. accrue the salary?

_____

126. Jerry is in the business of wholesaling certain plumbing parts. In his first year of operation, he purchases (in order of time) 100 of the parts at $1.00, 100 at $1.25, 100 at $1.50, and 100 at $1.60. Thus his total purchases are $535. At the end of the year, 120 of the parts still remain. How much is Jerry allowed to deduct as the cost of his goods sold if he uses:

a. FIFO?

_____

b. LIFO?

_____

127. Jack owns Blackacre, which has a basis of $6,000 and a value of $10,000. In Year 1, he sells it to Carla for $10,000, with a down payment of $2,000. The balance is payable in eight annual installments of $1,000 each. Each payment will also bear interest on the unpaid balance at the rate of 12% (which exceeds the applicable federal rate). Assume that Jack uses the cash method of accounting. The obligation is secured by Blackacre. Assume that Jack does not elect out of the installment

method of accounting. In Year 1, he receives only the $2,000 down payment. How much is includible in gross income? _____

128. Mutt and Jeff render services for Rocky in Year 1 for which Rocky is obligated to pay $50,000. He pays all of the money to Mutt. Mutt knows that Jeff is asserting a claim for some of this money, but Mutt intends to resist the claim. However, it is very likely that he will have to pay over half the money to Jeff. Finally, in Year 3, Jeff sues and recovers $25,000 from Mutt.

    a.   Must Mutt include the entire $50,000 in gross income in Year 1? _____

    b.   In Year 3, Mutt pays $25,000 to Jeff. Assume, however, that his Year 1 tax bracket was far higher than his Year 3 tax bracket. Is he allowed to amend his Year 1 return claiming a deduction for the payment to Jeff in that year? _____

    c.   Must Mutt claim the Year 3 deduction only at Year 3 tax rates? _____

129. Black & White ("B & W"), an accrual basis professional law corporation, was owed $100,000 by C, a cash basis client for work on a tax case. Had C paid the bill, C could have deducted it. In Year 1, B & W properly wrote off $100,000 as a bad debt because C was insolvent and could not pay. B & W's taxable income in Year 1 was $1 million. In Year 4, C found buried treasure and paid the debt.

    a.   What are the tax consequences to B & W in Year 1? _____

    b.   What are the tax consequences to C in Year 1? _____

    c.   What are the tax consequences to B & W in Year 4? _____

    d.   What are the tax consequences to C in Year 4? _____

130. X Co. is drilling for oil. It contracts in Year 1 with Hughes to drill a new well for $25,000. X Co. is an accrual method taxpayer. Hughes drills the well in Year 3. X Co. pays Hughes in Year 4. In what year can X Co. deduct the intangible drilling expense? _____

Answers to Review Questions

1.a. YES The $6 interest is included in Bobbi's income. Receiving loan proceeds is not income to Angelo and repayment of the principal of the loan is not income to Bobbi. [§§12-14, 17] The provision for imputed interest on gift loans [I.R.C. §7872] is not applicable because the interest rate exceeds the applicable federal rate. (If it were, Bobbi would have additional interest income.) [§239] An additional exception to section 7872 may also apply: When a gift loan is less than $10,000 and the proceeds are not invested in income-producing assets, interest is not imputed. [§241]

b. NO The $6 interest is not deductible to Angelo because personal interest is not deductible. The cost of his vacation is not deductible. Making a loan is not deductible by Bobbi and repaying the principal of the loan is not deductible by Angelo. [§§293, 572]

2. PROBABLY NOT The IRS does not seek to tax such items unless the taxpayer seeks a double deduction by donating them to charity. However, the IRS could tax these items under *Haverly* if it chose to do so. [§21]

3.a. YES An exchange of services generates income. Both Don and Edna must include $1,500 in income. [§26]

b. YES Don cannot deduct the cost of getting divorced, except for that part relating to tax advice. Since the problem does not indicate how much, if any, of Edna's services were for tax advice, Don cannot deduct anything. However, Edna can deduct the cost of accounting services for her practice as section 162 trade or business expense. [§§296, 338-340, 446-449]

4.a. YES Regardless of George's motivation, payments by employers to employees are not excludible gifts. [§§31-34]

b. NO Even if the payment was intended as compensation for services, the services of a valet are personal, not business, and would not be deductible. [§302]

c. YES Bequests to employees are taxable under I.R.C. section 102(c). [§45]

5.a. YES Under I.R.C. section 102(c), the amount would probably be treated as income regardless of the employer's motivation. In any event, since Zero has custom of paying such benefits, they are part of the decedent's compensation, not a gift. [§36]

b. YES It would appear to be an ordinary and necessary business expense—reasonable compensation. No facts are given to suggest that it is unreasonable compensation or a dividend. [§§37, 337]

6.a. **YES**   Prizes are includible in income under I.R.C. section 74. [§§49-50]

b. **YES**   These would seem to qualify as deductible expenses (under section 212)—incurred to produce income, although not part of a trade or business. [§437] Had Lem lost the contest, there is a chance that his deductions would have been disallowed as hobby losses under section 183. [§319] Note that if Lem's deduction is under section 212 instead of 162, it is a miscellaneous itemized deduction and subject to reduction under section 67. [§562]

7. **YES**   The amount not applied to tuition and books is taxable. [§§53-54]

8.a. **NO**   Life insurance proceeds are excludible under I.R.C. section 101(a). [§58]

b. **NO**   These are amounts paid to obtain excludible income and are consequently nondeductible—even if they are paid in a business or investment setting. [*See* I.R.C. §265(1)] [§§345, 601, 603]

c. **YES**   Life insurance policies purchased from an existing holder do not qualify for the exclusion. Oona's profit of $4,500 ($10,000 minus her basis of $5,500) would be taxable. [§65]

9. **YES**   Paul will be receiving a total of $150,000 over the 10 years. Clearly, $50,000 of this is interest; $100,000 is principal. Each payment would be broken down into one-third interest ($5,000) and two-thirds principal ($10,000). Thus, $5,000 of each payment is taxable. [§67]

10.a. **$375**   The investment in the contract is $10,000. The expected return is $16,000. The exclusion ratio is 10/16, or 0.625. Thus, $625 of each payment is excluded and $375 is taxable. [§69]

b. **YES, $9,375**   Steve recovered $625 of basis against the first payment, leaving $9,375 unrecovered. This is a loss deduction on the tax return for the year of his death. [§§70-71]

11.a. **NO**   Interest on state and municipal bonds is not taxable. [I.R.C. §103(a)] [§75]

b. **NO**   These are classed as nondeductible costs of obtaining tax-exempt income. [*See* I.R.C. §265(1), (2)] [§§601-602]

12.a. **NO**   Her income is below the threshold for including Social Security benefits in income. [§§78-80]

b. **NO**   SSI payments are excludible. [§79]

13.a. **YES**   Damages for defamation are taxable because they are not personal physical injuries under section 104(a)(2). [§89]

b. **YES**   Punitive damages are taxable whether arising from physical or nonphysical torts. [§89]

c.	**YES**	These seemingly would be an ordinary and necessary business expense. There are no public policy restrictions on deducting this item. [§§408-414, 424-436]
14.a.	**YES**	Under *Raytheon*, such payments are taxable (as capital gains) since the basis for the destroyed goodwill was zero. [§100]
b.	**YES**	Payments for lost profits are taxable. The section 186 exclusion does not apply to the payments since Zero got a tax benefit for its overpayments in past years. [§§101, 104]
c.	**YES**	Punitive damages are taxable. [§101]
d.	**NO**	It can deduct only $133,333. Under section 162(g), two-thirds of payments of civil damages in antitrust cases are not deductible if there has been a previous criminal conviction. [§436]
15.	**NO**	These items clearly fall within the exclusion of I.R.C. section 119 for meals and lodging furnished to the employee on the employer's premises for the convenience of the employer. [§§107-111]
16.a.	**YES**	Cancellation of debt produces taxable income. Here, Alpha was insolvent before the cancellation to the extent of $3,000. Consequently, instead of $4,000 income, it has income of only $1,000. Alpha must reduce various tax benefits such as loss carryovers by the amount of the debt cancellation income that was not recognized. [§§144-147]
b.	**YES**	It has a business bad debt deduction of $4,000. Since Piedmont is an accrual basis taxpayer, it had a basis for the debt of $10,000. [§§533-534]
17.a.	**YES**	$500 is taxable since this is not a "no additional cost service" as defined in I.R.C. section 132(b). It is too large to be considered a de minimis fringe benefit under section 132(e). The employer incurred substantial additional costs in rendering service. [§§116, 120]
b.	**NO**	This is a personal item and nondeductible. [§302]
18.a.	**$40,000**	Child support is not deductible. The $40,000 payments are deductible spousal support. [§§162, 169]
b.	**$40,000**	The rule of reciprocity controls: What is deductible to H is taxable to W. [§162]
19.	**$25,000 INCOME**	Under recapture, where first-year payments exceed average second- and third-year payments by more than $15,000, the excess over $15,000 is income to the payor (and deductible to the payee) in the third year. [§168]
20.	**NO**	This is an example of the principle of *Horst*; Diego has retained the property, giving up only the right to income from it. Consequently, he must be taxed on the income. [§191]

21.a. **YES**   This is the rule in *Blair*. [§§185, 194]

  b. **NO**   This is the rule in *Harrison v. Schaffner*. [§194]

22. **NO**   This is an example of *Lucas v. Earl*—income is taxed to the person who earns it. [§201]

23.a. **NO**   Sale of rights to compensation for personal services yields ordinary income, not capital gain. [§§201, 851]

  b. **NO**   Although Tex could give away the contract and shift the income (since Tex's personal services were not involved), he waited too long to do it. The contract is no longer contingent, and it is too late to shift the income through a transfer. [§191]

24. **YES**   This appears to comply with the requirements of section 704(e) for shifting income in family partnership. Capital is a material income-producing factor, Jean is receiving a reasonable salary, and the transfers to trusts for the children appear bona fide, assuming the trustees are truly independent. [§§214-219]

25.a. **YES**   Required by I.R.C. section 73. [§220]

  b. **YES**   Also required by I.R.C. section 73; this seems to be an appropriate ordinary and necessary expense for an actor. [§222]

  c. **YES**   This appears to be reasonable compensation for services. [§§415-417]

26. **NO**   In a community property state, the community property income of spouses must be divided equally between them if they file separate returns. [§§227-228]

27.a. **INCOME $15,000, DEDUCTION $15,000**   Under section 7872, interest is imputed when a corporation loans a shareholder money and fails to charge the applicable federal rate. This means that the appropriate amount of interest is treated as if it were paid by the corporation as a dividend, then repaid by the shareholder as interest. Thus, Enrique receives a $15,000 dividend (ordinary income) and an offsetting interest deduction (trade or business interest is deductible). [§§239-243]

  b. **INCOME OF $15,000**   The imputed dividend is not deductible, but X Corp. has imputed interest income of $15,000. [§§240, 243]

28. **NO**   The grantor, Giovanna, must treat the trust property as hers and pay tax on the income because she retained a reversionary interest. [I.R.C. §673] [§253]

29.a. **NO**   Powers to invade corpus limited by reasonably definite standards will not cause the income to be taxed to the grantor. [I.R.C. §674(b)(5)(A)] [§259]

b. **YES**   The grantor may not have powers to apportion income. [I.R.C. §674(a)] [§254]

c. **NO**   If a reasonably definite external standard of apportionment is spelled out, the grantor is not taxed on the trust income if he is not the trustee—even if the trustee is a relative of the grantor. [I.R.C. §674(d)] [§258]

d. **NO**   An independent trustee (such as the bank) may have power to apportion income or principal among the beneficiaries. The grantor will not be taxed as long as he is not a trustee and not more than half the trustees are his relatives or subordinates subservient to his wishes. [I.R.C. §674(c)] [§257]

e. **NO**   Income is not taxed to the grantor simply because he has the power to either distribute currently or accumulate income, provided that the accumulated income must eventually be paid to the person who would have received it currently, or to his estate or appointees. [I.R.C. §674(b)(6)] [§259]

30.a. **YES**   The grantor is taxed if he has the power to revoke. [I.R.C. §676] [§260]

b. **YES**   Tom is an "adverse party." The grantor is not taxed on the income if an adverse party must agree to revocation. [I.R.C. §676(a)] [§260]

31.a. **YES**   If the income either is or may be distributable to the grantor's spouse in the discretion of a nonadverse party, it is taxable to the grantor. [I.R.C. §677(a)] [§§261-262]

b. **NO**   Where income could be used for the support of someone whom the grantor is obligated to support other than his spouse, it is taxed to him only in the event that it is actually so used. [I.R.C. §677(b)] [§§266-268]

32.a. **YES**   If the grantor or a nonadverse party has the power to borrow corpus or the income without adequate interest or security, the income is taxed to the grantor. [I.R.C. §675(2)] [§271]

b. **NO**   As long as she has administrative powers of this kind only in a fiduciary capacity, she is not taxed on the income. [I.R.C. §675(4)] [§276]

33.a. **YES**   If someone has a general power of appointment over trust corpus, meaning that he could vest the trust income or corpus in himself, he is taxed on the income. [I.R.C. §678] [§277]

b. **NO**   Ivan is taxed on the income under section 674(a), since his powers to distribute corpus to the beneficiary are not limited by an ascertainable standard. Section 674 prevails over section 678, so Ivan is taxed, not Nicolai. [§277]

34.a. **NO**   Mary is taxable on the $25,000 as ordinary income. Under a simple trust, the amount required to be distributed to the beneficiaries is taxed to them whether or not distributed. [§282]

b. **YES**   The capital gain is taxed to the trust. [§282]

35. **$9,000**   In this complex trust, Paul is a "first tier" beneficiary whose distribution is taxable to the extent that distributable net income ("DNI") is equal to it. Consequently, Paul is taxed on his entire distribution. The remaining DNI of $9,000 is allocated to Roy. Consequently, $9,000 of the distribution to him is taxable. The remaining $6,000 distribution to him is treated as a tax-free distribution of corpus. [§§283-287]

36.a. **NO**   One can deduct only his own expenses, not the expenses of someone else. Furthermore, a stockholder is not treated as being in a trade or business, even though the corporation is. The expenditure would correctly be added to the basis of Arnie's stock and be deductible by the corporation. [§§294, 300]

b. **NO**   The move is clearly far enough to qualify, and the cost of moving household goods is deductible. The other items are not deductible, but the $1,000 commission reduces the amount realized on the sale of the home. [§§325-330]

37.a. **YES**   Under Rev. Rul. 99-7, the cost of the trip is deductible if we assume the registry is a regular place of business. [§§308-309]

b. **NO**   No part of the cost is deductible even though part of it would be allocated to transporting the bass. [§310]

c. **$300**   Since the trip was primarily for business, the entire cost of the airfare ($80) is deductible. However, one-third of the cost of the meals and lodging is not deductible since that part was travel for pleasure. Thus, only $240 of the lodging and $120 of the meals are deductible. In addition, the $120 must be reduced to $60 because only 50% of the cost of meals is deductible. [§311]

d. **NO**   Richard has neither a permanent residence nor a permanent place of business. Therefore, no matter how the word "home" is defined, he has no home from which to be away. [§§314-315]

e. **YES**   George is viewed as being away from home "temporarily," rather than "indefinitely." Therefore, he is entitled to deduct his lodging and 50% of his meals as well as his travel to Michigan. [§318]

38. **$28,000**   Under the passive loss rules, with the exception of the activities of a real estate professional (which Ralph is not), rental activity is always passive. The general rule is that passive loss can be deducted only against passive income (the dividends are portfolio, not passive, income). However, Ralph qualifies for the $25,000 allowance in section 469(i) (assuming he actively participates). This provision allows deduction of up to $25,000 loss on rental real estate if the taxpayer's adjusted gross income ("AGI") is under $100,000. The $25,000 allowance is phased out at a rate of 50 cents for each dollar by which AGI exceeds $100,000. Here, Ralph is $18,000 over, so the allowance

is reduced by $9,000 to $16,000. Thus, Ralph can deduct expenses up to his passive income ($12,000) plus $16,000, or $28,000. The remaining $2,000 of deductions are carried forward to be deducted against future passive income or when there is a taxable disposition of the house. [§§543-551]

39. **NO**

The origin of the dispute—Paul's mental state—is a personal matter, and the amount must be treated as personal rather than a business expense. It is not relevant that the results of losing would be destructive to one's business. (*See* the *Gilmore* case.) [§340]

40.a. **POSSIBLY**

The tuition may be subject to either the HOPE scholarship credit or the Lifetime Learning Credit. However, the educational expenses would not be deductible as a business expense because the education would qualify Wilhelm for a new trade or business. [§§341, 343, 722-725]

b. **YES**

This is training that maintains or improves skills required in Barbara's job. It does not qualify her for a new job. It is a miscellaneous itemized deduction subject to the 2% floor. [§§342, 562]

41.a. **NO**

The premiums on group term life insurance paid by an employer for an employee are exempt under I.R.C. section 79. The exclusion applies only with respect to life insurance up to $50,000. [§§123, 345]

b. **YES**

The employer is not allowed to deduct the premiums on insurance if it is the beneficiary, but it is entitled to deduct them if the employee is the beneficiary and (together with all other compensation) the compensation is reasonable. [§345]

42.a. **NO**

This creates an asset that will last for many years and is therefore not deductible as a business expense. It must be capitalized. [§§365-367]

b. **NO**

Under the I.R.C. section 263A and the *Idaho Power* case, the depreciation on the bulldozer is not currently deductible but must be added to the basis of the newly constructed building. [§§380-383]

43.a. **NO**

This must be capitalized as it creates an asset having a useful life of five years. She can amortize the prepayment and allocate it to the years during which she occupies the premises. [§387]

b. **PROBABLY YES**

Accrual basis taxpayers who receive prepayments must include them all in income when received, unless they fall within the Commissioner's rule permitting deferral of amounts received for services to be performed in the following year. A few cases cast doubt on this conclusion. [§§1024-1028] Note that in certain cases of increasing rents required by a lease, both the landlord and tenant must use the accrual method. [§§1030-1032]

44. **NO**

Under these facts, the so-called lease would be treated as a purchase. Therefore, the payments are not deductible as rent, but Zeke could claim depreciation on the machine. If he can prove that part of the payment should be treated as interest, he can deduct that part. [§388]

45.a. **YES**   The courts have held that fees paid to an employment agency are deductible business expenses even though no job is found, as long as the taxpayer is already employed in the same kind of business. [§398]

b. **YES**   Under I.R.C. section 174 and the *Snow* case, these amounts are currently deductible. [§401]

c. **NO**   The courts have held that the cost of searching for a new business to purchase is currently nondeductible. I.R.C. section 195 does not apply if no business is found. [§§396-397]

46.a. **NO**   This is treated as a nondeductible capital outlay, akin to the purchase of goodwill. The facts are similar to *Welch v. Helvering*. [§404]

b. **YES**   Although the payment of the debt is ordinarily not income to the creditor (assuming his basis for the debt is equal to the amount repaid), the fact that it was deducted as a bad debt in a prior year creates a different situation. This is an application of the "tax benefit rule." Assuming that the entire amount of the debt provided a tax benefit in a prior year, all of it is includible in income when it is repaid. [I.R.C. §111] [§§536-537, 1079-1084]

47.a. **NO**   Under I.R.C. section 104(a)(2), amounts received as damages for personal physical injury are excluded whether paid in a lump sum or periodic payments. [§89]

b. **NO**   Defco can deduct only $40,000 in Year 1. Under I.R.C. section 461(h)(2)(C), tort damages cannot be deducted by an accrual method taxpayer until they are paid, regardless of when the obligation arose. [§1041]

48.a. **YES**   Although payments that are illegal under state law are not usually deductible, this is true only if the law against them is generally enforced. Since this law is not generally enforced, the payment would appear to be deductible if it is "ordinary" for such payments to be made. [I.R.C. §162(c)] [§426]

b. **YES**   Illegal income is taxable the same as legal income. Even though the program director might have an obligation to turn the money over to the station, he nevertheless has taken it under claim of right and it is taxable to him. [§158]

49. **NO**   Under section 162(c)(2), a payment that would subject the payor to professional discipline is not deductible, assuming that the statute or rule is generally enforced. [§426]

50.a. **NO**   Fines are not deductible, even though they otherwise would qualify as business expenses and even though no fault is involved. [I.R.C. §162(f)] [§§431-432]

b. **YES** Attorneys' fees incurred in resisting criminal prosecution are deductible, assuming that the criminal act involved arose in business. This was clearly established by the *Tellier* case. [§§431-432]

51.a. **NO** No deduction or credit for political contributions is allowed. [§433]

b. **NO** Lobbying is not deductible. [§434]

52.a. **NO** Although he is also trying to get damages, the primary aspect of his lawsuit is to establish title. Consequently, the acquisition costs (including litigation expenditures) must be capitalized. This seems clearly established by the *Woodward* case. Presumably, however, if the litigation proves unsuccessful, Rex can deduct the amounts incurred both in looking for the mine and unsuccessfully suing as a business loss under I.R.C. section 165. [§§443-445, 493 *et seq.*]

b. **YES** This appears to be in lieu of lost profits and therefore would be taxed as ordinary income. [§§101-106]

53.a. **NO** Only the lessor is entitled to claim depreciation on the building since he paid for it. [§§459-460]

b. **YES** The tenant has made an economic investment in the building and is entitled to depreciate those assets. However, he must use the useful life of the improvement as the depreciation period, regardless of the term of the lease. [§460]

c. **NO** They have an unlimited useful life. [§458]

54.a. **NO** Under I.R.C. section 109, he does not realize or recognize any income on the construction of this building. [§758]

b. **39 YEARS** Although one must use the useful life of the building in this situation [§460], the lessee depreciates the property over the recovery period normally used for nonresidential real property under I.R.C. section 168(c)(1) [§465]. Thus, Sara should depreciate the building over 39, rather than 40, years.

c. **YES** Vic is entitled to depreciate this part of the purchase price, even though the tenant on the property is also depreciating exactly the same property. [§460]

55.a. **$2,400** Under straight-line depreciation, she can deduct one-fifth of cost, or 20%, per year. The half-year convention means only one-half of a full year's depreciation is deductible in the year of purchase. [§471]

b. **$4,800** Double-declining balance—twice the straight-line rate, or 40%. She can take half in the year of purchase. [§§468-469]

c. **$4,800** *See a., above.*

d. **$7,680**   Subtract the first year's depreciation ($4,800, *see* b., above) from the copier's basis ($24,000) and multiply the difference ($19,200) by 40%. [§469]

e. **$24,000 (in 2002) or $25,000 (in 2003)**   Special allowance for expensing small purchases. Amount is $24,000 in 2002, $25,000 in 2003 and subsequent years. [§477]

56.a. **$8,000**   Since the well cost $100,000, and was estimated to contain 100,000 barrels of oil, $1 is allocated to each barrel. Therefore, since 8,000 barrels were pumped, the cost depletion would be $8,000. [§486]

b. **$5,000**   Ordinarily, percentage depletion is based on 15% of the gross income (which would here produce a deduction of $6,000). However, the amount deductible is limited to 50% of the net income from the property. Here the net income is $10,000 ($40,000 gross income less $30,000 expenses), and 50% of that is $5,000. [§§487-489]

c. **YES**   Percentage depletion is not limited to basis. [§489]

d. **YES**   Percentage depletion in excess of basis is treated as a tax preference. [*See* I.R.C. §57(a)(1)] [§§489, 956]

57. **NO**   Demolition of a building produces no deductible loss whether or not the taxpayer intended to demolish a purchased building. [§502]

58. **NO**   Goodwill is amortized over a 15-year period; thus, Floyd is allowed an amortization deduction of $2,000 per year for purchased goodwill. However, even if it is now worthless, there is no closed and completed transaction that would allow a loss of the remaining $28,000 of basis to be realized. Probably only a sale or an abandonment of the entire business would satisfy this requirement. [§§473-474, 504-509]

59. **NO**   There are two potential grounds for attacking this transaction:

1) Losses incurred on sales between siblings (and other family members) are not deductible under I.R.C. section 267. [§§511, 514]

2) Another theory on which the Commissioner could disallow the loss might be that the whole transaction was a sham in the sense that Julius was always holding the property for Leon and there had been no real shift of ownership. However, this theory could be refuted by the fact that Julius actually lost $3,000 on the resale to Leon. [§518]

3) Note that the repurchase from Julius after two months does not invoke the wash sale provision of I.R.C. section 1091, which comes into play only upon a sale and repurchase within 30 days. [§517] Incidentally, Julius could not deduct his loss on the sale to Leon—I.R.C. section 267 prevents it. It

may well be that neither Julius nor Leon can ever deduct these losses since I.R.C. section 267 permits disallowed losses to be used only to offset gains on the property in the event it is later sold at a gain. [§§513-516]

60. **DEPENDS** The loss on a guarantee is treated as a bad debt. The theory is that Gloria makes payment to the bank and then by reason of subrogation, becomes a creditor of Mike. Assuming that Mike is insolvent, Gloria then can write off the claim as a bad debt. However, this appears to be a nonbusiness bad debt, which is deductible only as a short-term capital loss. If Gloria has no other capital transactions in this year, she will be limited to only a $3,000 deduction. [§§520-530, 826]

61.a. **YES** If she can prove partial worthlessness in Year 2 of a business bad debt, she can deduct the amount that becomes worthless in that year. [§528]

b. **YES** This is debt cancellation income. Assuming the exception for insolvency is not applicable, Dole must include $6,000 in income. [§§143-145, 536]

62. **PROBABLY NOT** Loans made by persons who are also stockholders are treated as nonbusiness bad debts (capital loss) since they arise in investment rather than in business. The fact that a corporation is in business does not mean that the creditor is in business. The facts of this case suggest that Larry did not need to make the loan to keep his job, since close family members controlled the corporation. Therefore, he cannot rely on the exception that gives business bad debt treatment to employees who make loans to the corporation to protect their jobs. [§§531-532]

63. **NO** As a cash basis taxpayer, she has no basis for this debt and therefore nothing is deductible by reason of its worthlessness. If she were on the accrual basis, she could deduct the amount of her basis (presumably the $20,000). Similarly, if she had actually loaned cash to John, she could deduct her basis. But as a cash basis taxpayer, she has no basis in a receivable obtained through the rendering of her services. [§534]

64. **$14,900** Certain deductions are subtracted from gross income to reach "adjusted gross income." These include capital losses and alimony. These two items total $1,100, and, consequently, adjusted gross income is $14,900. Other employee business expenses, such as union dues and uniforms, are deductible only from adjusted gross income and subject to the 2% floor. [§§554-555, 561]

65. **$40,000** Interest prepayments are not deductible immediately and must be amortized over the period for which the interest was prepaid. That provides a $40,000 deduction. Investment interest is deductible only to the extent of net investment income, but Jim has sufficient net investment income to absorb the interest. [I.R.C. §§163(d), 461(g)] [§§605-609]

66.	**YES**	Under the passive loss rules, Ray meets the material participation standards of the regulations and can deduct the loss. Spouses can combine their participation, and if their participation exceeds 500 hours, they meet the test. This assumes, however, that all of their participation was in fact appropriate for owners (not extra hours spent dishwashing just to get over 500). [§§543-547]
67.a.	**NO**	I.R.C. section 164(a). [§§612-617]
b.	**NO**	I.R.C. section 164(a). [§616]
c.	**NO**	I.R.C. section 164(a). [§616]
d.	**NO**	I.R.C. section 164(a). [§612]
68.a.	**YES**	It is permissible to deduct the gift of a remainder in a personal residence or a farm. The actuarial value of that remainder interest is deductible currently, assuming that depreciation on the property during the income beneficiary's lifetime is taken into account. [§625]
b.	**NO**	Such charitable remainders are deductible only if in the form of a "fixed annuity trust," or a "unitrust." A fixed annuity trust will pay a fixed dollar amount for Carol's lifetime, not merely all the income. A unitrust will pay a fixed percentage of the fair market value of the assets of the trust each year. The trust described in this problem does not qualify under either standard. A third form of interest in trust that is deductible is a "pooled income fund" in which many donors make contributions to the same trust, which has a charitable remainder. In this situation, it is permissible for all the income produced by the donor's assets to be paid to the income beneficiary for life. [§626]
69.a.	**$10,000**	Since this would be short-term capital gain, she must reduce the amount deductible by the entire amount of the short-term capital gain. [§§635-637]
b.	**$14,000**	Since this would be long-term capital gain, the entire amount is deductible. However, it should be noted that such gifts of long-term capital gain property cannot be deducted in excess of 30% of adjusted gross income, even though the gift is to a publicly supported charity like Public University. [§§629-630]
c.	**$10,000**	Even though long-term capital gain property is involved, the gift was of tangible personal property unrelated to the exempt purpose of the recipient. Consequently, the amount of the gain must be removed from the amount deductible. [§633]
70.a.	**$20,000**	This is computed by subtracting the amount the charity paid from the full fair market value of the property. [§§640-641]
b.	**YES**	In this case of a bargain sale to charity, he cannot allocate his entire basis against the amount received from the charity. Since the charity paid only

one-fifth of the fair market value, he can apply only one-fifth of his basis against the amount received. Therefore, the basis usable is only $1,000, and he has long-term capital gain of $4,000. [§641]

71. **$100**

Total expenses equal $1,750. Seven and one-half percent of AGI is $1,650. Excess is $100. [§665]

72.a. **THREE**

Mike and Susan have exemptions for themselves, and they can claim an exemption for Bob. Although he earned over the exemption amount, that is not disqualifying since he is under age 19 and his parents supplied more than one-half of his support. The fact that Carol earned more than the exemption amount is disqualifying since she is neither a student nor under 19. Even though her parents supplied more than one-half of her support, they cannot claim her as an exemption. [§668]

b. **NO**

The fact that his parents claim him as a dependent prevents him from claiming an exemption for himself. [§668]

73.a. **YES**

The custodial parent is entitled to the exemption. [§672]

b. **NO**

The noncustodial parent may claim the exemption only if the custodial parent signs a waiver and the noncustodial parent attaches it to his return. [§673]

74. **$870 CREDIT**

Mary receives a credit (not a deduction) equal to 29% of $3,000, or $870. Although Mary has child care costs of $4,800, her credit is subject to a $3,000 statutory cap. Additionally, the maximum percentage of 35% is reduced by 1% for each $2,000 or fraction thereof by which AGI exceeds $15,000. Mary has AGI of $26,000; thus, the reduction to the maximum percentage is 6% ($26,000 - $15,000 = $11,000 ÷ $2,000 = 5.5%, which is rounded up to 6%). [§§704-709]

75. **$200**

He can deduct the lesser of the adjusted basis ($1,000) or the difference between the value before ($700) and after ($0). Furthermore, the loss must be reduced by $100, leaving a $600 deduction. However, casualty losses are deductible only to the extent they exceed 10% of AGI (10% of $4,000 equals $400). [§§676-677]

76. **$83,900**

Casualty loss deduction is: the lesser of adjusted basis ($150,000) or decline in value ($225,000) less insurance recovery, less $100, and less 10% of AGI. Thus, the calculation here is as follows: $150,000 (adjusted basis) - $60,000 (insurance recovery) = $90,000; $90,000 - $100 = $89,900; $89,900 - $6,000 (10% of AGI) = $83,900. [§§676-680]

77. **$103,000**

The mortgage and the brokerage commission are included in basis. However, the contingent liability is not. If he later has to pay the contingent liability, it would be added to basis at that time. [§§726-732]

78.a. **$82,400 GAIN**

This is a long-term capital gain. Deborah's basis, for the purposes of computing both gain and loss, is the same as Sarah's—$10,000. However, she is entitled to add a portion of the gift tax paid to basis. The portion is a fraction based on the net appreciation in the gift; 4,000 × 90,000/100,000, or $3,600. Thus Deborah's basis is $13,600. When the property is sold for $96,000, it produces a gain of $82,400. Deborah's gain is long term because she "tacks" Sarah's holding period onto her own. [§§737-738]

b. **$7,000 LOSS**

This is a long-term capital loss. Where the property is worth less than Sarah's basis at the time of the gift, the basis for determining *loss* is the fair market value at the date of the gift ($8,000). (The basis for determining *gain* would be $10,000.) Also in this situation the gift tax (if any) cannot be added to basis since there is no unrealized appreciation in the property. [§737]

c. **NEITHER GAIN NOR LOSS**

Her basis for determining loss is $8,000. Since she sells the property for $9,250, there is no loss. Her basis for determining gain is $10,000, so there is no gain. [§737]

79.a. **$1 MILLION**

Kojak's basis would be $1 million since basis equals fair market value at date of death. Note that in 2010, this rule is slated to change so that the legatee's basis for inherited property is the same as the decedent's basis (subject to many exceptions). [§§740-741]

b. **$9,000**

Basis equals fair market value at date of death. [§§740-741]

80.a. **NO**

Amortization of a life interest or a term interest received by gift or inheritance is not allowed. [I.R.C. §273] [§749]

b. **CAPITAL GAIN OF $41,000**

He is not allowed any basis for the sale of this interest. [I.R.C. §1001(e)] However, he does have capital gain under the *McAllister* case. [§747]

c. **$1,000 CAPITAL GAIN**

He is allowed to use the basis of $40,000 when both life tenant and remainderman together sell their interests. [§748]

d. **YES**

The purchaser of a life estate is entitled to amortize it over the useful life of the asset—which would be the life expectancy of the income beneficiary. [§750]

81.a. **$100,000**

Both halves of the community property receive a new basis under I.R.C. section 1014(b)(6). Note that in 2010, this rule is slated to change so that the legatee's basis for inherited property is the same as the decedent's basis (subject to many exceptions). [§§741, 743]

b. **$25,000**

The portion of the joint tenancy property that is not included in the decedent's estate does not receive a new basis. [§745]

c. **$100,000** Since Herbert's one-half was included in his estate for tax purposes, it receives a new basis. [§745]

82.a. **$15,000** This item is called "income in respect of a decedent" and is fully taxed to whomever receives it. [*See* I.R.C. §691] The item does not receive a new basis under I.R.C. section 1014. The effect of labeling it "income in respect of a decedent" is to assure that it has the same basis as it had to the decedent—that is, zero. This item is clearly income in respect of a decedent because it represents payment for services rendered by the decedent prior to his death but which, under his method of accounting, was not taxable to him at that time. [§§751-754]

b. **$13,000** The estate is allowed to deduct for income tax purposes the estate tax paid in respect to this item. [§754]

83.a. **$9,500** Basis is reduced by the greater of the depreciation allowed or allowable. In this case, more was "allowed" than was allowable, so the entire $10,000 claimed reduces basis. [§756]

b. **$11,500** In this case the amount allowable ($8,000) was greater than the amount allowed ($3,000); therefore, basis is reduced by the amount allowable. [§756]

84. **NO** The amount of the overall basis that can be attributed to the air rights is indeterminable. Consequently, David should reduce his basis for the building to $84,000. Later, when the building is sold, this adjustment will cause his ultimate gain to increase or his ultimate loss to decrease. [§759]

85.a. **YES** She is deemed to have realized $95,000 on the foreclosure, and, consequently, has a $13,000 long-term capital gain (or section 1231 gain). [§767]

b. **NO** Mortgaging property is not a realizing transaction, even though the amount borrowed is in excess of basis. [§763]

86. **PROBABLY NOT** This is an example of an "open transaction," although the IRS is likely to dispute this. Since the amount of the profits to be received is not readily determinable (although it can be roughly estimated), Winston should offset $15,000 received against his basis, which will reduce it to $7,000. The next $7,000 he receives on account of the profits' interest will reduce his basis to zero. Thereafter, each dollar will be taxed as capital gain. [§782] This transaction can be accounted for under the installment method of section 453 since the installment method is available for open transactions. This would be done by equally apportioning Winston's basis over the 10-year payment period. Indeed, the installment method would be used unless the taxpayer elected out of it. [§§779, 782, 1055-1056] Note also that interest must be imputed here since the parties failed to provide for it. [§923] The IRS's position would be that Winston has a capital gain of $73,000 ($95,000 amount realized less $22,000 basis).

87.a. **NO**   This is a nonrecognizing transfer under I.R.C. section 1041. [§816]

    b. **NO**   Transfers between spouses (or between former spouses incident to a divorce) are treated as gifts to the recipient. [§§816-819]

    c. **$8,000**   Basis stays the same after a transfer described in I.R.C. section 1041. [§818]

88.a. **$60,000**   Although his realized gain is $150,000, this is a transaction described in I.R.C. section 1031—exchange of property of a "like kind" to that given up. Consequently, gain or loss is recognized only to the extent of the "boot" received, which is the $60,000 in cash. [§§786, 796]

    b. **$20,000**   This again is an I.R.C. section 1031 exchange, but the boot received ($60,000) exceeds the realized gain ($20,000). No more than the realized gain could ever be recognized. [§796]

    c. **NONE**   Since this is a section 1031 exchange, no loss can be recognized. [§796]

    d. **$200,000** The formula is old basis ($200,000) plus gain recognized ($60,000) minus boot received ($60,000), or $200,000. [§798]

    e. **$290,000** The formula is old basis ($330,000) minus boot received ($60,000) plus gain recognized ($20,000), or $290,000. [§798]

    f. **$360,000** The formula is old basis ($420,000) minus boot received ($60,000), or $360,000. [§798]

89.a. **NO**   If she elects to use section 1033 and the reinvestment occurred within two years, she need not recognize the gain. However, she failed to reinvest $1,500 of the proceeds, so $1,500 gain would be recognized. [§804]

    b. **YES**   The vacation cottage and the Ferrari are not property that is "similar or related in service or use." Consequently the entire gain is recognized. [§805]

90.a. **NONE**   Under I.R.C. section 121, a single person can exclude up to $250,000 of gain on sale of a principal residence if during the five-year period ending on the date of the sale it has been both owned and used as a principal residence for two years or more. [§§810-811]

    b. **$220,000** The basis of the new house is its purchase price. [§729]

91.a. **$350,000** Wanda meets the requirements of I.R.C. section 121 for her share. She is single and can exclude $250,000. However, her share of the gain was $600,000 (her half of the difference between the $1,400,000 sales price and the $200,000 purchase price), so $350,000 is taxable. [§§810-811]

    b. **$350,000** Under I.R.C. section 121(d)(3)(B), Harry is allowed to treat the house as his principal residence during the years he no longer lived there. Therefore he qualifies for exclusion under section 121. However, he cannot exclude $500,000, even though he filed a joint return with Mary, because Mary does not meet the ownership and use requirements of section 121. [§§813-815]

92. **NO**   This is a clear case in which the property is held primarily for sale to customers in the ordinary course of business. This is evidenced by the large number of sales, the fact that he purchased large pieces of property and split them up into smaller pieces, the improvements he made, his practices in prior years, and his personal involvement in selling the property. This is not a case in which he appears to have had several purposes, such as farming, as opposed to selling. It is simply a case in which the nature of his activities clearly shows that the property is being held primarily for sale rather than for investment. [§§832-836]

93. **YES**   This seems to be clearly an investment. None of the facts point to Luis's having held the property primarily for sale to customers in the ordinary course of business. As far as we know, this is the only transaction of this type that he has entered into. He has no personal involvement in improving or in selling the land. The increase in value occurred because of extrinsic factors, not his efforts. This is clearly a capital gain. [§833]

94. **YES**   Under *Malat v. Riddell*, even though Vicky holds other property for sale to customers, it is possible to establish a different purpose for a particular parcel. Here one must measure whether her purpose of developing and leasing the property was more important than her purpose of selling it. Since it seems clear that her primary purpose was development, not sale, it is a capital gain. [§835]

95.a. **YES**   Different standards are applied to stock traders than to land dealers. Despite the volume of his trading, Warren is still treated as holding capital assets; his stocks are not held primarily for sale to customers in the ordinary course of business. The result would be different if Warren were a "dealer" of securities (for example, by acting as a floor specialist on the exchange or by holding stocks in inventory and selling to customers for a commission). [§§837-840]

   b. **YES**   These would be deductible under I.R.C. section 212(1) as expenses incurred for the production or collection of income, or under section 212(2) as expenses incurred for the management, conservation, or maintenance of property held for the production of income. However, the 2% floor is applicable. [§§437, 561]

96.a. **NO**   Copyrights and other literary, musical, or artistic property are not capital assets in the hands of the taxpayer whose personal efforts created them. [I.R.C. §1221(a)(3)] [§846]

   b. **YES**   Under I.R.C. section 1235, inventors are entitled to long-term capital gain on the sale of their invention. It would not matter whether the purchase price was to be paid in the form of a royalty based upon the number of instruments manufactured; the royalties would still be capital gains. Furthermore, it would not matter how many such inventions Betty previously had made. They would still be capital gains. [§849]

97. **NO**   These assets are classified as ordinary income assets under section 1221(3), meaning that if the President had sold them, he would receive ordinary income. Therefore, he is entitled to deduct only their basis, not their market value, when he gives them to charity. Presumably his basis in these letters and memoranda is zero, and, therefore, he would be entitled to no deduction. [§§635, 847]

98. **YES**   Under *Arkansas Best*, this stock is a capital asset regardless of the business reason for buying it. [§843]

99. **NO**   This is similar to the *P.G. Lake* case. When the taxpayer anticipates ordinary income by selling the rights to income while keeping the underlying income-producing asset, he receives ordinary income, not capital gain. [§855]

100. **YES**   Unlike the previous case, he has sold his entire interest. Even though it is only a right to income, the fact that he sells the entire interest, without retaining anything, is sufficient to give him capital gain under the *McAllister* case. Note that under I.R.C. section 1001(e), Zahi is given a zero basis. [§§856-857]

101.a. **YES**   Allen is treated as having sold the right to collect rent, while retaining the reversion, and this is taxable as ordinary income without basis recovery. This was established in the *Hort* case. [§862]

b. **YES**   The lessee has sold his entire interest in the property, and it is treated as a capital asset. Section 1241 establishes that the lessee has a sale or exchange for capital gain purposes. [§§861, 902]

102. **NO**   The contingent right to money was received for personal services. The sale of the right to compensation for personal services produces ordinary income. [§864]

103. **YES**   Under the "lookback" rule, the money is treated as capital gain because it is referable to a previous transaction that produced capital loss. [§871]

104.a. **$95,000**   The amount paid for the option is part of his purchase price. [§735]

b. **NO**   Since it is an option to purchase a capital asset, its lapse is treated as capital loss under I.R.C. section 1234. [§852]

c. **NO**   It is ordinary income because Paul has not sold or exchanged a capital asset. [§852]

d. **YES**	The option to purchase a capital asset is itself a capital asset. [§850]
105. **NO**	The consideration must be fragmented and the analysis must be made asset by asset. The gain on the furniture and books ($2,000) is ordinary income because of depreciation recaptured under I.R.C. section 1245. The accounts receivable produce ordinary income since they are payment for services. [*See* I.R.C. §1221(4)] The goodwill produces capital gain. The covenant not to compete produces ordinary income. Therefore, the gain is $20,000 ordinary income and $5,000 capital gain. [§§844, 873-877, 933-934]
106. **NO**	These are both section 1231 assets. Since the losses ($6,000) on section 1231 assets exceed the gains ($3,000), both the loss and the gain are given ordinary, not capital, treatment. [§§888-892]
107. **NO**	If gains on casualties involving business or investment assets exceed losses, both gains and losses are within section 1231. Here the only casualty transaction produces a gain. However, the net of all section 1231 transactions is a loss: consequently, the casualty gain is ordinary income. [§§888-892]
108.a. **NO**	I.R.C. section 1253 provides that if the franchisor retains these kinds of controls, it is treated as ordinary income to him. [§899]
b. **YES**	A franchise is amortizable over a 15-year term. Hence, $1,000 per year is deductible. [§474]
109.a. **YES**	Fred did not collect on the note, but rather sold it. [§907] The note appears to be a capital asset [§829], and the sale to Roy is treated as a sale or exchange. [§896]
b. **YES**	Collection of a debt instrument (such as a promissory note) is treated as a sale or exchange to the creditor. [§§907-908]
c. **YES**	He appears to have $5 of debt cancellation income. [§142]
110. **YES IN PART**	These were the facts in the *Brown* case, which held that the seller was entitled to capital gain. This was so even though the seller continued to manage the business and had all the risks of loss if the business failed. However, part of the money received by Laura in fact would be treated as ordinary income in this situation because it is a sale with the price to be paid in the future, but without providing for interest. This requires that interest be imputed under I.R.C. section 483. Consequently, each payment would be treated as ordinary income to Laura. [§§911-913, 925]
111. **YES**	Jomo can deduct 50% of his $3,800,000 gain under section 1202. Thus, only $1,900,000 is included in income. However, 7% of the excluded amount is treated as a tax preference under the alternative minimum tax. [§§918-921]

112. **$7,000** The capital gain is includible in income; the capital loss is deductible to the extent of capital gain plus $3,000. The remainder of the capital loss ($17,000) will be a carryforward to future years. [§§821-828]

113. **NO** This requires the application of section 483—imputed interest. (Section 1274 does not apply to any transaction under $250,000.) The parties have failed to provide for any interest and therefore it will be imputed. Assume the applicable rate is 10% (and ignore the requirement of semi-annual compounding). Interest at the rate of 10% on $10,000 for 18 months is about $1,500. Consequently, $1,500 will be interest income (ordinary) to Rory, and Ryan will have a $1,500 interest deduction (subject to the limit of the investment interest limitation or the passive loss rules, whichever is applicable). Rory's capital gain will be the amount realized ($8,500) minus basis ($1,000), or $7,500. [§923]

114.a. **YES** Although ordinarily the tractor would presumably be considered section 1231 property, on which the gains would be capital (if it were the only section 1231 transaction that year), the provision for recapture of depreciation would apply here. Section 1245 requires the entire $1,200 gain to be taxed as ordinary income regardless of whether the depreciation was straight-line or accelerated. [§§933-936]

   b. **NO** It is ordinary income only up to the amount of the depreciation ($8,000). The balance of the gain of $2,000 would be taxed under section 1231 and (assuming there are no section 1231 losses) would be capital gain. [§936]

   c. **NO** It is capital loss because the section 1231 gains exceed the section 1231 losses. Therefore, all transactions are capital. Recapture of depreciation has no application if the property is sold at a loss. [§§933-936]

   d. **NO** This is a section 1031 exchange of property for like-kind property. No gain or loss is recognized, and therefore there is no opportunity for depreciation to be recaptured. If Zeke had received any "boot" in this transaction, it would have been treated as ordinary income because of the recapture of depreciation. [§938]

115. **YES** Don's AMTI is $280,000, because the bargain element in an incentive stock option is a tax preference. The exemption on a joint return is $45,000, which is phased out at a rate of 25% of the excess of AMTI over $150,000. In Don's case, this means that the $45,000 exemption is reduced by $32,500 (25% of $130,000) to $12,500, making the amount subject to AMT $267,500 ($280,000 - $12,500). The AMT is 26% of the first $175,000 plus 28% of the amount over $175,000. Thus, Don's AMT would be $71,400 (26% × $175,000 = $45,500, 28% × $92,500 ($267,500 - $175,000) = $25,900, $45,500 + $25,900 = $71,400). Given that his regular tax was only $57,000, he must pay the AMT instead (an additional $14,400). [§§945-957]

116.a. YES   Paul has capital gain equal to the fair market value of the note less his basis. The regulations require that the note be valued at $10,000 (the value of the property given up) rather than its actual fair market value of $8,500. Thus, Paul has capital gain of $9,000. [§780]

b. YES   To an accrual basis taxpayer, the date of actual payment and the value of the note are irrelevant. Paul acquired a right to be paid in Year 1, and therefore must accrue the $9,000 capital gain in that year. [§1014]

c. YES   The stock is treated as the equivalent of cash and thus is income when received by a cash basis taxpayer. [§§960, 1014]

117.a. YES   This is an example of constructive receipt. The money was available; Cassie had a right to it and the power to obtain it, but she turned her back on the money. It is taxable in Year 1. [§963]

b. NO   It is permissible for a cash basis taxpayer to contract not to receive money until a later year. No income is recognized until the money is paid. [§§969-970]

118. YES   The placing of the money in trust, beyond Zero's control, causes it to be treated as the equivalent of cash to Suman. Thus, it is taxed in Year 1. [§974]

119.a. NO   Under a *qualified* pension or profit-sharing plan, the amounts paid into the plan are not taxable until ultimately received by the employee. [§§977, 980]

b. YES   Contributions to a qualified plan are deductible in the year paid. [§977]

c. NO   The trust is a tax-exempt entity. [§978]

120.a. NO   In almost all cases, the grant of a stock option is not a taxable event. In the absence of an established market for options, the market value would not generally be clearly ascertainable. [§995]

b. YES   The exercise of a stock option is a taxable event (assuming that the earlier grant of the option was not taxed). Pete has purchased 100 shares for $100 per share when the real value is $130. Therefore, he has income of $3,000. This is ordinary income since it is compensation for services. [§996]

c. YEAR 3   It receives a $3,000 deduction in Year 3. [§997]

d. $13,000   His basis consists of the amount paid plus the amount included in income. [§996]

e. NO   Under I.R.C. section 83, the stock received would be nontransferable and subject to a substantial risk of forfeiture. It would not be currently taxable. [§§983-984]

f. **YES** Under the terms of section 83, the stock is taxable as ordinary income at its fair market value when it first becomes transferable or nonforfeitable. Thus, Pete would have $12,000 of income in Year 4 (fair market value of $22,000 less the amount paid—$10,000). [§984]

121.a. **YES** Lloyd, a cash basis taxpayer, must include money in income when it is received. [§1002]

b. **NO** Although the Supreme Court has established the general rule that prepayments of income must be included by accrual basis taxpayers in the year in which they receive the money, the Code has established a relatively narrow area in which deferral is permitted. As to advance payments for services, if the services are to be performed by the end of the year following payment, the taxpayer can defer to that year the portion of the payment attributable to it. [§§1023-1028]

c. **YES** The general rule requiring an accrual basis taxpayer to include immediately all prepayments for services applies to this situation. The special exemption provided by the IRS applies only if the services are to be completed by the end of the following year. Since this is more than a one-year prepayment, the IRS's special dispensation does not apply. [§§1023-1028]

122. **NO** There is a special rule concerning dividends to an accrual basis taxpayer. They are included in income only when received, even though the dividend in this case would accrue on December 15 by ordinary accounting standards. [§1029]

123.a. **NO** Under the accrual method, nothing is accrued until all the events have occurred that establish the right to the income. The contract would be viewed as a single right to payment, and nothing would be accrued until all the events had occurred that establish the right to receive all of the compensation. [§1019]

b. **NO** It is not necessary to accrue as income money due from an insolvent debtor. [§§1021-1022]

124. **NO** Even though it is likely that Louis will have to pay the money, all the events have not occurred that establish his obligation to do so. It is not permissible to accrue estimated future expenses, even though under accounting practice, it might be mandatory to do so. In this case, not only is the obligation not yet fixed, but the amount of the damages is also probably not reasonably ascertainable—which is also required before an expense can be accrued. [§§1034, 1043]

125.a. **YES** She will probably be treated as in constructive receipt. The corporation is obligated to pay her the salary, and she has the power to require the treasurer to write the check. [§§963, 966]

b. **YES**   Ordinarily, the rule under I.R.C. section 267 is that an accrual basis tax-payer may not accrue an expense payable to a related person (including an owner of more than 50% of its stock) if the creditor is on the cash basis, un-til payment is actually made. This rule would be applicable here except for the fact that Laura was probably required to include the amount in income under the doctrine of constructive receipt. Consequently, it would follow that Zero Corp. is entitled to a deduction in Year 1. [§§1044-1045]

126.a. **$345**   Under FIFO, the inventory is considered to consist of the last item pur-chased, which is 100 parts at $1.60 ($160) and 20 at $1.50 ($30). Thus, the $535 cost of goods sold is reduced by the inventory of $190. [§§1049-1051]

b. **$410**   Under LIFO, the ending inventory is considered to be the first items pur-chased. Consequently, there are 100 parts at $1 ($100) and 20 purchased at $1.25 ($25), or a total of $125. Thus, cost of goods sold would be $410. [§§1052-1053]

127. **$800**   Compute a fraction in which the gross profit ($4,000) is the numerator and the total contract price ($10,000) is the denominator. This fraction is multi-plied by the payments received each year to compute the amount includible in income. The interest payments, as they are received, are all ordinary income. [§§1055-1059]

128.a. **YES**   He has received it under claim of right and must include it in income notwith-standing the risk that he will not be able to retain it. [§§999-1000]

b. **NO**   This would be a violation of the annual accounting concept. Since the repay-ment occurred in Year 3, it can be deducted only in that year. [§1075]

c. **NO**   Under I.R.C. section 1341, he has an option: either deduct on his Year 3 re-turn or reduce his Year 3 taxes by the amount of tax he would have saved if he had deducted in Year 1. [§1076]

129.a. **$100,000 DEDUCTION**   As an accrual basis taxpayer, B & W had included the $100,000 in income; it had a basis of $100,000. When the debt became worthless, it was a business bad debt (ordinary deduction). [§528]

b. **NONE**   There is no debt cancellation income if the debtor could have deducted the pay-ment if he had made it. [§147]

c. **$100,000 INCOME**   Recovery of an amount previously deducted is income in the year of recovery if the prior deduction resulted in a tax saving. Contra if no tax benefit. [§§1079-1080]

d. **$100,000 DEDUCTION**   A cash basis taxpayer gets a deduction when the amount is paid. [§959]

130. **YEAR 3** Under I.R.C. section 461(h)(2)(A), no deduction is allowed to an accrual taxpayer until economic performance occurs—which means when the services are actually performed. In Year 3, economic performance had occurred and also all events had occurred that establish X's obligation to pay; the actual date of payment is irrelevant. Note that drilling expenses for an oil well are deductible immediately; they do not have to be capitalized and depreciated over the useful life of the well. [§§490, 1038-1040]

Exam Questions
and Answers

QUESTION I

Barnes is a Native American. More than 30 years ago, he bought a house in Butte, Montana, where he has lived ever since. He is unmarried. He paid $20,000 for the house, paying $500 down and executing a note and first mortgage for the $19,500 balance. He has made timely payments of principal and interest on the note and has reduced its principal balance to $14,500. The house became very valuable because of development in the area. On June 15 of Year 5, Barnes sold it for $280,000 cash plus assumption of the mortgage.

Spence owns 60 rented houses in Helena, Montana. He spends all of his working time taking care of the houses and looking for profitable sales. There are no "for sale" signs on the houses. Interested buyers are referred to Spence's broker. The broker is self-employed; working for Spence consumes about 5% of his time. Because the Helena housing market has been poor, Spence has sold only one house during the last three years, but has purchased 16 houses during that time.

Spence's house on Oak St. was purchased for $40,000 in Year 1. In Year 2, Spence leased it to Tennant for $400 per month. The lease runs until December 31 of Year 6. Spence has claimed $5,000 in depreciation on the house on Oak St.

Barnes had to move to Helena and began looking for a house there in April of Year 5. He discovered from Spence's broker that the house on Oak St. could be purchased for $75,000. After speaking to Tennant, Barnes discovered that Tennant would surrender his lease for $750. Spence refused to sell to Barnes. Barnes suspects racial discrimination.

Under Montana law, the housing commission can order a house to be sold to a buyer if it finds that the seller refused to sell because of racial discrimination. The commission can also order the seller to pay a $3,000 penalty to the buyer. After holding a hearing, the commission ordered Spence to sell the house on Oak St. to Barnes for $75,000 and ordered him to pay a $3,000 penalty to Barnes.

On June 5 of Year 5, Barnes, Spence, and Tennant settled their affairs. Barnes handed Tennant $750 and paid Spence $72,000 (that is, $75,000 less the $3,000 penalty). Barnes handed Spence a deed to the Oak St. house. On June 10, Barnes moved into the house.

What are the income tax consequences in Year 5 to Barnes, Spence, and Tennant?

QUESTION II

Oliver W. Holmes, a prominent Boston lawyer, had great difficulty in recruiting law school graduates for his exciting practice (which consisted of making claims against railroads for damaged freight). He felt that recruiting might improve if he financed a scholarship program. Consequently, he arranged to fund a scholarship for one needy law student throughout his or her three years of law school. The scholarship would pay $800 per month (during the school year) to the recipient to cover living expenses, not tuition. The recipient's only obligations were to work at Holmes's office the summers between the first and second years and the second and third years of law school and to do research for Holmes on request. (For such research, the recipient would be compensated at the rate of $10 per hour.) In June of Year 1, Holmes sent Harvard Law School a check for $19,200 (i.e., $800 per month for eight months a year for three years).

In Year 1 through Year 5, Holmes's adjusted gross income was $25,000 before taking into account any of the transactions mentioned in this problem.

Paul Prolific, who entered Harvard Law School in the Fall of Year 1, was selected by the Dean as the first recipient of the Oliver W. Holmes Scholarship. He had a wife and five young children and was broke. Each month during the school year from October of Year 1 to May of Year 2, Harvard issued a check to Prolific for $800. He was never asked to do any research during the school year.

Prolific worked at Holmes's office during the summers of Year 2 and Year 3, receiving a salary of $1,500 per month. (You may assume that the $1,500 payments are taxable to Prolific as ordinary income and deductible by Holmes.)

In October of Year 2, Ann Allen, who had been Prolific's secretary at Holmes's office, found herself pregnant and accused Prolific of being the father. She brought a paternity suit to compel Prolific to support the child. Holmes investigated Ms. Allen's charges and decided that they were unwarranted. He thereupon fired her. Holmes assumed the burden of Prolific's defense without charge, since he felt himself somewhat at fault in exposing someone of Prolific's tender years to a person like Ms. Allen.

The costs of the defense (all of which were paid by Holmes in Year 3) were $8,000 (court costs, investigator's fees, and the salaries of attorneys in Holmes's office who worked on the matter). In June of Year 3, the court held that Prolific was not the father of Ms. Allen's child.

After he graduated in June of Year 4, Prolific rejected Holmes's offer of permanent employment and took a job with Penn Central Railway in the freight claims department. In Year 5, Prolific wrote to Holmes, stating his appreciation for all Holmes had done for him. He enclosed a check for $1,000 to partially reimburse Holmes for the costs of defending the paternity suit.

What are the income tax consequences to Holmes and to Prolific in Year 1, Year 2, Year 3, and Year 5? (Ignore consequences to Ann Allen.) Discuss.

QUESTION III

Laura has been a tenant for 10 years in the Hilgard Arms, a 100-unit apartment house; she occupies her apartment on a month-to-month rental agreement. Rex, owner of the Hilgard Arms, decided to convert the building to condominiums, which he plans to offer for sale. Local law allows apartments to be converted to condominiums, but requires the owner to pay each tenant $2,500 to reimburse them for the inconvenience of moving and the possibly higher rent they must pay elsewhere. Rex pays Laura $2,500 in pursuance of this law.

A.   How should Laura treat the $2,500 for tax purposes?

B.   How should Rex treat the $2,500?

QUESTION IV

Tailor Corporation, which tailor-makes business suits, made a contract with Grunt Steel Company, which provided that Tailor would make suits for Grunt executives. Each suit has a fair market value of $500. Tailor Corporation will lease these suits to Grunt for $200 per year, and Grunt will provide them free of charge to its executives. The leases run for three years. At the end of the term, Grunt will return the suits to Tailor Corporation, but (since they will be worn out and since they were custom-made) you can assume that they would be worthless at the end of the lease term. Ray, vice president of Grunt, got a new tailor-made suit in Year 1 worth $500. Grunt paid Tailor Corporation $200 as rental in Year 1 on Ray's suit. Tailor's costs of making the suit were $240. All taxpayers use the cash method of accounting.

A.   What income tax consequences to Ray in Year 1?

B.   What income tax consequences to Grunt in Year 1?

C.   What income tax consequences to Tailor Corporation in Year 1?

QUESTION V

Turbo Corporation manufactures hydraulic grunches and has earned substantial profits for the last 20 years. Turbo has a large physical plant with expensive and sophisticated machinery. It has accumulated earnings and profits equal to $400,000, and has never paid a dividend. It uses the accrual method of accounting and the calendar year. Its current policy is to pay out most of its profits as salary and bonus to its executives. All of the executives use the cash method of accounting and the calendar year.

All of the executives of Turbo are the sons and daughters of Max Kirk. Max has been the chief executive officer of Turbo for 10 years. He works a 12-hour day, six days a week. Max owns 25% of the stock of Turbo, and his sons and daughters own the balance. In Year 1, Max was 62 years old and single. He plans to retire in Year 3.

In Year 1, Max received a salary of $125,000. He also was voted a $50,000 bonus in December of Year 1 by the directors. The bonus was payable immediately. However, Max did not get around to requesting that a check be drawn for $50,000 until June 15, Year 2. Max was also entitled to $24,000 of additional salary in Year 1, which he deferred until later years under the deferred compensation plan (described below). Research indicates that the chief executive officers of other hydraulic grunch companies earn between $50,000 and $100,000 per year.

In March of Year 1, the directors of Turbo adopted a deferred compensation plan. Under this plan, each executive can elect to defer up to $3,000 per month of current salary to a future year or years. The election must be made by the 15th of a month, with respect to the salary payable during the immediately following month. Pursuant to this plan, Max elected in April of Year 1 that $3,000 per month of each month's salary should be retained by the corporation and paid to him in 10 installments beginning in Year 4. Thus, $24,000 ($3,000 per month for eight months) of Max's salary was not paid to him in Year 1.

What are the income tax consequences to Max and Turbo in Year 1 and Year 2?

QUESTION VI

Blackacre and Whiteacre are both unimproved parcels of land. Beth purchased Whiteacre in 1992 for $74,000. In 2005, when it was worth $56,000, she transferred it to her friend, Marc. Whiteacre was Beth's only significant asset and she wanted to get on welfare, so she had to divest herself of her property. Beth and Marc understood that if Beth wanted to get Whiteacre back, she only had to ask. The transfer was not recorded.

Hal and Gretel acquired Blackacre as community property in 1984 by exchanging their home for it. The home had a basis of $25,000 and a value of $70,000. Blackacre was worth $70,000 in 1984. In 1995, Hal died at the age of 42, leaving his community one-half interest in Blackacre to Gretel. The value of Blackacre in 1995 was $66,000.

In 2006, Marc and Gretel exchanged Whiteacre for Blackacre. Marc and Beth discussed the exchange and Beth approved of it. In 2006, Whiteacre was worth $61,000. Blackacre was worth $40,000. Gretel transferred $10,000 in cash and an AT&T bond worth $11,000 (basis: $13,200) to Marc. What are the income tax consequences of the facts above to Beth, Marc, Hal, and Gretel?

QUESTION VII

Jenny operates a tree surgery business. Paul is going to purchase the entire business for $20,000 in cash. In addition, he will assume $9,200 of Jenny's business liabilities.

The following is a table of the assets of Jenny's business (all of which have been held more than one year):

ASSET	BASIS	VALUE
Lease on office*	$ 0	$ 5,000
Office furniture**	4,000	7,200
Trucks***	16,000	9,000
Goodwill	0	8,000
Total	$20,000	$29,200

*Assume the lease is treated as real property used in the business.

**$5,000 is the depreciation on the furniture.

***$9,000 is the depreciation on the trucks.

Assuming that Jenny's taxable income (without reference to the above) was $30,000, what is her taxable income after taking account of the sale of her business?

QUESTION VIII

On January 1 of Year 2, Bill bought an apartment house (the "Dallas Arms") from Sam. Bill put $20,000 down and took the property subject to a $100,000 nonrecourse first mortgage loan owed to Coast Savings. Bill also gave Sam a note for an additional $30,000, payable on July 1 of Year 5. This was Sam's only asset sale in Year 2.

The note to Sam is nonrecourse and is secured by a second mortgage on Dallas Arms. The note to Coast Savings bears interest at 10%, and the note to Sam bears interest at 18%. Bill made payments to Coast Savings as they became due. In Year 2, principal payments to Coast Savings totaled $2,000 and interest payments to Coast Savings totaled $10,000.

Sam's adjusted basis for Dallas Arms was $60,000. He had claimed straight-line depreciation of $50,000 during his 12 years of ownership.

Tina, a tenant in Dallas Arms, signed a lease on January 1 of Year 1. Tina is rather eccentric and likes to pay bills before they are due. Consequently, in Year 1, she prepaid two years' rent. The total prepayment was $12,000. To account for the fact that a year still remained for which Tina had prepaid rent, Sam paid Bill $6,000 at the time of the sale of Dallas Arms.

On December 31 of Year 2, Tina asked Bill if she could renew her lease for another two years (for Years 3 and 4) at the same rental price, and Tina stated that she desired to prepay the two years' rent ($12,000) immediately. Bill said he did not want to discuss the rent payment until January of Year 3.

Also on December 31 of Year 2, Bill gave Sam a promissory note for $5,400—the amount that Bill owed in interest for Year 2. The note is payable on April 1 of Year 3, bears an interest rate of 20%, and is secured by a third mortgage on Dallas Arms. The note had a fair market value of $5,000 on December 31 of Year 2.

Both Bill and Sam use the cash method of accounting and the calendar year. What are the income tax consequences to Bill and Sam of the facts above? Ignore consequences to Tina and ignore imputed interest.

QUESTION IX

On December 31 of Year 2, Ellen (who is not a professional bicycle thief) stole Rick's racing bike, which was then worth $1,400. The bike was not insured. Rick had bought the bike new on March 15 of Year 1 for $1,000. The bike was so good, and so few were made, that used bikes rose in value. The useful life of the bike was about seven years. Rick used the bike both for pleasure and for riding in bicycle races in which money prizes were given. In the typical bike race, 1,000 people would enter and the top five finishers would get prizes. Rick never finished in the top 200 in a bike race. Rick's AGI in Year 2 was $6,000. Because his itemized deductions did not exceed the standard deduction in Year 2, Rick got no benefit from the resulting casualty loss deduction.

Ellen tried to fence the bike but decided to wait until the market improved. In the meantime, she used the bike for pleasure riding. One day, in Year 3, as she was riding at the beach, Rick saw her and, after a brief struggle, reclaimed the bike, which by then was worth $1,600. Rick also called the police. Ellen was prosecuted for petty theft and paid an attorney $500 in Year 3 to defend her. Ellen resisted the theft charge because, if found guilty, she would probably lose her job as a probation officer. Ellen was acquitted.

What are the tax consequences to Rick and Ellen by reason of the facts above?

ANSWER TO QUESTION I

A. Barnes

Sale and Purchase of House: Barnes's basis for his Butte house is $20,000 (original purchase price, including mortgage). The amount realized on the sale is $294,500 (assumption of mortgage plus cash). The realized gain is $274,500. Under I.R.C. section 121, because the property has been Barnes's principal residence for at least two of the five years preceding the sale, Barnes can exclude $250,000 of his gain. The remaining $24,500 is taxable as long-term capital gain. The fact that he reinvested in another house is irrelevant.

The basis of the Oak St. house is its purchase price ($75,000) plus the amount paid to buy Tennant's rights as a lessee ($750). Thus the total basis is $75,750. The purchase of the house and the penalty are treated separately even though they were netted out by the parties.

Taxation of the Penalty: The $3,000 penalty is taxable. Since racial discrimination is not a physical injury, section 104(a)(2) is inapplicable.

B. Tennant

Tennant's sale of his leasehold interest produces a $750 long-term capital gain. A leasehold is a capital asset to the tenant, provided he sells his entire interest therein. Since the lease is being sold to a third party, not the lessor, it is clear that there is a sale or exchange. (And even if it were sold to the lessor, section 1241 makes it clear that there is a sale or exchange.)

C. Spence

Sale of the House: It is important to treat the sale of the house and payment of the penalty as separate transactions. Spence's adjusted basis for the house is $35,000 ($45,000 purchase price less $5,000 depreciation). The sale price was $75,000; thus, the realized gain is $40,000.

If the house were held for sale to customers in the ordinary course of business, the gain would be ordinary income, not capital gain under section 1231(b)(1)(B) (if rental is treated as being a trade or business) or section 1221 (if rental is not a trade or business).

Factors to Consider: Spence seems more interested in renting the houses than in selling them—all of them are rented, and he spends a great deal of time on renting. This suggests they are not being held for sale. Moreover, Spence has not made any strong efforts to sell, since he does not display any signs and uses an independent broker (rather than an employee) to transact sales. Also, only one sale has been made in three years, further suggesting that the houses are not being held for sale. On the other hand, it could be argued that Spence is renting the houses only to pay his costs and that he is in fact primarily interested in buying and selling as fast as possible (the lack of sales recently being due to the stagnant market). On balance, it appears that Spence has a strong case for capital gains.

Payment of the Penalty: Is the penalty a deductible expense (under section 162 if Spence is in a trade or business or section 212 if he is an investor)? Presumably the payment of such penalties by housing dealers is ordinary (*i.e.*, customary) and necessary (in the sense that payment of the penalty once it was assessed was a necessity). It might be argued that it arose out of Spence's personal life, rather than his business life, since evidently he allows his prejudices to get in the way of business, but this argument seems weak since the penalty is traceable to a business transaction. It might also be argued that the penalty should be treated as a selling expense, which would reduce capital gain rather than allow for a deduction, but this also seems weak because Spence would have had to pay the penalty even if the sale had not gone through (*i.e.*, had Barnes bought a different house).

There is no public policy obstacle to deduction—section 162(f) disallows only fines or penalties paid to a government; section 162(g) disallows only treble damage payments under the antitrust laws; and section 162(c) disallows only deduction of illegal payments (obviously payment of the penalty was not illegal; indeed, it was required by state law). Thus, payment of the penalty is probably deductible by Spence.

ANSWER TO QUESTION II

A. Scholarship

Holmes: The payment of $19,200 to Harvard might qualify as a charitable contribution. If so, it would be deductible, but only in an amount equal to 50% of adjusted gross income, or $12,500. The balance ($6,700) is not currently deductible, but could be carried forward and deducted in the following year.

On the other hand, this is arguably *not* a charitable contribution, in the sense that the donor expects a significant quid pro quo (a guaranteed research assistant and summer clerk as well as a likely permanent recruit). Where there is a direct business benefit to be gained, the outlay is not a charitable contribution, but might be deducted as a business expense under section 162(b). Moreover, it could be argued that this was a grant from Holmes directly to Prolific rather than Harvard—in which case, it would be disallowed because it was not a gift to an organized charity.

Analyzing the payment under section 162, it is seemingly not ordinary for lawyers in Boston to arrange for scholarships; on the contrary, it is extraordinary and unusual. Moreover, the payment probably should be capitalized: It does not yield an immediate benefit—the primary benefit will be realized only after three years when Prolific graduates from law school. Thus, the deduction would have to wait for three years. On the other hand, perhaps it could be amortized over the three-year period, since it does provide some advantages during that time (*e.g.*, a summer clerk and availability of a research assistant).

When Prolific finally turned down Holmes's offer of employment, the $19,200 (if previously capitalized and not amortized) could be deducted as an ordinary business loss under section 165.

Prolific: Scholarships are taxable unless applied directly to tuition or books. Even if this payment were applied to tuition, it could be argued that it is really a payment for services, not a payment for studying. However, since Prolific was being adequately compensated for any work he did for Holmes, it would appear that the payment would qualify as a scholarship (if it were applied to tuition).

B. Paternity Suit

Holmes: Deduction of the $8,000 might be disallowed for the reason that Holmes is paying someone else's expenses, not his own; however, since the dispute arose out of an employment situation, perhaps this rule would not be applied. It would seem appropriate for an employer to pay an employee's litigation costs where the litigation is traceable to the employment. By the same token, these payments were probably "ordinary" within the meaning of section 162. They produce an immediate benefit and hence would not have to be capitalized. (If held to be a gift to Prolific (below), only $25 could be deducted under section 274(b).)

Prolific: Since the litigation costs related to freeing him from potential child-support liabilities, they would seem to be Prolific's expenses, and the payment of his expenses by his employer should be treated as gross income. Paul might argue that the payments are gifts, excludible under section 102, but that argument will not prevail. Payments by an employer on behalf of an employee cannot be treated as gifts.

Prolific could also argue that these payments were for the convenience of the employer, similar to reimbursement of an employee's travel costs. However, these expenses hardly seem to be within the narrow scope of the "convenience of the employer doctrine," which does not seem to encompass any more than travel, entertainment, and meals and lodging that are closely related to the employment situation and necessarily must be borne to keep the business going.

In any event, Prolific **cannot deduct** the costs. Under *Gilmore,* a paternity dispute surely arises out of the personal part of his life (not the business part), even though there were some connections to the business setting (Ann was his secretary).

C. Repayment

Holmes: If Holmes deducted the $8,000 in the past, the unexpected recovery of $1,000 would be taxable income, unless he did not receive a tax benefit from the deduction. Presumably, however, there was a tax benefit (either in Year 3 or, by way of a net operating loss carryover or carryback, in some other year). Thus, the recovery is taxable.

Prolific: Prolific could argue that reimbursing Holmes for the litigation costs was an ordinary and necessary expense—*i.e.*, it will help Prolific in business by establishing his good character. But this would suggest that the payments should be capitalized, as in *Welch v. Helvering*, as analogous to the purchase of goodwill of indeterminate life. In response, Paul would contend that the payments were akin to deductible advertising. On balance, however, the payments are probably not deductible—either because they are not ordinary, because they have to be capitalized, or because they are only personal (*i.e.*, traceable to the earlier paternity suit that arose out of the personal part of Paul's life).

Assuming Paul can deduct the payment, he would obviously prefer to deduct it in Year 5 (when he is in a higher bracket) than in Year 3. Since Year 5 is the payment year, it is the correct year to deduct the payment (it is improper to reopen Year 3). In the unlikely event that Paul was in a higher bracket in Year 3 than Year 5, he might try to apply section 1341, which allows the payor to select the tax bracket of the payment year or the income year. However, section 1341 is inapplicable because it was never "established" that Paul had to return the money. In addition, section 1341 applies only to payments over $3,000.

ANSWER TO QUESTION III

A. Laura

Laura has been enriched by $2,500 and at first glance would seem to have gross income of that amount. She has received a windfall, and windfalls produced by statutory policies are taxable under *Glenshaw Glass*. To avoid including the $2,500, Laura might argue that she has received a gift, but this argument clearly fails—Rex was forced by statute to make the payment, so it cannot meet the disinterested generosity standard of *Duberstein*.

A more plausible argument might analogize the payment to a government subsidy or welfare payment. When these are paid by the government and are responsive to the recipient's need, they are not included in income—even though no statute so provides. Here the payment is made by an individual, not the government, but the same argument could be made. However, this argument seems unpersuasive—after all, Rex and Laura are simply contracting parties and a payment required by law made by one party to another seems quite remote from the welfare analogy. Besides, there is no way of knowing whether Laura is really needy at all or how seriously she will be harmed by the eviction.

Another argument Laura might offer is that her moving costs, and her higher rent, are nondeductible outlays (moving costs are deductible only in connection with changing jobs). The refund of a nondeductible outlay should not be taxable under the tax benefit rule. Of course, she receives the reimbursement here before incurring the costs, so perhaps the tax benefit rule would not apply. Moreover, the $2,500 is an arbitrary amount, not related at all to the actual moving cost or higher rent. Perhaps Laura might try, under this theory, to exclude the portion of the $2,500 that in fact is spent on moving costs and higher rent (although for what period she should measure the rent is not clear).

Still another argument Laura might offer is that the payment should be analogized to a personal injury recovery. Under the pre-section-104 case law, tort recoveries for intangible injuries, such as defamation and invasion of privacy, were not taxed, based on a dubious theory that they were a recovery of capital. Here, the law creates a sort of tort (condominium conversion) and awards arbitrary damages that are supposed to approximate the victim's losses. However, this argument is undercut by the fact that the parties' relationship seems more a function of contract than tort. In addition, Laura received the $2,500 before she had incurred the costs of moving—which is not typical of tort recoveries and which ordinarily precludes exclusion of damages either under the case law or statutory personal injury exclusions. On the other hand, the payment is made after the tort had occurred—the decision to evict the tenant and convert to condominiums—so perhaps the personal injury cases could still be used. Probably, section 104(a)(2) would be viewed as overruling the prior case law. Since Laura did not suffer a physical injury, she would not be permitted to exclude the payment under that section.

If the $2,500 is taxable to Laura, she could argue that it is taxable as long-term capital gain. A lease is a capital asset in the hands of the tenant and, if one argues that a month-to-month tenancy is the same as a lease, the $2,500 could certainly be considered an amount realized in a sale or exchange of the lease (an asset held more than one year). Section 1241 makes it clear that the amount received on cancellation of a lease is treated as a sale or exchange to the lessee. However, the month-to-month agreement falls far short of a lease—it is the antithesis of a lease—and might well not be held to be "property" under section 1221. On the other hand, the statute has conferred a sort of property-like protection on the tenancy, and so arguably has turned it into a property for capital gain purposes.

B. Rex

Rex cannot deduct the $2,500 payment. It clearly must be capitalized and added to the basis of the apartment. It is an acquisition cost of an asset held for sale. (But for the capitalization problem, the payment would be deductible as an ordinary and necessary business expense, the deductibility of which is not barred by any public policy provision.)

ANSWER TO QUESTION IV

A. Ray

If the form of the transaction is given effect, Ray would be treated as receiving the free use of the business suit by reason of his employment with Grunt, and he should include the fair rental value of the suit in income (presumably $200 of ordinary income in Year 1). Although many fringe benefits are excluded from income, this one does not seem to fit. The amount is hardly de minimis, and it is not a "working condition fringe" because the employee cannot deduct it (*see* below). Thus, section 132 is of no help. And if the $200 is includible in income, Ray has no offsetting deduction since business suits are not deductible as a business expense—only clothing not suitable for street wear can be treated as business expense.

However, the transaction probably should be recharacterized as an outright transfer of the suit to Grunt, followed by an outright transfer to Ray—not as a lease by Grunt. The economics of the transfer suggest: the suit will be worthless at the end of the "lease" term, the transaction seems peculiar (nobody leases suits, they buy them), and there is at least the possibility of tax avoidance purpose here (*i.e.*, it is a way of giving an employee immediate use of valuable property without an immediate tax or with tax spread out over the time the property is used). Thus the transaction should be treated in accordance with its true substance, not its form, as an outright transfer by Tailor to Grunt and by Grunt to Ray. In that case, Ray has income of $500.

B. Grunt

If the transaction is treated as a lease by Grunt, followed by a transfer that makes the suits available to Ray, Grunt should deduct the $200 rental it pays as ordinary and necessary business expense (or as compensation to Ray). If the transaction is treated as if Grunt purchased, rather than leased the suits (as explained above), it would have bought an asset for $500. If one assumes that Grunt continued to own the suit and made it available to Ray, the suit could be depreciated over a three-year useful life. Accelerated depreciation under ACRS would be $166.75 (0.67 rate for one-half year) in Year 1. Since Grunt is obligated to pay $600 over three years, the extra $100 should be treated as interest and deducted. It is not clear just how the $200 payment made in Year 1 should be broken down into principal and interest, but it would be logical to treat the interest as payable in equal amounts in each of the three years, in which case, Grunt gets a $33 interest deduction in Year 1.

If Grunt is treated as having purchased the suit, then transferred it outright to Ray, it would not depreciate the suit since Grunt would not own it. Instead Grunt should be treated as if it sold the suit to Ray in discharge of his claim for compensation. Since the suit has a value of $500, which is also its basis, Grunt has no gain or loss on the transfer. In addition, it should take a $500 deduction for compensation (assuming that it is reasonable compensation). (To see this more clearly, pretend that Grunt had sold the suit for cash—which would produce no gain or loss—and transferred the cash to Ray; the latter cash transfer is a payment of compensation.)

C. Tailor Corporation

Tailor Corporation would have rental income of $200 in Year 1 and would depreciate the suit over a three-year useful life. However, if the transaction is recharacterized as a sale, rather than a lease, Tailor Corporation has income of $260 in Year 1 ($500 sale price minus $240 manufacturing costs). (This assumes that Grunt's promise to pay in the future is worth its face value.) In addition, it will have interest income in an amount that matches Grunt's deduction. Tailor cannot use the installment method because it is holding the suits for sale. The income would certainly be ordinary income, as the suits were held for sale to customers in the ordinary course of Tailor's business.

ANSWER TO QUESTION V

A. Excessive Compensation

Max was entitled to Year 1 compensation of $175,000, although $24,000 was deferred. However, Turbo Corporation may deduct compensation costs only if the compensation is deemed reasonable. In this case, "reasonable compensation" may be less. Other hydraulic grunch manufacturers pay their chief executive officers only $50,000 to $100,000 per year. However, these companies may not be comparable, given that Max works long hours and has been very successful for Turbo Corporation. Additionally, under *Exacto Spring*, the test is whether an independent investor, considering the investor's return on equity, would have been willing to pay Max $175,000. Given Turbo's high profits, the answer may be yes, in which case the compensation would be deemed reasonable and Turbo would be able to deduct the compensation costs. On the other hand, under *McCandless*, Turbo has failed to pay dividends, suggesting that part of the salary must be allocated to a reasonable return on capital (and thus taxed as a dividend). The year-end bonus is particularly suspicious in this regard. If any part of the compensation was unreasonable, Turbo is denied a deduction for that part, and that part of the compensation is taxed as a dividend (ordinary income) to Max.

B. Deductibility of Bonus

Under I.R.C. section 267, Max is treated as owning 100% of the stock. Therefore, Turbo is subject to the rule denying deduction for accrued compensation until it is paid. Under that rule, the $50,000 bonus is deductible by Turbo in Year 2. Max is taxed on the $50,000 bonus in Year 2 when he receives it.

It is arguable that Max constructively received the entire bonus in Year 1, since it was immediately payable and as chief operating officer he had both the right and the power to have the check drawn immediately. If it was constructively received in Year 1, it was taxable to Max in Year 1 and Turbo can deduct it in Year 1.

C. Deferred Compensation

The unfunded deferred compensation plan is effective to delay taxation of the deferred compensation until the years in which it is paid. IRS rulings allow elective plans, provided the election is made before the year in which the work is done. Presumably the same principle would apply to a monthly deferral. Under this approach, Max would not be taxed until the money was actually received in Year 4 and Turbo cannot deduct it until it is actually paid in Year 4. [I.R.C. §404(a)(5)]

ANSWER TO QUESTION VI

A. Beth-Marc 2005

If the transfer to Marc is given effect for tax purposes, Beth does not realize her loss because a gift is not a realizing transfer. Similarly, Marc does not include the value of Whiteacre in income since a gift is excluded under I.R.C. section 102. However, it is likely that the transfer would not be given effect for tax purposes, since Beth can get it back anytime she wants and simply made the transfer to commit welfare fraud. Failure to record the transfer is very relevant to this determination. For economic purposes, she would still be considered the owner of the property; her transfer would be a sham (which is defined as a transaction in which, for practical purposes, nothing really happened). At most, the transfer would be considered to create a revocable trust, the income of which is taxed to the grantor. [I.R.C. §676]

B. Hal-Gretel 1984

The exchange of the home for Blackacre was not a nonrecognition exchange under I.R.C. section 1031 because that section requires both properties to be held for investment or business. Since the home was used for personal purposes, the exchange does not qualify. The exchange also did not qualify for rollover under the now repealed section 1034, since Blackacre was investment property, not a principal residence. Thus the sale of the home was taxable; Hal and Gretel had a capital gain of $45,000. They are treated as if they purchased Blackacre for cash. Thus its basis was $70,000.

C. Hal-Gretel 1995

Neither Hal nor his estate recognizes gain upon transferring property by reason of death, and Gretel does not include the value of inherited property. However, in the case of community property, both the decedent's and the survivor's halves are given a new basis of the value of the property at the date of death. [I.R.C. §1014(b)(6)] Consequently, Gretel's basis for Blackacre is $66,000.

D. 2006 Exchange

Here there is a clear I.R.C. section 1031 exchange of like kind property.

Gretel: Gretel has a realized loss of $26,000 on Blackacre (basis is $66,000, value is $40,000). However, she cannot recognize this loss because of section 1031. She does recognize the loss on her AT&T bond since it is not like kind property. Thus, she has a capital loss of $2,200. Her basis for Whiteacre is her old basis for all the property transferred ($66,000 + $13,200), plus cash paid out ($10,000), plus gain recognized ($0), less loss recognized ($2,200), or a total of $87,000. (*Check the answer:* If she now sold Whiteacre for its value of $61,000, she would have a recognized loss of $26,000; this is exactly the amount of the realized loss on the exchange that she previously could not deduct. Thus, $87,000 is the correct basis for Whiteacre.)

Beth: Assuming that Beth, and not Marc, is the owner of Whiteacre for tax purposes, any tax consequences should be attributed to Beth. Beth has a realized loss of $13,000 on the exchange ($74,000 basis less $61,000 value) but cannot recognize it because of I.R.C. section 1031, even though she receives boot.

Her basis for Blackacre and for the AT&T bond is her old basis ($74,000), less cash received ($10,000), or $64,000. This amount is allocated first to the AT&T bond in its fair market value ($11,000); the balance is allocated to Blackacre ($53,000). (*Check the result:* If Blackacre is now sold for its value of $40,000, she will have a $13,000 recognized loss—exactly the amount she was not allowed to recognize on the exchange.)

ANSWER TO QUESTION VII

The amount realized on the sale is $29,200—assumption of liabilities is the same as receiving cash. It is necessary to break down the transaction asset-by-asset; a business is not treated as a single unit for tax purposes.

The sale of the lease produces $5,000 of gain under I.R.C. section 1231 (since it is real property used in a trade or business). The furniture produces $3,200 of ordinary income because of depreciation recapture. The trucks produce $7,000 of section 1231 loss. (They are depreciable property used in business, and there is no depreciation recapture when property is sold at a loss.) The goodwill produces a long-term capital gain of $8,000 (goodwill is not a section 1231 asset since it is not subject to depreciation under section 167—although it is depreciable in Paul's hands under section 197).

Thus, taxable income is $39,200: Add to $30,000 taxable income, the ordinary income ($3,200) and the gains ($13,000); subtract the loss ($7,000). The sum is $39,200. Since section 1231 losses exceed gains, both section 1231 transactions are ordinary and the loss is fully deductible.

ANSWER TO QUESTION VIII

A. Sam

Purchase: Sam's realized gain is $90,000 (amount realized, which includes both the note to Coast and to himself, of $150,000; basis of $60,000). To avoid recognizing all of the gain, he will probably choose to use the installment method of taxation. (He must use that method unless he affirmatively elects out of it.) Under the installment method, he must include the excess of the Coast note ($100,000) over his basis ($60,000) in both the payments and the total contract price. The total contract price therefore is $40,000 (excess of Coast note over basis) + cash received ($20,000) + note received ($30,000) or $90,000. The gross profit is also $90,000. Thus, 100% of payments received are taxable. In Year 2, he receives $20,000 in cash and $40,000 representing excess of mortgage over basis, or a total of $60,000. Consequently, Sam has long-term capital gain of $60,000. He has no depreciation recapture under section 1250 since he used straight-line depreciation. Because Sam does not have $5 million in installment sales during Year 2, he does not pay interest on the deferred tax. Note that Sam's capital gain is taxed at a rate of 25% (compared with the usual rate of 20%) to the extent of depreciation taken on the property ($50,000). The balance of his gain ($40,000) would be taxed at a rate of 20%.

B. Tina's Prepaid Rent in Year 1

When Tina prepaid $12,000 in rent to Sam in Year 1, Sam had to take the entire amount into income. However, when Sam repays the $6,000 unearned portion to Bill, he is entitled to deduct $6,000. He should not, however, be required to reduce the sale price by $6,000 (which would have the effect of denying him a deduction but reducing his capital gain on the sale). The rent item is logically separate from the purchase of the building and should be accounted for separately.

The amount was taken into income on the theory that Sam would retain it. When he has to transfer it to a buyer of the building, he no longer has that use, and a deduction under either I.R.C. section 162 or section 165 is appropriate.

Compare, for example, the treatment of amounts received under claim of right that must later be repaid; the payor can deduct the repayment. It seems unlikely, however, that Sam can take advantage of section 1341 on the repayment since it was never established that he did not have an "unrestricted right" to such item. [I.R.C. §1341(a)(2)]

Bill should take the $6,000 received from Sam into income as prepaid rent. He should not treat it as a reduction in his purchase price. From his point of view, it is just rental received.

C. Tina's Prepaid Rent for Years 3 and 4

The issue is whether Bill constructively received $12,000 in prepaid rent on December 31 of Year 2 from Tina. Although he did "turn his back" on income, it could be strongly argued that the constructive receipt doctrine is not applicable. This situation is akin to deferred compensation in which an employer is willing to pay an employee immediately but the employee insists on a contract deferring the amount. The employee is not currently taxed. [Rev. Rul. 60-31] Here, until a new lease is signed, Bill has no right to any money from Tina and no agreement has yet been signed. Notwithstanding Tina's willingness to prepay rent immediately, it is likely that Bill has successfully deferred the income until Year 3.

D. Interest Payments

Bill can deduct the $10,000 in interest paid to Coast but not the $2,000 in principal. As to the interest due to Sam, Bill cannot deduct it. Giving a note—even a negotiable one—is not considered a payment by a cash basis taxpayer. However, Sam must include in income the fair market value of the note. A secured promissory note is the equivalent of cash; so Sam has interest income of $5,000 upon receipt of this note. Sam has additional income in Year 3 of $400 when the note is paid (plus interest income on the note).

ANSWER TO QUESTION IX

A. Rick—Basis

Rick bought the bike for $1,000. If the bike was an asset used in his trade or business, he can claim depreciation. Under ACRS, presumably the bike is five-year property (since its useful life is seven years). Thus if Rick used straight-line depreciation, he could claim $100 of depreciation in both Year 1 and Year 2 (half-year convention for year of acquisition and disposition).

However, it is unlikely that the bike would be treated as a depreciable asset because it is unlikely that bike racing would be considered Rick's trade or business. Rick has never come close to making any money at it. The problem specifies that he uses the bike partly for pleasure. Under section 183, the test is whether there was a significant profit motivation. Based on the facts given us, which should be analyzed carefully under the section 183 regulations, it would probably be found that Rick had no such intention. Consequently, he cannot depreciate the bike and its basis remains $1,000.

B. Theft Deduction

When the bike is stolen, Rick can deduct its adjusted basis ($1,000) or its fair market value ($1,400), whichever is less, as a casualty loss. He must reduce this amount by an additional $100 and by 10% of AGI (or $600). (If the bike were a business asset, he would not reduce it by $100 or 10% of AGI.) Thus, Rick would have had a $300 casualty loss deduction in Year 2 but does not because his itemized deductions are less than the standard deduction. If the bike is considered a business asset, Rick would have an above-the-line loss deduction equal to the adjusted basis of the bike (probably $800). He could deduct this item in addition to the standard deduction.

C. Theft Income

When Ellen steals the bike, she has income of $1,400, despite the obligation to return the bike. *James* has firmly established the taxability of stolen goods. (Her basis for the bike is $1,400.)

D. Return of the Bike

When Ellen returns the bike in Year 3, she should deduct the amount previously included in income. It is not likely that she can deduct $1,600 (the value of the bike at the date of return). Because essentially accounting adjustments are involved, it would seem more reasonable to allow a deduction that simply offsets the earlier income item. However, she cannot use section 1341 for the repayment since it never "appeared that the taxpayer had an unrestricted right to such item" as required by section 1341(a) and also the amount is less than $3,000. Another approach would be to treat the return as a realization of $1,600, producing $200 of short-term capital gain and a $1,600 loss, which would be a nondeductible personal loss.

Rick would ordinarily have to include $300 in income; under the tax benefit rule, when an item previously deducted has been returned, it produces income. The measure of the income is the amount deducted, not the value of the bike at the time it is returned. However, Rick received no tax benefit from the deduction in Year 2, so would not include anything in income in Year 3. [I.R.C. §111] If Rick had been entitled to treat the theft as a business loss of $800, which would have produced a tax benefit, he would be required to include $800 in income in Year 3.

E. Ellen's Attorneys' Fees

These might be deductible under section 212(1). Under *Gilmore,* the fact that she paid the costs to keep her job is irrelevant. She is not in the trade or business of bike theft, so she cannot deduct them under section 162. However, the theft was a profit-seeking transaction so the origin of the later criminal case was an attempt to produce income, which would make the legal fees deductible under section 212. No public policy rule bars deduction of attorneys' fees.

Tables of Citations

CITATIONS TO INTERNAL REVENUE CODE (I.R.C.)

I.R.C.	Text Reference	I.R.C.	Text Reference	I.R.C.	Text Reference
1	§§694, 945	56(a)(1)	§951	71(b)(1)(C)	§165
1(a)	§695	56(b)(1)(A)(i)	§952	71(b)(1)(D)	§166
1(b)	§695	56(b)(1)(A)(ii)	§953	71(b)(2)	§163
1(c)	§695	56(b)(1)(B)	§950	71(c)	§535
1(d)	§§237, 695	56(b)(1)(C)	§955	71(c)(1)	§169
1(f)	§695	56(b)(1)(E)	§954	71(c)(2)	§170
1(f)(8)	§234	56(b)(1)(F)	§954	72	§68
1(g)	§224	57	§956	72(b)(3)	§71
1(h)	§822	57(a)(7)	§921	73	§220
1(h)(4)(A)	§825	57(a)(8)	§489	73(b)	§222
1(h)(6)	§823	57(a)(11)	§491	74(a)	§50
1(h)(11)	§824	61	§§9, 27	74(b)	§51
1(h)(11)(D)(i)	§608	62	§§297, 554	74(c)	§52
1(i)	§695	62(a)(1)	§555	79	§123
2	§227	62(a)(2)(A)	§555	82	§§121, 329
2(b)	§238	62(a)(2)(B)	§555	83	§§975, 983, 996
2(c)	§238	62(a)(2)(D)	§555	83(a)	§§42, 991
21	§704	62(a)(3)	§555	83(b)	§990
21(b)	§705	62(a)(4)	§§440, 555	83(c)(3)	§989
21(c)	§709	62(a)(5)	§555	83(d)	§986
21(d)(2)	§710	62(a)(7)	§690	83(e)(3)	§42
21(e)(5)	§711	62(a)(10)	§§162, 555, 689	83(h)	§§985, 991
21(e)(9)	§707	62(a)(17)	§§555, 600	84	§199
22	§§699, 700, 701	62(a)(19)	§97	85	§83
23	§721	62(b)	§555	86	§79
24	§712	63	§566	86(d)(1)(A)	§79
24(b)	§713	63(c)(2)(A)	§§234, 568	101(a)	§§58, 59
24(c)(1)	§714	63(c)(3)	§569	101(a)(2)	§65
24(d)	§716	63(c)(4)	§567	101(c)	§67
24(h)	§721	63(c)(5)	§570	101(d)	§67
25A	§722	63(f)	§569	101(g)	§62
27	§698	67	§§297, 321, 341, 440, 562	102	§§34, 186, 337
31	§697			102(a)	§28
32	§§132, 718	67(b)	§952	102(b)(1)	§47
38(b)	§703	68	§§565, 954	102(b)(2)	§§48, 749
44F	§401	68(f)(2)	§565	102(c)	§§31, 33, 34, 36, 45
51	§703	71	§§268, 689	103	§75
55	§945	71(a)	§162	103(b)	§77
55(b)(3)	§948	71(b)(1)(B)	§164	103(b)(1)	§75
55(d)(3)	§947			104(a)	§91

I.R.C.	Text Reference	I.R.C.	Text Reference	I.R.C.	Text Reference
104(a)(2)	§§89, 93, 94, 96, 97, 99, 601	132(h)(5)	§122	166(a)(2)	§528
		132(m)	§122	166(d)	§529
104(a)(3)	§84	135	§129	167	§§450, 883
105(a)	§88	141	§75	167(a)(1)	§297
105(c)	§87	151(c)	§668	167(a)(2)	§297
105(d)	§86	151(d)(3)	§674	167(c)(2)	§460
105(g)	§86	151(d)(3)(E)	§674	167(f)	§457
106	§86	152(a)	§668	167(g)	§457
107	§131	152(b)(5)	§668	167(h)	§§463, 464
108(a)	§143	152(c)	§§670, 714	168	§450
108(a)(1)(D)	§146	152(c)(3)	§715	168(a)(3)(C)	§471
108(b)	§145	152(e)(1)	§672	168(a)(5)	§471
108(c)	§146	152(e)(2)	§673	168(b)	§469
108(d)(3)	§143	162	§§296, 297, 337, 340, 424, 431, 438, 439, 440, 490, 519, 1080	168(d)	§470
108(e)(2)	§147			168(d)(2)	§476
108(e)(5)	§155			168(d)(3)	§470
108(e)(6)	§154	162(a)	§§318, 616	168(d)(4)(B)	§476
108(f)(1)	§149	162(a)(1)	§415	168(e)(3)(A)	§465
108(f)(2)	§149	162(a)(3)	§386	168(i)(6)	§460
109	§§127, 758	162(c)(1)	§425	168(i)(14)	§465
111	§§537, 870	162(c)(2)	§426	168(k)	§472
111(a)	§1079	162(c)(3)	§427	170(a)(3)	§627
111(c)	§1083	162(e)	§434	170(b)(1)	§619
112	§132	162(e)(2)	§433	170(b)(1)(D)	§630
117	§53	162(f)	§§431, 519	170(b)(2)	§620
117(b)	§54	162(g)	§436	170(c)	§618
117(c)	§54	162(l)	§666	170(d)	§619
117(d)	§55	162(m)	§423	170(e)(1)(A)	§§635, 827
118(a)	§56	163	§579	170(e)(1)(B)(i)	§632
118(b)	§57	163(d)	§607	170(e)(1)(B)(ii)	§633
119	§114	163(d)(4)(B)	§608	170(e)(1)(B)(iii)	§634
119(a)	§107	163(h)	§244	170(e)(2)	§641
119(b)(3)	§113	163(h)(3)	§592	170(e)(3)	§637
119(b)(4)	§111	163(h)(3)(B)	§593	170(e)(4)	§637
121	§§810, 812	163(h)(4)	§592	170(e)(5)	§632
121(a)	§811	163(h)(4)(A)	§595	170(f)(2)	§626
121(b)(2)	§813	163(h)(4)(C)	§594	170(f)(2)(B)	§628
121(b)(3)	§812	164	§612	170(f)(3)	§647
121(d)(1)	§813	164(b)	§617	170(f)(8)	§623
121(d)(3)(A)	§814	164(b)(5)	§615	170(f)(11)	§638
121(d)(3)(B)	§815	164(d)	§613	170(f)(12)	§639
121(d)(10)	§811	165	§§493, 519	170(i)	§645
123	§128	165(c)	§941	170(j)	§652
131	§133	165(c)(1)	§§297, 497, 676	170(l)	§649
132	§§115, 122	165(c)(2)	§§297, 498, 676	172	§1085
132(b)	§116	165(c)(3)	§676	172(d)(4)	§297
132(c)	§§42, 117	165(d)	§§160, 298, 501	174	§§401, 494
132(d)	§118	165(e)	§510	179	§§477, 480, 481
132(e)	§120	165(h)(1)	§676	182	§906
132(f)	§119	165(h)(2)(A)	§§687, 890	183	§§319, 323, 454, 906
132(f)(4)	§119	165(h)(2)(B)	§§686, 890	183(b)	§321
132(g)	§§121, 329	165(h)(4)	§685	183(d)	§320
132(h)(1)	§117	165(i)	§510	186	§101
132(h)(2)	§122	166(a)	§528	195	§§392, 393, 394, 400

I.R.C.	Text Reference	I.R.C.	Text Reference	I.R.C.	Text Reference
195(c)(1)	§395	267(b)(4)	§514	404	§977
197	§§405, 456, 457, 473, 474, 475, 875, 883	267(b)(6)	§514	404(a)(3)	§981
		267(b)(7)	§514	404(a)(5)	§971
198	§§378, 379	267(b)(9)	§514	405	§977
212	§§300, 340, 341, 354, 437, 438, 440, 441, 442, 490, 555, 616	267(c)(4)	§§514, 1045	406	§977
		267(d)	§516	407	§977
		267(e)	§1046	408(m)	§825
212(1)	§§97, 297, 448	273	§749	408A	§692
212(2)	§297	274	§35	410	§980
212(3)	§§341, 449	274(a)	§331	415	§981
213	§§653, 654	274(a)(1)(B)	§333	422	§998
213(a)	§665	274(a)(2)(A)	§333	442	§1074
213(b)	§654	274(a)(3)	§333	443(i)	§1074
213(d)(1)(A)	§654	274(b)	§337	446	§958
213(d)(1)(B)	§654	274(b)(1)	§37	446(b)	§958
213(d)(1)(C)	§658	274(d)	§334	446(c)	§958
213(d)(2)	§§654, 656	274(h)	§312	447	§1011
213(d)(3)	§653	274(h)(7)	§442	448	§1017
213(d)(9)	§654	274(j)	§52	448(b)(1)	§1017
213(e)(1)(C)	§654	274(k)	§335	448(b)(3)	§1017
213(e)(2)	§654	274(m)(2)	§311	448(c)	§1017
215	§§162, 689	274(m)(3)	§313	448(d)(1)	§1017
217	§§325, 555	274(n)	§§304, 317, 331, 335	448(d)(2)	§1017
217(b)	§328	275	§617	448(d)(3)	§1017
217(c)	§326	278	§1011	453	§§1055, 1068
217(c)(2)	§327	279	§609	453(b)(1)	§1063
217(d)	§327	280A	§§347, 356	453(b)(2)	§1063
219(b)(5)	§690	280A(c)(1)	§§309, 348, 351, 353	453(d)	§1056
219(f)(1)	§690	280A(c)(2)	§352	453(e)	§1062
219(g)	§691	280A(c)(4)	§352	453(f)(1)	§1062
221	§596	280A(c)(5)	§§355, 362	453(f)(4)	§1061
223	§663	280A(d)	§358	453(f)(5)	§1061
248	§400	280A(d)(1)	§595	453(i)	§1059
262	§§302, 941	280A(d)(3)	§§359, 360	453(j)	§1060
263	§365	280A(e)	§361	453A	§§1064, 1067
263(c)	§491	280A(g)	§363	453A(b)(2)	§1065
263A	§§380, 383, 384, 385, 386	280B	§502	453B(a)	§1070
		280E	§428	453B(c)	§1071
263A(b)(2)	§384	280F	§478	453B(g)	§1072
263A(f)	§382	280F(a)	§480	454	§129
263A(h)	§385	280F(b)	§479	455	§1025
264	§577	280F(c)	§386	456	§1025
264(a)(1)	§345	280F(d)(3)	§481	461(f)	§1034
264(a)(2)	§603	336	§1080	461(g)	§§605, 1010
264(a)(3)	§603	341	§880	461(g)(2)	§§606, 1010
264(c)	§603	351(d)	§153	461(h)	§1036
265(a)(1)	§601	401	§977	461(h)(2)	§1041
265(a)(2)	§602	401(a)(4)	§980	461(h)(2)(A)	§1039
267	§§511, 513, 514, 516, 518, 940	401(a)(5)	§980	461(h)(2)(B)	§1040
		402	§977	461(h)(2)(C)	§§99, 1041
267(a)(2)	§1044	402(a)	§977	461(h)(3)	§1042
267(b)	§§801, 1045	402(a)(1)	§74	461(h)(4)	§1033
267(b)(1)	§1045	402(b)(1)	§975	461(i)(3)	§1017
267(b)(2)	§§514, 802, 1045	403	§977	464	§1011

I.R.C.	Text Reference	I.R.C.	Text Reference	I.R.C.	Text Reference
465	§§452, 541, 944	672(e)	§253	1015(d)(6)	§738
465(a)	§538	673	§253	1016	§755
465(b)	§539	674	§§254, 255	1016(a)(2)(B)	§757
465(c)	§540	674(b)	§259	1017	§145
467	§1030	674(b)(3)	§259	1019	§§127, 758
467(b)	§1032	674(b)(5)	§259	1022	§741
467(b)(1)(A)	§1031	674(b)(6)	§259	1031	§§495, 789, 790, 793,
467(e)(1)	§1032	674(b)(7)	§259		796, 808, 809, 811, 938
469	§§451, 543, 610, 943	674(c)	§257	1031(a)	§786
469(c)(7)	§550	674(d)	§258	1031(a)(3)	§792
472	§1052	675	§269	1031(b)	§796
472(c)	§1052	675(1)	§270	1031(c)	§796
475(a)	§839	675(2)	§271	1031(d)	§798
475(d)(3)	§839	675(3)	§272	1031(f)(1)	§801
475(f)	§840	675(4)	§276	1031(f)(2)	§802
482	§§206, 207, 208	676	§260	1031(h)	§787
483	§§25, 248, 588, 923, 924,	677	§261	1032	§56
	925, 927, 929, 930, 1058	677(a)(1)	§268	1033	§§804, 806, 807,
483(d)(2)	§930	677(a)(3)	§265		808, 809, 889, 938
483(e)	§931	678	§277	1033(a)	§805
501	§171	678(b)	§277	1033(g)	§809
501(c)(3)	§§171, 173	678(c)	§277	1034	§810
501(c)(4)	§174	678(d)	§277	1038	§820
501(c)(5)	§174	682	§§168, 268	1041	§§66, 511, 512, 518,
501(c)(6)	§174	691	§751		814, 816, 817, 819
508(e)	§179	691(a)(4)	§1071	1041(a)(1)	§40
509	§179	691(a)(5)	§1071	1041(b)(2)	§818
511	§176	691(c)	§754	1041(c)	§819
514	§§178, 913	704(e)	§§216, 218, 219	1060	§877
527	§180	704(e)(2)	§217	1091	§§517, 518, 942
530	§693	706(b)(1)(B)	§1074	1202(a)	§918
611	§§483, 486	741	§880	1202(b)(1)	§919
612	§486	751	§880	1202(c)	§920
613	§487	901	§698	1202(d)	§920
613(b)	§487	902	§698	1202(e)	§920
613(A)	§488	903	§698	1211	§555
615	§492	904	§698	1211(b)	§826
616	§492	905	§698	1212	§826
642(b)	§288	911	§§125, 225	1221	§§829, 830, 868
642(c)	§621	911(c)	§125	1221(a)(1)	§§831, 835, 837,
643(a)	§280	1001	§762		848
651(a)	§281	1001(b)	§769	1221(a)(2)	§881
652(a)	§282	1001(c)	§784	1221(a)(3)	§846
662(a)(1)	§284	1001(e)	§857	1221(a)(4)	§844
662(a)(2)	§285	1001(e)(2)	§747	1221(a)(7)	§§841, 843
663(a)	§286	1001(e)(3)	§748	1221(a)(8)	§881
665	§290	1002	§784	1221(b)(2)	§841
666	§290	1012	§§728, 729	1221(b)(3)	§846
667	§§290, 291	1013	§728	1222(11)	§822
668	§290	1014	§§728, 740, 741, 751	1231	§§845, 881, 882, 884,
669	§290	1014(b)(6)	§743		885, 886, 887, 888, 889,
671	§§250, 251	1014(b)(9)	§745		890, 891, 892, 895,
672(a)	§255	1014(c)	§751		910, 936, 1059
672(b)	§255	1015	§§728, 737	1231(a)(4)C)	§888

I.R.C.	Text Reference	I.R.C.	Text Reference	I.R.C.	Text Reference
1231(b)	§884	1271(a)(1)	§907	6013(d)	§235
1231(c)	§887	1271(b)(1)	§907	6015(b)	§236
1234	§§850, 852, 902	1272	§909	6015(c)	§236
1234(A)	§902	1273	§909	6015(d)	§236
1235	§849	1274	§§25, 248, 588, 909,	6115	§651
1235(a)	§849		923, 924, 925, 927,	6201(c)	§221
1235(d)	§849		928, 1058	6315	§697
1237	§836	1274(c)(3)	§925	6511(d)(1)	§526
1239	§§893, 895	1275	§909	6661(b)(2)(C)(ii)	§1017
1241	§902	1275(b)	§932	6714	§651
1245	§§482, 936, 1059	1286	§192	7701(g)	§773
1245(a)	§935	1341	§§421, 1001, 1076,	7702B	§658
1245(a)(1)	§936		1077	7702B(c)	§62
1245(a)(2)	§936	1378	§1074	7703(b)	§238
1245(b)	§938	2040	§745	7872	§§25, 239, 240, 241,
1250	§§937, 1059	4940	§179		242, 243, 245, 248, 587
1250(d)	§938	4941	§179	7872(a)	§§244, 246
1253(a)	§899	4942	§179	7872(b)	§247
1253(e)	§900	4943	§179	7872(c)	§240
1254	§491	4944	§179	7872(c)(2)	§241
1256(b)(3)(B)	§1017	4945	§179	7872(c)(3)	§241
1271	§908	6013	§227	7872(d)	§241

CITATIONS TO REVENUE RULINGS

Rev. Rul.	Text Reference	Rev. Rul.	Text Reference	Rev. Rul.	Text Reference
53-162	§643	71-425	§82	82-94	§575
56-531	§861	73-529	§315	82-149	§429
57-418	§396	74-22	§18	82-166	§788
60-31	§969	74-23	§18	89-23	§383
64-328	§346	74-77	§95	89-68	§341
65-57	§59	74-323	§426	90-16	§777
65-261	§868	75-120	§398	92-99	§155
66-7	§916	75-380	§310	93-86	§318
66-167	§46	75-432	§314	94-12	§376
67-297	§584	76-75	§573	94-38	§379
69-188	§585	78-38	§1013	99-7	§309
69-650	§970	78-39	§1013	99-23	§394
70-45	§875	79-24	§26		
70-54	§61	79-220	§99		

Table of Cases

Hughes Properties, Inc., United States v. - **§1036**

Hutchinson Baseball Enterprises, Inc. v. Commissioner - **§172**

Hyplains Dressed Beef Inc. v. Commissioner - **§1045**

I

Idaho Power Co., Commissioner v. - **§§383, 662**

Inaja Land Co. v. Commissioner - **§759**

Indianapolis Power & Light Co., Commissioner v. - **§1003**

INDOPCO, Inc. v. Commissioner - **§§369, 370, 371, 372, 374, 376, 400**

International Shoe Machinery Co. v. United States - **§885**

Irwin v. Gavit - **§48**

J

Jacob v. United States - **§109**

Jacobson, Commissioner v. - **§148**

James v. United States - **§§158, 159, 1000**

Johnson v. Commissioner - **§765**

Johnson & Son, Inc. v. Commissioner - **§189**

Jordan Marsh Co. v. Commissioner - **§795**

K

Kaiser, United States v. - **§39**

Kem v. Commissioner - **§460**

Kenseth v. Commissioner - **§952**

King v. Commissioner - **§673**

Kinney v. Commissioner - **§442**

Kinsey v. Commissioner - **§198**

Kirby Lumber Co., United States v. - **§142**

Klamath Medical Service Bureau v. Commissioner - **§420**

Knetsch v. United States - **§§576, 577, 578, 579, 580**

Kornhauser v. United States - **§303**

Kowalski, Commissioner v. - **§§111, 114**

L

Larchfield Corp. v. United States - **§444**

Lark Sales Co. v. Commissioner - **§444**

Latham Park Manor, Inc. v. Commissioner - **§207**

Lavery v. Commissioner - **§964**

Leslie Co. v. Commissioner - **§§495, 795**

Lester, Commissioner v. - **§170**

Lewis, United States v. - **§§1000, 1075**

Liant Record Inc. v. Commissioner - **§808**

Liddle v. Commissioner - **§458**

Lilly v. Commissioner - **§430**

Linde, Commissioner v. - **§751**

Lindeman v. Commissioner - **§108**

LoBue, Commissioner v. - **§§42, 993**

Loewi v. Ryan - **§527**

Lovejoy v. Commissioner - **§584**

Lucas v. Earl - **§§201, 228**

Lutter v. Commissioner- **§669**

Lyeth v. Hoey - **§44**

M

McAllister v. Commissioner - **§§747, 857**

McCandless Tire Service v. United States - **§422**

McDonald v. Commissioner (1944) - **§399**

McDonald v. Commissioner (1928) - **§95**

McFall v. Commissioner - **§864**

McWilliams v. Commissioner - **§515**

Maginnis, United States v. - **§855**

Malat v. Riddell - **§835**

Mallinckrodt v. Nunan - **§277**

Maloney v. Spencer - **§532**

Markey v. Commissioner - **§316**

Matz v. Commissioner - **§904**

Mayerson v. Commissioner - **§733**

Mazzei v. Commissioner - **§519**

Merchants National Bank v. Commissioner - **§870**

Merians v. Commissioner - **§341**

Merriam, United States v. - **§46**

Merritt v. Commissioner - **§515**

Midland Empire Packing Co. v. Commissioner - **§379**

Miller v. Commissioner (2000) - **§673**

Miller v. Commissioner (1962) - **§868**

Minor v. United States - **§§974, 975**

Minzer, Commissioner v. - **§24**

Moller v. United States - **§§354, 438, 840**

Mooney Aircraft Inc. v. United States - **§1037**

Moritz v. Commissioner - **§6**

Morrill v. United States - **§262**

Moss v. Commissioner - **§336**

Murphy v. United States - **§§7, 96**

Muse v. Commissioner - **§327**

N

Nahey v. Commissioner - **§907**

Newark Morning Ledger Co. v. United States - **§§456, 473**

Nichols v. Commissioner - **§399**

Nickerson v. Commissioner - **§319**

Nor-Cal Adjusters v. Commissioner - **§§416, 422**

North American Oil Consolidated v. Burnet - **§§999, 1000**

O

Ochs v. Commissioner - **§659**

O'Daniel's Estate v. Commissioner - **§751**

O'Gilvie v. Commissioner - **§93**

Old Colony Trust Co. v. Commissioner - **§136**

Olk v. United States - **§38**

Oswald v. Commissioner - **§421**

Ottawa Silica Co. v. United States - **§648**

PQ

P.G. Lake, Commissioner v. - **§§195, 855**

Paine v. Commissioner - **§681**

Palmer v. Bender - **§485**

Parker v. Delaney - **§767**

Patton v. Commissioner - **§416**

Penn Mutual Indemnity Co. v. Commissioner - **§7**

Pepper v. Commissioner - **§412**

Peterson, Commissioner v. - **§751**

Peurifoy v. Commissioner- **§318**

Pevsner v. Commissioner - **§364**

Philadelphia Park Amusement Co. v. United States - **§780**

Phillips, Commissioner v. - **§867**

Pittston Co., Commissioner v. - **§901**

Pleasant Summit Land Corp. v. Commissioner - **§§578, 732**

PNC Bancorp, Inc. v. Commissioner - **§§373, 374**

Poe v. Seaborn - **§§228, 231**

Pohoski v. Commissioner - **§551**

Poirier & McLane Corp. v. Commissioner - **§1034**

Pollock v. Farmers Loan & Trust Co. - **§2**

Popov v. Commissioner - **§350**

Pounds v. United States - **§864**

Poyner v. Commissioner - **§36**

Preslar v. Commissioner - **§155**

Prosman v. Commissioner - **§952**

Pulvers v. Commissioner- **§680**

Putnam v. Commissioner - **§523**

R

Ranciato v. Commissioner - **§320**

Raymond Bertolini Trucking Co. v. Commissioner - **§414**

Raytheon Production Corp. v. Commissioner - **§100**

Reporter Publishing v. Commissioner - **§505**

Riach v. Frank - **§661**

Richmond Television Corp. v. United States - **§392**

Roberts v. Commissioner - **§38**

Robinson v. Commissioner- **§969**

Rochelle, United States v. - **§158**

Rogers v. United States - **§418**

Rose v. Commissioner - **§§301, 322, 323, 454, 580**

Rosenspan v. United States - **§314**

Ross v. Commissioner - **§968**

Rozpad v. Commissioner - **§89**

Rubin v. Commissioner - **§208**

Rudolph v. United States - **§137**

S

Saia Electric Inc. v. Commissioner - **§421**

Sakol v. Commissioner - **§988**

Sanders v. Commissioner - **§307**

Schlude v. Commissioner - **§1024**

Schuster v. Commissioner - **§204**

Sharon v. Commissioner - **§§342, 402**

Skelly Oil Co., United States v. - **§1078**

Sklar v. Commissioner - **§648**

Smith v. Commissioner - **§704**

Smith, Estate of v. Commissioner - **§188**

Smyth v. Barneson - **§522**

Snow v. Commissioner - **§401**

Sobel Liquors, Inc. v. Commissioner - **§429**

Soliman, Commissioner v. - **§§350, 351**

South Carolina v. Baker - **§76**

Southern Pacific Transportation Co. v. Commissioner - **§433**

Southwest Exploration, Commissioner v. - **§485**

Stanton v. United States - **§§33, 34**

Starker v. United States - **§§791, 792**

Starr's Estate v. Commissioner - **§389**

Stephens v. Commissioner - **§§431, 519**

Stidger, Commissioner v. - **§314**

Stranahan's Estate v. Commissioner - **§855**

Strauss v. Commissioner - **§205**

Sullivan, Commissioner v. - **§§299, 430**

Sunnen, Commissioner v. - **§211**

Surasky v. United States - **§441**

T

Tank Truck Rentals, Inc. v. Commissioner - **§432**

Tellier, Commissioner v. - **§§413, 431**

Teschner v. Commissioner - **§203**

Thor Power Tool Co. v. Commissioner - **§§510, 1051**

Toavis v. Commissioner - **§131**

Trujillo v. Commissioner - **§614**

Tufts, Commissioner v. - **§§730, 773, 776**

U

U.S. Freightways Corp. v. Commissioner - **§§407, 1009**

United States v. - *see name of party*

United States Steel Corp. v. United States - **§150**

University Properties, Inc. v. Commissioner - **§387**

Unvert v. Commissioner - **§1081**

V

Van Cleave v. United States - **§1076**

Van Suetendael v. Commissioner - **§837**

Van Zandt v. Commissioner - **§213**

Varied Investments Inc. v. United States - **§1034**

Veit v. Commissioner - **§970**

Venture Funding Ltd. v. Commissioner - **§985**

WX

Waddell v. Commissioner - **§§453, 539**

Index

Subject	I.R.C. Section	Text Section
goodwill, acquiring	197	§§404-406
lease vs. sale of equipment		§§388-390
legal fees, organization of business	195; 248	§§400, 445
litigation costs related to property		§§443-445
patents, copyrights, trademarks, purchase of	174	§401
property produced or sold	263A	§§380-385
qualified creative expense exception	263(A)(h)	§385
rental prepayments		§387
search for business, successful	195	§§393-394

CAPITAL GAINS AND LOSSES

Subject	I.R.C. Section	Text Section
alternative minimum tax	55; 56; 57	§948
business interests, sale of	197; 341; 741; 751; 1060	§§873-880
capital assets, defined	1221	§829
capital loss, deduction of	1211(b); 1212	§826
charitable contributions	170(e)(1)(A)	§827
collectibles	1(h)(4)(A); 408(m)	§825
contract rights, sale of		§§858-867
depreciable property used in trade or business. *See also* Quasi-capital assets	167; 1221(a)(2); 1231	§§845, 881-883
dividends	1(h)(11)	§824
gift to political organization	84	§199
goodwill, sale of	197; 1060	§§875, 877, 883
holding period of capital assets, determination of	1(h); 1222	§§822, 915-917
involuntary conversions	1033; 1231	§§803-809, 910
life estates, sale of		§857
long-term gains, defined		§§915-916
noncapital gains or losses, sale or exchange of		
personal services		§§864-865
right to income		§§854-857
options	1234	§§850-852
patents	1235	§849
real property subdivided and sold exception	1237	§836
real property used in trade or business	167; 1221(a)(2); 1231	§§845, 881-883
sale or exchange, requirement of. *See also* "Sale or exchange" of capital asset		§§896-914
sales of real estate	1(h)(6)	§823
short-term gains, defined		§915
small business stock	57(a)(7); 1202(a)-(e)	§§918-921
special computations		
disallowed losses. *See also* Losses, nondeductible	165(c); 262; 267; 465; 469; 1091	§§939-944
imputed interest	483; 1274	§§923-932
recapture of depreciation	1245; 1250	§§933-938
tax rates	1(h); 408(m); 1211(b); 1212; 1222	§§821-826

CASH BASIS

Subject	I.R.C. Section	Text Section
		§§959-1013
cash equivalents		§§960-962
promissory note or deferred payment		§962
stock or property as compensation	83; 422	§§961, 983-998
claim of right doctrine	1341	§§999-1001
repayment in later year. *See also* Annual accounting periods	1341	§§1075-1078
constructive receipt doctrine	402; 404	§§963-976
deferred compensation	402; 404	§§969-976
interest not withdrawn		§965

Subject	I.R.C. Section	Text Section
CONSTRUCTIVE RECEIPT DOCTRINE	402; 404	§§963-976
See also Cash basis		
CONTRIBUTIONS		
See Charitable contributions		
CORPORATIONS		
accrual method	448	§1017
charitable deduction by	170(b)(2)	§620
sale of		§§878-880
CREDITS AGAINST TAX		
adoption credit	23	§721
child care expense credit. *See also* Child care expenses,		
credit for	21	§§704-711
child tax credit	24	§§712-717
"child" defined	24(c)(1); 152(c)	§§714-715
disabled child	152(c)(3)	§715
divorced parents		§717
phaseouts	24(b)	§713
refundable	24(d)	§716
deductions, distinguished from		§292
defined		§§292, 696
disabled persons	22; 152(c)(3)	§§702, 715
earned income credit	32	§§718-720
education credits		§§722-725
HOPE scholarship credit	25A	§§723-724
lifetime learning credit	25A	§724
phaseouts		§725
elderly	22	§§699-701
foreign tax credit	27; 901-905	§698
taxes withheld and prepaid	31; 6315	§697
work incentive credit	38(b); 51	§703

D

Subject	I.R.C. Section	Text Section
DAMAGES		
See Exclusions from gross income; damage payments		
DEDUCTIONS		
adjusted gross income		§§554-565
"above the line" deductions	62(a)	§555
"below the line" deductions		§§556-561
defined	62	§554
itemized deductions		§§562-565
phaseout	68	§565
alimony	71; 62(a)(10); 215	§689
alternative minimum tax and	56(a)(1), (b)(1)	§§949-955
bad debts. *See* Bad debts		
business and investment expenses. *See also* Expenses	162; 212	§§296-551
casualty and theft loses. *See* Losses	165(c), (h)	§§676-687
charitable contributions. *See also* Charitable contributions		§§618-652
credits, distinguished from		§292
defined		§292
dependents	63(c)(5)	§570

Subject	I.R.C. Section	Text Section
nondeductible	164(b); 275	§617
property taxes	164(d)	§613
two percent floor	67	§§561-562, 564
DEFERRED COMPENSATION	402(b); 404(a)(5)	§§969-976
DEPENDENT		
defined	151-152	§668
divorced parents, agreement concerning	152(e)	§§672-673
exemption for. *See also* Exemptions	151-152	§§668-673
DEPLETION		
by whom deductible		§485
cost method	611-612	§486
deduction for wasting asset	611	§483
depletable property		§484
drilling costs	263(c); 615-616	§§480-492
mineral deposits	615-616	§492
percentage method	613	§§487-489
tax advantages		§489
DEPRECIATION AND AMORTIZATION		
accelerated cost recovery system ("ACRS")	168	§450
computation of		§§465-476
accelerated method	168(b), (d)(3)	§§468-470
intangibles, amortization of	197	§§473-475
real property	168(d)(2), (4)(B)	§476
recovery periods	168(e)(3)(A), (i)(14)	§465
salvage value		§466
stimulus bill—extra depreciation		§472
straight line method	168(a)(3)(C), (5)	§§467, 471
consumer items limited deductions	280F	§§478-481
depreciable property		§§455-458
books, films, sound recordings, software	167(f); 197	§457
intangibles	197	§456
"limited useful life"		§455
works of art		§458
election to expense	179	§477
limitations		§§451-454
"at risk"	465	§452
generic tax shelters	183	§454
passive loss rules	469	§451
property worth less than debt		§453
recapture of	1245; 1250	§§933-938
reduction of basis effect		§482
who may deduct		§§459-464
future interest holder	167(h)	§463
landlord-tenant	167(c)(2); 168(i)(6)	§460
purchaser		§462
sale-leaseback		§461
trustee-beneficiary	167(h)	§464
DIVORCE		
See also Support payments		
deductibility of expenses of	212(1), (3)	§§446-449
exemption for children	152(e)	§§672-673
marital property divisions	121(d)(3); 1041	§§814-819
no gain or loss	1041	§§512, 814-819

Subject	I.R.C. Section	Text Section
sales between spouses	1041	§§816-819

Subject	I.R.C. Section	Text Section
EXPENSES		
acquisition of business	195	§§391-407
acquiring goodwill	197	§§404-406
bar exam		§402
employment agency fees		§§398-399
running for office distinguished		§399
incorporation and reorganization		§400
legal fees	195; 248	§§400, 445
patents, copyrights, and trademarks	174	§401
search for		§§396-397
selling costs		§403
short-term prepayments		§407
start-up costs	195	§§392-395
bribes	162(c)	§§425-427
business gifts	274(b)	§337
"businesses" operated for pleasure	183	§§319-324
child care	21	§§704-711
compensation, reasonableness of	162(a)(1)	§§415-423
creative expense	263A(h)	§385
current expenses vs. capital outlay	263	§§365-407
distinguishing test		§§366-367
long-term benefits–*INDOPCO*		§§369-375
property produced or sold	263A	§§380-385
resisting hostile takeovers		§375
drilling costs	57(a)(11); 162; 212; 263(c); 615-616	§§490-492
educational		§§342-343
employment agency fees		§§398-399
entertainment	274	§§331-336
meals	274(k), (n)	§§335-336
environmental cleanups	198	§§378-379
fines and penalties	162(f)	§§431-432
home office	280A	§§347-355
deduction limitation	280A(c)(5)	§355
exclusive business use	280A(c)(1)	§348
investors' costs	212	§354
principal place of business	280(A)	§§349-355
taxpayer is employee	280A(c)(1)	§353
insurance premiums	264	§§344-346
life	264(a)(1)	§§345-346
property		§344
investor costs	212	§354
litigation	212(3)	§§338-341, 443-445
lobbying	162(e)	§§433-434
medical, dental, etc.	213	§§653-666
moving	82; 132(g); 217	§§325-330
deductions allowed	217(b)	§328
distance limitations	217(c)	§326
full-time employee	217(c)(2), (d)	§327
move must be permanent		§330
reimbursement for	82; 132(g)	§329
ordinary and necessary		§§408-423
compensation	162(a)(1)	§§415-423
defined		§409

Subject	I.R.C. Section	Text Section
voluntariness of payment		§§411-414
personal expenses, distinguished from business	262	§§302-303
production of income, expenses for	212	§§437-449
divorce and property settlement, costs of		§§446-449
litigation		§§443-445
proxy fights	212	§441
stockholder's travel	212; 274(h)(7)	§442
public policy limitations	162	§§424-436
antitrust violations	162(g)	§436
bribes	162(c)(1)	§425
civil damage payments		§§435-436
drug dealers	280E	§428
fines		§§431-432
illegal rebate exception		§§429-430
lobbying	162(e)(2)	§§433-434
medical kickbacks	162(c)(3)	§427
rent payments	162(a)(3); 263A; 280F(c)	§§386-390
lease as sale		§§388-390
repairs		§§376-379
requirements for deductibility		§296
salaries, reasonableness of	162(a)(1), (m)	§§415-423
selling costs		§403
tax shelters		§§301, 322-324
trade or business	62; 67; 162; 165; 167(a); 172(d)(4); 212(1)-(2)	§§297-301
defined		§298
legality of		§299
nature of taxpayer		§300
tax shelters		§301
traveling and living expenses. *See also* Travel expenses	162(a)(2); 274(n)	§§304-318
uniforms		§364
vacation homes	280A	§§356-363

F

FOREIGN TAXES, CREDIT FOR	27; 901-905	§698

FRINGE BENEFITS

See Compensation for personal services, fringe benefits

G

GAIN OR LOSS ON SALE OR EXCHANGE

See also "Sale or exchange" of capital assets

basis for determining. *See* Basis of property

boot	1031(b)	§§796-798
mortgage repossessions	1038	§820
personal residence, sale of	121; 1034	§§810-815
spouses, sale between	1041	§§816-819
capital vs. ordinary	170(e)(1)(A); 178; 475; 1211; 1212; 1221; 1222; 1234-1236	§§821-914
computation of, amount of	165(c); 262; 267; 465; 469; 483; 1091; 1245; 1250; 1274	§§918-944
nonrecognition of	121; 1031; 1033; 1034; 1038; 1041	§§785-820

Subject	I.R.C. Section	Text Section
includible items		
alimony, separate maintenance, and child support	62(a)(10); 71(a), (b), (c); 215; 682	§§161-170
any increase in net worth		§134
cancellation of indebtedness	108	§§142-157
compensation for services rendered		§135
expenses of employees. *See also* Expenses		§§137-141
frequent flier miles		§126
meals and lodgings		§§109, 138-141
reimbursements		§137
unreimbursed		§140
fringe benefits	132	§§115-123
moving expenses	132(g)	§121
retirement advice	132(h)(2), (m)	§122
transportation	132(f)	§119
gambling winnings	165(d)	§160
income from illegal activities		§§158-159
payment of employee's income taxes		§136
reimbursements		§§98, 137-141
kiddie tax	1(g)	§§224-226
net worth concept		§§11-22
no income		
borrowing		§17
loan repayment		§§13-15
return of capital		§16
trust income		§18
unsolicitated property		§21
noncash income		§19
punitive damages	104(a)	§§89, 93
strike benefits		§39
windfalls		§20
GROUP TERM LIFE INSURANCE	79	§123

H

HEAD OF HOUSEHOLD, TAX ON	2(b), (c); 7703(b)	§238
HOLDING PERIOD OF CAPITAL ASSETS	1(h); 1222	§§822, 915-917
HOME OFFICES, EXPENSE DEDUCTIONS	280A	§§347-355
HUSBAND AND WIFE, JOINT RETURN	1(d); 2; 6013	§§227-237
effect of		§230
joint and several liability	6013(d)	§§235-236
divorced or separated spouse	6015(c), (d)	§236
innocent spouse rule	6015(b)	§236
marriage and single penalty		§§232-234
gradual elimination	1(f)(8); 63(c)(2)(A)	§234
quickie divorce		§233
not mandatory	1(d)	§237
right to file	2, 6013	§227
sale of residence exclusion	121(b)(2), (d)(1)	§813
sales between	1041	§§816-819

I

IMPUTED INCOME		§§23-26

Subject	I.R.C. Section	Text Section
sale to related person	453(e), (f)(1)	§1062
sale of property only	453	§1055
INTEREST		
below-market interest on loans. *See also* Below-market interest on loans	483; 7872	§§239-248
deductibility of	62(a)(17); 163; 221; 264; 265; 279; 280A(d)(1); 461(g); 469; 483; 1274; 7872	§§572-610
business purpose	163	§§579-580
excess investment interest	163(d); 279	§§607-609
family loans		§581
imputed interest	483; 1274; 7872	§§239-241, 248, 586-588
below-market interest on loans. *See also* Below-market interest on loans	7872	§§239-248
computation	483; 1274	§§923-932
deductibility for business debts		§§586-588
deferred payments on property sales	483; 1274	§§923-932
farms and residences	483	§925
installment payments on property sales	483; 1274	§1058
included in gross income		§14
nondeductibility of	1(h); 62(a)(17); 163(d), (h); 221; 264; 265; 279; 280A(d)(1); 461(g); 469	§§590-610
personal interest	163(h)	§§591-600
prepaid interest	461(g)	§§605-606, 1010
residence loans	56(b)(1)(C), (e); 163(h)(3), (4); 280(A)	§§592-595, 955
tax-free		
higher education	135; 454	§129
state and local bonds	103; 141	§§75-77
INVENTORIES		
methods of computing	472	§§1047-1054
not capital assets	1221(a)(1)	§§830-843
INVESTOR EXPENSES		
See Nonbusiness expenses for production of income		
INVOLUNTARY CONVERSIONS	1033	§§803-809
See also Gain or loss on sale or exchange		

J		
JOINT RETURNS	2; 121(b)(2), (d)(1); 6013	§§227-230, 813

K		
KICKBACKS	162	§§424-430
KIDDIE TAX	1(g)	§§224-226

L		
LESSEE, IMPROVEMENTS BY		
adjusted basis	109	§758
basis of property to lessor	1019	§127

Subject	I.R.C. Section	Text Section
lobbying costs	162(e)	§434
losses between closely related taxpayers	267; 1041	§§511-516, 940
personal expenses	262	§302
purchase of goodwill	197	§§404-405
running for office		§§399, 433
unreasonable compensation	162(a)(1), (m)	§§415-423

NONRECOGNITION OF GAIN OR LOSS
See Gain or loss on sale or exchange

NONTAXABLE ITEMS
See Exclusions from gross income

O

OBSOLESCENCE
See Depreciation and amortization

OFFICE AT HOME	280A	§§347-355
See also Expenses		

OPTIONS, GAIN OR LOSS ON	1234	§§850-852

ORDINARY AND NECESSARY EXPENSE		§§408-423
defined		§409
determinative factors		§§410-414

P

PARTNERSHIPS		
family partnerships	704(e)	§§214-219
sale of	741; 751	§§878-880

PASSIVE LOSSES		§§543-551, 610, 943
See also Losses		
interest on disallowed	469	§§610, 943

PATENTS		
character of asset	1235	§849
shifting royalty income		§§211-212

PENSIONS AND PROFIT-SHARING PLANS, QUALIFIED	401-407	§§977-982

PERSONAL EXEMPTIONS		§667
phaseout	151(d)	§674

PERSONAL SERVICE INCOME
See Compensation for personal services

PRIVATE FOUNDATIONS	170(b), (e)	§§619, 632

PUBLIC POLICY		
expenses disallowed by reason of	162	§§424-436
losses disallowed by reason of	165	§519

Q

QUASI-CAPITAL ASSETS	1221(a)(2), (8); 1231	§§881-895
casualties, special rules for	165(h)(2); 1033; 1231	§§888-890
computation of gain and loss	1231(c)	§§886-887
property used in trade or business	167; 1221(a)(2); 1231	§§881-883

Subject	I.R.C. Section	Text Section
aborted sales		§897
contract rights	1234; 1234A; 1241	§§901-902
foreclosure		§903
franchises, trademarks and trade names	1253(a), (e)	§§899-900
involuntary conversion	1231	§910
mineral interests		§898
not affected by seller's retention of control	514	§§911-914
payment to creditor	1271(a)(1), (b)(1); 1272-1275	§§907-909
worthless debts or securities	182-183	§906

SCHOLARSHIPS	117	§§53-55

SOLE PROPRIETORSHIPS, SALE OF	197	§§873-877

STOCK OPTIONS, EMPLOYEE'S	83; 422	§§42, 983-998

SUPPORT PAYMENTS

Subject	I.R.C. Section	Text Section
child support	71(c)(1), (2)	§§169-170
spousal		§§161-168
alimony trusts	682	§168
cohabitation between parties	71(b)(1)(C)	§165
general rule	62(a)(10); 71(a); 215	§162
judicial decree required	71(b)(2)	§163
payments cease at death	71(b)(1)(D)	§166
recapture of payments		§167

T

TAX BENEFIT RULE

Subject	I.R.C. Section	Text Section
carryforwards	111(c)	§1083
classification of assets		§870
erroneous deduction		§1081
"recovery" defined		§1080
recovery of bad debts	111	§537
statement of rule	111(a)	§1079
tax brackets		§1084

TAX EXEMPT ORGANIZATIONS	501	§§171-182
charitable	501(c)(3)	§§172-173
description of	501(c)	§§171-175
political organizations	527	§§180-182
private foundations	508(e); 509; 4940-4945	§179
racial discrimination disqualification		§175
unions, fraternities, and civic leagues	501(c)(4)-(6)	§174
unrelated business income	511	§§176-178
debt-financed property	514	§178
rental		§177

TAX PREFERENCE, ITEMS OF	57	§§956-957

TAX RATES

See Rates of tax

TAX SHELTERS

Subject	I.R.C. Section	Text Section
accrual method required	448; 461(i)(3); 1256(b)(3)(B); 6661(b)(2)(C)(ii)	§1017
"at risk" limitations	465	§§538-542
business operated for pleasure	183	§§322-324

Subject	I.R.C. Section	Text Section
flagrant		§301
generic		§§322-324, 580

TAXES

Subject	I.R.C. Section	Text Section
See also Alternative minimum tax		
deduction for	163	§§566-571
business and investment expense	162; 212	§616
disability insurance		§614
general sales tax	164(b)(5)	§615
property taxes	164(d)	§613
foreign, credit for	27; 901-905	§698
nondeductible	56(b)(1)(A)(ii); 164(b); 275	§§617, 953

TRAVEL EXPENSES

Subject	I.R.C. Section	Text Section
	162(a)(2); 274(n)	§§304-318
"away from home"		§§314-318
business reason for home		§318
homeless persons		§315
several offices		§316
"sleep or rest" rule		§317
"temporary vs. indefinite" rule	162(a)	§318
meals		§317
"pursuit of trade or business"	274(h), (m)(2), (3)	§§305-313
combined business and pleasure	274(m)(2)	§311
commuting		§§306-310
foreign meetings	274(h)	§312
spouse expenses	274(m)(3)	§313
stockholder's travel	212; 274(h)(7)	§442

TRUSTS

Subject	I.R.C. Section	Text Section
alimony trusts	682	§§168, 268
assignments of income		§194
beneficiary, tax to	667	§§279, 283-285, 291
"*Clifford* trusts"	671; 678	§§209-210, 250-277
distributable net income, defined	643(a)	§280
estate and gift taxes		§252
loans to grantor	675	§§271-275
separate taxable entity		§§278-291
beneficiary or trust taxed		§279
complex trusts	642(b); 662(a)(1), (2); 663(a)	§§283-288
decedent's estates as		§283
simple trusts	651(a); 652(a)	§§281-282
throwback rule	665-669	§§289-291
tax effect	671	§§251-252
trusts taxable to grantor	671	§§250-277
administrative control by grantor	675	§§269-276
borrowing from trust	675(1)-(3)	§§271-275
income for benefit of grantor or spouse	677; 682	§§261-268
support of dependents		§§266-267
power to alter beneficiary	674	§§254-259
external standards exception	674(d)	§258
independent trustees' powers exception	674(c)	§257
reasonable alterations exception	674(b)	§259
power to revoke	676	§260
reversionary interest	672(e); 673	§253
trusts taxable to person other than grantor	678	§277

Subject	I.R.C. Section	Text Section
U		
UNADJUSTED BASIS		
See Basis of property		
VWXYZ		
VACATION HOMES	280A	§§356-363

Notes

Notes

Notes